LET'S GO

www.letsgo.com

# BERLIN, PRAGUE & BUDAPEST

**researcher-writers**
Sophia Angelis
Nelson Greaves
Vanda Gyuris

**staff writers**
Juan Cantu
Meghan Houser
Dorothy McLeod
William N. White
Qichen Zhang

**research manager**
Colleen O'Brien

**editor**
Sarah Berlow

**managing editor**
Daniel C. Barbero

# CONTENTS

**DISCOVER BERLIN,
PRAGUE & BUDAPEST** .......................... 1
when to go                2
what to do                2
suggested itineraries     6
how to use this book      13
**BERLIN** .............................................. 15
orientation               16
accommodations            24
sights                    35
food                      53
nightlife                 63
arts and culture          74
shopping                  76
essentials                80
berlin 101                83
**PRAGUE** .............................................. 89
orientation               90
accommodations            96
sights                    104
food                      119
nightlife                 141
arts and culture          149
shopping                  150
essentials                153
prague 101                154
**BUDAPEST** ...................................... 159
orientation               160
accommodations            165
sights                    172

food                      182
nightlife                 196
arts and culture          203
shopping                  204
essentials                207
budapest 101              209
**EXCURSIONS** .................................... 215
germany                   216
czech republic            222
hungary                   227
**ESSENTIALS** ..................................... 231
planning your trip        232
money                     236
safety and health         239
getting around            241
keeping in touch          242
climate                   245
measurements              246
language                  246
**BEYOND TOURISM** ............................ 253
studying                  254
volunteering              257
working                   259
**INDEX** .............................................. 261
map index                 263
**QUICK REFERENCE** ........................... 270

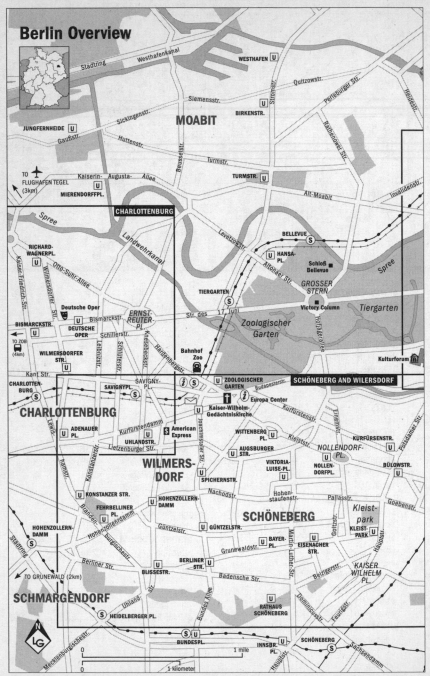

# Berlin Overview

MOABIT

CHARLOTTENBURG

WESTHAFEN Ⓤ

Städtring
Westhafenkanal

Quitzowstr.
Siemensstr.
Strohmstr.
Perleberger Str.
Heidestr.
BIRKENSTR.
Sickingenstr.
Gaußstr.
Huttenstr.
Turmstr.
Beusselstr.
TURMSTR. Ⓤ
JUNGFERNHEIDE Ⓤ
Kaiserin- Augusta- Allee
Alt-Moabit
Invalidenstr.

TO
FLUGHAFEN TEGEL
(3km)
MIERENDORFFPL.

Spree
Landwehrkanal
Levetzowstr.
BELLEVUE Ⓢ
HANSA- PL.
Altonaer Str.
Schloß Bellevue ■
Spree

RICHARD-WAGNERPL. Ⓤ
Otto-Suhr-Allee
Wilmersdorfer Str.
Kaiser-Friedrich-Str.

Deutsche Oper 🎭
Bismarckstr.
ERNST-REUTER-PL.
Str. des 17 Juni
GROSSER STERN
Victory Column ■
Tiergarten

BISMARCKSTR. Ⓤ
DEUTSCHE OPER Ⓤ
Schillerstr.
Leibnizstr.
Schlüterstr.
Krummestr.
Hardenbergstr.
Hofjägerallee
Zoologischer Garten

TO ZOB
(4km)
WILMERSDORFER STR.

Kant Str.
CHARLOTTENBURG Ⓢ
Lewishamstr.
SAVIGNYPL. Ⓢ
SAVIGNY-PL.
Bahnhof Zoo 🚆
ⓘ Ⓢ ZOOLOGISCHER GARTEN Ⓤ
Budapesterstr.
SCHÖNEBERG AND WILERSDORF

CHARLOTTENBURG
✉
Kaiser-Wilhelm-Gedächtniskirche 🕇
Europa Center
Kurfürstenstr.
Einemstr.
KURFÜRSENSTR. Ⓤ
Potsdamer Str.

ADENAUER PL. Ⓤ
Kurfürstendamm
UHLANDSTR. Ⓤ
American Express Ⓢ
Joachimstaler Str.
WITTENBERG PL. Ⓤ
Kleiststr.
NOLLENDORF-PL.
NOLLENDORFPL. Ⓤ
BÜLOWSTR. Ⓤ

Konstanzerstr.
Lietzenburger Str.
AUGSBURGER STR. Ⓤ
VIKTORIA-LUISE-PL.

WILMERSDORF
SPICHERNSTR. Ⓤ
Nachodstr.
Hohenstaufenstr.
Pallasstr.
Goebenstr.
Kleistpark
KLEIST-PARK Ⓤ
Haupt str.

KONSTANZER STR. Ⓤ
FEHRBELLINER PL. Ⓤ
Brandenburgischestr.
HOHENZOLLERN-DAMM
Hohenzollerndamm
GÜNTZELSTR. Ⓤ
Grolmanstr.
SCHÖNEBERG

HOHENZOLLERN-DAMM
Berliner Str.
Güntzelstr.
Grunewaldstr.
BAYER-PL. Ⓤ
Martin-Luther-Str.
EISENACHER STR. Ⓤ
Belziger str.
KAISER WILHELM PL.

Städtring
TO GRUNEWALD (2km)
Uhland str.
BERLINER STR. Ⓤ
BLISSESTR. Ⓤ
Badensche Str.

SCHMARGENDORF
Mecklenburgischestr.
Bundes Allee
HEIDELBERGER PL. Ⓢ
RATHAUS SCHÖNEBERG
Dominicusstr.
Feuristr.

N
LG

0                    1 mile
0          1 kilometer

BUNDESPL. Ⓢ Ⓤ
INNSBR. PL. Ⓤ
Haupt str.
SCHÖNEBERG Ⓢ
Sachsendamm

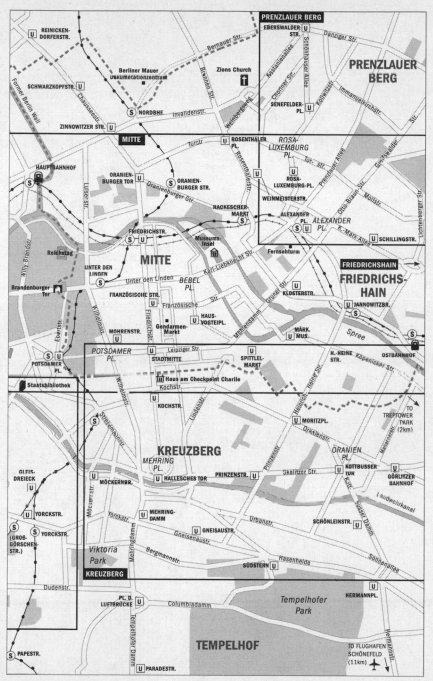

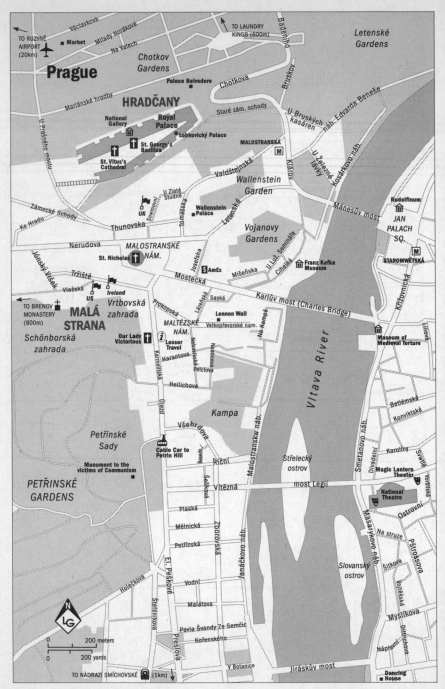

TO RUZYNĚ AIRPORT (20km)

Market

Václavkova

Milady Horákové

Na Valech

Badeního

TO LAUNDRY KINGS (600m)

Letenské Gardens

Chotkov Gardens

**Prague**

Palace Belvedere

Chotkova

Bruskov

Mariánské hradby

**HRADČANY**

Staré zám. schody

U Bruských kasáren

nábř. Edvarda Beneše

National Gallery

Royal Palace

Lobkovický Palace

St. George's Basilica

MALOSTRANSKÁ Ⓜ

U Prašného mostu

St. Vitus's Cathedral

Klárov

U železné lávky

U žel. lávky Kosárkovo náb.

Zámecké Schody

Ke Hradu

U Zlaté Studně

Wallenstein Garden

Valdštejnská

Mánesův most

Rudolfinum

JAN PALACH SQ.

Thunovska

UK

Wallenstein Palace

Letenská

Nerudova

Vojanovy Gardens

Ⓜ STAROMĚSTSKÁ

Jánský Vršek

**MALOSTRANSKÉ NÁM.**

St. Nicholas

Josefska

U Luž. Semináře

Cihelná

Franz Kafka Museum

Tržiště

Ireland

US

Vlašská

AmEx

Mišeňská

Mostecká

Karlův most (Charles Bridge)

Křižovnická

Lihová

**MALÁ STRANA**

Vrtbovská zahrada

Prokopská

Lázeňská

Saská

Na Kampě

TO BRENOV MONASTERY (800m)

Schönborská zahrada

MALTÉZSKÉ NÁM.

Lennon Wall

Velkopřevorské nam.

Museum of Medieval Torture

Our Lady Victorious

Lesser Travel

Karmelitská

Nebovidská

Nosticova

Pelclova

Harantova

Vltava River

Betlémská

Konviktská

Hellichova

**Kampa**

Malostranské náb.

Karoliny

Smetanovo náb.

Divadelní

Sitwté

Svaté

Magic Lantern Theater

Petřínské Sady

Všehrdova

Cable Car to Petrin Hill

Úezd

Řiční

Seříková

Vítězná

Střelecký ostrov

most Legií

National Theater

Ostrovní

Monument to the victims of Communism

**PETŘINSKÉ GARDENS**

Na struze

Plaská

Zborovská

Mělnická

Petřínská

Janáčkovo náb.

Slovanský ostrov

Masarykovo náb.

Vořišová

Pštrossova

Sitkova

Vojtěšská

Holečkova

El. Peškové

Vodní

Malátova

Myslíkova

Diitřichova

Štefánikova

Pavla Švandy Ze Semčic

Kořenského

Preslová

Náplavní

N LG

0     200 meters

0     200 yards

V Botanice

Jiráskův most

Dancing House

TO NÁDRAŽÍ SMÍCHOVSKÉ 🚆 (1km)

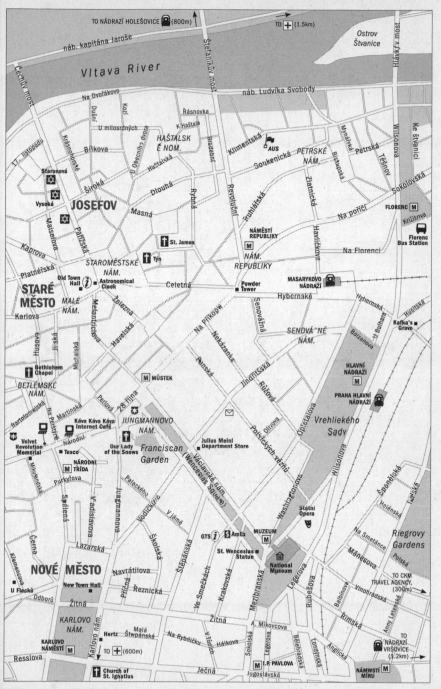

TO NÁDRAŽÍ HOLEŠOVICE (800m)

TO (1.5km)

Ostrov Štvanice

náb. kapitána Jaroše

Štefánikův most

Hlávkův most

Vltava River

náb. Ludvíka Svobody

Na Dvořákově

Dušní

Kozí

Rásnovka

Ke štvanici

Wilsonova

Čechův most

lt. listopadu

Krásnohorské

Bílkova

Široká

U Obecního dvora

K Haštalě

HAŠTALSK É NOM.

Hradební

Klimentská

AUS

Soukenická

PETRSKÉ NÁM.

Petrská

Bišnusská

Myslbek

Petrská

Těšnov

Sokolovská

Staronová

Vysoká

JOSEFOV

Haštalská

Dlouhá

Rybná

Masná

Revoluční

Truhlářská

Zlatnická

Na poříčí

FLORENC

Křižíkova

Florenc Bus Station

Maiselova

Pařížská

St. James

NÁMĚSTÍ REPUBLIKY

Havlíčkova

Na Florenci

Kaprova

Platnéřská

STAROMĚSTSKÉ NÁM.

Tyn

NÁM. REPUBLIKY

Na Florenci

STARÉ MĚSTO

Old Town Hall

Astronomical Clock

Celetná

Powder Tower

MASARYKOVO NÁDRAŽÍ

MALÉ NÁM.

Železná

Hybernská

Hybernská

Husická

Karlova

Metantrichova

Havelská

Na Příkopě

SENOVÁ NÉ NÁM.

Božanova

Kafka's Grave

Nekázanke

HLAVNÍ NÁDRAŽÍ

Bethlehem Chapel

Michalská

MÚSTEK

Panská

Jindřišská

Růžova

PRAHA HLAVNÍ NÁDRAŽÍ

BETLÉMSKÉ NÁM.

Perlová

28. října

Olivova

Opletalova

Bartolomějská

Martinská

Káva Káva Káva Internet Café

JUNGMANNOVO NÁM.

Vrehlieckého Sady

Na Perštýně

Národní

Julius Meinl Department Store

Politických věžňů

Velvet Revolution Memorial

Tesco

Our Lady of the Snows

Franciscan Garden

Wilsonova

NÁRODNÍ TŘÍDA

Purkyňova

Václavské nám. (Wenceslas Square)

Mikulandská

Spálená

Vladislavova

Jungmannova

Palackého

Washingtonova

Štátní Opera

Španělská

Helénská

Černá

Lazarská

Vodičkova

V jámě

GTS

AmEx

MUZEUM

Riegrovy Gardens

Polská

NOVÉ MĚSTO

Navrátilova

Příčná

Štěpánská

Řeznická

Krakovská

St. Wenceslas Statue

Mezibranská

Legerova

National Museum

Rubešova

Mánesova

TO CKM TRAVEL AGENCY (300m)

Vinohradská

New Town Hall

Ve Smečkách

Anny Letenské

U Fleků

Kremencova

Odborů

Žitná

KARLOVO NÁM.

Hertz

Malá Štwpánská

Na Rybníčku

A. Mikovcova

Sokolská

Balbínova

Římská

Rumunská

Karlovo nám.

TO NÁDRAŽÍ VRŠOVICE (1.2km)

KARLOVO NÁMĚSTÍ

TO (600m)

Hálkova

Anglická

Balbínská

Longinova

Resslova

Church of St. Ignatius

Ječná

Žitná

I.P. PAVLOVA

Jugoslávská

NÁMWSTÍ MÍRU

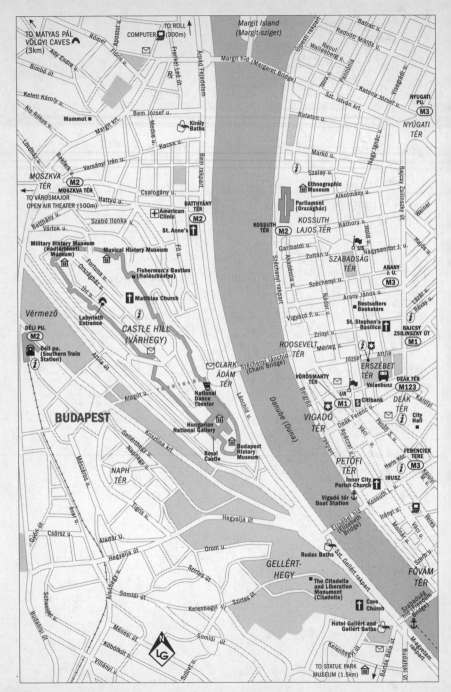

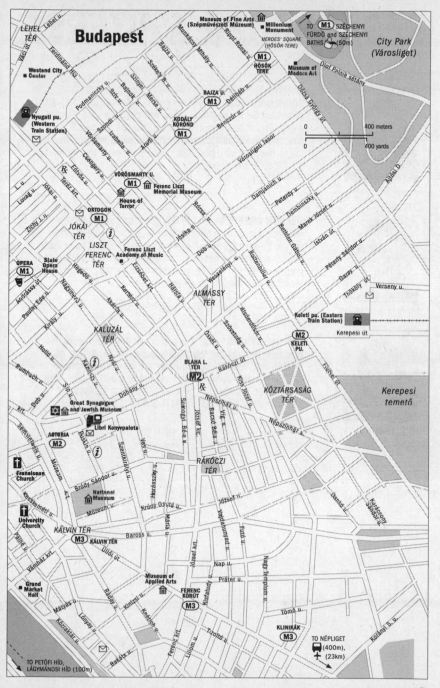

# Budapest

LEHEL TÉR

Museum of Fine Arts (Szépművészeti Múzeum)
Millenium Monument
HEROES' SQUARE (HÖSÖK-TERE)

M1 SZÉCHENYI FÜRDÖ and SZÉCHENYI BATHS (50m)

City Park (Városliget)

Westend City Center

Nyugati pu. (Western Train Station)

M1 HÖSÖK TERE
Museum of Modern Art

BAJZA U. M1

M1 KODÁLY KÖRÖND

400 meters
400 yards

VÖRÖSMARTY U. M1
Ferenc Liszt Memorial Museum
House of Terror

OKTOGON M1

JÓKAI TÉR

OPERA M1
State Opera House

LISZT FERENC TÉR
Ferenc Liszt Academy of Music

KALUZÁL TÉR

ALMÁSSY TÉR

Keleti pu. (Eastern Train Station)
Kerepesi út
M2 KELETI PU.

Verseny u.

BLAHA L. TÉR M2

KÖZTÁRSASÁG TÉR

Kerepesi temetö

Great Synagogue and Jewish Museum

Libri Könyvpalota

ASTORIA M2

Franciscan Church

University Church

KÁLVIN TÉR

National Museum

RÁKÓCZI TÉR

M3 KÁLVIN TÉR

Baross u.

Grand Market Hall

Museum of Applied Arts

FERENC KÖRÚT
M3

KLINIKÁK M3

TO NÉPLIGET (400m), (23km)

TO PETÖFI HÍD, LÁGYMÁNOSI HÍD (100m)

# RESEARCHER-WRITERS

**SOPHIA ANGELIS.** Freshman phenom Sophie tore through northeast Germany, holding her own on a team of Harvard grads. While last-minute German lessons helped Sophie navigate small villages and big cities alike, her outdoorsy California spirit and photographic eye are what truly helped her discover the country.

**NELSON GREAVES.** On the few occasions that Nelson was able to suppress his attraction to Czech women and addiction to Eastern European cuisine, he pumped out copy that left his editors in stitches. Come the fall, the recent Harvard grad will move to California, to start writing the screenplays for all of your favorite TV shows.

**VANDA GYURIS.** This Let's Go veteran planned her research around the World Cup schedule, watching each match with lively local septuagenarians. With her Harvard degree in hand, Vanda is off to China to teach English—but she'll undoubtedly take frequent vacations to Portugal to showcase her badass California surfing skills.

# BERLIN, PRAGUE & BUDAPEST

Throughout Berlin, Prague, and Budapest, the vestiges of imperial glory and Communist rule can be found on the same block. Castles stand staunchly beside concrete Soviet monuments, overlooking the graves of 20th century writers and medieval poets.

The '90s sparked the transformation of these three central European Metropolises into alternative, electrifying urban hangouts. Döner kebabs, *bockwurst*, and Czech cheeses are peddled side by side, while Hungarian locals frequent Turkish bathhouses. Freewheeling youth and a relentless drive toward the modern means endless streets of hip hangouts and vehemently chill attitude, making the cities some of the best student urban destinations in Europe. And even though the locals might be too cool for school they do appreciate a tenacity to learn, from Czechs who cheer your blatantly wrong attempts at their language to Berlin's widely-renowned language and music schools.

Locals want you to come too. Whether they're sharing beers at a lowkey pub or inviting you to a local party, the citizens will open their arms to you.

# when to go

All three cities are tourist-friendly and can be visited year-round. Summers are filled with tourists and cheaper accommodations may be difficult to find; the upside is that most outdoor concerts and festivals are happening. Spring and autumn are calmer both weather- and crowd-wise, but be aware that this region is infamous for its spring and early summer precipitation. Winters are often bitterly cold, so only plan on going if you're prepared to handle snow.

# what to do

## BOTTOMS UP

Berlin, Prague, and Budapest all have a variety of nightlife scenes. From jazzy and laid-back to all-out crazy, you can find what you're craving. Make sure to try local brews as well as some crazier mixed drinks some of these clubs and bars serve up.

- **A TRANE:** Berlin's hottest jazz club has featured greats like Herbie Hancock and Wynton Marsalis (p. 63).
- **CROSS CLUB:** One of the coolest clubs in Europe, boasts three bizarre floors with music to match (Prague; p. 147).
- **RADOST FX:** Strange drinks from the glowing bar, zebra print couches, and vegetarian munchies will have you coming back for more (Prague; p. 146).
- **SZIMPLA KERT:** Surround yourself in Surrealism with film and crepes (Budapest; p. 198).
- **CORVINTETŐ:** Watch sunrise over Budapest while partying at this hip club (p. 200).

### top five places to get cozy with ☭communism

**5. BERLINER MAUER DOKUMENTATIONZENTRUM:** Head here to learn what papers you'll need to check through Checkpoint Charlie.

**4. KLUB DER REPUBLIC:** Soviet artifacts line the walls of this legendary dance club in Berlin.

**3. MUSEUM OF COMMUNISM:** This will give you an in-depth history lesson on the Communist regime in Czechoslovakia.

**2. SOVIET MONUMENT:** This massive obelisk commemorates the Russian soldiers who liberated the city from the Germans in WWII.

**1. CHECKPOINT CHARLIE:** This tourist trap once had significance as the entrance point into the American sector from East Berlin. Now, it is a prime tourist destination where photo-snapping lemmings pay €3 to take pictures of Germans in American uniforms.

*discover berlin, prague & budapest*

discover berlin, prague & budapest

# RAINY DAY RETREATS

Barely escaped the torrential downpour? Fear not. Many of the coolest cafes in the three cities are famous in their own right, not to mention incredible decor, specialty teas, and illustrious customers.

- **SCHWARZES CAFE:** The boho cafe is almost always open and lets you switch continuously between absinthe and breakfast (Berlin; p. 53).

- **GLOBE BOOKSTORE:** Expats flock to this bookstore-cafe for its American fare and English book collection (Prague; p. 151).

- **CAFÉ ŠLAGR:** The baked goods here make you realize what a certain other nation's *patisseries* are emluating (Prague; p. 134).

- **CAFE ALIBI:** This place lets you enjoy traditional Budapest away from obnoxious tourists (Budapest; p. 182).

- **1000 TEA:** Enjoy tranquility and an instant sense of Zen (Budapest; p. 183).

# METROPOLIS ART

Somtimes a city's best art is in its skyline and avenues, so get your nose out of the guidebook and set your eyes on street level.

- **REICHSTAG:** Most of 20th-century German politics happened under its cool glass dome. Walk up the spiral path to watch history in the making (Berlin; p. 43).

- **DANCING HOUSE:** People finally appreciate the swaying building, which was way too ahead of its time (Prague; p. 106).

- **PARLIAMENT:** It looks more like a cathedral than a government building; decide whether Hungary Is holy or unholy at its Gothic home (Budapest; p. 172).

- **HEROES' SQUARE:** Sufficiently grand for commemorating the chieftains of Hungarian tribes, it also has some great concerts and events during the summer (Budapest; p. 175).

- **CASTLE LABYRINTHS:** Wind your way through Neanderthal abodes (Budapest; p. 178).

- **ASTRONOMICAL CLOCK:** Check the time (if you can see it through the crowd) on Prague's most famous ticker (p. 108).

# BEYOND TOURISM

If you plan on spending an extended period of time traveling or you're the antsy alternative type that wants more than just pretty architecture, you'll want to check this section out. Volunteering, learning a new language, and even finding a job or internship are within your reach. Even with a brief itinerary you can find activities that are right up your philanthropic alley.

- **PAPRIKA IT UP:** Pepper your cooking skills with courses in Budapest (p. 256).

- **GREEN LIVING:** Prague is in need of your green thumb in helping out with the city's ecological development (p. 258).

- **SNACKST DU INGELSCH?** Don't understand what that means? You will after an intensive German language program (p. 256).

- **THINK ENGLISH IS THE WORLD'S OFFICIAL LANGUAGE?:** Consider teaching it in Germany (p. 259).

what to do · beyond tourism

- **BEST STREET ART:** Prague's telephone poles.
- **BEST WATER WORKS:** Křížík's Fountain in Prague is an aquatic masterpiece and feat of colored effects.
- **LARGEST DISPLAY OF FAITH:** Budapest's Great Synagogue is the largest synagogue in Europe.
- **BEST CULTURAL CHEAPSKATE BOOKWORM HANGOUT:** Berlin's St. George's Bookstore has the largest selection of secondhand books in Berlin, not to mention free readings, concerts, movie nights, and other events.
- **BEST OSTENTATIOUS ROMP SIGHT:** Berlin's Pfaueninsel (Peacock Island) was used by Friedrich Wilhelm II to flock around with his mistress and peacocks.
- **BEST MUSIC MELANGE:** Prague's bizarre Cross Club plays different music genres in its various rooms. Words can't do it justice, so trust us and go.
- **PRETTIEST KITSCH STORE:** Budapest's Great Market Hall has all manners of trinkets and exhaustive rows of produce under a colorful tiled roof.

# suggested itineraries

## THE BEST OF BERLIN, PRAGUE & BUDAPEST (3 WEEKS)

To tackle the three cities, focus on each neighborhood in turn; for example, splitting sights between East and West Berlin is a solid way to see the contrast of the two and also see the remains of the Berlin Wall. Some areas have more to see than others, while others have one big attraction. Budapest is split by the Danube River into Buda and Pest, and can be explored that way. In Prague, explore the underappreciated vibrant Vinohrady, from its fortress to its nightlife, then make your way to Holešovice, another hidden gem of a neighborhood, to gape at Křížík's Fountain.

**1. BERLIN (6 DAYS):** Peacock Island's lake vistas won't leave your feathers ruffled. More somber war-related monuments will, but don't let that stop you from taking it all in. Spend your first day adjusting to the city by making a trip to **Fassbender& Rauch Chocolatiers** and strolling through part of **Tiergarten**. Take the next few days visiting museums like **Gemäldegalerie** for an amazing collection of art and **Deutsche Historisches Museum** (German History Museum). Pig out on Turkish food, swig it all down with a local brew and buy a discount ticket to one of the many sporting events, concerts, and shows available. Two days before, take a trip to **Spreewald Forest** (see below). Take your last day to say farewell to the city by walking the dome in **Berliner Dom**. Public transportation in Berlin is great, but consider trying another mode like bicycling or even boating.

**2. SPREEWALD FOREST (1 DAY):** Take a side trip from Berlin and canoe your way through what could only be a magical forest.

**3. PRAGUE (7 DAYS):** Wild parties, affordable chow, and a breathtaking skyline will convince you that this city was founded for students. Begin your first night in Prague at a bar with some new hostel friends. Take the next day to travel through Nové Město and check out the New Town Hall, all the while stopping at cheap and delicious eateries. Gradually make your way through to Staré Město along the **Charles Bridge**

for a Prague-tastic view. Take the rest of your trip to marvel at **Prague Castle** and **Saint Vitus's Cathedral** by day; gape at the unreal clubs by night.

**4. BUDAPEST (7 DAYS):** Hold yourself over with goulash while you run around in search of Soviet mementos. Take the first two days of your trip to relax at the Kiraly Baths and **Gödör Klub,** a venue that takes the word "underground" literally. This will all prepare you for the **House of Terror** and the **Millenium Monument.** Take a breather at **Great Market Hall** and **1000 Tea.** The next day head into **Pál-völgyi** and **Mátyás Caves** and take on **The Sandwich of Death** (not for the claustrophobic). After that, you'll want to see **Parliament** and realize the city is perfectly civilized despite the Neanderthal city beneath. On the last night, watch the sunrise from the roof of **Corvintető,** one of Budapest's hip clubs.

# CAVORTING WITH KAFKA (1 WEEK)

Prague=Kafka, or at least that's what every Czech will try to tell you. Metamorphose your own trip by infusing some Kafka appreciation.

**1. KAFKA STATUE:** "Rude!" will be the first thing out of your mouth when you see the author pointing fingers.

**2. DUM U MINUTY (HOUSE OF THE MINUTE):** See where baby Kafka began his life.

**3. NATIONAL GALLERY AT GOLTZ-KINSKY PALACE:** Stroll from his childhood home to this buildling, where Kafka walked everyday to attend school.

**4. FRANZ KAFKA MUSEUM:** Learn how Franz's neighbors put up with him; the museum focuses on Kafka's life in its relation to Prague.

**5. CAFÉ LOUVRE:** Visit Kafka's favorite teenage hangouts.

**6. GRAND HOTEL EUROPA:** Kafka gave a reading of "The Judgment" here.

**7. KAFKA'S GRAVE:** Where the legend be buried.

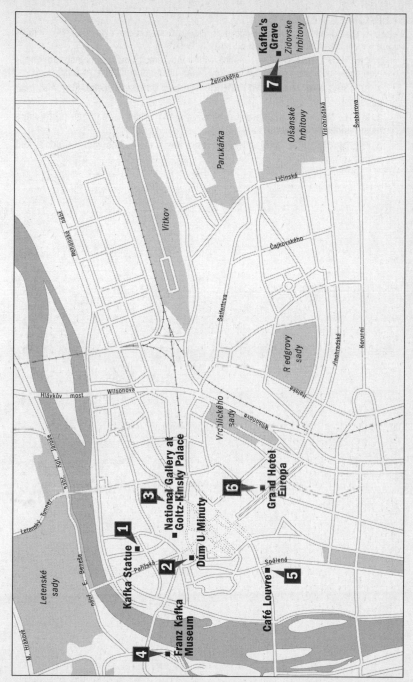

**Kafka's Grave** 7
Židovské hřbitovy

Želivského

Parukářka

Olšanské hřbitovy

Vítkov

Vinohradská

Šrobárova

Ličinská

Čajkovského

Rohanské nábř.

Seifertova

R edgrovy sady

Jičínská

Vinohradská

Korunní

Hlávkův most

Wilsonova

Vrchlického sady

National Gallery at Goltz-Kinsky Palace 3

Grand Hotel Europa 6

Dům U Minuty

Kafka Statue 1

2 Pařížská

5 Café Louvre
Spálená

Letenské sady

nábř. E. Beneše

Franz Kafka Museum 4

M. Horákové

# BEER-LIN (1 WEEK)

We admit that there are amazing sights in Berlin that you can't pass up. But what's wrong with a little shmoozing and boozing in between?

**1. CHARLOTTENBURG:** After dealing with yuppy preps and the mainstream shopping strip, you'll want to keep it low-key (read: beer, not cocktails) at **Salz**.

**2. SCHÖNEBERG AND WILMERSDORF:** The best gay party scene. Ever. And beer abounds!

**3. MITTE: Week-End** will have you partying until the sun rises in one of the city's most happening neighborhoods.

**4. FRIEDRICHSHAIN: Berghain/Panorama Bar** is the techno club you don't want to miss.

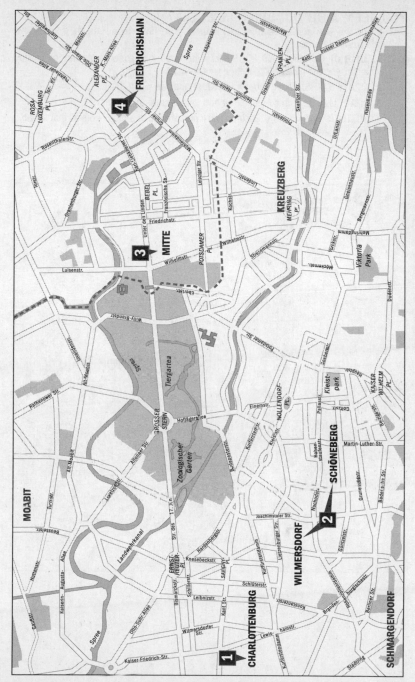

## YOU SEEM A BIT OCCUPIED (1 WEEK)

Check out the Ottoman presence in Budapest. You have to admit, they left some fantastic things behind.

**1. TOMB OF GÜL BAB AND ROSE HILL:** An ornate octagonal tomb and the nearby rose gardens will have you re-writing your will.

**2. KIRALY BATHS:** Siege-proof baths! Just what we wanted!

**3. CITADELLA:** Take in some history and architecture to feel more legit.

**4. HUMMUS BAR:** Yumm...Besides, you'll probably need a break from all that kebab.

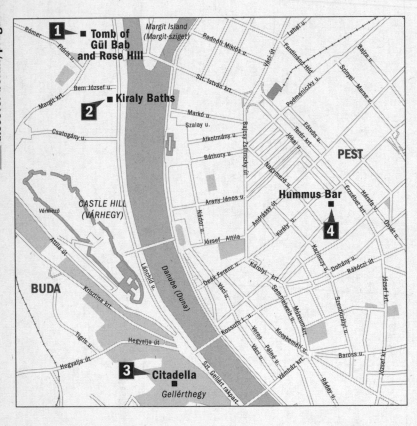

# how to use this book

## CHAPTERS

In the next few pages, the travel coverage chapters—the meat of any *Let's Go* book—begins with Berlin. After Berlin, Prague takes over, followed closely by Budapest. Last but not least, excursions from Prague and Budapest are available to those who have conquered the two Metropolises, or just need to get away.

But that's not all, folks. We also have a few extra chapters for you to peruse:

| CHAPTER | DESCRIPTION |
|---|---|
| Discover Berlin, Prague & Budapest | Discover tells you what to do, when to do it, and where to go for it. The absolute coolest things about any destination get highlighted in this chapter at the front of all *Let's Go* books. |
| Essentials | Essentials contains the practical info you need before, during, and after your trip—visas, regional transportation, health and safety, phrasebooks, and more. |
| Beyond Tourism | As students ourselves, we at *Let's Go* encourage studying abroad, or going beyond tourism more generally, every chance we get. This chapter lists ideas for how to study, volunteer, or work abroad with other young travelers in Berlin, Prague, and Budapest to get more out of your trip. |

## LISTINGS

Listings—a.k.a. reviews of individual establishments—constitute a majority of *Let's Go* coverage. Our Researcher-Writers list establishments in order from **best to worst value**—not necessarily quality. (Obviously a five-star hotel is nicer than a hostel, but it would probably be ranked lower because it's not as good a value.) Listings pack in a lot of information, but it's easy to digest if you know how they're constructed:

**ESTABLISHMENT NAME** 💳💵♿🚫📶🍸❄☀▼ type of establishment ❶

Address ☎phone number 🖥website

Editorial review goes here.

*✥ Directions to the establishment. ℹ Other practical information about the establishment, like age restrictions at a club or whether breakfast is included at a hostel. [$] Prices for goods or services. ⏰ Hours or schedules.*

## ICONS

First things first: places and things that we absolutely love, sappily cherish, generally obsess over, and wholeheartedly endorse are denoted by the all-empowering **👍Let's Go thumbs-up.** In addition, the icons scattered throughout a listing (as you saw in the sample above) can tell you a lot about an establishment. The following icons answer a series of yes-no questions about a place:

| | | | | | |
|---|---|---|---|---|---|
| 💳 | Credit cards accepted | 💵 | Cash only | ♿ | Wheelchair-accessible |
| 🚫 | Not wheelchair-accessible | 📶 | Internet access available | 🍸 | Alcohol served |
| ❄ | Air-conditioned | ☀ | Outdoor seating available | ▼ | GLBT or GLBT-friendly |

The rest are visual cues to help you navigate each listing:

| | | | | | |
|---|---|---|---|---|---|
| ☎ | Phone numbers | 🖥 | Websites | ✥ | Directions |
| ℹ | Other hard info | [$] | Prices | ⏰ | Hours |

## OTHER USEFUL STUFF

**Area codes** for each destination appear opposite the name of the city and are denoted by the ☎ icon. Finally, in order to pack the book with as much information as possible, we have used a few **standard abbreviations.** "Strasse" is abbreviated "str.," while

"Pl." is short for "Platz." "Kč" denotes the Czech currency koruna, while "Ft" marks the Hungarian forint. The "€" sign denotes the European euro.

## PRICE DIVERSITY

A final set of icons corresponds to what we call our "price diversity" scale, which approximates how much money you can expect to spend at a given establishment. For **accommodations,** we base our range on the cheapest price for which a single traveler can stay for one night. For **food,** we estimate the average amount one traveler will spend in one sitting. The table below tells you what you'll *typically* find in Berlin, Prague, and Budapest at the corresponding price range, but keep in mind that no system can allow for the quirks of individual establishments.

| ACCOMMO-DATIONS | BERLIN | PRAGUE | BUDAPEST | WHAT YOU'RE LIKELY TO FIND |
|---|---|---|---|---|
| ❶ | under €15 | under 440 Kč | under 3000Ft | Campgrounds and dorm rooms, both in hostels and actual universities. Expect bunk beds and a communal bath. You may have to provide or rent towels and sheets. |
| ❷ | €15-23 | 440-650Kč | 3000-4000Ft | Upper-end hostels or lower-end hotels. You may have a private bathroom, or there may be a sink in your room and a communal shower in the hall. |
| ❸ | €24-30 | 651-800Kč | 4001-5700Ft | A small room with a private bath. Should have decent amenities, such as phone and TV. Breakfast may be included. |
| ❹ | €31-35 | 801-1100Kč | 5701-9000Ft | Should have bigger rooms than a ❸, with more amenities or in a more convenient location. Breakfast probably included. |
| ❺ | over €35 | over 1100Kč | over 9000Ft | Large hotels or upscale chains. If it's a ❺ and it doesn't have the perks you want (and more), you've paid too much. |
| FOOD | BERLIN | PRAGUE | BUDAPEST | WHAT YOU'RE LIKELY TO FIND |
| ❶ | under €4 | under 110Kč | under 1200Ft | Probably street food or a fast-food joint, but also university cafeterias and bakeries (yum). Usually takeout, but you may have the option of sitting down. |
| ❷ | €4-8 | 110-220Kč | 1200-1800Ft | Sandwiches, pizza, appetizers at a bar, or low-priced entrees. Most ethnic eateries are a ❷. Either takeout or a sit-down meal, but only slightly more fashionable decor. |
| ❸ | €9-12 | 221-340Kč | 1801-2400Ft | Mid-priced entrees, seafood, and exotic pasta dishes. More upscale ethnic eateries. Since you'll have the luxury of a waiter, tip will set you back a little extra. |
| ❹ | €13-20 | 341-450Kč | 2401-3500Ft | A somewhat fancy restaurant. Entrees tend to be heartier or more elaborate, but you're really paying for decor and ambience. Few restaurants in this range have a dress code, but some may look down on T-shirts and sandals. |
| ❺ | over €20 | over 450Kč | over 3500Ft | Your meal might cost more than your room, but there's a reason—it's something fabulous, famous, or both. Slacks and dress shirts may be expected. Offers foreign-sounding food and a decent wine list. |

discover berlin, prague & budapest

# BERLIN

Congratulations on your decision to visit Berlin. Your wussy friends went to Paris. Your snob friends left for London. Your tacky friends chose Florence. And your fat friends stayed home. But you chose Berlin, which makes two things true of you: 1. You're smarter than your friends. 2. You're bad at choosing friends. Everything that rocks in the other European capitals does so in Berlin, but here the beat is faster, the groove is harder, and all of it is covered in more mustard than Mr. French could dream. First, Berlin has normal history; the Prussians ruled from Berlin's canal-lined boulevards, built the Berliner Dom, pimped out opera houses, and collected enough art to make the Louvre green with envy.

But Berlin also has more recent history, part of which was the implosion of its older history in WWII, then there whole"wall" thing where the Soviets literally cut the city in half. In short, "change" more than anything else continues to define Berlin. As a city simultaneously abandoned and dominated by authority, Berlin became a haven of punks and anarchists in the '70s and '80s. When the wall came down, that sharp culture was suddenly forced to have a playdate with legitimacy as East and West reunited and sought to establish common ground.

In 1999, the German government moved from Bonn to Berlin, and suddenly Berlin's graffiti-filled streets were full of briefcase-carrying bureaucrats. Embracing change and pushing forward has also made Berlin the "cool" capital of Europe.

Your friends are morons.

## greatest hits

- **COLD WAR KIDS.** Admire the Berlin Wall murals painted by artists from around the world at the East Side Gallery (p. 50).
- **TAKE ME TO THE RIVER.** Party like T. Pain (on a boat!) with rum and pizza at Club der Visionaere (p.72).
- **SASSY GAY FRIEND.** Take the weekly pub quiz with the hottest members of Berlin's GLBT community at Hafen (p. 65).
- **SHOP IT TO ME.** Barter with bakers and brewers at the biweekly Turkish market (p. 77).

Hit up the Bahnof Zoo and the schloß in Charlottenburg, but bounce as soon as the sun goes down. Shake the geriatrics, sip wine alongside PYTs at Solsi e Morsi, and befriend the legendary bar owner. Continue to paint the town—or at least Prenzlauer Berg—red at Klub Der Republic, a bar that proves that drinking can be educational, but maybe only if you're studying all of the Soviet-era artifacts hanging on the walls. After your tektonik dance marathon, cool off with some ice cream from Caramello Eis, a student haunt that claims to serve up the best chocolate ice cream in all of Berlin. When your daily schedule begins to reek of LiLo's party addiction, take a shot of culture instead at Berliner Philharmonisches Orchester; standing room at a show costs only €7.

# orientation

## CHARLOTTENBURG

Should you forget that Berlin is an old European capital, venture into West Berlin's Charlottenburg. Originally a separate town founded around the grounds of Friedrich I's palace, it was an affluent cultural center during the Weimar years as well as the Berlin Wall era thanks to Anglo-American support. The neighborhood retains that old-world opulence, from its upscale Beaux-Arts apartments to the shamefully ex-

travagant **Kurfürstendamm,** Berlin's main shopping strip. **Ku'damm,** as the locals call it, runs east to west through southern Charlottenburg. It's also home to Europe's largest department store, **KaDeWe,** which comprises five massive floors that keep patrons dressed to a tee and their pantries similarly so with truffle oil. Close to central Charlottenburg is the large **Bahnof Zoo,** a Berlin family favorite, which may join the Ku'damm (and its never-ending flow of teenagers darting in and out of H and M) as the youngest and liveliest areas in Charlottenburg. Other sights include part of the Tiergarten, the sprawling Zoologischer Garten, the Spree River in the northwest, and the **Schloß Charlottenburg** to the west. Otherwise, the higher neighborhood rents keep out most young people and students, so the Charlottenburg crowd is quiet and somewhat older, and the nightlife options are few and far between.

## SCHÖNEBERG AND WILMERSDORF

South of Ku'damm, Schöneberg and Wilmersdorf are primarily middle class, residential neighborhoods, remarkable for their world class mellow cafe culture, bistro tables, relaxed diners, and coffee shops spilling onto virtually every cobblestone street. Nowhere else in Berlin, and perhaps in all of Germany, is the gay community quite as contentedly outrageous as in the area immediately surrounding **Nollendorfplatz.** The gay nightlife scene, ranging from dark and smoky bars to chic and sleek clubs, is diverse in decor and music, but also laid-back and welcoming. To the west lies one of Berlin's most convenient outdoor getaways: **Grunewald,** popular with city-dwellers trading in their daily commute for peaceful strolls with the family dog along pine-lined dirt trails, is reachable by bus and tram in just about 20 minutes.

## MITTE

Mitte is without a doubt the most important district in Berlin. It has the **Brandenburg Gate,** the **Reichstag,** the **Jewish Memorial,** the **Column of Victory,** and the **Berliner Dom.** It has the best cultural institutions; **Museum Island** stacks the world's best musuems practically on top of each other. And somehow Mitte manages to multitask as a center for Berlin hipsterdom as well, with sick clubs, indie movie theaters, excellent food, and more walking plaid than that nightmare where the tablecloths came alive. Then, of course, there's the forest-like **Tiergarten** at the center of Mitte, which shelters sunbathers, barbecuers, and grasping lovers. The main street, **Strasse des 17 Juni,** serves as a populist gathering place where carnivals, markets, protests, and public viewings of the World Cup take precedent over traffic. However, what's most fun about Mitte is tracing the history of Berlin down its streets and through its old and new buildings (which are often combined). The **Berlin Wall** ran directly through Mitte, and East and West Germany made a habit of comparing the sizes of their manhood over the wall. The communists built the Berlin Fernsehturm (TV Tower) as a sign of dominance it's still the tallest building in Europe. The Americans responded with Congress Hall, now the House of World Cultures, an architectural wonder that's earned the nickname "pregnant oyster." Elsewhere, at the "Topography of Terror" museum, one of the longest standing stretches of the Berlin Wall streaks above the ruins of Hitler's war offices. And even with all this history to fall back on, Mitte continues to construct and reconstruct icons. The **Berlin Schloß,** the Hohenzollern Imperial Palace that was destroyed in the 1950s, is scheduled to re-open in 2018.

## PRENZLAUER BERG

What was once Berlin's overlooked Beirke, replete with crumbling cement and graffiti-covered Soviet-era buildings, is rapidly transforming into perhaps the trendiest area in the city. Attracted by low rents, students and artists stormed the neighborhood after reunification, giving the area a bohemian vibe with a unique DDR spin. Today, the streets are owned by well-dressed schoolchildren and their young, effortlessly hip parents, and the city blocks are interrupted by countless small parks, playgrounds, and costly secondhand stores. In Prenzlauer Berg, everything used to

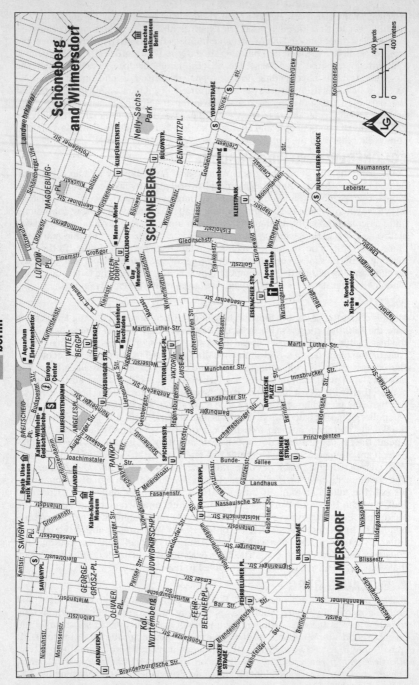

Schöneberg and Wilmersdorf

Deutsches Technikmuseum Berlin

Katzbachstr.

Monumentenbrücke

Kolonnenstr.

400 yards
400 meters

0
0

Nelly-Sachs-Park

YORCKSTRASSE

Yorck str.

JULIUS-LEBER-BRÜCKE

Naumannstr.

Leberstr.

BÜLOWSTR.

DENNEWITZPL.

Goebenstr.

Crellestr.

Monumentenstr.

str.

Hauptstr.

Lesbenberatung

KLEISTPARK

Pallasstr.

Winterfeldstr.

Eisstr.

Grunewaldstr.

Warbergstr.

Taunusstr.

Ebersstr.

SCHÖNEBERG

Gleditschstr.

Frankenstr.

Golzstr.

Goltzstr.

Apostle Paulus Kirche

Eisenacher Str.

Wartburgstr.

Barbarossastr.

St. Norbert Kirche Cemetery

Hauptstr.

Martin-Luther-Str.

Martin Luther-Str.

Hohenstaufen Str.

Münchener Str.

Innsbrucker Str.

Landshuter Str.

BAYERISCHE PLATZ

Berlin

Badensche

Aschaffenburger Str.

Prinzregenten

BERLINER STRASSE

Bundes-    sallee

Landhaus

WILMERSDORF

Nassauische Str.

Gasteiner Str.

Am Volkspark

Hildegardstr.

Blissestr.

BLISSESTRASSE

Mehlitzstr.

Barstr.

Mannheimer Str.

Berliner

Brandenburgische Str.

18    www.letsgo.com

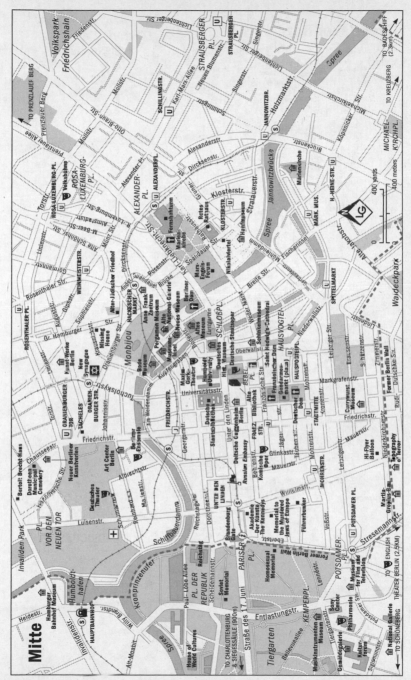

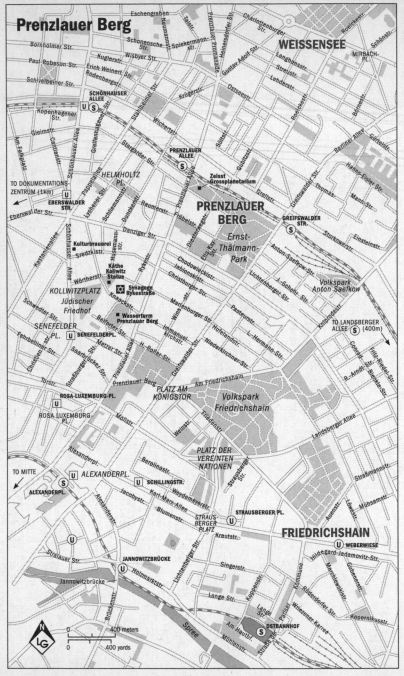

# Prenzlauer Berg

Eschengraben

Neumannstr.

Talstr.

Charlottenburger Str.

Roelckestr.

Schönstr.

**WEISSENSEE**

Bornholmer Str.

Schönensche Str.

Spiekermann-str.

Prenzlauer Promenade

Heinersdorfer Str.

Gustav Adolf Str.

Ostseestr.

Langhansstr.

MIRBACH-PL.

Kuglerstr.

Wisbyer Str.

Paul-Robeson Str.

Erich Weinert Str.

Rodenbergstr.

Krügerstr.

Streustr.

Lehderstr.

Roelckestr.

Börnestr.

Schivelbeiner Str.

**SCHÖNHAUSER ALLEE**

Ⓤ Ⓢ

Stahlhelmer Str.

Wichertstr.

Sültstr.

Gubitzstr.

Berliner Allee

Gürtelstr.

Am Falkplatz

Kopenhagener Str.

Schönhauser Allee

Greifenhagener Str.

**PRENZLAUER ALLEE** Ⓢ

Prenzlauer Allee

Greifswalder Str.

Thomas-

Hans-Eisler Str.

Mann-Str.

Gleimstr.

Cantianstr.

Stargarder Str.

**Zeiss Grossplanetarium**

Greifswalder Str.

Einsteinstr.

TO DOKUMENTATIONS-ZENTRUM (1km)

**EBERSWALDER STR.** Ⓤ

**HELMHOLTZ PL.**

Pappelallee

Lychener Str.

Schliemannstr.

Raumerstr.

Fröbelstr.

Danziger Str.

**PRENZLAUER BERG**

**GREIFSWALDER STR.** Ⓢ

Starkowerstr.

Eberswalder Str.

Kastanienallee

Schönhauser Allee

Dunckerstr.

Danziger Str.

Ⓢ

**Ernst-Thälmann-Park**

Anton-Saefkow-Str.

J.-Schehr-Str.

**Volkspark Anton Saefkow**

**Kulturbrauerei** ■

Sredzkistr.

Husemannstr.

Chodowieckistr.

Jablonskistr.

Christburger Str.

Lichtenberger Str.

**Käthe Kollwitz Statue** ■

Wörtherstr.

Knaackstr.

✡ **Synagoge Rykestraße**

Marienburger Str.

Pastrurstr.

Kniprodestr.

**KOLLWITZPLATZ**

*Jüdischer Friedhof*

Belforter Str.

■ **Wasserturm Prenzlauer Berg**

Winsstr.

Immanuel-kirchstr.

Hufelandstr.

L. Hermann-Str.

TO LANDSBERGER ALLEE Ⓢ (400m)

Schwedter Str.

**SENEFELDER PL.**

Metzer Str.

Kollwitzstr.

Diedenhofer Str.

Rhinower Str.

H.-Roller-Str.

Greifswalder Str.

Niederkirchner Str.

Conrad-Blenheim Str.

Fritz-Riedel-Str.

Fehrbelliner Str.

**SENEFELDERPL.** Ⓤ

Saarbrücker Str.

Prenzlauer Berg

R.-Arndt-Str.

Christinenstr.

Strassburger Str.

Torstr.

Prenzlauer Berg

Am Friedrichshain

**PLATZ AM KÖNIGSTOR**

*Volkspark Friedrichshain*

Landsberger Allee

**ROSA-LUXEMBURG-PL.** Ⓤ

Mollstr.

Weinstr.

Friedenstr.

**ROSA LUXEMBURG PL.**

Alexanderpl.

Berolinastr.

**PLATZ DER VEREINTEN NATIONEN**

Straussberger Str.

Straßmannstr.

TO MITTE

Ⓤ **ALEXANDERPL.**

Ⓤ **SCHILLINGSTR.**

Weydemeyerstr.

**ALEXANDERPL.** Ⓢ

Jacobystr.

Alexanderstr.

Karl-Marx-Allee

Blumenstr.

**STRAUSBERGER PL.** Ⓤ

Auerstr.

Mühsamstr.

**FRIEDRICHSHAIN**

Ⓤ

**STRAUS-BERGER PLATZ**

Krautstr.

Ⓤ **WEBERWIESE**

Stralauer Str.

**JANNOWITZBRÜCKE**

Ⓤ

Holzmarktstr.

Lichtenberger Str.

Singerstr.

Hildegard-Jadamovitz-Str.

Marchlewski-str.

Koppenstr.

Kommune

Rüdersdorfer Str.

Wedekindstr.

Gubenerstr.

*Jannowitzbrücke*

Brückenstr.

Lange Str.

Lange Str.

Palisaden

Warschauer Karree

Kopernikusstr.

S p r e e

Am Hauptbf.

**OSTBAHNHOF** Ⓢ

Mühlenstr.

Straße der

N

LG

0    400 meters

0    400 yards

berlin

be something else. Delicious brunches are served every summer in what were once butcher shops, students party in a horse stable turned nightclub, and cheap cocktails are served from a bar countertop in a former linoleum showroom. For this neighborhood, what's cool is ironic, and what's ironic is the bare-bones, stuck in the'70s, USSR cement siding, burnt-orange shag carpeting past. Cafe-bar owners know what's hip, so even as relics of Prenzlauer Berg's are rapidly disappearing, mismatched sofas and floral wallpaper remain the shabby-chic decorating standard. The bar scene is to Prenzlauer Berg as club culture is to Friedrichshain. After dark, Prenzlauer Berg turns into a not-to-be-missed extravaganza of hole-in-the-wall basement concerts, laid-back wine tastings, and trendy, vegan cafes.

Geographically, Prenzlauer Berg is east of the city center, overlapping in some places with Mitte to the west. Cheaper bars cluster around the **Kastanienallee**, while the area around Lettestr. is ideal for checking out the'70s decorating revival. Only two U-Bahn lines and a single S-Bahn line cut through the area, so plan on trams or walking to explore the berg.

## FRIEDRICHSHAIN

Friedrichshain's low rents and DDR edge draw a crowd of punk-rock types ever eastward. From the longest remnant of the Berlin Wall that runs along the river to the oppressive, towering architecture of the neighborhood's central axis, **Frankfurter Allee**, the presence of the former Soviet Union is still strong. Nowhere is that hard edge felt as sharply as in Friedrichshain's famous hardcore nightlife monopolizing every rundown train station and abandoned factory along the Spree, turning graffitied cement sheds into wild raves and electro hangouts. However, some locals complain that gentrification has found its way even here, as traditional residential buildings pop up and chic 20-somethings set up shop on the cafe-ridden **Simon-Dach-Strasse** and **Boxhagenerplatz**. But however legitimate those observations may be, Friedrichshain is still wonderfully inexpensive and fantastically out of the ordinary. Travelers should keep an eye out at night, as Friedrichshain is still a little rough around the edges and even desolate in some spots.

## KREUZBERG

If Mitte is Manhattan, Kreuzberg is Brooklyn. Gritty graffiti covers everything here, and the younger population skulks around chowing down street food good enough for the Last Supper. The parties start later, go later, and sometimes never stop. Kreuzberg once ruled as the center of punkdom and counterculture in Berlin. It was occupied by *hausbesetzer* (squatters) in the 1920s and '70s, until a conservative city government forcibly evicted them in the early '80s. Riots ensued, and during Reagan's 1985 visit to the city, authorities so feared protests in Kreuzberg that they locked down the entire district. While these days find it a bit tamer, the alternative heart of Kreuzberg remains. Underground clubs turn on when the lights go down in abandoned basements, burned-out apartment buildings, and shaky rooftop terraces; the clubs that party the hardest in Berlin all find shelter in Kreuzberg. Kreuzberg is also notably home to Berlin's enormous Turkish population. Döner kebabs, those shawarma sandwich-like miracles, go for €2-3 all across this district, and the Turkish Market along the southern bank of the Landwehrkanal is one of the most exciting, raucous, cheap, and authentic markets in Western Europe. If you want to learn things about Berlin, go to Mitte. If you want to not remember your entire trip, come to Kreuzberg.

orientation • kreuzberg

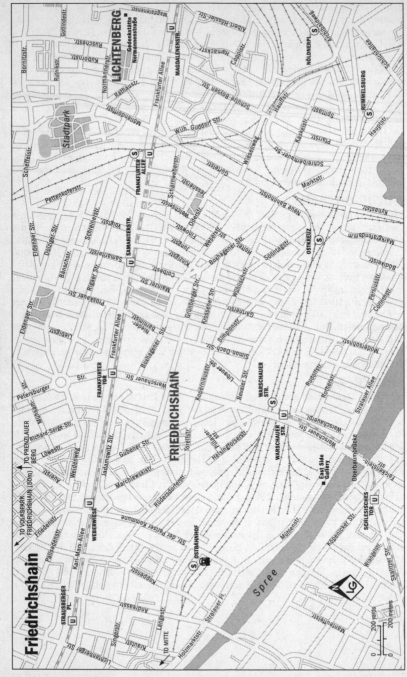

# Friedrichshain

**berlin**

LICHTENBERG

Gedenkstätte
Normannenstraße

Stadtpark

FRIEDRICHSHAIN

FRANKFURTER
ALLEE

FRANKFURTER
TOR

SAMARITERSTR.

WEBERWIESE

STRAUSBERGER
PL.

OSTBAHNHOF

WARSCHAUER
STR.

WARSCHAUER
STR.

OSTKREUZ

RUMMELSBURG

NÖLDNERPL

SCHLESISCHES
TOR

East Side
Gallery

Spree

TO VOLKSPARK
FRIEDRICHSHAIN (50m)

TO PRENZLAUER
BERG

TO MITTE

Oberbaumbrücke

0    200 yards

0    200 meters

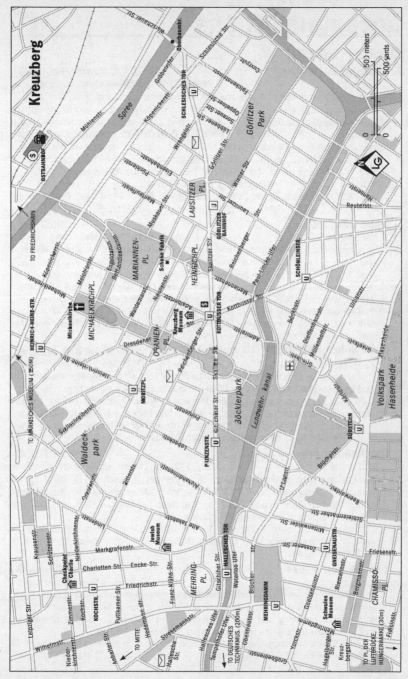

Kreuzberg

# accommodations

## CHARLOTTENBURG

### 👍 BEROLINA BACKPACKER — 💳📶 HOSTEL [2]

Stuttgarter P. 17 ☎030 32 70 90 72 💻www.berolinabackpacker.de

This quiet hostel keeps things elegant with pastel walls and bunk-free dorms. Backpackers enjoy the high ceilings and big windows; some rooms even have balconies and intricate molding. Surrounding cafes and close proximity to the S-Bahn make up for its distance from the rush of the city. Communal and private kitchens *(communal €1 per day, private €9.50)* available for use. Relax and enjoy a breakfast buffet *(€7)*, or the "backpackers' breakfast" *(a roll with sausage, cheese and coffee; €3)* in the popular and newly decorated pale blue dining area.

*🚇 S3, S5, S9, or S75: Charlottenburg. ℹ Internet €0.50 per 15min. Wi-Fi included. $ 5 bed dorms €10-13.50; singles €29.50-35.50; doubles €37-47; triples €39-64; quads €46-60. ⏰ Reception 24hr. Check-out 11am.*

### A AND O HOSTEL — 🍸🚭 HOSTEL [1]

Joachimstaler Str. 1-3 ☎030 809 47 53 00 💻www.aohostels.com

On a busy, commercial street, A and O may not have an ideal location unless you plan on frequenting the Erotik Museum 40m away, but it has reliable rooms and close proximity to the Bahnhof Zoo transit hub. The lobby and bar are packed nightly, as is the roof patio despite its resemblance to a dilapidated mini-golf course. Rooms have metal bunks, big windows, personal lockers, and ensuite baths.

*🚇 30m from Bahnhof Zoo. ℹ Wi-Fi €5 per day. Breakfast buffet €6. Linens €6. $ 8-10 bed dorms from €10; smaller dorms from €15. Doubles from €25; singles from €39. Prices may change significantly in busy months. ⏰ Reception 24hr.*

### FRAUENHOTEL ARTEMISIA — 💳🚭📶 HOTEL [4]

Brandenburgische Str. ☎030 873 89 05 💻www.frauenhotel-berlin.de

This elegant hotel for women only was the first of its kind in Germany. A quiet rooftop terrace with sweeping views of Berlin is adjacent to a sunny breakfast room. Rooms are spacious, with large windows and molding around the ceiling. Named after Italian painter Artemisia Gentileschi, the hotel hosts rotating art exhibitions.

*🚇 U7: Konstanzer Str. ℹ Breakfast buffet €8. Wi-Fi included. $ Singles €49-54, with bath €64-79; doubles €78/78-108. Additional beds for €20. ⏰ Reception daily 7am-10pm.*

### JUGENDHOTEL BERLIN — 💳 HOSTEL [3]

Kaiserdamm 3 ☎030 322 10 11 💻www.sportjugendhotel-berlin.de

Though mostly booked by traveling school groups, Jugendhotel Berlin is a good option for the traveler short on places to stay. Clean rooms with lots of light suffer from an unfortunate lack of decoration and character. All rooms have full baths, and over half have outdoor balconies.

*🚇 U2: Sophie-Charlotte-Pl. ℹ Breakfast and bed linens included. Substantial discounts for groups of 10 people or more, email for details. $ Singles €36-€46; doubles €33; triples €29-30. ⏰ Reception 24hr.*

### CITY PENSION BERLIN — 💳📶 PENSION [3]

Stuttgarter Pl. 9 ☎493 03 27 74 10 💻www.city-pension.de

In exchange for the extra euros, travelers at City Pension get an ensuite bath, television, and large rooms sans bunk beds. Near the S-Bahn and accentuated with elegant molding and watered glass, City Pension is a fancier non-hostel option for group travelers that can keep you all under budget.

*🚇 S3, S5, S7, or S75: Charlottenburg, or U7: Wilmersdorfer Str. ℹ Wi-Fi and breakfast included. $ Singles €54; doubles €76; 3-bed rooms €89; 4-bed €104; 5-bed €120. ⏰ Reception 24hr.*

### HOTEL PENSION CITYBLICK

PENSION [3]

Kantstr. 71 ☎030 32 30 32 82 🖳www.hotel-cityblick.de

The value of proximity to public transportation can never be underestimated. There's that and more, including rich ochre decor, surprisingly large rooms, and exposed timbers. An adjacent restaurant clinches the deal. The eating area is warm and friendly. Just be aware that prices may vary steeply from one week (or even one day) to the next. To avoid surprises, email ahead to verify costs at hotel-cityblick@gmx.de.

*S3, S5, S7 or S75: Charlottenberg, or U7: Wilmersdorferstr. $ Singles from €45; doubles from €60; triples from €80; quads from €90. ⏰ Reception 8am-10pm.*

**close to home**

Pensions are family-owned guest houses. They are cheaper than hotels, but more expensive than hostels. Many offer long-term rates.

## SCHÖNEBERG AND WILMERSDORF

### JUGENDHOTEL BERLINCITY

HOSTEL [3]

Crellerstr. 22 ☎030 78 70 21 30 🖳www.jugendhotel-berlin.de

Located on a quiet street and bordered by trees, this Jugendhotel Berlincity has first-class rooms, but no dorms. This hostel is a splurge for solo travelers and small groups (think arching-brick-ceilings-and-dark-wood-floors kind of splurge), and usually larger groups get more reasonable rates. The hostel has a strict no smoking and no alcohol policy.

*U7: Kleistpark. i Wi-Fi €1 per 30min., €5 per day. Sheets and breakfast included. $ Singles €38, with bath €52; doubles from €60/79; triples €87/102; quads €112/126; quints €124/150; 6-person rooms €146/168. ⏰ Reception 24hr.*

### JETPAK

HOSTEL [1]

Pücklerstr. 54 ☎030 83 25 🖳www.jetpak.de

JetPAK is way out in the boonies; if you're even remotely concerned about having a somewhat central location, think hard before booking here. That said, there's a lot that sets this hostel apart, and might make it worth the walk, bus, or train. Converted from an old German army camp, the hostel has been warmed up with colorful walls and comfortable beds and sofas, and is now more convincing as a summer camp. With showers heated by the hostel's own solar panels, this JetPAK is also one of Berlin's most environmentally conscious places to kick back and reap the benefits of nature.

*U3: Fehrbelliner Pl. or U9: Güntzselstr., then bus #115 (dir. Neuripppiner Str.): Pücklerstr. Follow the signs to Grunewald, and turn left on Pücklerstr. Turn left again when the JetPAK sign directs you, just before the road turns to dirt. i Breakfast, linens, and Internet included. $ 8-bed dorms €14; doubles €23.*

### ART-HOTEL CONNECTION

▼ HOTEL [4]

Fuggerstr. 33 ☎030 210 21 88 00 🖳www.arthotel-connection.de

Recently redecorated with deep purple walls, crystal chandeliers, and dark wood floors, this hotel is (almost) nothing but class. A gay hotel that describes itself as "hetero-friendly," Art-Hotel boasts some of the most sophisticated style in Schöneberg. But lest we get too serious, this hotel also offers "playrooms," with slings and other sex toys.

*U1, U2 or U15: Wittenbergpl. $ Mar-Oct singles €48; doubles €64; "playrooms" €99. Nov.-Feb. €43/59/89. ⏰ Reception 8am-10pm.*

### JETPAK CITY HOSTEL — 💳🚭 HOSTEL [2]

Pariserstr. 58 — ☎030 784 43 60 💻www.jetpak.de

There's nothing like large rooms with pine bunks, large windows, and brightly colored walls to lessen the institutional hostel feel. Owned by the same people who started the JetPAK in Grunewald, this hostel is much more central and practical for the city traveler, if not quite so one-of-a-kind. But after all, real estate hints at the importance of "location, location, location." The bathrooms are newly tiled, and the common room has couches and a foosball table. Most JetPAK travelers book ahead of time online.

*🚇 U3 or U9: Spichernstr. i Linens included. Most breakfast items, including croissants, €1. $ 8-bed dorms from €18; 6 bed dorms from €19; 4 bed dorms from €20. ⏰ Reception 8am-midnight.*

### JUGENDGÄSTEHAUS CENTRAL — 💳♿ HOSTEL [2]

Nikolsburger Str. 2-4 — ☎030 873 01 88 89 💻www.jugendgaestehaus-central.de

With a little more charm than the average *jugendgästehaus*, a few fun murals brighten this otherwise sparse hostel. The common room has a pool and foosball table and a TV for guests. A friendly, English-speaking staff that's actually helpful makes this otherwise ordinary hostel, usually reserved by groups, a slightly better option for backpackers.

*🚇 U9: Güntzelstr. i Sheets €2.50 for stays of less than 3 nights. More than 3 nights, sheets included. $ Mar-Oct €24 with breakfast included, with half-board €28, with full board €30. Nov-Feb €20/24/26. For a single room, add €5.50 per night. ⏰ Reception 24hr.*

### JUGENDHOTEL VIER JAHRESZEITEN — 💵🚭 HOSTEL [2]

Bundasallee 31a — ☎030 873 30 14 💻www.jugendhotel-4j.de

These rooms may be a little lacking in character with white walls and sparse decoration, but we always fall hard for bathrooms that actually have baths! Two rooms share a bathroom, with three common rooms and eating spaces on the first floor. Mostly popular with school groups, but also takes in a fair number of backpackers.

*🚇 U7 to "Güntzelstr." i Breakfast and sheets included. $ Doubles €22.50; 6-bed rooms €22.50 per night. ⏰ Reception 24hr.*

### CVJM JUGENDGÄSTEHAUS — 💵♿📶 HOSTEL [2]

Einemstr. 10 — ☎030 26 49 10 88 💻www.cvjm-jugendgaestehaus.de

From the outside, CVJM, a YMCA hostel, is sterile and plain. The interior is slightly warmer and always well-cleaned, with pine beds and large windows, if still lacking creative decoration. But there's not much to criticize about the top-floor common room, which has an open fireplace and views of Berlin. Hostel is usually booked for school groups. Quiet hours from 11pm.

*🚇 U1, U3, U4, or U9: Nollendorfpl. i Breakfast, Wi-Fi, and linens included. Lunch €3.20 extra. $ Mar-Oct singles €35; doubles €27.50; 3-bed rooms €25.50; 4-bed rooms €24.50. ⏰ Reception M-F 9am-6pm.*

### ARTA LENZ HOTEL — 💳🚭 HOTEL [3]

Xantener Str. 8 — ☎030 88 91 79 24 💻www.arta-lenz-hotel.de

Arta Lenz Hotel is a step up from most of the surrounding hostels in comfort, but far from opulent. A few rooms, including reception and the main entryway, reflect West Berlin's affluent past and the wealth on the nearby Kurfürstendamm, with granite walls, dark wood paneling, and marble floors. The rooms also have high ceilings with simple decorative carving around the top, but underwhelm with bland furnishings. Still, especially for groups of multiple travelers, Arta Lenz offers reliable, clean rooms for a very reasonable cost. Call ahead or check the website for prices: they can vary significantly.

*🚇 U7 to "Adenauerpl." i Breakfast included. Internet €5 per day. $ Singles from €39; doubles from €49; triples from €59; quads from €69. ⏰ Reception 24hr.*

# How are you doing Germany?

**A)** Like a berlin party animal.

**B)** Like a HIPPIE ... in Berlin

**C)** like a capital city SPACE COWBOY

**D)** ROCKIN' ALL OVER in BERLIN

**E)** flying into Frankfurt Airport

**F)** sleep easy in Munich

## OLIVAER APART HOTEL
                 ❤🚫 HOTEL ❸
Konstanzer Str. 1       ☎030 885 86 0 ✉www.olivaer-apart-hotel.de

With all new, sleek modern furniture, and dark wood paneling on ground floor walls, Olivaer is certainly more refined than any hostel in Schöneberg. That said, its rooms lack character, with nondescript white wallpaper, red carpeting, and simple beds. Rooms are all well-maintained, and bathrooms are decorated with marble tiled floors and shower stalls. And after a day of walking all over decadent *Schlöβer*, who couldn't use some trodding on marble? Sometimes "third beds" are fold out couches; check by email or phone, or at reception to find out what you're getting. Prices vary, so call ahead.

 ❦ *U7 to "Adenauerpl." i Breakfast included. Internet access for a fee. Ⓢ Singles from €39; doubles from €49; triples from €59; quads from €79; quints from €99.*

# MITTE

Travelers with a limited number of nights should especially think about paying the few extra bucks a night for a place in Mitte. Most of the hostels are nice, and a few of them are literally minutes away from major sights.

### ▨ CIRCUS HOSTEL
                ♿(ŋ)✵ HOSTEL ❷
Weinbergswet 1A    ☎030 20 00 39 39 (Skype: circus-berlin) ✉www.circus-berlin.de

A cushy place with luxurious beds in the hippest part of Mitte, Circus has a chill cafe, a great bar with nightly specials, DJs, and a pimping karaoke night. Wi-Fi only works well in rooms, and the lack of a"chill-out area" leaves more net-addicted guests wanting, but forgive us for nitpicking. Breakfast is generous and all you can eat, and the mattresses are like clouds. Rooms come with a load of "extras"; the podcast audio tours, jogging route maps, quality food recommendations, and outstandingly helpful staff really do make a difference.

 ❦ *U8: Rosenthaler Pl. i Linens included. Segways €35 per day. Bikes €12 per day. Breakfast €5. Towels €1. Luggage lockers €10 deposit. Ⓢ 8- to 10-bed dorms €19; 4-bed dorms €23. Singles €43; doubles €28. ⏰ Reception 24hr.*

### ▨ HELTER SKELTER
             ❤🚫(ŋ)✵ HOSTEL ❶
Kalkscheunenstr. 4-5    ☎030 28 04 49 97 ✉www.helterskelterhostel.de

The receptionist's warning: "The bar's open all day, but if you're too drunk at breakfast, we cut you off." A bit dirty, a bit worn, but that's just because every night here is wild. If hostel-wide drinking games and late nights are your thing, then take a chance on this place, and years from now you'll remember it as a Berlin highlight.

 ❦ *U6: Oranienburger Tor. From the station, head south on Friedrichstr. and take a left on Johannisstr. The hostel is on the 3rd fl. through a courtyard. Follow the signs. i Linens, towel, coffee, tea, and Wi-Fi included. Breakfast €3 (free for guests staying longer than 3 days). Smoking allowed in common area. Kitchen available. First 10min. on computer free, €1 per 30min. after. Key deposit €5. Ⓢ Megadorm €10-14. Singles €34; doubles €22-27. ⏰ Reception 24hr. Check-in 2pm. Check-out noon.*

### BAXPAX DOWNTOWN HOTEL/HOSTEL
      ❤♿(ŋ)✵ HOSTEL, HOTEL ❷
Ziegelstr. 28        ☎30 27 87 48 80 ✉www.baxpax.de

Baxpax Downtown has a bag full of fun hostel tricks. Two aboveground pools are revealed in the summer (one on the lower patio, the other on the roof, where, by the way, there's a sweet minibar). Downstairs has its own bar, where a giant stuffed moose head keeps court. The hangout room has a pinball machine, and the patio has a bizzare 6m long bed in case you want to get weird with your friends.

 ❦ *U6: Oranienburger Tor. From the station, head south on Friedrichstr., then turn left on Ziegelstr. i Key deposit €5. Linens €2.50. Towel €1, free in doubles and singles. Breakfast €5.50. Laundry self-service €5, full-service €8. Non-smoking. Ⓢ 20-bed dorms €10-31; 5-bed dorms with private shower €16-36. Singles €29-92; doubles €54-132. ⏰ Reception 24hr. Check-in 3pm. Check-out 11am.*

## WOMBAT'S CITY HOSTEL

HOSTEL 2

Alte Schönhauser Str. 2 ☎030 84 71 08 20 www.wombats-hostels.com

Mod, spotless, comfortable, with a rooftop bar and terrace—if Wombats is wrong, we don't want to be right. Hotel-like amenities exclude the possibility of clutch deals, but relax on the beanbags in the lobby and consider that you get what you pay for—that is, except for your first drink at the bar, which is free. The apartments with mini kitchens are nice enough to live in long-term.

*U2: Rosa-Luxemburg-Pl. [i] Linens, lockers, luggage storage, and Wi-Fi included. Towel €2, free in doubles and apartments. 8 Internet stations; €.50 per 20min. Breakfast €3.70. Laundry €4.50. Guest kitchen. Non-smoking. $ 4- to 6-bed dorms €20-24; doubles €58-70; apartments €40-50 per person. Reception 24hr. Check-in 2pm. Check-out 10am.*

## CITYSTAY

HOSTEL 2

Rosenstr. 16 ☎030 23 62 40 31 www.citystay.de

Besides being the most centrally located hostel in Berlin, a beautiful, well-kept courtyard and an expansive cafe lounge separate this hostel from the pack. Rooms are nice enough with huge windows and adequate beds. But you know what's really nice? A 2min. walk to Museum Island and Unter der Linden.

*U5, U8, S5, S7, S9, S75: Alexander Pl. [i] Laundry €5. 5 computers in lobby; €3 per hr. Lockers €10 deposit. Sheets €2.50, free with ISIC. Towel €5 deposit. 2 women-only dorms. $ 8-bed dorms €17; 4-bed dorms €21; doubles €50, with private shower €65. Reception 24hr. Check-in 2pm. Check-out 10am.*

## ST. CHRISTOPHER'S

HOSTEL 2

Rosa Luxembourg Str. 41 ☎030 81 45 39 60 www.st-christophers.co.uk

It's rare you find a hostel bar with drinks as cheap as €1 Jager shots, but St. Christopher's delivers this and, subsequently, many a wild night. The Wi-Fi-equipped bar, lobby, and loft spaces blow most hostels out of the water. Rooms are spacious and clean and smell nice, though the same can't always be said of your roommates.

*U2: Rosa-Luxemburg-Pl. [i] Breakfast, luggage storage, lockers, and linens included. Towels €1. Internet €2 per hr. Non smoking. $ Prices change in real time based upon availability. Dorms €12-20; doubles €35-50; quads €60-96. Reception 24hr. Check-in 2pm. Check-out 10am. Bar open daily until 3am.*

## BAXPAX MITTE

HOSTEL 2

Chausseestr. 102 ☎30 28 39 09 65 www.baxpax.de/mittes-backpacker

Baxpax Mitte rewards travelers who favor flavor over luxury. A group of traveling artists spread their love over the rooms to create a series of themed sanctuaries like the Garden of Eden, which has carpet-lined walls, or the Four Elements room with floors of water, beds of fire, earth tracked in by your dormmates, and air of air. The poetry room continues to develop as guests add their own original works: "Let's Go knows/That it should stick/To prose." No beds are actually made of fire.

*U6: Zinnowitzer Str. [i] Guest kitchen available. Linens €2.50. Key deposit €10. Towel €1. Full service laundry €7. Breakfast €5.50. 2 Internet kiosks €2 per hr. Happy hour at small in-house bar 7-8pm. Non-smoking. $ 7- to 9-bed dorms €13-19; 4-bed dorms €19-26. Singles €37-39; doubles €58-62, with private toilet €46-68. Reception 24hr. Check-in 3pm. Check-out 11am.*

## HEART OF GOLD HOSTEL

HOSTEL 1

Johannisstr. 11 ☎030 29 00 33 00 www.heartofgold-hostel.de

With a rundown *The Hitchhiker's Guide to the Galaxy* theme, Heart of Gold Hostel makes a bunch of references to its source material that most travelers won't get. Don't worry—not everyone can appreciate literature. The dorms aren't very plush, but enormous windows and wild space-themed rooms will distract you from that.

*S1, S2, S25: Oranienburger Str. Or U6: Oranienburger Tor. [i] Wi-Fi, lockers, and towel included. Breakfast €3.50, free for guests staying more than 3 days. Laundry €4. Key deposit €5. Linens deposit €5. Padlock deposit €10. $ Megadorms €22; 4-bed dorms €12. Singles €40; doubles €60. Reception 24hr. Check-in 2pm. Check-out noon.*

**CITY HOSTEL BERLIN** 💳♿📶🍸⛅ HOSTEL ❷

Glinka Str. 5-7 ☎030 238 86 68 52 💻www.cityhostel-berlin.com

City Hostel Berlin feels a little old and institutionalized for having only been around a few years. Although it can't produce an awesome social environment, the beds are nice and the bathrooms are clean. A nice little bar with cheap and delicious snacks stays open late but doesn't exactly encourage revelry. Great "family rooms" with a bunk and a double bed available.

*✣ U2: Mohrenstr. ℹ 6 Internet stations €0.50 per hour. Breakfast, luggage storage, safe box, Wi-Fi, lockers, linens, and towels included. Bike rental available. $ Dorms €17-22; doubles with shower €48-54. ⏰ Reception 24hr. Check-in 3pm. Check-out 10am. Bar open 6pm-late.*

**THREE LITTLE PIGS HOSTEL** 🚫💳🚫♿🍸 HOSTEL ❷

Stresemannstr. 66 ☎030 32 66 29 55 💻www.three-little-pigs.de

An enormous 100-year-old former abbey serves as this hostel's lobby. Pushed back from the road through a series of courtyards, Three Little Pigs feels removed from the bustle of the city. Sturdy benches and long oak tables make it feel more like a medieval drinking hall than a hostel. Rooms and mattresses could be plusher but are entirely adequate, and the outdoor terrace is heaven on warm days.

*✣ S1, S2, or S25: Anhalter Bahnhof. ℹ Wi-Fi and lockers included. Laundry €5. Bike rental €12 per day. 4 computers with Internet access €2 per hr. Breakfast €5. Linens €2.50. Towel €1. Guest kitchen. Parking facilities available. $ 6- to 8-bed dorms €11-17; Singles €34-36; doubles €44-48. ⏰ Reception 24hr. Check-in 3pm. Check-out 11am.*

## PRENZLAUER BERG

👍 **PFEFFERBETT** 🚫💳♿📶🍸 HOSTEL ❷

Christinenstr. 18-19 ☎030 93 93 58 58 💻www.pfefferbett.de

This old, 19th-century brick building is tasteful with a modern edge. The lobby's towering ceilings are supported by brick arches, and the garden out back has a patio popular for socializing. Bathrooms are newly tiled, and spacious rooms have a fun style, with thick stripes running around the walls. Lounge room has a pool, foosball table, and fireplace.

*✣ U2: Senefelderpl. ℹ Breakfast items from €1. Linens €2.50. $ Mar-Oct 8-bed dorms €16; 6-bed €20; 4-bed dorms with bath €25; singles with bath €58; doubles with bath €78. Nov-Feb 8-bed dorms €12; 6-bed €15; 4-bed dorms with bath €20; singles with bath Nov-Feb €47; doubles with €64. ⏰ Reception 24hr.*

👍 **EAST SEVEN HOSTEL** 💳♿📶🍸 HOSTEL ❷

Schwedter Str. 7 ☎030 93 62 22 40 💻www.eastseven.de

Orange and olive walls make this retro hostel a cool, bunk-free place to stay. The indoor lounge area with comfortable sofas and the back patio with a grill are well-used hangouts for backpackers who appreciate cold beer specials *(€1)*. Rooms are spacious, with hardwood floors, old windows, and subtle-hued stripes that would make Martha Stewart proud.

*✣ U2: Senefelderpl. ℹ Free Wi-Fi; Internet terminals €0.50 per 20min. Linens included. Bike rental €10 per day. $ Mar-Oct 8-bed dorms €18; 4-bed dorms with bath €22; singles €38; doubles €26; triples €22. Nov-Feb 8-bed dorms €14; 4-bed dorms with bath €19; singles €31; doubles €22; triples €19. ⏰ Reception 7am-midnight.*

**ALCATRAZ** 🚫💳🚫♿📶 HOSTEL ❷

Schönehauser Allee 133A ☎030 48 49 68 15 💻www.alcatraz-backpacker.de

Alcatraz is hardly an inescapable prison, but you probably wouldn't mind spending a life sentence here. This hostel's graffiti-chic, spray-painted exterior is as lively as the sociable "chill out room," fully stocked with a foosball table and television. Alcatraz has 80 beds in carefully decorated rooms that contrast the chaos of the common areas. All rooms have ensuite baths, big windows, light yellow walls, and pine bunks.

*✣ U2: Eberswalder Str. ℹ Wi-Fi included. Fully equipped kitchen. Linens €2. Bike rental €10 per*

*day.* $ *Mar-Oct 8-bed dorms €16; 4-bed €18; singles €40; doubles €50; triples €69. Nov-Feb 8-bed dorms €13; 4-bed dorms €15; singles €35; doubles €44; triples €57.* ⏰ *Reception 24hr.*

**LETTE'M SLEEP HOSTEL** HOSTEL [2]

Lettestr. 7 ☎030 44 73 36 23 💻www.backpackers.de

Located opposite a small park and between the popular bars of the lively Helmholtzpl., this brightly painted hostel is situated perfectly in the middle of Prenzlauer Berg's afternoon and early evening cafe scene. The big kitchen, complete with comfy red couches, a television, and a selection of DVDs, is home base for the hostel's young backpackers. Rooms are spacious and well-lit, with personal lockers and sinks in every room.

*U2: Eberswalder Str.* **i** *Linens and Wi-Fi included.* $ *Apr-Oct 4- to 7-bed dorms €17-23; doubles with sheets and a small kitchenette €55; triples €60. Nov-Mar 4- to 7-bed dorms €11-20; doubles with sheets and a small kitchenette €40; triples €60.* ⏰ *Reception 24hr.*

**MEININGER** HOTEL [3]

Schönehauser Allee 19 💻www.meininger-hotels.com

Meninger is having an identity crisis; the establishment self-identifies as a hotel but charges by the person to fill up its dorms. Decorated in red and white, this neat and clean ho(s)tel is all reliability. Boasting bright white walls, spotless rooms, lots of windows, and just-outside proximity to the U-Bahn station, you really can't lose. Special deals for families.

*U2: Senefelderpl.* **i** *Free Wi-Fi, or €1 per 20min. at terminals. Breakfast €5.50. Sheets included. All bathrooms ensuite.* $ *3- to 6-bed dorms €28; women-only or small dorms €19; singles €52; doubles €70. Children 6-12 pay 50% of per person fee.* ⏰ *Reception 24hr. Check-out 1pm.*

**AURORA-HOSTEL** HOSTEL [3]

Pappelallee 21 ☎030 46 99 59 30 💻www.aurora-hostel.com

There's not much to set this small hostel apart, other than an unbeatable location. Walls are white and generally lack decoration, and linoleum floors don't lend character, but this spotless hostel has one quirk: guests can pick a colored light bulb to shine in their window, making the outside of the hostel its own aurora by night.

*U2: Eberswalder Str.* $ *3-bed dorms €64.50; singles €30; doubles €49.* ⏰ *Reception 8am-10pm.*

## FRIEDRICHSHAIN

Friedrichshain has built a reputation for itself as Berlin's neighborhood for inexpensive student-friendly housing. Luckily, travelers will enjoy the same wide range of youthful, cheap options for accommodations.

**ALL IN HOSTEL** HOSTEL [1]

Grünberger Str. 54 ☎030 288 76 83 💻www.all-in-hostel.com

A bright, open lounge with a welcoming staff make you feel right at home. Rooms have crowded bunks but compensate with high ceilings and big windows. The location is unbeatable—right in the thick of Friedrichshain's popular cafes and bars on a quiet, arboreal street. The crowded lounge area, with big, comfortable couches, is great for socializing.

*U5: Franfurter Tor.* **i** *Wi-Fi €1 per hr., hostel terminal €1 per 20min. Breakfast €5. Sheets €3 for 1st night only.* $ *10-bed dorms €10; 6-bed dorms with bath €18. Singles with bath €39; doubles with bath €44.* ⏰ *Reception 24hr.*

**GLOBETROTTER HOSTEL ODYSSEE** HOSTEL [1]

Grünberger Str. 23 ☎030 29 00 00 81 💻www.globetrotterhostel

Right in the middle of Friedrichshain's bars and restaurants, Globetrotter Odyssee is decorated with quirky medieval statues and vaulted ceilings. Muraled walls and rock music in the lounge (furnished with a pool table) give the hostel an East Berlin edge.

*U5: Franfurter Tor.* **i** *Free Wi-Fi, hostel terminals €0.50 per 20min. Breakfast €8. Sheets €3* *deposit. Credit card min. €25. $ Mar-Oct 8-bed dorms €13.50; 6-bed €15.50; 4-bed €17.50; 3-bed €19.50; singles €36; doubles €47. Nov-Feb 8-bed dorms €10; 6-bed €12; 4-bed €14; 3-bed €16; singles €29, doubles €39. ⏰ Reception 24hr.*

**U INN BERLIN HOSTEL** 🛏🚭📶 HOSTEL [2]

Finowstr. 36 ☎030 33 02 44 10 🖥info@uinnberlinhostel.com

This small hostel has only 40 beds and is set off a quiet street in Friedrichshain. Rooms are spacious, with pine bunks and brightly colored walls. U Inn Berlin doesn't consider itself a party hostel; there's a no-alcohol policy, and quiet hours start at 10pm. This hostel's speciality is creating a community for its small number of guests, with events like free German cooking lessons every Friday at 7pm.

*🚇 U5: Franfurter Tor. i Linens €2. Breakfast €2. Hostel terminals €1 per 20min. €0.50 daily supplement to pay for "greening" the cleaning supplies and buying fair-trade, organic coffee. $ Apr-Oct 8-bed dorms €15; 5-bed €18; 4-bed €19; 3-bed €23; singles €29; doubles €50. Nov-Mar 8-bed dorms €13; 5-bed €16; 4-bed €17; 3-bed €21; singles €25; doubles €46. ⏰ Reception 7am-1am.*

**PEGASUS HOSTEL BERLIN** 🛏🚭📶 HOSTEL [1]

Str. der Pariser Kommune 35 ☎030 297 73 60 🖥www.pegasushostel.de

Set around a courtyard with picnic tables, this hostel has a laid-back atmosphere, but is full of young energy. Towering orange and yellow walls are decorated with canvases of student artwork. There are private lockers in all the rooms. The top floor rooms include loft beds, set right underneath large skylights.

*🚇 U5: Weberwiese. i Linens included. Breakfast €6. $ 8- to 10-bed dorms €13; 6-bed €15; quads from €68; triples from €57. Prices vary significantly; call or email ahead to confirm. ⏰ Reception 24hr.*

**A AND O HOSTEL** 🛏♿📶 HOSTEL [1]

Boxhagener Str. 73 ☎030 80 94 7 54 00 🖥www.aohostels.com

With over 450 beds, this A and O feels like more like a self-sufficient youth community than a hostel. A bright, airy lounge and bar have their own, separate building with foosball and pool tables. Travelers sleep in towering buildings that surround a courtyard. The backyard has a tar volleyball court and single basketball hoop for pick-up games. This A and O might still have some of that chain-hostel look with pre-fab beds and minimal decoration on the walls, but a few quirky touches, like student-made statues in the living area, give it more character.

*🚇 U5: Frankfurter Allee. Alternatively, S3, S5, S7, S9 or S75: Ostdreuz. i Breakfast €4. Sheets €3 1st night. Wi-Fi €1 per hr., €8 per week. $ 4- to 8-bed dorms from €10; singles from €19. Prices vary significantly; in the high season, dorms cost as much as €20 per person. Additional €2 for ensuite bath. ⏰ Reception 24hr.*

**SUNFLOWER HOSTEL** 🛏♿📶 HOSTEL [1]

Helsingforser Str. 17 ☎030 44 04 42 50 🖥www.sunflower-hostel.de

This relaxed, eclectic hostel is decorated in dark blue and vivid orange with vines hanging from the ceiling and a small pond with running water in the lounge. The spotless rooms with high ceilings, striped walls, big windows and personal lockers are a marked contrast to the studied chaos of the common areas. The staff invites guests to ask about Berlin; use them as a great resource for Friedrichshain nightlife. This hostel is close to the action on the river but farther away from cafes and bars in the Simon-Dach area.

*🚇 U1, S3, S5, S7, S9 or S75: Warschauer Str. i Breakfast €3. Laundry €4.50. Linens and padlocks €3 deposit. $ 7- to 8-bed dorms €10-14.50; 5- to 6-bed dorms €12.50-16.50. Singles €30-36.50; doubles €38-46.50; triples €51-61.50; quads €60-79.50. ⏰ Reception 24hr.*

**EASTERN COMFORT HOSTEL** 🛏🚭📶 HOSTEL [2]

Mühlenstr. 73-77 ☎030 66 76 38 06 🖥www.eatern-comfort.com

Stop flipping copies at Kinko's and grab your swim trunks and your flippy-floppies. This hostel is straight flowing on the Spree on the deep blue East Berlin side of the river. Guests rent rooms in cabins, with fold-down beds in dorm rooms and portals for windows. The truly adventurous can rent a tent and sleep on the top deck for the cheapest view of the big blue watery road. Every Wednesday, travelers enjoy a Language Party, where guests get together to experience the hostel's international clientele.

✚ *U1, S3, S5, S7, S9, or S75: Warschauer Str.* ℹ *Wi-Fi included. Breakfast €4.50. Internet €3 per hr. Linens €5. 2-night bookings only on the weekends.* ⑤ *4- or 5-bed dorms €16; 4-bed dorms with bath €19. Singles with bath €50; doubles with bath €58; triples with bath €69. Tents €12.* ⓩ *Reception 8am-midnight.*

## OSTEL ♥((ɕ)) HOSTEL ❷

Wriezener Karree 5 ☎030 25 76 86 60 ▣www.ostel.eu

No, it's not a typo. The oddly abbreviated "Ostel" is also distinctive for a lime green exterior in a newly constructed, stucco-sided, small high-rise, built close to the river but far from Friedrichshain's restaurants and bars. This recently-decorated hostel prides itself on its "DDR Design," but unless that's code for a business-hotel vibe, we're a little lost. Pre-fab beds and small stripes of wallpaper decorate this neat and clean hostel's walls. Some rooms have balconies.

✚ *S3, S5, S7, S9, or S75: Ostbahnhof.* ℹ *Linens and towels included. Breakfast €6.50.* ⑤ *8-bed dorms €15; singles €33; doubles €54.* ⓩ *Reception 24hr.*

# KREUZBERG

Accommodations in Kreuzberg tend to a bit grungier than other parts of the city, but the hostels also have a much better sense of community. Staying in Kreuzberg lets travelers live in a rich community while still being close to the city's major sights.

## ▨ METROPOL HOSTEL ♥&Ұ HOSTEL ❷

Mehringdamm 32 ▣www.Metropolhostel-berlin.com

The newest addition to the Kreuzberg hostel scene wasn't entirely finished when *Let's Go* stopped by, but the results thus far are pretty promising. The hallways feel a bit like a hospital, but the rooms themselves sometimes verge on near-hotel accommodations. Superb mattresses, clean floors, newly painted walls, and spotless bathrooms all work to this end. Oh, and those century-old-looking doors are actually 100 years old. The building is a historical site and the doors cannot be replaced.

✚ *U6 or U7: Mehringdamm.* ℹ *Shower and toilet in every room. Breakfast, linens, lockers, luggage storage, safe box, and towels included.* ⑤ *6- to 10-bed dorms €9-14; singles €39-49; doubles €40 50.* ⓩ *Reception 24hr. Check-in 2pm. Check-out 10am.*

## HOSTEL X BERGER ☺⊗((ɕ))Ұ HOSTEL ❶

Schlesischestr. 22 ☎030 69 53 18 63 ▣www.hostelxberger.com

For the quickest jump to the coolest clubs in Berlin, no one outdoes Hostel X Berger, located right along the canal. While the accommodations are far from new, the rooms somehow feel relaxed, like you've already lived there. A foggy downstairs smoke room with a pool table works like an underground club, while a quiet study upstairs makes good space to work. Rooms are also designed to let you play hard, with a late check-out time and free coffee for the after-party blues.

✚ *U1: Schlesisches Tor. From the U-bahn, head south on Schlesischestr.* ℹ *Luggage storage and Wi-Fi included. 2 computers with free Internet. Linens €2. Towel €1. Laundry €4. Lock rental €1. Key deposit €6. Guest kitchen open until 9:30pm.* ⑤ *4-bed dorms €17-18; 16-bed dorms €11-12. Singles €32-36; doubles €40-46.* ⓩ *Reception 24hr. Check-in 4pm. Check-out 2pm.*

## BAXPAX KREUZBERG ☺&((ɕ))Ұ⌂ HOSTEL ❷

Skalitzer Str. 104 ☎030 69 51 83 22 ▣www.baxpax.de

This old-school backpacker hostel offers far from the royal treatment, but a weary traveler will find a bed, lively drunk guests, and staff accustomed to drunk guests. Rooms are themed around countries—someone literally sleeps in a VW bug in the German room. A rooftop terrace connected to the guest kitchen is brilliant in the daytime but unfortunately closes at 10pm. Shoddy Wi-Fi is a major turn-off, but the signal is enough to check mail. Staff wakes you up if you sleep past check-out...not that we would know.

🍴 *U1: Görlitzer Bahnhof.* ℹ️ *Breakfast options €1-2.50. Linens and towel €2.50. Internet €2 per hr. Laundry €7. Lockers, luggage storage, and safebox included. Guests can smoke in the common room after 6pm.* Ⓢ *32-bed dorms €9-14; 8-bed €10-17; 4-bed €14-20. Singles €26-37; doubles with bath €24-30.* 🕐 *Reception 24hr. Check-in 3pm. Check-out 11am.*

## HOSTEL 36 ROOMS
◎Ⓧ⦅ᵗᵖ⦆Ⓨ HOSTEL ❶

Spreewaldpl. 8    ☎030 53 08 63 98 🖥️www.36rooms.com

Nice large rooms and a beautiful outdoor patio are somewhat robbed of fun by the hostel's no-outside-alcohol policy. Guests can beer it at the hostel bar or wait until Thursday, Friday and Saturday, when one of Kreuzberg's hippest underground clubs rocks in the hostel's basement. Hot travelers can dip in the wave pool across the street at the hostel's discounted price *(€2 per hr.)*. Old World rooms have chandeliers and great views of the nearby park. Unfortunately some also have an Old World smell.

🍴 *U1: Görlitzer Bahnhof.* ℹ️ *Locker rental €2. Linens and towel €2.50. Bike rental €10 per day. Key deposit €10.* Ⓢ *8-bed dorms €14-17; 4-bed €18-21. Singles €35-39; doubles €50-58.* 🕐 *Reception 24hr. Check-in 1pm. Check-out 11am. Patio and kitchen open until 10pm.*

## COMEBACK PACKERS HOSTEL
◎Ⓧ⦅ᵗᵖ⦆Ⓨ HOSTEL ❶

Alabertstr. 97    ☎030 60 05 75 27 🖥️www.comebackpackers.com

As you climb the fish-smelling stairs, you'd never guess that this relaxed hostel waited at the top, just chilling there. The large common room feels more like your mother's kitchen and stays open all night. Guests can jump out the windows...onto the roof for a smoke or some sun at the picnic tables. The showers are pretty exposed—as in, people will definitely see you naked, and you definitely should not pee because everyone will know, and it will be embarrassing. Anyway—beds are adequate and tend to not be bunked. Rooms are large, wood-floored, and climb-on-the-roof-able, but otherwise unremarkable. The only remarkable thing is the goose lamp in the goose room. It's a goose. But it's also a lamp. Staff has a very German sense of humor.

🍴 *U1 or U8: Kotbusser Tor.* ℹ️ *Coffee, linens, and Wi-Fi included. Key deposit €10. Full-service laundry €5. Towel €2. Continental breakfast (€3) must be requested.* Ⓢ *Dorms €14-20.* 🕐 *Reception 24hr. Check-in 3pm. Check-out 1pm.*

## MEININGER
🏄&♿Ⓨ HOSTEL ❷

Hallesches Ufer 30    ☎030 66 63 61 00 🖥️www.meininger-hotels.com

Meininger might not be the cheapest hostel around, but it provides top-notch service. Most impressive is that Meininger balances hip with professionalism. Graffiti-lined walls lead to a quaint guest kitchen that never closes, all-you-can-eat breakfast is served on a beautiful roof terrace, and a relaxed bar/workspace serves up drinks daily from 7pm. The beds don't break any comfort records, but the rooms definitely beat the average: each has a TV and carpets are all unstained. Potsdammer pl. and many of the great sites in lower Mitte are just a hop away, assuming you have developed hopping muscles.

🍴 *U1 or U6: Hallesches Tor.* ℹ️ *Linens and lockers included. Late riser fee €5. Breakfast €4. Laundry €5. Towel €1, plus €5 deposit. Lock deposit €5.* Ⓢ *8-bed dorms €18-21; 4-bed €23-24. Singles €49-55; doubles €66-72.* 🕐 *Reception 24hr. Check-in 2pm. Check-out 10am. Late check-out 1pm. Roof terrace open until 10pm.*

## ALETTO'S
🏄&♿Ⓨ⌂ HOSTEL ❷

Tempelhofer Ufer 8-9    ☎030 25 93 04 80 🖥️www.aletto.de

In spite of a logo that resembles a horned dildo, Aletto keeps it clean for groups of travelers. Even though its rooms come in denominations for one to eight people, each room is private and must be booked in its entirety. The Hostel Oscar nominees for Best Amenities at an Aletto hostel in Kreuzberg are: large free breakfast, starring eggs; the mini-cinema, starring free DVD rentals; and the snappy common spaces, starring free Wi-Fi, a full service bar, and a foosball table. Matresses are a cut above average, and proud pictures of the horned dildo enchant every room.

✦ *U1 or U6: Hallesches Tor.* ℹ *Linens, luggage storage, and towels included. ATM available. Internet €2 per hr.* Ⓢ *All prices are per room. 4-bed dorms €16-29; 6-bed €90-156. Singles €35-55; doubles €39-75.* ⓩ *Reception 24hr. Check-in 2pm. Check-out noon.*

## BERLIN BOUTIQUE HOSTEL
➜⊗(ꞏꞏ)👤 HOSTEL ❶

Gneisenaustr. 109-110 ☎030 69 81 92 37 🖥www.boutique-hostel.de

If boutiques are small and fancy, then this tiny hostel lives up to at least half of its name. With only 32 beds, Boutique lacks a sense of real hostel community, and even though it's small, it could benefit from a few more toilets and showers. Additionally, if you need a lot of help in life (which you won't because you bought this really comprehensive travel guide), the lack of 24hr. reception can be a bummer. But for travelers who don't care, the rooms are cheap, clean, and even have some charm, with tall French doors and high ceilings in some of them. A small lounge area has a DVD collection and a flatscreen TV.

✦ *U6 or U7: Mehringdamm.* ℹ *Luggage storage and Wi-Fi included. Irons and hair dryers available at front desk.* Ⓢ *12-bed dorms €12-13; 6-bed €14-15. Doubles €50-60.* ⓩ *Reception 8am-11pm. Check-in 2pm. Check-out noon. Travelers can arrange for late arrival.*

# sights

## CHARLOTTENBURG

Most of Berlin's sights are located outside of residential Charlottenburg, closer to the center of the city. That said, Charlottenburg has certain sights that recommend themselves to the traveler with more than a day or two to spend in Berlin. Unique museums, grand palaces, and one of the world's most historic stadiums are spread out all over the neighborhood.

### 🖼 KÄTHE-KOLLWITZ-MUSEUM
MUSEUM

Fasanenstr. 24 ☎030 32 69 06 00 🖥www.kaethe-kollwitz.de

Through both World Wars, Käthe Kollwitz, a member of the Berlin Sezession (Secession) movement and one of Germany's most prominent 20th century artists, protested war and the situation of the working class with haunting sketches, etchings, sculpture and charcoal drawings of death, poverty, and starvation. The series of works entitled, "A Weaver's Revolt," on the 2nd floor are the drawings that skyrocketed Kollwitz to fame. The death of the artist's own son, who was killed in Russia during WWII, provides a wrenching emotional authenticity to her depictions of death, pregnancy, and starvation, and her own revealing self-portraits.

✦ *U1: "Uhlandstr."* Ⓢ *Admission €6, students €3.* ⓩ *Open daily 11am-6pm.*

### 🖼 SCHLOß CHARLOTTENBURG
PALACE

Spandauer Damm 10-22 ☎030 320 9275

This expansive Baroque palace, commissioned by Friedrich I in the 1600s as a gift for his wife, Sophia-Charlotte, stands impressively at the end of a long treelined walkway on the outer north end of Charlottenberg. The Schloß is made up of several parts. **Altes Schloß,** the oldest section (marked by a blue dome in the middle of the courtyard), has rooms chock full of historic furnishings (much of it reconstructed due to war damage) and elaborate gold guilding. **Neuer Flügel** (New Wing), includes the marble receiving rooms and the more somber royal chambers. **Neuer Pavillion** houses a museum dedicated to Prussian architect Karl Friedrich Schinkel. Other sections include the **Belvedere,** a small building housing the royal family's porcelain collection, and the **Mausoleum,** the final resting place for most of the family. Behind the palace extends the exquisitely manicured

Schloßgarten, full of small lakes, footbridges and fountains.

*➔ Bus #M45 from Bahnhof Zoo to Luisenpl./Schloß Charlottenburg or U2: Sophie-Charlotte Pl. $ Altes Schloß €10, students €7; Neuer Flügel €6/5; Belvedere €2/1.50; Mausoleum free. Audio tours available in English included. ⏰ Altes Schloß open Apr-Oct Tu-Su 10am-6pm; Nov-Mar Tu-Su 10am-5pm. Neuer Flügel open year-round M and W-Su 10am-5pm. Belvedere and Mausoleum open Apr-Oct daily 10am-6pm, Nov-Mar daily noon-5pm.*

**MUSEUM BERGGRUEN** MUSEUM

Schloßstr. 1 ☎030 326 95 80

Think Picasso is a jerk whose art didn't deserve the hype it got? This intimate three-floor museum will put away your anti-Picasso sentiments. The first and second floor are Picasso-packed, with added bonuses of French Impressionist Matisse's art and African masks. The third floor showcases paintings by Bauhaus teacher Paul Klee and Alberto Giacometti's super-skinny sculptures of human forms.

*➔ Bus #M45 from Bahnhof Zoo to Luisenpl./Schloß Charlottenburg or U2: Sophie-Charlotte Pl. $ €12, €6 students, children free. Audio guide included. ⏰ Open Tu-Su 10am-6pm.*

**BRÖHANMUSEUM** MUSEUM

Schloßstr. 1A ☎030 32 69 06 00 💻www.broehanmuseum.de

If you're wondering where all the stuff you couldn't sell at your great-aunt's estate sale went, here it is. The Bröhanmuseum showcases epic brös ißing brös... Just kidding, we mean Art Nouveau and Art Deco paintings, housewares, and furniture. Along with figurines and lampshades that resemble knicknacks you sneered at (and now regret not buying) at neighborhood garage sales, the ground floor also pairs several groupings of period furniture with paintings from the same era (1889-1939). The first floor is a small gallery dedicated to the Modernist Berlin *Sezession* painters, though occasionally upstaged by oddly chosen shocking green walls, and the top floor houses special exhibitions.

*➔ Bus #M45 from Bahnhof Zoo to Luisenpl./Schloß Charlottenburg or U2: Sophie-Charlotte Pl. The museum is next to the Bergguen, across from the Schloß. $ Admission €6, students €4. ⏰ Open Tu-Su 10am-6pm.*



**OLYMPIASTADION** STADIUM

Olympischer Pl. 3 (Visitor Center) ☎030 25 00 23 22 💻www.olypiastadion-berlin.de

This massive Nazi-built stadium comes in a close second to Tempelhof Airport in the list of monumental Third Reich buildings in Berlin. It was erected for the infamous 1936 Olympic Games, in which African-American track and field athlete Jesse Owens won four gold medals. Hitler refused to congratulate Owens, who has since been honored with a Berlin street, Jesse-Ownes-Allee and his name has been engraved into the side of the stadium with the other 1936 gold medal winners. The six stone pillars flanking the stadium were originally intended to signify the unity of the six "tribes" of ethnicities that Hitler believed fed into true German heritage. Recent uses have included the 2006 World Cup final. The independently operated **Glockenturm** (bell tower) provides a great lookout point and houses an exhibit on the history of German athletics.

*➔ S5, S7, or U2: Olympia-Stadion. For Glockenturm, S5 or S7: Pichelsburg. $ €4, students €3. Tour with guide €8, students €7, children under 6 free. ⏰ Open daily Mar 20-May 9am-7pm, June-Sept 15 9am-8pm, Sept 16-Oct 31 9am-7pm, Nov-Mar 19 9am-4pm.*

**KAISER-WILHELM-GEDÄCHTNISKIRCH (MEMORIAL CHURCH)** CHURCH

Centre of the Breitscheidpl. ☎030 218 5023

This partially destroyed church was left standing after World War II as a reminder of the devastation of war. With gaping holes where the large circular stained glass used to fit, this is a moving testament to the price Germany paid. Part neo-Romanesque and Byzantine style, part war-ravaged, cracked colorful mosaics line the interior, which you can compare to a small exhibit that shows the

## fütball faithful

I am An American Who Doesn't Watch Soccer. Yes, one of those. Back home, there are millions of us people who don't much care for eleven sweaty men kicking a ball around to each other, with the 90-minute drone of sporting monotony punctuated (if you're lucky!) once or twice by the excitement of a goal. My brother and I watched the past two World Cup tournaments periodically; we considered a game a success if we managed to pay attention long enough to see a goal scored.

But on Sunday night, I decided to go undercover as A German Who Would Follow Her Team to the Edge of the Earth. The city of Berlin was broadcasting the first game against Australia live outside Olympic Stadium, to a crowd of 200,000 bloodthirsty (and beerthirsty) Deutschelanders.

Blending in was surprisingly easy. Even if I sometimes feared that the 199,999 people standing around me would suddenly collectively figure me out, I managed to conceal my nationality for those three crazy hours. I sang along to cheers whose words I didn't understand, I jumped up and down with people I'd never met, and I drank good beer in the spirit of international cooperation.

The night couldn't have gone better. Four times Germany scored on Australia, and every time the crowd went absolutely wild. I'd actually never seen anything like it. And that was all it took. I'm hooked. I love soccer. Actually, no—I love *fütball.* I'm swapping in my Birkenstocks for cleats, and I'm never leaving my hostel without my shin guards. And I'm carrying around a red card for the next German that says Americans don't care about soccer.

*Sophia Angelis*

church in happier days and horrific photos of the city in the wake of WWII. Across from Memorial Church stands the New Church, constructed in 1992 with a plain exterior and blue stained glass interior.

*➜ On the Kurfürstendamm in the centre of the Dreitscheidpl. ⏰ Exhibit open M-Sa 10am-4pm. Church open daily 9am-7pm.*

**ZOOLOGISCHER GARTEN** ZOO

8 Hardenberg Pl. ☎030 25 40 10 💻www.zoo-berlin.de

Germany's oldest zoo houses around 14,000 animals of 1500 species, most in open-air habitats connected by winding pathways under dense cover of trees and brush. While you're there, pay your respects to the world-famous polar bear ▣**Knut,** or he may go nuts. Originally deemed the cutest polar bear alive, Knut has been diagnosed by animal specialists as a psychopath addicted to human attention. Luckily, he's still pretty cute.

*➜ U2 or U9: Zoological Garten, or S5, S7 or S75: Bahnhof Zoo. Main entrance is across from the Europa Center. $ €12, students €9, children €6. Combination to zoo and aquarium €18/14/9. ⏰ Open daily from 9am-7pm (last entry 6pm). Animal houses open 9am-6pm.*

**AQUARIUM** AQUARIUM

Budapester Str. 32 ☎030 25 40 10 💻www.aquarium-berlin.de.

Within the walls of the zoo, but independently accessible, is an aquarium with three floors of fish, reptiles, amphibians and insects. Highlights include the pychadelic jellyfish and the slimey carp petting zoo.

*➜ U2 or U9: Zoological Garten, or S5, S7 or S75: Bahnhof Zoo. $ €12, students €9, children €6. See above for aquarium-zoo combination tickets. ⏰ Open daily 9am-6pm.*

**BEATE UHSE EROTIK MUSEUM** MUSEUM

Joachimstalerstr. 4 ☎030 886 06 66 💻www.erotikmuseum.de

The world's largest sex museum contains over 5,000 sex artifacts from around the world. Attracting a quarter of a million visitors per year, it is Berlin's fifth most popular tourist attraction.Visitors come to see erotica ranging from explicit carvings on a 17th century Italian deer-hunting knife to a 1955 calender featuring Marilyn Monroe in her birthday suit. A small exhibit describes the life of Beate Uhse, a pilot-turned-entrepeneur who started Europe's first and largest sex-shop chain, then decided to get historical about the whole thing and founded the museum.

*🚇 S5, S7 or S75: Bahnhof Zoo. [$] €14 per person, €25 couples. €10 students with ID, or with WelcomeCard. Make it an orgy (€10 per person for groups of 10 and over), or bring grandpa (€10 seniors). ⏰ Open daily 9am-midnight.*

## SCHÖNEBERG AND WILMERSDORF

Schöneberg sights are a mix of gorgeous parks and whatever cultural bits and pieces ended up in this largely residential neighborhood. Travelers with limited time in Berlin should note that attractions here are few and far between, and aren't easily and efficiently visited.

**👍 GRUNEWALD AND THE JAGDSCHLOß** ♿ PARK

Am Grunewaldsee 29 (Access from Pücklerstr.) ☎030 813 35 97 💻www.spsg.de

This 3 sq. km park, with winding paths through wild underbrush, gridded pines, and a peaceful lake, is popular dog-walking turf and a great change from the rest of the bustling Berlin. About a 1km walk into the woods is the **Jadgschloß,** a restored royal hunting lodge that houses a gallery of portaits and paintings by German artists like Graff and Cranach. The house is the picture of understated elegance, surrounded by even more blooming botany. The one-room hunting lodge is worth skipping, unless you find pottery shards particularly gripping. Instead, walk around the grounds, or take a hike north in the forest to **Teufelsberg** ("Devil's Mountain"), the highest point in Berlin, made of rubble from World War II piled over a Nazi military school.

*🚇 U3 or U7: Fehrbelliner Pl., or S45 or S46: Hohenzollerndamm then bus #115 (dir. Neuruppiner Str. of Spanische Alle/Potsdamer): Pücklerstr. Turn left on Pücklerstr. following the signs and continue straight into the forest to reach the lodge. ℹ Check the Jadgschloß visitor's center for a map. [$] Admission to the hunting lodge €4, €3 students. Tours in German offered on the weekends €1. ⏰ Open Tu-Su 10am-6pm.*

**BRÜCKE MUSEUM** MUSEUM

Bussardsteig 9 ☎030 831 20 29 💻www.brueckemusuem.de

This museum displays an uncommon collection of Brücke art, German impressionism inspired by its French contemporaries. The brief *Die Brücke* ("The Bridge") stylistic period was characterized by bright, fierce colors. The Brücke Museum building, inside the Grunewald forest, is a work of contemporary art itself. The staff loves the collection (which says something), and often rotates special exhibitions displaying pieces related to the Brücke period, including the obvious French Impressionist works, but also world art, such as African craft works.

*🚇 U3 or U7: Fehberlliner Pl., then bus #115 (dir. Neuruppiner Str. to Spanische Allee/Potsdammer): Pücklerstr. [$] €4, €3 students. For a ticket including special exhibits, €5/4. ⏰ Open M and W-Su 11am-5pm.*

**GAY MEMORIAL** MEMORIAL

Just outside the Nollendorf U-Bahn station

Blink and you might miss it. This unassuming, unmarked memorial is shaped like a Crayola crayon, and striped with as many colors as a box of the art supply. The small monument commemorates the homosexuals killed in World War II.

*🚇 U1, U3, U4, or U9: Nollendorfpl.*

### ST. NORBERT KIRCHE CEMETERY — CEMETERY

Access from Belzinger Str., between Martin-Luther-Str. and Eisenacher Str.

Sunken in a few feet from street level and walled off by unlocked gates, this enchanting cemetery brings R.I.P. to the living. With a mix between manicured shrubs and a patch of wild, over-grown ivy in front of every tomb, a quick stop here on a busy day is beautiful. An adjoining children's playground outside the gates brightens things up. We wouldn't say this is worth a trip itself, but the cemetery is good for a stroll after stepping out of one of Schöneberg's popular cafes.

*🚇 U7: Eisenacherstr. ⏰ Gate usually locked by 6pm.*

### VIKTORIA-LUISE-PLATZ — PARK

On Motzstr., where it intersects Winterfeldstr.

This relaxed hangout is just a block south of the lively scene on Fuggerstr. Named after the daughter of Wilhelm II, this park channels the extravagance of an older bourgeois Berlin. A large central fountain is encircled by hedges, and a semi-circular stone-worked arch with detailed columns marks one end. This is a favorite summer picnic spot for locals, thanks to the city-maintained gardens.

*🚇 U4: Viktoria-Luise-Pl.*

### APOSTLE PAULUS KIRCHE — CHURCH

Klixstr. 2 (Grunewaldstr.) ☎030 781 12 80 💻www.apostel-paulus-gemeinde.de

Apostle Paulus Kirche is the best known and perhaps most architecturally significant church in all of Schöneberg. Black and dark green brickwork intricately patterns the exterior a series of gothic arches. The church is often used by community choirs and a range of other performers who visit for the acclaimed acoustics.

*🚇 U7: Eisenacher Str. ℹ Check website for information on upcoming events. Ⓢ Church only open during service hours; Su at 10am, meditative morning prayers every M from 9:15-9:30am.*

## MITTE

Like any KFC, Mitte contains 95% good stuff and 5% crap. Stick with the recommendations, and you'll be fine. You're on your own with KFC.

### 🏛 PERGAMON MUSEUM — 🎟♿ MUSEUM

Am Kupfergraben 5 ☎0302 090 55 77 💻www.smb.museum

If it kept its two main exhibits, the Pergamon temple and the Ishtar Gate, the rest of this museum could show off cotton balls and it'd still be worth it. The museum reconstructs the Pergamon temple nearly to its full size, and the battle mural on the wall displays jagged toothed snakes ripping off heroes' arms while titans rip lions' mouths apart. The Mesopotamian Ishtar Gate, reconstructed tile by-original-tile, rises 30m into the air, then stretches 100m down a hallway. You'll hardly believe it.

*🚇 U2, U5, U8: Alexanderpl. Ⓢ €10, students €5. Free Th after 6pm. ⏰ Open M-W 10am-6pm, Th 10am-10pm, F-Su 10am-6pm.*

### 🏛 TOPOGRAPHY OF TERROR — ♿🍸 MUSEUM

Niederkirchner Str. 8 ☎0302 545 09 50 💻www.topographie.de

This exhibit opened May 2010 and looks at the origins, development, and deployment of Nazi terror from 1930 to 1946. This detailed, personalized, fair, and informative exhibition provides one of the best insights into Nazi strategies and the extent of the horror. No detail (or image) is deemed off-limits, and travelers with weak stomachs are warned. That said, the conclusions of this exhibit are so incredibly important and so poorly understood that a trip here should really be considered a must. A bookshop, cafe, and library take up the bottom floor, while a segment of the Berlin Wall and the excavated foundations of Hitler's old terror headquarters fill out an enormous, otherwise empty, courtyard.

*🚇 U2: Potsdamer Pl. From the Metro, head east on Leipziegerstr. and take a right on Wilhelm-Leipziegerstr. The exhibit is directly across from the Hi-Flyer. Ⓢ Free. ⏰ Open daily 10am-8pm.*

## MEMORIAL TO THE MURDERED JEWS OF EUROPE — ♿ MEMORIAL

Cora-Berliner-Str. 1 ☎0302 639 43 11 🖥www.stiftung-denkmal.de

Imposing concrete blocks equidistant from each other commemorate the Jews who were killed by the National Socialists. If you're looking for reflection or somberness, you won't find it aboveground, where kids play hide and seek, tourists nap on blocks, and policemen from the nearby American embassy work in a paranoid frenzy to keep cars from stopping. See the memorial quickly, then head below ground for a moving, informative exhibit on the Jewish history of WWII. Especially devastating is the "family" room, which presents pre-war Jewish family portraits and then investigates the individual fates of the family members. The last room continuously plays one of thousands of compiled mini-biographies of individuals killed in the Holocaust. To read the bios of every murdered Jew would take over six years.

*U2: Potsdamer Pl. From the Metro, walk north on Ebertstr. $ Free. ⏰ Open daily Apr-Sept 10am-8pm; Oct-Mar 10am-7pm.*

## HOMOSEXUAL MEMORIAL — ♿ MEMORIAL

On Ebertstr. 🖥www.stiftung-denkmal.de/en/homosexualmemorial

While Berlin now accepts homosexuality like few places do in the world, it wasn't so until 1969, before which homosexuality was illegal under a law passed by the Nazis. As a result, homosexuals were not included in many memorials against Nazi violence. This memorial, which opened in 2008, consists of a giant block with a screen that plays a video of two men kissing on loop—though part of the memorial, this video is set to change every two years.

*U2: Potsdamer Pl. From the Metro, walk north on Ebertstr. The memorial will be on your left, in the garden. ⏰ Open 24hr.*

## HOUSE OF WORLD CULTURES — ♿🍸 EXHIBIT HALL

John-Foster-Dulles-Allee 10 ☎3039 78 70 🖥www.hkw.de

Originally built by the Americans to show off to the nearby East Berliners, the House of World Cultures now hosts festivals, movie screenings, lectures, and an incredible anarchist bookstore in a bizarre structure that's been affectionately called "The Pregnant Clam." The formless statue in the pool out front becomes a butterfly when you view its reflection.

*U55: Bundestag. From the Metro, head southwest down Paul Löbe Allee. $ Free. Event prices vary. ⏰ Open daily 10am-7pm. Exhibitions open M 11am-7pm, W-Su 11am-7pm.*

## NEUES MUSEUM — ♿ MUSEUM

Bodestr. 1 🖥www.neues-museum.de

One of the top museums in the city, this collection of Egyptian and Greek antiquities goes beyond what you'd expect. Mummies abound, sarcophogi run rampant, and somewhere in it all, that famous bust of Nefertiti—yeah, that one—sits glowing in her own room. The building was heavily damaged in the war, and this new New Museum does a brilliant job of incorporating the old structure into a fantastically modern creation. To avoid the lines, reserve a ticket online.

*U6: Friedrichstr. S5,S7,S75,or S9: Hackescher Markt. ℹ Tickets correspond to a time, and after they've been purchased visitors must return at the time printed on their ticket. No line Th 6-8pm. $ €10, students €5. Free Th after 6pm. ⏰ Open M-W 10am-6pm, Th-Sa 10am-8pm, Su 10am-6pm.*

## SOVIET MEMORIAL — ♿ MEMORIAL

Str. des 17 Juni

WWII tanks and anti-aircraft guns flank this memorial built by the Soviets in 1945. It is estimated that between eight to 10 million Soviets died fighting in the war, including 80,000 who died in the Battle of Berlin. The memorial is expected to be finished by late 2010.

*Bus #100: Pl. der Republik. Head south through Tiergarten to Str. des 17 Juni and take a right. $ Free. ⏰ Open 24hr.*

**BRANDENBERG GATE** ♿ GATE

Pariser Pl. ☎0302 263 30 17

During the day, tourists swarm this famous 18th-century gate; the wise traveler will return at night to see it lit in a blaze of gold. Friederich Wilhelm II built the gate as a symbol of military victory, but Germans these days prefer to shy away from that designation, you know, because of WWI and, uh, WWII. A system of gates once surrounded it, but today only this most famous gate remains.

*🚇 U55: Brandenburg Tor. 💲 Free. ⏰ Open 24hr.*

**HUMBOLDT UNIVERSITY** ♿ UNIVERSITY

Unter den Linden 6

Home to some of the greatest thinkers of the modern age, including Freud and Einstein, this university is closed to the public and doesn't make much of a sight touring-wise, but it's neat to stop by and feel like you're somehow being involved in something. During the day, vendors sell used books out in front. Maybe you'll find Einstein's old unread copy of *The Mayor of Casterbridge*.

*🚇 U2: Hausvogteipl. From the Metro, walk north along Oberwalstraße.*

**THE KENNEDYS** 💳♿ MUSEUM

Pariser Pl. 4A ☎030 20 65 35 70 💻www.thekennedys.de

A mostly photographic exhibit of this family that had such strong ties to Berlin. Incomprehensibly, this musuem has a book of its entire exhibit in the lobby and bookstore. Just look through this and save the money. The museum also features various temporary exhibitions.

*🚇 Bus TXL 100/200. 💲 €7, students €3.50. ⏰ Open daily 10am-6pm.*

**VICTORY COLUMN** 💳🚭🍸 MONUMENT

Großer Stern 1 ☎030 391 29 61 💻www.monument-tales.de

This 27m tall monument celebrates Prussia's victory over France in 1880. The statue of Victoria at the top is made of melted-down French cannons, and during WWII, Hitler had the statue moved to its present location to increase its visibility. The column is under renovation; an exhibition that examines the significance of various "monuments" built throughout the world is expected to be finished in 2011.

*🚇 U9:Hansapl. ℹ Present your ticket at the cafe to get a €0.50 discount on all drinks. 💲 €2.20, students €1.50. ⏰ Open Apr-Oct M-F 9:30am-6:30pm, Sa-Su 9:30am-7pm; Nov-Mar M-F 10am-5pm, Sa-Su 10am-5:30pm.*

**NEUE WACHE** ♿ MEMORIAL

Unter den Linden 4 ☎030 25 00 25

This building was built as a guard house for the nearby city palace (hence, "New Watch"). The building has been used as a number of memorials since then, and in 1969 the remains of an unknown soldier and an unknown concentration camp victim were laid to rest here. Since 1993 the Neue Wache has served as the central memorial of the Federal Republic of Germany for the Victims of War and Tyranny. A statue of a mother holding her dead son stands alone in the center of an enormous empty room.

*🚇 U2: Hausvogteipl. From the Metro, walk north along Oberwalstr. 💲 Free. ⏰ Open daily 10am-6pm. The interior of the monument is still visible when the building's gate is closed.*

**BEBELPLATZ** ♿ SQUARE

Bebelpl.

In 1933, a crazed group of Nazi students raided the Humboldt library and burned over 20,000 volumes of "un-German" books written by Jews, communists, and homosexuals. A plaque displays Heinreich Heines's prophetic words: "Only where they burn books, will they eventually burn people." Visitors can look down through a glass window into a library full of empty white shelves. It's spooky.

*🚇 U2: Hausvogteipl. From the Metro, walk north along Oberwalstr.*

### SCHLOßPLATZ ♿ SQUARE

Schloßpl.

Schloßplatz manages to be a sight where castles themselves are feuding. The Berliner Schloß, the Hohenzollern imperial palace stood on this spot until the communists tore it down in 1950 to build the Palast der Republick. After reunification, the Palast der Republick was torn down, this time to make way for a replica of the Berliner Schloß. The new building will house the collections of Humboldt University among other exhibitions. Construction is set to start in 2013 and finish in 2019. Currently, the field sits open in some parts, while others are under excavation. A nearby visitors center has German-only information on the forthcoming building.

*🚇 U2: Hausvogteipl. From the Metro, walk north along Oberwalstr. and take a right on Französische Str. Continue it across the canal bridge. ⏰ Visitors center open daily 10am-6pm.*

### FERNSHEHTURM 🍸 TOWER

Panoramastr. 1A ☎030 242 3333 💻www.tv-turm.de

At 368m, the Fernshehturm, literally"TV Tower," trumps all other sky-ticklers in the EU. It's shaped like a lame 1950s space probe on purpose; commies wanted folk to think of Sputnik when they saw it. In the DDR's defense, it wasn't its biggest miscalculation. This supposed "triumph of Soviet technology" was actually completed by Swedish engineers when construction faltered. Elevators now shoot more than a million people each year to a height of 200m where they can dig a 360° panorama, grab a drink at the bar, or stomach an incredibly pricey meal. The height plays especially well in Berlin, which has few tall buildings.

*🚇 U2, U5, U8: Alexanderpl. $ €10.50, under 16 €6.50. ⏰ Open daily Mar-Oct 9am-midnight; Nov-Feb 10am-midnight.*

### ROTES RATHAUS CITY HALL

Rathausstr. 15 ☎0309 02 60

This imposing red brick structure looks like the world's most intense East Coast private high school, but it used to be the East Berlin City Hall and now houses the Berlin Senate. Senate? In Berlin? But Berlin's a city! Well, actually, traveler, Berlin is one of the 16 states that make up the Federal Republic of Germany. Each district of Berlin has a mayor, and individual state senators who conduct business at the Rotes Rathaus. It's closed to the public and currently under construction, expected to finish in 2010.

*🚇 U2: Klosterstr. From the Metro, head north.*

### MARIENKIRCHE CHURCH

Karl-Liebknecht-Str. 8 ☎0302 500 25 💻www.marienkirche-berlin.de

The oldest still-standing medieval church in Berlin (est. 1270) has one of the most frightening murals you'll ever see: a line of saints and kings perform the dance of death alongside a line of skeletons who look more like space creatures from *The X-Files*. There's a Dan Brown novel here waiting to be written.

*🚇 U2, U5, U8: Alexanderpl. $ Free. ⏰ Open daily in summer 10am-9pm; in winter 10am-6pm.*

### SAINT HEDWIG'S CATHEDRAL CATHEDRAL

Hinter der Katholischen Kirche 3 ☎0302 03 48 10 💻www.hedwigs-kathedrale.de

Named after Harry Potter's owl (not really), the biggest and oldest Catholic cathedral in the city also looks like no cathedral you've seen before. Round like a *yurt*, this church's altar is actually a level down, while the seats are located on the ground level. The interior has also been recently renovated with a cool Space-Age roof and hanging sets of 10 glowing balls that make the place feel like something out of Kubrick. Still, the place is rich in history, having been established as a haven for Catholics by Frederick II in 1773.

*🚇 U2: Hausvogteipl. From the Metro, walk north along Oberwalstr. Look for the copper dome. $ Free. ⏰ Open M-F 10am-5pm, Sa 10am-4:30pm, Su 1-5pm.*

### REICHSTAG ✉♿🍸 PARLIAMENT

Pl. der Republik 1 ☎0302 273 21 52 🖳www.bundestag.de

Visitors to the German parliament building can climb the roof's 1200-ton glass dome that looks down into the main chamber as a symbol of the "openness" of German democracy. It also serves to focus sunlight into the government chambers via an aggressive spire of mirrored fragments that juts down toward the floor. A free, automated audio tour tracks your movements up and down the nearly 300m ramp. Stop off at the very top for a swell view of the Berlin skyline and to marvel at the fact that this dome—and therefore the Reichstag—has no roof. Rain, snow, and sleet all fall into the building and land in a giant "cone" located on the dome's floor. Visitors can trek around the roof terrace to avoid the solar panels that make the Reichstag the world's only zero-emission congress. Across the way stand a series of futuristic government offices that have been affectionately termed "the Washing Machine." If viewing democracy makes you hungry, stop at the restaurant located on the roof.

*# Bus #100: Pl. der Republik. $ Free. ⏰ Open daily 8am-10pm.*

### SCHLOß BELLEVUE PALACE

Spreeweg 1 ☎0302 00 00

This palace, home of the German president, was the first Neoclassical building in Germany. What? That doesn't excite you? Then try this: when there's a gala, watch from the street as the privileged drink cocktails.

*#U9: Hansapl. From the Metro, head east past the Victory Column. ⏰ Never open to you.*

### HI-FLYER BALLOON ✉♿🍸 HOT-AIR BALLOON

Wilhelmstr. ☎0302 266 788 11 🖳www.air-service-berlin.de

The best thing that can be said about the Hi-Flyer Balloon is that it actually gets cooler as you approach it. What looks like an annoying, touristy balloon becomes a pretty enormous, annoying, touristy balloon. Even so, if you want a 15min. trip 150m into the air, this balloon obliges. Always call ahead to see if weather conditions allow for flying.

*# U6: Kochstr. $ €19, students €13. ⏰ Open daily Apr-Oct 10am-10pm; Nov-Mar 11am-6pm.*

### BERLINER DOM 🎧♿ CHURCH

Am Lustgarten ☎0302 026 91 19 🖳www.berlinerdom.de

You'll probably spend the whole time thinking how big a bowl of cereal the inverted dome would make; in other words, it's a fantastically enormous dome and a ridiculously beautiful church. "Dom" means cathedral in German; since this 1905 church belongs to the Protestants, it's technically not a cathedral, but in terms of grandeur it blows away most cathedrals you've seen. A museum upstairs shows various failed incarnations of the church, and if you climb some sketchy-feeling backstairs, you can actually get to a roof terrace lookout. Don't forget the basement with the most luxurious crypt you've ever seen, housing the ghosts of lightweights like the Hohenzollern kings.

*#U2, U5, U8: Alexanderpl. $ €5, students €3. ⏰ Open Apr-Sept M-Sa 9am-8pm, Su noon-8pm; Oct-Mar Ma-Sa 9am-7pm, Su noon-7pm.*

### ALTES MUSEUM 🎧♿ MUSEUM

Am Lustgarten 🖳www.smb.museum

A newly organized collection of Roman and Estruscan antiquities now takes up the entire first floor of this incredible musuem. Though this museum's cool in another context, those who've seen its flashier cousins, the Pergamon and the Neues, might be a bit disappointed. Check it if you've got the time; skip it if you don't.

*# U2, U5, U8: Alexanderpl. $ €8, students €4. Free Th after 6pm. ⏰ Open M-W 10am-6pm, Th 10am-10pm, F-Su 10am-6pm.*

### ALTE NATIONAL GALERIE
🚫♿ GALLERY

Bodestr. 1-3 ☎0302 090 55 77 💻www.smb.museum

This fantastic, small collection of mostly German art does special justice to masters like Adolph Menzel. While the building also houses several Monets, Van Goghs, and some Cézannes, the wealth of the place is in its German collection. Music fans will note the famous portrait of Richard Wagner.

*⇄ U2, U5, U8: Alcxanderpl. $ €8, students €4. Free Th after 6pm. ⏰ Open M-W 10am-6pm, Th 10am-10pm, F-Su 10am-6pm.*

### BODE MUSEUM
💵♿ MUSEUM

Am Kupfergraben 1 ☎0302 090 55 77 💻www.smb.museum

Though interesting to some folk, the Bode Museum largely contains medieval art and Christian iconography, and if we have to explain to you why this is cool, you probably won't find it cool. The gorgeous building, which looks like it's floating on the water, is worth a free entrance on a Thursday night, but unless 100 depictions of Christ is your thing, your time's better spent elsewhere.

*⇄ U2, U5, U8: Alexanderpl. $ €8, students €4. Free Th after 6pm. ⏰ Open M-W 10am-6pm, Th 10am-10pm, F-Su 10am-6pm.*

### AKADEMIE DER KÜNSTE
🚫♿ MUSEUM

Pariser Pl. 4 ☎0302 005 70 💻www.adk.de

Exhibits rotate every two months in this eye-pleasing modern museum that serves as the headquarters for the Akademie der Künste, an society of famous German artists. Exhibits tend toward the bold and progressive in media ranging from photo to design to traditional painting. Incredibly, the walls of this exhibit hall are the original 17th-century pieces, and the modern hall has been built around it.

*⇄ Bus #100 or #200 to Brandenburg Tor. $ €5, students €3-4. Free 1st Su of the month. ⏰ Open Tu-Su 11am-10pm.*



### TIERGARTEN
♿🍸 PARK

Tiergarten

Stretching from the Brandenburg Gate in the east to the Bahnhof Zoo in the west, this Balrog-sized park is at the heart of Berlin and contains some of its most famous iconic monuments including the Column of Victory and the Soviet War Memorial. Str. des 17 Juni bisects the park from east to west, and frequently hosts parades or celebrations. During the 2010 World Cup, the city blocked off the entire street from June to July and presented the World Cup on 10 enormous screens to daily hordes of thousands of fans. It was drunk and it was loud. The park also contains some beautiful paths and gardens that can offer solace from the hipster invasion.

*⇄ Bus #100 or #200: Brandenburg Tor.*

### DOROTHEEN MUNICIPAL CEMETERY
♿ CEMETERY

Chausseestr. 125

Hegel, one of the most important historians of the 19th century, lies dead here along with Bertold Brecht, who might be the most important playwright of the 1900s. If graves don't get your blood running, this body grove also makes a great park. A map near the entrance points out graves of interest.

*⇄ U6: Oranienburger Tor. From the U-Bahn, head north on Chausseestr. ⏰ Open daily 8am-dusk.*

### UNTER DER LINDEN
♿ STREET

Unter Der Linden

Many of Berlin's most famous sites, including Bebelplatz, the Neue Wache, and the Berlin Opera House, lie along this wide boulevard, which dates back to the 16th century, when it was a palace path leading to the royal hunting grounds. The street gets its name from the rows of linden trees that run through the middle. Today, the path makes perfect grounds for biking, especially at night, while during the day small cafes and ice-cream shops feed the mostly tourist crowd roaming the grounds. The statue of Frederick the Great starts the row of trees, and nothing less than the Brandenburg Gate ends it. If you're lucky—and somewhat unlucky—a group of drunk Aussies will pedal by on the 10-person bicycle-beer bar that runs up and down this street.

*🚇 Bus #100 or #200: Brandenburg Tor.*

### TACHELES — GALLERY

Oranienburger Str. 53

An unforgettable experience day or night, this bombed-out department store has become a living, breathing street-art Metropolis. Bars, galleries, a movie theater, faux beach exterior, and sculpture garden/workshop all exist where every available space is covered in graffiti art, human piss, or both. *But it's worth it.* Seating options in the outside bars range from lifeguard towers to forklifts.

*🚇 U6: Oranienburger Tor. [S] Free to enter; most galleries cost €1-5. ⏰ Open 8am-late.*

### CENTRUM JUDAICUM: NEW SYNAGOGUE — SYNAGOGUE

Oranienburger Str. 28-30 ☎88028 316 💻centrumjudaicum.de

The New Synagogue, built in 1866, was once one of the most awesome Jewish temples in Europe, with 3200 seats and a 50m dome. Almost completely destroyed, first by Nazi violence, then by American bombs, after 1989 the building's exterior and dome were restored, and the building became the museum, cultural center, and miniature synagogue that it remains today. The exhibit on the original synagogue is small and only justified by a pre-existing interest in the building's history. The dome, too, disappoints somewhat, and most visitors will be satisfied with a strut past the front.

*🚇 U6: Oranienburger Tor. i Information in English. [S] Permanent exhibition €3, reduced €2. Dome €1.50, reduced €1. ⏰ Open Apr-Sept M 10am-8pm, Tu-Th 10am-6pm, F 10am-5pm, Su 10am-8pm; Oct and Mar M 10am-8pm, Tu-Th 10am-6pm, F 10am-2pm, Su 10am-8pm; Nov-Feb M-Th 10am-6pm, F 10am-2pm, Su 10am-6pm.*

### POTSDAMER PLATZ — SQUARE

Potsdamer Pl.

Berlin's answer to Times Sq. feels like the inside of the Death Star, since an enormous antenna-like spoke sticks down from what seems a giant satellite dish. This new commerical center of Berlin sees fancy tourist-heavy restaurants serve unexciting food beside a fountain that actually is exciting. The square additionally has three movie theaters, a Sony Design store, and a museum dedicated to German film history.

*🚇 U2: Potsdamer Pl. [S] Free. ⏰ Hours vary.*

### NEUE NATIONAL GALLERIE — MUSEUM

Potsdamer Str. 50 ☎0302 66 42 45 10 💻www.smb.museum

The be-all end-all of early 20th century painting in Berlin, this museum's building is almost as famous as its collection. Strange temporary exhibits live upstairs in the so-called "Temple of Light and Glass" designed by Mies van der Rohe, while the basement holds a treasure trove of primarily German paintings and sculptures. Works by Edward Munch, Franz Marc, and Max Ernst are just a few of the highlights. Sadly, in the 1930s, key works were labeled "degenerate" by the Nazis and have since disappeared from the collection. Missing works appear as black-and-white photocopies and are still hung throughout the gallery.

*🚇 U2: Potsdamer Pl. i Audio tour included in the price of admission. [S] €10, students €5. Free Th after 6pm. ⏰ Open M-W 10am-6pm, Th 10am-10pm, F-Sa 10am-6pm.*

### MUSEUM FOR FILM AND TELEVISION — MUSEUM

Potsdamer Str. 2 ☎30 300 903 0 💻www.deutsche-kinemathek.de

A fun little exhibit on the history of German cinema, with a special emphasis on the work of Fritz Lang and Marlene Dietrich. Not a must-see, but the production photos and set drawings of *The Cabinet of Dr. Caligari* and *Metropolis* are

# tiergarten

**1. ZOOLOGICAL GARDEN.** The oldest and most popular zoo in Germany is home to almost 1,500 species of flora and fauna. Frederick William IV, King of Prussia, donated animals from the pheasantry and menagerie of the Tiergarten to comprise the zoo's starter collection.

**2. COLUMN OF VICTORY.** Heinrich Strack designed the column to commemorate Prussian victory in the Danish-Prussian War. The 35-ton bronze statue of Victoria was later added to celebrate victories in the Austro-Prussian and Franco-Prussian Wars. The Prussians won a lot of wars.

**3. NEW NATIONAL GALLERY.** The "temple of light and glass" houses a collection that ranges from early modern art to pieces from the 1960s—not just light and glass. Plan ahead if you're hoping to see a particular work; when temporary exhibitions are on show, the permanent collection is closed.

**4. CULTURAL FORUM.** This building complex—comprised of the Philharmonic Hall, the Musical Instrument Museum, and the Chamber Music Hall—is the perfect place to get your groove back.

**5. REICHSTAG.** After German reunification, intensive restoration brought the meeting place of the German Parliament to its present-day splendor. Climb to the roof and peer through the building's 1200-ton glass dome to witness some democracy.

**6. BRANDENBURG GATE.** On November 9, 2009, 1000 foam dominoes were lined up along the former route of the Berlin Wall, and converged here to celebrate the "Festival of Freedom"—the 20th anniversary of the wall's fall.

worth the admission price alone. Film buffs will be rewarded, and film gruffs will still find a few things to tickle them. A TV library lets visitors watch old German TV. If you thought their *wars* were crazy...

⇆ *U2: Potsdamer Pl.* [$] *€5, students €3. Audio tour €4/3.* ⏰ *Open Tu-W 10am-6pm, Th 10am-8pm, F-Su 10am-6pm.*

### ZIONS CHURCH

⊗ CHURCH

Zionskirchstr. 44 ☎0308 870 98 70 💻www.zionskirche-berlin.de

This quiet little church in North Mitte suffered damage and looting after the war and only recently have modest renovation efforts begun. While the 140-year-old church may not have the history of some of Berlin's houses of worship, its neglect makes a visit here all the more worthwhile. A beautiful tower rises high from a natural hill while the church's interior remains unadorned, empty, and candlelit.

⇆ *U8: Roenthaler Pl. From the Metro, head northeast on Weinbergsweg.* [$] *Free.* ⏰ *Open daily 9am-7pm.*

### BERTOLD BRECHT HAUS

🚫⊗ MUSEUM

Chausseestr. 125 ☎030 200 57 1844 💻www.adk.de

Bertold Brecht revolutionized theater with such masterworks as the *Three Penny Opera*, and this tour lets you glimpse into his personal life. While Brecht only lived (and died) here from 1953 to 1956, the same is true of his other addresses—Brecht "changed countries as often as shoes," so don't feel like you're getting a raw deal. Preserved by his wife, the Brechtian actress Helen Weigel, Brecht's apartment (two studies and the bedroom where he croaked) contains his library and other small artifacts of note. Come with an English-speaking crew so they do the tour in English; otherwise you'll be stuck reading along and wondering if the Germans are mocking you each time they laugh.

⇆ *U6: Oranienburger Tor. From the U-Bahn, head north on Chausseestr. The house will be on your left. There isn't a good sign or anything, so look for the address.* **i** *All tours are guided.* [$] *€4, students €2.50.* ⏰ *Tours every 30min. Tu 10-11:30am, 2-3:30pm. W 10-11:30am. Th 10-11:30am, 5-6:30pm. F 10am, 10:30am, and 11:30am. Sa 10-noon, 1-3:30pm. Su 11am, noon, 1, 2, 3, 4, 5, and 6pm.*

### HACKESCHER MARKT

♿🍸 SQUARE

Hackescher Markt

Grungy electric didgeridoo acts rock off against angsty singer/songwriters who trade chords with father/son jazz duos. Vendors hawk wares and street artists juggle fire in this beautiful square that runs along the train tracks. Tons of outdoor restaurants. Plaid is everywhere and there's an American Apparel for kids. Yikes.

⇆ *S5, S7, S9, S75: Hackescher Markt.*

### HAMBURGER BANHOFF MUSEUM

🚫♿🍸 MUSEUM

Invalidenstr. 50-51 ☎03039 78 34 39 💻www.hamburgerbahnhof.de

This modern art museum does a good job of mixing traditionally recognized modern masterworks (Andy Warhol, etc.) with whacked out temporary exhibitions. Maybe you'll enter a room where clowns throw basketballs at you from TV screens. Maybe you find a room filled with a large black tunnel and you'll feel sorry for the security guard who works here alone with this tunnel. While you should avoid getting his job, the museum itself is massive, stretching the entire length of the old station house. If modern art even slightly tickles you, this joint's worth a look.

⇆ *S5, S7, S9, or S75: Hauptbahnhof.* [$] *€12, students €6.* ⏰ *Open Tu-F 10am-6pm, Sa 11am-8pm, Su 11am-6pm.*

### DEUTSCHER DOM

🚫⊗ MUSEUM

Gendarmenmarkt 1-2 ☎0302 273 04 31 💻 www.bundestag.de

Originally an 18th-century Protestant church, this building was completely destroyed during the war. It has now been rebuilt and houses a museum of German government called "Milestones, Setbacks, Sidetracks." The exhibit is only in German, and though the free English audio tour helps, the main enjoyment of this building comes from considering its estimation of Nazi dictatorship as a "setback" and looking up the narrow belltower from the lobby.

*U2: Hausvogteipl. $ Free. ⏰ Open daily Oct-Apr 10am-6pm; May-Sept 10am-7pm.*

### GENDARMENMARKT ♿ 🍸 SQUARE

Gendarmenmarkt

The plaza that includes the Deutscher Dome also contains Koncerthaus Berlin, where the Berlin Philharmonic Symphony plays, and the Französischer Dom, an 18th-century church built for French Huguenots (Protestants). In July, the Berlin Symphony Orchestra plays free night concerts outside, while the tower of the Französischer Dom provides a view of the city. Easily one of the most beautiful squares in Europe. For a kick, read some of the menus of the fancy cafes around the square that try to be"bourgeois hip" and offer such pairings as currywurst and champagne.

*U2: Hausvogteipl. $ Französischer Dom Tower €2.50. ⏰ Tower open daily 10am-6pm.*

### CURRYWURST MUSEUM 🎟 ♿ 🍸 MUSEUM

Schützenstr. 70 ☎0308 871 86 30 💻www.currywurstmuseum.de

The hilarious Currywurst Museum expertly traces the origins of this Berlin treat from a small kitchen in Germany to the mouths of Berliners everywhere. Exhibits are very hands-on (squeeze a ketchup bottle and it sings to you) and sometimes mouths-on, since each ticket comes with a sample of the wurst in question. A gift shop sells sausages, hats, shirts, spices, and more. Good story and great resource for the currywurst scholar.

*U2, U6: Stadtmitte. $ €11, students €7. Entrance includes a cup of currywurst. ⏰ Open daily 10am-10pm.*

## PRENZLAUER BERG

### BERLINER MAUER DOKUMENTATIONZENTRUM MUSEUM, MONUMENT

Bernauer Str. 111 ☎030 464 1030 💻www.berliner-mauer-dokumentationzentrum.de

A remembrance complex, museum, chapel, and entire city block of the preserved Berlin Wall, two concrete barriers separated by the open *Todesstreife*, or death strip, come together in a memorial to "victims of the communist tyranny." The church is made of an inner oval of poured cement walls, lit from above by a large skylight, with gaps that look out over a field of tall grasses and poppies. The museum has assembled a comprehensive collection of all things Wall. Exhibits include photos, film clips, and sound bites. Climb up a staircase to see the wall from above.

*U8: Bernauer Str. $ Free. ⏰ Open Tu-Su Apr-Oct 9:30am-7pm; Nov-Mar 9:30am-6pm.*

### JÜDISCHER FRIEDHOF CEMETERY

On Schönehauser Allee; enter by the Lapidarium

Prenzlauer Berg was one of the major centers of Jewish Berlin during the 19th and early 20th centuries. The ivy-covered Jewish cemetery contains the graves of Giacomo Meyerbeer and Max Liebermann and is studded by impressively high, dark tombs under towering old trees. Nearby, **Synagogue Rykstrasse** *(Rykestr. 53)* is one of Berlin's loveliest synagogues. It was spared on *Kristallnacht* thanks to its inconspicuous location. Unfortunately, visitors are not allowed in, as the synagogue still operates as a school.

*U2: Senefelderpl. $ Free. ⏰ Open M-Th 8am-4pm, F 8am-1pm.*

### KOLLWITZPLATZ PARK, MONUMENT

Directly below Wörther Str.

This little triangle of greenery is one big playground, with toddlers climbing over tree stumps, jungle gyms, and even the lap of Käthe Kollwtiz's statue. Close by, a magical little playground with a small bridge, stream, and willow trees is another popular destination for young moms with energetic kids. Non-parents are drawn by the upscale market on Saturdays, where vendors sell everything from boar meat sausage to handmade ravioli.

*U2: Senefelderpl. $ Free.*

**ZEISS-GROSSPLANETARIUM** PLANETARIUM

Prenzlauer Allee 80 ☎030 421 84 50 🖳www.astw.de

In 1987 this planetarium opened as the most modern facility of its kind in the DDR. Compared to its peers in the West, it seems about as technologically advanced as a tricycle, but it can still show you the stars. No exhibits here, only shows; check the website or call in advance for times.

*🚉 S8, S41, S42, or tram M2: Prenzlauer Allee. From the stop, the planetarium is across the bridge. $ €5, students €4. ⏰ Open Tu 9am-noon, W 9am-noon and 1:30-3pm, Th 9am-noon, F 7-9pm, Sa 2:30-9pm, Su 1:30-5pm.*

**KULTURBRAUEREI** COMMUNITY SPACE

Schönehauser Allee 36 ☎030 44 43 56 20 🖳www.kulturbrauerei-berlin.de

A former brewery, the Kulturbrauerei now calls itself the "cultural melting pot" of a diverse Berlin. Home to offices, restaurants, and a cinema, this old brick building tower and courtyard hosts community events, including salsa lessons and local theater performances. For the traveler, this space might be best enjoyed as a brief peek at the interesting architecture.

*🚉 U2: Senefelderpl.*

**WASSERTURM PRENZLAUER BERG** PARK, WATER TOWER

Berlin's oldest water tower was built to supply the rapidly growing population of workers in Prenzlauer Berg with water. Below the tower were the homes of the former machinery operators, still occupied today as apartments. The area around the tower has since been converted into a park with excellent views of Prenzlauer Berg, the TV Tower, and suntanning Germans.

*🚉 U2: Senefelderpl. Between Knaackstr. and Belforter Str. in Kollwitzkiez.*

## FRIEDRICHSHAIN

### VOLKSPARK — PARK

Volkspark is the second-largest park in Berlin and its oldest. This 52-hectare park is too big to feel crowded, even with masses of dog-walkers and suntanners filling the paths and grassy lawns. Since opening in 1840, monuments and memorials have been added here and there around the green spaces. In 1913 the **Fairy Fountain** was added, representing 10 characters from the book *The Brothers Grimm*. The rubble from two bunkers that were bombed and destroyed in World War II was piled into a war monument in 1950, now called **Mont Klemont**, and is sometimes used as a platform for open-air concerts and movie screenings in the summer. Statues that commemorate the Polish soldiers and German anti-fascists were built in 1972.

*S8 or S10: Landsberger Allee. Alternatively, U5: Strausbgr. Pl. Bounded by Am Friedrichshain to the north, Danziger Str. to the east, Landsberger Allee to the south, and Friedenstr. Str. to the south.*

### EAST SIDE GALLERY — MONUMENT

Along Mühlenstr. www.eastsidegallery.com

The longest remaining portion of the Berlin Wall, this 1.3km stretch of cement slabs has been converted into the world's largest open-air art gallery. The Cold War graffiti wasn't preserved; instead, the current murals were painted by an international group of artists who gathered in 1989 to celebrate the end of the city's division. One of the most famous contributors is artist Dmitri Wrubel, who depicted a wet kiss between Leonid Brezhnev and East German leader Eric Honecker. The stretch of street remains unsupervised and, on the Warschauer Str. side, open at all hours, but vandalism is surprisingly rare.

*U1, U15, S3, S5, S6, S7, S9, or S75: Warschauer Str. Alternatively, S5, S7, S9, or S75: Ostbahnhof. From the stops, walk back toward the river. $ Free.*

### STASI MUSEUM — MUSEUM

Ruschestr. 103, Haus 1 ☎030 553 68 54 www.stasimuseum.de

The Lichetenberg suburb harbors perhaps the most hated and feared building of the DDR regime: the headquarters of the East German secret police, the **Staatssicherheit** or **Stasi.** During the Cold War, the Stasi kept dossiers on some six million of East Germany's own citizens, an amazing feat and a testament to the huge number of civilian informers in a country of only 16 million people. On January 15, 1990, a crowd of 100,000 Berliners stormed and vandalized the building to celebrate the demise of the police state. Since a 1991 law made the records public, the "Horror Files" have rocked Germany, exposing millions of informants and wrecking careers, marriages, and friendships at every level of German society. Officially known today as the **Forschungs-und Gedenkstätte Normannenstrasse,** the building retains its oppressive Orwellian gloom and much of its worn 1970s aesthetic. The exhibit displays the extensive offices of Erich Mielke, the loathed Minister for State Security from 1957 to 1989, a large collection of tiny microphones and hidden cameras used for surveillance by the Stasi, and a replica of a Stasi prison cell.

*U5: Magdalenenstr. $ €4, students €3. Exhibits in German; English information booklet €3. Open M-F 11am-6pm, Sa-Su 2-6pm.*

### KARL-MARX-ALLEE — STREET

Formerly known as Stalinallee, this was the main drag of the East German Potempkin Village, where party members staged elaborate military parades. Built in the early 1950s, it is flanked by hideous gray pre-fab buildings and wedding-cake style "people's palaces" at Strausberger Pl. Covered in gleaming white plastic tiles and aluminum railings dyed gold, these "palaces" were clearly designed to impress. At the end of Strausberger Pl., the two Stalin-styled **Frankenfurter Tors** flank the street.

*U5: Strausbgr. Pl. or Frankfurter Tor. Starting at the intersection of Karl-Marx-Allee and Litchtenbergger Str., and running to the intersection of Karl-Marx-Allee and Petersburger Str.*

## KREUZBERG

While sights don't quite compare to the grand historical scope of Mitte, there is still a fair amount to see in this more real section of town. The greenery in itself is an amazing sight.

### DEUTSCHES TECHNIKMUSEUM BERLIN — MUSEUM

Trebbiner Str. 9 ☎03090 25 40 www.sdtb.de

Don't tell the National Air and Space Museum about this place. With 30 full-sized airplanes, 20 boats—including a full-sized Viking relic—and a train from every decade since 1880, this museum could be a city in itself. Most impressive are the large mechanical demonstrations conducted throughout the day. The museum also has a garden with two windmills and a brewery.

*U1 or U2: Gleisdreieck. i Many exhibits in English. $ €4.50, students €2.50. Open Tu-F 9am-5:30pm, Sa-Su 10am-6pm.*

### OBERBAUMBRÜCKE — BRIDGE

Twin brick towers rise from this double-decker bridge that spans the Spree River. Once a border crossing into East Berlin, it now connects Kreuzberg to Friedrichshain. Residents of the rival neighbohoods duke it out on the bridge every July 27, when thousands of people chuck rotten vegetables at each other.

*U1 or U15: Schlesisches Tor.*

### MOLECULE MAN — STATUE

Between the bridges Elsenbrücke and Oberbaumbrücke

It's a bird! It's a plane! It's a statue that looks like three men hugging! "Molecule" refers to the porous grating the statue is constructed from, and "Man" refers to the junk between his legs. Designed by American artist Jonathan Borofsky in 1999, the 30m tall statue sitting in the middle of the river symbolizes unity.

*S8, S9, S41, S42, or S85: Treptower Park.*

### ARENA POOL — POOL

Eichenstr. 4 ☎03053 320 30 www.arena-berlin.de

In the summer it's a pool floating in the river. In the winter it's a sauna. Year-round, it's awesome. Arena Pool has a bar, club, party boat, and enough Speedo-clad German men to forever give you nightmares.

*S8, S9, S41, S42, or S85: Treptower Park. i Admission warrants unlimited pool entrance and access to bar and locker room. $ Adults €4, students €3. Open daily 8am-late.*

### TEMPELHOFER PARK — PARK

At Columbiadamm and Tempelhofdamm ☎03070 09 06 88 www.gruen-berlin.de

This expansive park was an airport, and also the drop point for the Berlin Air lift, until 2008 when it closed forever. In 2010, the space was converted into a park where runways became jog trails and beer gardens replaced those weird caterpillar-like cart things that hold your luggage.

*U6: Pl. der Luftbrücke. i The dog that you brought with you on your backpacking trip must stay on a leash. $ Free. Open dawn-dusk.*

### CHECKPOINT CHARLIE — HISTORIC SIGHT

Zimmerstr. and Friedrichstr.

This tourist trap once had significance as the entrance point into the American sector from East Berlin. For reasons unknown to Let's Go, it has recently become a prime tourist destination, where buses of photo-snapping lemmings buy into this scheme. Germans in American uniforms stand in the middle of the street and charge you €3 to take a picture of them; this is the most lucrative business since prostitution. A set of placards along Kochstr. provide a somewhat interesting history on the checkpoint and the various escapes it saw. Skip the musuem.

*U6: Kochstraße $ Free. Open 24hr.*

**BERGMANSTRASSE** ♿ STREET

Bergmanstr. between Merringdamm and Zorrenstr.

A bubbling commercial street where street vendors mix with specialty restaurants, hip clothing stores, and a series of conspicuous Whole Foods knock-off stores.

*🚇 Pl. der Luftbrücke. From the U-bahn, head north up Merringdamm.*

**JEWISH MUSEUM** 🎟♿🍸⛅ MUSEUM

Lindenstr. 9-14 ☎0302 599 33 00 💻www.jmberlin.de

Modern, interactive exhibits treat subjects ranging from explanations of the Torah to the philosophies of Moses Mendelssohn to the anatomy of Jewish discrimination under Charles V. Architect Daniel Libeskind designed the museum's building to reflect the discomfort, pain, and inherent voids in Jewish history. While most attempts at "conceptual buildings" suck grandly, this one amazingly succeeds and the effect is moving, disorienting, and thought-provoking. No two surfaces are parallel to each other; the floor is uneven, and the doors and windows seem like portals from a nightmare.

*🚇 U1 or U6: Hallesches Tor. From the station, head east on Gitschinerstr. and take a left at Lindenstr. [$] €5, students €2.50. Audio tours €2. ⏰ Open M 10am-10pm, Tu-Su 10am-8pm. Last entry 1hr. before close.*

**SCHWULES MUSEUM (GAY MUSEUM)** 🍸 MUSEUM

Mehringdamm 61 ☎0306 959 90 50 💻www.schwulesmuseum.de

This little indie-feeling museum is actually state-supported, making it the world's only state-funded exhibit on homosexual persecution. Temporary exhibits take up over half of the museum, and displays are far from extensive, but the museum

## palace prowl

Come for the beer. Come for the bratwurst. Come for the museums. Come for the music. There are, at last count, a million reasons to come to Berlin. But palaces just aren't one of them. Berlin has about as many royal castles in its city limits as, say, Philadelphia.

And what is perhaps slightly odd by American standards is absolutely shocking by castle-crowded, palace-packed European city ones. Don't get me wrong–Berlin is full of Baroque, Romantic, and otherwise intricately detailed, elaborate buildings of the first class. It's just that almost none of them were built by or lived in by kings.

I had no idea where all the palaces went. Until today. When I found them. All of them. In a single 600-acre space.

**Potsdam.** There, I said it–now you know. The castles are in Potsdam. It was here, about a half hour from the city center, that Friedrich II built himself a gilded playground of incredible schloßes, Chinese teahouses, windmills, and whatever the heck else he wanted (being king, you see, he didn't have to worry about permits). And all these stunning buildings are in a single royal park: the **Sanssouci.** Bike paths and walking trails weave through the beautifully planned park, filled with meadows of tall grasses, jasmine bushes, towering chestnut trees...and then wham! All of a sudden you're standing at the front door of a palace. It's unbelievable. It's breathtaking. It's the most wonderful feeling of discovery and awe and reverence for what are, I can guarantee you, some of the most beautiful buildings you'll ever see. It's Disneyland with palaces instead of rides, bike paths instead of lines, and (it is Germany, after all), overpriced beer instead of overpriced ice cream.

*Sophia Angelis*

does offer a history rarely presented. The permanent exhibit focuses on German homosexual history from 1800 to the present.

✦ *U6 or U7: Mehringdamm. From the station, head south on Merhringdamm. The museum will be through a courtyard on your left.* ℹ *English exhibit guide available.* Ⓢ *€5, students €3.* ☑ *Open Tu-F 2-6pm, Sa 2-7pm.*

## rule of thumb

While ordering beer (or anything else), be careful which finger you use to indicate "one." As you may have seen in *Inglourious Basterds*, Germans use the 👍thumb to ask for one, while adding the pointer finger means two. Simply holding up the second finger may earn you some confused looks from the occasional bartender.

# food

## CHARLOTTENBURG

Charlottenburg's history of wealth and opulence is still visible to the visitor in the upscale Ku'damm or in its elegant hotels. It's not surprising that inexpensive meals are difficult to come by. In north Charlottenburg, the neighborhood called Moabit (right next to Mitte) is home to strong Middle Eastern and Asian ethnic communities. For cheap, authentic Turkish or Vietnamese food, it may be worth the trip of 20min. from the Zoo.

### 🔲 SCHWARZES CAFE
Kantstr. 148

☻✆Ⓨ♨ BAR, RESTAURANT ❸

☎030 313 80 38

Pharmacies, grocery stores, and even whole neighborhoods might close down at night, but Schwarzes Cafe will still be open. Drink absinthe after dark inside the frescoed walls of the area's most popular boho cafe. The artistically peeling paint on the floors will increasingly bewilder as the absinthe gets to your head. Chase it down with breakfast when the sun comes up, or at a mere bohemian hour: all meals are served around the clock.

✦ *S3, S5, S7, S9, or S75: Savignypl.* Ⓢ *Weekly specials €7-13 served 11:30am-8pm. Breakfast €5-8.50. Cash only.* ☑ *Open M 24hr., Tu 4am-10am, W-Su 24hr.*

### ABBAS
Huttenstr. 71

☻♨ MIDDLE EASTERN ❶

☎030 34 34 77 70

Abbas and the restaurants around it belong to Arabic and Asian immigrants attracted by the area's low rent. This sprawling sweet and nut shop sells a wide range of authentic Middle Eastern desserts on the cheap, from chocolate-covered lentils to pistachio-cashew pastries. Try its specialty baklava *(€1.30 for 2 pieces).*

✦ *Bus M27: Turmstr./Beusseistr.* Ⓢ *Cash only.* ☑ *Open M-Th 10am-5pm, F and Sa noon-8pm.*

### MARIBEL
Kantstr. 70

♥☻Ⓨ♨ RESTAURANT, BAR ❸

☎030 31 00 48 73 🖳www.restaurant-maribel.de

A lovely corner restaurant with floor-to-ceiling French doors that open onto the sidewalk on sunny days, Maribel is one of the best deals for families and those with exceptionally big appetites. For Saturday and Sunday brunch *(10am-4pm),* enjoy an all-you-can-eat spread of sophisticated cheeses (sophisticated can also mean pungent), sauteed vegetables, breads, pastries, salami, and smoked salmon *(adults €9.50, ages 7-14 €4, children under 6 free).* Breakfast *(including omelettes, €4.80)* served daily until 4pm. Lunch menu served from 11:30am to close.

✦ *U7: Wilmersdorfer Str., or S3, S5, S7 or S75: Charlottenburg.* Ⓢ *Entrees €7-11.* ☑ *Open M-Sa 9am-1am, Su 10am-1am.*

food · charlottenburg

**PARIS BAR** 💳🍸☀ BAR, RESTAURANT ❹

Kantstr. 152 ☎030 313 80 52

One of former West Berlin's favorite gathering places is still a hot spot for hip artists, popular politicians, uber-celebs being "normal people," and students who can only afford the desserts. With warm lighting, dark wood, and a well-stocked bar, this restaurant is an option for any budget—just supplement a dish off the starter menu with some dirt-cheap döner later.

*➡ U1: Uhlandstr. $ Soups from €5.50; starters €6.50-14.50; entrees €12-25. ⏰ Open daily noon-2am. Kitchen closes at 1am.*

**MENSA TU** 🥗☀ CAFETERIA ❶

Hardenbergerstr. 34 ☎030 939 39 74 39

It's a cafeteria, but the Hardenbergerstr. Mensa offers the cheapest hot meal around, with three-entree choices as well as vegetarian options. And our favorite part: your portion size is as much food as you can fit on a plate. Accordingly, it's overrun by university students. A slightly higher-priced cafeteria is downstairs; avoid it.

*➡ U2: Ernst-Reuter-Pl., bus #245: Steinpl., a 10min. walk from Bahnhof Zoo. $ Meals €3-4, students €2-3. ⏰ Downstairs cafeteria open M-F 11am-2:30pm. Upstairs open M-F 11:30am-3:30pm, coffee bar M-F 11am-6pm, and cake shop M-F 7:30am-2:30pm.*

**LA PETIT FRANCE CROISSANTERIE** 🥗☀ CAFE ❶

Nürnberger Str. 24A ☎017 817 11 38 26

Fresh, inexpensive lunches are sometimes difficult to come by in sprawling Charlottenburg. This pocket-sized French bistro has some stellar baguettes and classic Francophone music to transport you across the Rhein. Try the small baguettes with a variety of toppings, including tomato, mozzarella and basil *(€2.50; large €3.30)*. Or try a light quiche and salad combo *(€4.50)*.

*➡ U3 to Ausgburger Str. ⏰ Open M-Sa 8am-6:30pm.*

**FAM DANG** 🥗☀ THAI AND VIETNAMESE ❶

Hutten Str. 5 ☎030 75 56 75 26

Located in a predominantly Vietnamese area, Fam Dang's bright rooms, outdoor patio, and ridiculously inexpensive daily menu make it a must. The highlight is the standing soup menu, with large bowls of Thai and Vietnamese favorites *(€5)*. The entree menu rotates daily, but prices are in the same ballpark.

*➡ Bus M27: Turnstr./Beusselstr. $ Entrees €5 or less. ⏰ Open M-F 11:30-9pm, Sa 2pm-9pm.*

## SCHÖNEBERG AND WILMERSDORF

Schöneberg's relaxed cafe culture is best experienced around the intersection of **Maaßenstrasse** and **Winterfeldstrasse.** More popular cafes and inexpensive restaurants crowd the **Akazienstrasse,** from the U-Bahn station at Eisenacherstr., to Hauptstr.

👍 **CAFE BILDERBUCH** 🥗📶 CAFE ❷

Akazienstr. 28 ☎030 78 70 60 57 🖥www.cafe-bilderbruch.de

Even if you couldn't eat here, Cafe Bilderbuch's antique cabinets, fringed lamps, deep-cushioned sofas, and adjoining library would still make this a place to visit. Fortunately, their unbeatable Sunday brunch buffets *(€8)* have us shoving grandmothers out of the way to get in the door. The dinner specials *(€5-8.50)* are always affordable and never stuffy.

*➡ U7: Eisenacher Str. i Free Wi-Fi. $ Soup from €3.70. Salads from €6. Entrees €8. Coffee €1.50. ⏰ Open M-Th 9am-1am, F-Sa 9am-2am, Su 10am-1am. Kitchen closes Su-F 11pm, Sa midnight.*

👍 **BAHARAT FALAFEL** 🥗☀ TURKISH ❶

Winterfeldtstr. 37 ☎030 216 83 01

This isn't your average *döner* stand. First, because it doesn't serve *döner*. Second, because this vegetarian Turkish restaurant makes all its falafel fried to order, in fluffy pita with lots of tomatoes, lettuce, and mango or chili sauce *(€3-4)*. Wash Baharat's plates, with hummus, tabouleh, and salad, all down with fresh-squeezed *Gute Laune Saft (good-mood juice, €1-2)*. Indoor seating with bright walls and flowers on the table, or an outdoor bench under a striped awning.

✦ *U1, U3, U4 or U9: Nollendorfpl.* Ⓢ *Entrees €6-8.* ⏲ *Open M-Sa 11am-2am, Su noon-2am.*

### 🍽 HIMALI
●🍴♨ TIBETAN, NEPALESE ❷

Crellerstr. 45 ☎030 78 71 61 75 ■www.himali-restaurant.de

Nepali and Tibetan classics are cooked up and served piping hot from a tandoori oven. Food is never short on spices, either in quantity or variety, which are grown and ground by hand. This restaurant offers a huge range of vegetarian dishes, curried or grilled, with tofu, vegetables and *naan* with your choice of seasonings. The Nepali tea *(€2.50)* is to die for.

✦ *U7: Kleistpark.* Ⓢ *Entrees €6.50-10.* ⏲ *Open daily noon-midnight.*

### DOUBLE EYE
●🍴 CAFE ❶

Akazienstr. 22 ☎017 94 56 69 60 ■www.doubleeye.de

For coffee purists, this is an inexpensive way to enjoy the best kind of brew. This coffee bar is packed all day with locals, who come for the no-syrup-added, only-best-quality-cream daily brews. Baristas prepare each espresso with surgical precision and take pride on their top quality "latte-art" designs traced into the inch deep foam. They've got victory plaques behind the bar to back up that smack.

✦ *U7: Eisenacher Str.* Ⓢ *Cappuccinos €1.80. Macchiatos €2.* ⏲ *Open daily 8.45am-5:30pm, Sa 9am-6pm.*

### CAFE BERIO
●🍴♨▼ VIENNESE ❷

Maaßenstr. 7 ☎030 216 19 46 ■www.cafe-berio.de

French doors open to the streets and let passerby look in on this constantly jam-packed Viennese-style cafe. Frequented by a mostly gay clientele, Cafe Berio is a favorite stop-off point before a night of clubbing. The two-floor cafe is best known for their breakfast menu *(€3-11)*, two-for-one happy hour drinks *(M-Th and Su 7pm-midnight, F-Sa 7-9pm)*, and obscenely extensive menu of dessert options, with cakes and tortes *(from €2)*.

✦ *U1, U3, U4, or U9: Nollendorfpl.* Ⓢ *Entrees €5-9.* ⏲ *Open M-Th 8am-midnight, F-Sa 8am-1am, Su 8am-midnight. Kitchen open daily 8am-11pm.*

### CAFE EINSTEIN
●🍴♨ CAFE ❹

Kurfurstenstr. 58 ☎030 261 5096 ■www.cafeeinstein.com

Cafe Einstein is Berlin's premiere Viennese coffeeshop, and an obligatory stop for tourists and intelligent, good-looking Let's Go travelers alike. Large windows ingeniously look out onto Einstein's private garden, which you can enjoy along with splurge-worthy home roasted coffee *(cappuccino €4.30, milchkaffee €3.80)*. A small cake or torte is the least expensive way to enjoy the cafe's wood paneled and detailed molding, and will set you back about €4.

✦ *U1, U3, U4, or U9: Nollendorfpl.* Ⓢ *Entrees €14.50-22. Breakfast from €5.80, €12.80 for a Sunday brunch bar. Mixed drinks at the bar Lebensstern from €9.* ⏲ *Open daily 6am-1am. The bar Lenesstern is open 7pm-late.*

### BAR TOLUCCI
●🍴♨ TUSCAN ❷

Eisenacher Str. 86 ☎030 214 16 07 ■www.bar-tolucci.de

With stone-oven cooked pizzas *(from €5.50)* and outdoor seating on wood-slated bistro tables along the quiet streetcorner, this restaurant is casual eating and generous portions at their finest. Surround yourself with photographs from Italian filmmaker Bertolucci's films with the inside seating, or seclude yourself in the small garden.

✦ *U7: Eisenacher Str.* Ⓢ *Pizzas €5.50-8.20. Entrees €6-7.* ⏲ *Open daily noon-1am, garden noon-midnight. Oven in use M-F from 5pm, and Sa-Su from noon.*

**YOGI-HAUS** 🌿🍸☀ INDIAN [2]

Belziger Str. 42 ☎030 782 92 23 💻www.restaurant-yogihaus.de

In an ethnic food scene dominated by Turkish cuisine, Yogi-Haus is a welcome deviation from the *döner* and falafel norm. Find it tucked in-between a gaggle of cafes next to a small park. The two outdoor seating patios overlooking trees and quiet roads may help you connect with your inner yogi. The authentically Indian cuisine will definitely jumpstart your discovery of the stomach *chakra*.

*🚇 U7: Eisenacher Str. The restaurant is on the corner of Ecke Eisenacher Str. $ Traditional Indian soups €2.30-3.10. Vegetarian entrees €4.80-6.50. Chicken and lamb curry dishes €5.50-8. ⏰ Open daily noon-midnight.*

**SEILDS** 🌿🍸☀ ROMANTIC [4]

Gotenstr. 1 ☎030 78 09 79 97 💻www.seilds-berlin.de

This airy, out of the way restaurant oozes romance. Outside, the triangular patio shaded by trees makes an ideal chill-out date after a particularly bad argument. Inside, local art on red walls and candlelight sets the scene for a *Lady and the Tramp* sequel. If you're looking to lighten your wallet, this is a good place to indulge.

*🚇 S1: Julius-Leber-Brücke. $ Soups from €6, weekly specials €10-19. Beer from €2.80. ⏰ Open M-Sa noon-1am, Su 9-1am.*

**VIET RICE** 🌿 VIETNAMESE [1]

Martin-Luther-Str. 99 ☎152 03 11 00 63 💻www.vietrice.de

This stark Vietnamese restaurant may have tried and failed to make itself "elegant," but the food is still great and incredibly cheap. Uncomfortable seating and too many tables can make sit-down meals a nightmare, but as an upscale takeout place, without the extra cost, Viet Rice is unbeatable. A short menu includes many Vietnamese staples, like veal soup with coriander *(€5)*. Watch your food being made in the large, updated kitchen.

*🚇 U4: Rathaus Schöneberg. $ Full entrees €3.60-5.60. ⏰ Open daily 11:30am-11pm.*



## MITTE

**BERLINER MARCUS BRÄU** 💳♿🍸 GERMAN [2]

1-3 Münzstr. ☎0302 47 69 85 💻www.marcus-brau.de

This corner shack's been brewing its own beer and liqueurs since before its country tried to conquer the world. The liqueurs, especially the coffee liqueur, taste as good as your mom smells, assuming she smells great. The food isn't exactly free, and the decor isn't exactly Ritz Carlton, but it's authentic, hearty, and German. Try the beer *(from €3 for 5L)*; it's among the best in the city.

*🚇 U2, U5, U8, S5, S7, S9, or S75: Alexanderpl. $ Entrees €7.50-9. Drinks €1-7. ⏰ Open daily noon-late.*

**GOOD MORNING VIETNAM** 💳♿🍸☀ VIETNAMESE [2]

Alte Schonhauser 60 ☎030 30 88 29 73 💻www.good-morning-vietnam.de

The name is great. Explanation for the name is even better: "A yesterday's movie title, a salutation that reminds us of the past, a past full of starvation and war..." Brimming with such great food, this restaurant is hardly about starvation. Entrees *(€7)*, are cheaper than much-hyped Monsieur Vuong's down the street, and include crispy duck, mango chicken skewers, and tofu platters.

*🚇 U2: Rosa-Luxemburg-Pl. $ Entrees €7-7.50. ⏰ Open daily noon-midnight.*

**MONSIEUR VUONG** 💳♿🍸☀ VIETNAMESE [3]

Alte Schonhauserstr. 46 ☎030 99 29 69 24 💻www.monsieurvuong.de

Other people will be talking about it, and the food is good, but don't feel like you must make it to this wildly popular Vietnamese bistro. The menu changes every two days, keeping a crew of regulars coming back to try the forthcoming noodle and rish dishes, but popularity has unnecessarily jacked up the prices.

The only exception is the fantastic and reasonable Vietnamese coffee *(€2)* made with condensed milk and a little bit of love.

*🚇 U2: Rosa-Luxemburg-Pl. **i** Only the outdoor seating is wheelchair-accessible. $ Entrees €7.40-9.80. ⏰ Open daily noon-midnight.*

**DOLORES BURRITOS** 🥦☀ MEXICAN FUSION [1]

Rosa-Luxemburg-Str. 7 ☎030 28 09 95 97

Modeled after the Mexican fusion of Baja Fresh or Chipotle, this "California Burrito" shop sells hulking tubes under €5. While we won't go as far as calling these suckers "Californian," the place does a good job of supplying a real spread of chipotle chicken *(€1)*, spiced *carnitas* *(€1.30)*, and vegetables *(€0.80)* and lets you combine them in burrito *(€4)*, bowl *(€4)*, or quesadilla *(€3.70)* form. The staff could be nicer, but with the rush of students they're dealing with, you hardly blame them.

*🚇 U2, U5, U8, S5, S7, S9, or S75: Alexanderpl. $ Burritos around €5; prices vary depending on your ingredients. ⏰ Open M-Sa 11:30am-10pm, Su 1-10pm.*

**TIPICA** 💳📶☀ MEXICAN [1]

Rosenstr. 19 ☎030 25 09 94 40 💻www.tipica.mx

Tipica is built around a "do-it-yourself" taco menu. Large portions of meat, cilantro, onion, and lime come with four tortillas; you add the sides and salsas to roll your own creations. The meats get crazy, even including a veal taco, but the portions are large, and friends like to come and mix and match. Get any meat Alcurbie style—fried with peppers, onions, and bacon—for no extra charge.

*🚇 S5, S7, S9, or S75: Hackescher Markt. From the station, head east and turn right at An der Spandauer Brucke immediately after the Markt. Follow it 100m or so as it curves around to the right. **i** Only outdoor seating is wheelchair-accessible. $ Tacos €4-7. Sides €2. Salsas €1. ⏰ Open M-Th 11am-11pm, F-Sa 11am-1am, Su 11am-11pm.*

**ARAB ESKE** 💳♿🍸☀ LEBANESE [1]

Kastanienallee 59 ☎030 44 01 27 70 💻www.arabeske.berlin.de

A solid meal at a great price with no frills and one thrill (the salad dressing! No joke, it kills). Safe bets include shawarma *(€5.50)*, which comes with hummus and salad. Vegetarians can find comfort in falafel *(€4)* and the fact that they only indirectly contribute to the deaths of millions of innocent animals.

*🚇 U8: Rosenthaler Pl. From the U-Bahn, head northeast up Weinbergsweg. $ Entrees €4-6. ⏰ Open daily 11am-late*

**HUMBOLDT UNIVERSITY NEW LIBRARY** 🥦♿🍸 CAFETERIA [1]

Geschwister-Scholl-Str. 1 ☎03020 939 93 99

In the thick of Mitte tourist mecca—where a cup of coffee costs €4—sits the quiet, seemingly off-limits library of Humbodlt University. You'll find no one but students inside this tiny cafeteria (conveniently located before the security checkpoint) that has the lowest prices anywhere in central Berlin. Bockwurst *(€1.50)*, salads with chicken and egg *(€1)*, and coffee *(€0.60-2)* must be state-subsidized at these prices. They even have a tray of powders for constructing your very own "curry bockwurst."

*🚇 U6: Friedrichstraße. From the station, take Friedrichstraße north and take a right just past the tracks. $ Entrees €1-2. ⏰ Open M-F 9am-8pm, Sa-Su noon-5pm.*

**FASSBENDER AND RAUSCH CHOCOLATIERS** 💳♿🍸 CHOCOLATERIE [1]

Charlottenstr. 60 ☎0302 045 84 43 💻www.fassbender-rausch.de

To prepare for his fall into Wonka's chocolate river, Augustus Gloop jumped into F and R's chocolate volcano (real), took a ride on their chocolate *Titanic* (real, though it might be the *Lusitania*), and commented on the Baroque idealism of their chocolate Berliner Dom. A stimulating, bustling, enormous chocolate house where every inch is filled with confections so delicious, they're physically arousing. Truffles *(€0.50-0.80)* come in 100 flavors, and it's hard to go wrong with any of them.

❖ *U2 or U6: Stadmitte.* ⓢ *Chocolate €0.50-300.* ⏰ *Open M-Sa 10am-8pm, Su 11am-8pm.*

## GALERIA GOURMET—GALERIA KAUFHOF    ⬤♿ GROCERIES ❷
Alexanderpl. 9                          ☎0302 474 30 💻www.galeria-kaufhof.de

The entire bottom floor of this seven-story department store devotes itself to laying out the anatomy of the German diet. Take this time to spy all the whacked-out foods the Germans enjoy at this Deutsche version of Whole Foods, like 10 types of pickled herring, more sausages than you thought the world had pigs, and a great assortment of relatively cheap German wine *(€2-200)*. Sandwiches *(€4-6)*, warm sausages *(€2-5)*, and other prepared food can be taken to nearby Alexanderpl. and enjoyed from a bench.

❖ *U2, U5, or U8: Alexanderpl.* ⓢ *Prepared food €4-8.* ⏰ *Open M-W 9:30am-8pm, Th-Su 9:30am-10pm.*

## CURRY 61                                ⬤♿ CURRYWURST ❶
Oranienburgerstr. 6                        ☎0302 636 99 41 💻www.curry61.de

There's a horde of currywurst stands across this city, but God did not make them all equal. Curry 61 is your best bet in Mitte since the supposed originator of currywurst mysteriously went out of business for a few months. Try the 🔲**spicy with skin.**

❖ *S5, S7, S9, or S75: Hackescher Markt.* ⓢ *Currywurst €1.70.* ⏰ *Open M-Sa 11am-1pm.*

## ROSENTHAL GRILL                          ⬤♿🍴 CAFE ❶
Torstr. 125                                ☎0302 83 21 53

Outstanding deals and quality Berlin street food at a nice outdoor cafe. Big eaters: an entire chicken costs €5. Döner kebabs (which are like a gyro, but made with cabbage) and pizzas are also great.

❖ *U8: Rosenthaler Pl.* ⓢ *Menu €1-6.* ⏰ *Open 24hr.*

# PRENZLAUER BERG

## 🔳 W-IMBISS                              ⬤⑴🍴 VEGETARIAN ❶
Katanienallee 49                           ☎030 48 49 26 57

Maybe it's Indian food, or maybe it's Mexican. We can't really tell, but one thing we do know: this food is good. W-Imbiss specializes in fusing ethnic food types to make something interestingly novel, and damn good. Their specialty is the *naan* pizza—freshly baked bread in a tandoori oven spread with anything from pesto to avocado to chipotle sauce and served piled high with arugula and feta or mozzarella. W-Imbiss also sells cold wraps and quesadillas to an international crowd.

❖ *U8: Voltastr.* ⓢ *Pizza €2-5.50. Wraps €4-5.* ⏰ *Open May-Aug daily noon-midnight; Sept-Apr daily 12:30-11:30pm.*

## 🔳 HANS WURST                            ⬤🍴 VEGAN ❷
Dunckerstr. 2A                             ☎030 41 71 78 22

This small cafe serves only organic, vegan foods with no flavor enhancers. Readings, DJs, and acoustic concerts spice up the evenings in this minimally decorated, laid-back venue. The menu changes daily, with seasonal and innovative offerings. Try the tofu burger on toast with original, spicy sauces.

❖ *U2: Eberswalder Str. Or M10: Husemannstr.* ⓢ *Entrees €3.70-8. Tofu burger €4.* ⏰ *Open M-Th noon-midnight, F-Sa noon-late.*

## DAS FILM CAFE                            ⬤🍴 BURGERS, THEATER ❷
Schliemannstr. 15                          ☎030 810 11 90 50 💻www.dasfilmcafe.de

Das Film Cafe serves up homemade burgers to fans hungry for a good meal and even better movies. This cafe has two screenings a night in a small, high-resolution theater downstairs, usually around 8pm and 10pm, and prides itself on selecting films with an international, independent flair. Films are never dubbed over and are usually shown in English.

🚇 *U2: Eberswalder Str.* $ *Tickets €4.50, students €4. Burgers €7. Hummus plates €5.50. Cappuccino €2.* ⏰ *Open M-F 2:30pm-late, Sa-Su 11:30am-late.*

**THE BIRD** 🍴🍸☀ BURGERS ❷

Am Falkpl. 5 ☎030 51 05 32 83

With a bar made of old wood and exposed brick walls, this seemingly quintessential European restaurant is anything but. Opened by two New York transplants, The Bird makes some of the only honest-to-goodness, criminally huge burgers in Berlin. Everything is made from scratch daily, including the sauce for the aptly named "napalm wings." Locals appreciate "Angry Hour," 6-8pm, when all beer is buy one, get one free.

🚇 *U8: Voltastr.* $ *Burgers €9-12. Wings €6.* ⏰ *Open M-Sa 6pm-late, Su noon-late.*

**CAFE RESTAURANT MIRÓ** 🍴🍸☀ MEDITERRANEAN ❷

Raumerstr. 29 ☎030 44 73 30 13 💻www.miro-restaurant.de

Cafe Miró captures the essence of the Mediterranean, whose food it proudly serves in a candlelit, pillow-laden room. Brick walls and cobalt blue details set the scene for your love affair with feta and oregano. The Greek omelettes *(€5.20)* are incredibly popular.

🚇 *U2: Eberswalder Str.* $ *Entrees €8.50-15.50. Appetizers and salads €4-9. Soups €3.20-3.70. Su brunch €8.* ⏰ *Open M-F 3pm-late, Sa-Su 10am-late. Brunch Su 10am-4pm. Kitchen open until midnight.*

**LIEBLING** 🍴🍸☀ CAFE ❶

Raumer Str. 36A ☎030 41 19 82 09

This corner cafe is all elegance, with a little edge. An alternative crowd chills out and sips on gin and coffee in the completely white-on-white interior plastered with mosaic tile. Enjoy a typically-Berlin *milchkaffee* on a bistro table on a quiet street or stick around 'til dark to watch the chairs fill with guests sipping aperitifs and liquor.

🚇 *U2: Eberswalder Str.* $ *Milchkaffee €2.50. Apertifs €2.50-4. Mixed drinks €2-3.50.* ⏰ *Open M-F 9am-late, Sa-Su noon-late.*

**BABEL** 🍴☀ MIDDLE EASTERN ❶

Kastanienalle 33 ☎030 44 03 13 18

With the exception of Che Guevara's portrait, which hangs over the front door, Babel is a perfect Middle Eastern eatery. Locals obsessed with the falafel keep this neighborhood joint busy at all hours, eating at outside packed tables or inside under dangling garlic. Scarf down some döner to the beat of Middle Eastern tunes.

🚇 *U8: Bernauer Str.* $ *Falafel €3-6.* ⏰ *Open daily 11am-2am.*

**SOUPANOVA** 🍴🍸☀ SOUP ❶

Stargader Str. 24 💻www.soupanova.de

Creative soups here begin with a broth base from a variety of choices, including Thai coconut milk and miso. Then add tofu, wonton, or chicken to make it a meal. Full of vegetarian options and zany floral patterns.

🚇 *U2: Eberswalder Str.* $ *Soup €4-5.* ⏰ *Open daily 6pm-late.*

**CAFE IMNU** 🍴🍸☀ CAFE ❷

Lychener Str. 41 ☎0304 471 88 98

Located just across from one of Prenzlauer Berg's best-known parks, Cafe ImNu is a serene place to enjoy an early breakfast or midday meal. Juices are squeezed fresh to order, including the sweet strawberry-kiwi-banana blend *(€3.80)*. The vegetarian breakfast comes with pasta, mozzarella, tomatoes, pesto, yogurt, honey, and a garden salad.

🚇 *U2: Eberswalder Str.* $ *Breakfast €5.10-8. Baguette sandwiches €3.20-4.10.* ⏰ *Open daily 8am-7pm.*

## FRIEDRICHSHAIN

Friedrichshain is famous for its inexpensive, student-centered living, and its restaurants, bars and cafes don't disappoint. In the area bounded by Frankfurter-Allee to the north, Jennerstr. to the east, Simon-Dach-Str. to the west, and Wühlschischerstr. to the south, streets overflow with bistro tables, outdoor umbrellas, and cheap food.

### 👍 FRITTIERSALON — 🥦🍸☁ GERMAN ❶

Boxhagener Str. 104 — ☎030 25 93 39 06

Yes, we know, ever since you set foot in Berlin, you've been drowning in bratwurst, currywurst, and fried potatoes. But for anyone in Friedrichshain, this all-organic "frying salon" is unique enough to merit a visit. In addition to a traditional prize-winning Berliner currywurst, this restaurant serves a number of German classics with a twist: try the wheat-based vegetarian currywurst or bratwurst or a hamburger or veggie burger with strawberries and avocado. All sauces and french fries are homemade, and all dishes are cooked to order.

*🚇 U5: Frankfurter Tor. Ⓢ Bratwurst and currywurst €2.20. Burgers €6. ⏰ Open M 6pm-late, Tu-F noon-late, Sa-Su 1pm-late.*

### 👍 CARAMELLO EIS — 🥦☁ ICE CREAM ❶

Wühlischerstr. 31 — ☎030 50 34 31 05 💻www.caramello-eis.de

Caramello Eis scoops some of the best ice cream in town all night long to a following of devoted students. All of Caramello's ice cream is handmade, organic, and vegan. Don't leave Friedrichshain without trying the dark chocolate *eis* with chili powder; the staff says it's the best chocolate ice cream in all of Berlin, and we're not about to argue.

*🚇 U5: Frankfurter Tor. Ⓢ Cones €1. ⏰ Open daily 11am-late.*

### AUNT BENNY — 🥦📶☁ CAFE ❶

Oderstr. 7 — ☎030 66 40 53 00

Frequented by moms who take their children to the playground across the street, students who love Wi-Fi, and anyone who's serious about the art of making carrot cake, this cafe is always buzzing with energy. Regulars are almost aggressive with their enthusiasm for the cafe's *bricher-muesli*—a kind of Swiss cereal, containing nuts, fresh apples, and oats, soaked overnight, served with yogurt, and usually sold out by 4pm.

*🚇 U5: Frankfurter Allee. Ⓢ Smoothies €4.20-4.80. Bagels €1.60. Coffee €1.60. Su brunch €8. ⏰ Open Tu-F 9am-7pm, Sa-Su 10am-7pm.*

### HOPS AND BARLEY — 🥦🍸☁ MICROBREWERY ❶

Wühlischstr. 22/23 — ☎030 29 36 75 34 💻www.hopsandbarley-berlin.de

This microbrewery makes its own cider, pilsner, and lager on site for hordes of thirsty locals. The bar gets particularly packed for German club football games, when the bar opens early *(3pm)* and stays open late. The guys here also make their own bread daily, so no German, or wandering traveler, has to drink good beer on an empty stomach.

*🚇 U5: Frankfurter Allee. Ⓢ 0.3L beer €1.90. 0.5L beer €2.80. ⏰ Open 5pm-late.*

### INTIMES KINO-CAFE — 🥦🍸☁ CAFE ❷

Boxhagener Str. 107 — ☎030 29 66 64 57

A portrait on the wall pays homage to Che Guevara, for a reason that the staff either doesn't know or won't tell. A large photograph of Havana that looks weirdly like East Berlin covers another wall. A large variety of vegetarian entrees (more than just pasta!) and outdoor tables overrun with locals in the summertime make this restaurant a standout.

*🚇 U5: Frankfurter Tor. Ⓢ Vegetarian casseroles and gratin €7-9.10. Tarte flambées €4.50-7. ⏰ Open daily 10am-midnight.*

**YOBARCA** — FROZEN YOGURT [1]
Simon-Dach-Str. 40 ☎0170 969 97 37 💻www.yobarca.com

This is the first frozen-yogurt place opened in Friedrichshain, and while the locals might still be figuring it out, we love it. Try toppings from blueberries and blackberries to pineapple and passion-fruit sauce. Started by an Italian ice-cream maker, this froyo cafe is outfitted in shocking yellow walls and chairs strewn around a small patio on a busy, shaded Friedrichshain street.

*🚇 U5: Frankfurter Tor. $ Small yogurt with 1 topping €2.50. Bubble tea €2.50. Extra toppings €0.50. ⏰ Open daily 10am-10pm.*

**CAFE CORTADO** — CAFE [1]
Simon-Dach-Str. 9

Flowers and boardgames on breezy patio tables and a cozy, sofa-covered backroom draw a young crowd with a taste for international coffee blends. Cafe Cortado's mosaic bar serves up Turkish and Portuguese coffee by day and beer and cocktails by night. A variety of chai teas and a berry torte, made fresh daily, are favorites.

*🚇 U5: Frankfurter Allee. $ Beer €3. Mixed drinks from €6. ⏰ Open M-F 9am-9pm, Sa-Su 9am-midnight.*

**LEMONGRASS** — THAI [1]
Simon-Dach-Str. 2 ☎030 20 05 69 75

Located on a popular street with shops and restaurants, this criminally cheap Thai restaurant serves up classic favorites in a relaxed, green-striped kitchen. Bistro tables crowd the outdoor patio, and small tables inside look over the kitchen. Portions are huge, so pick your view and relax while enjoying authentic Asian specialities.

*🚇 U5: Frankfurter Tor. $ Soups from €2.80. Entrees €6.50-8. ⏰ Open daily noon-midnight.*

**STRANDGUT BERLIN** — RESTOBAR [1]
Mühlenstr. 61 ☎030 70 08 55 66 💻www.strandgut-berlin.com

There's something a little inauthentic about sitting on a beach next to the Spree, but we're not letting that keep us from enjoying a little piece of paradise (however contrived) in the middle of Berlin. Imported sand and lounge chairs line the river, shaded by trees and umbrellas. A beach-house-style bar and restaurant serve up quick, cheap food to frighteningly pale Germans working on their tan.

*🚇 U1, S3, S5, S7, S9 or S75: Warschauer Str. $ Beer €3. Mixed drinks €6. Soda €2. Hamburgers €3.50. Salads €2. ⏰ Open M-F 10am-10pm, Sa-Su 10am-4pm. Restaurant open noon-late.*

**DER FLIEGENDER TISCH** — ITALIAN [2]
Mainzer Str. 10 ☎030 02 97 76 48

This cozy candlelit eatery serves inexpensive Italian food to local devotees. The pizza is cooked fresh in a Dutch oven. The restaurant's fans swear by their risotto *(€5.60-6.50)*. Meals are served on small, crowded tables in a darkened room with a central bar and understated Tuscan decor.

*🚇 U5: Samariter Str. $ Pizza €5. Pasta €4.30-6.60. ⏰ Open daily 5pm-midnight.*

## KREUZBERG

Good food lives and dies all over Kreuzberg, but the best food is stacked up in the area near **Oranienestrasse.**

**CAFE MORGANLAND** — CAFE [1]
Skalitzer Str. 35 ☎03061 132 91 💻www.cafemorgenland.eu

Its Parisian breakfast—a fresh butter croissant, a large dish of perfect vanilla custard with fresh fruit, and the best milk coffee you've ever had—breaks the laws of economics. The all-you-can-eat brunch buffet *(€9.50)* on the weekends will literally make your jaw drop: eight types of meat, five types of bread, 15 spreads, sausages, eggs, curries, potatoes, fish, vegetables, fruits—it's paradise.

Solid international fare fills out the rest of the menu.

*🚇 U1: Görlitzer Bahnhof. $ Entrees €5-15. ⏰ Open daily 10am-1am.*

### 👍 RESTAURANT RISSANI
🍸 MIDDLE EASTERN ❶

Spreewaldpl. 4 ☎3061 62 94 33

A lot of döner kebab places around town call themselves authentic. Well, Rissani doesn't serve döners—they call them chicken shawarma sandwiches—but they're twice as delicious and half as expensive *(€2)*. Dinner plates, with shawarma, falafel, tabbouleh, hummus, and salad will make you forget your bad day.

*🚇 U1: Görlitzer Bahnhof. From the station, head east down Skalitzer str. and take a right at Spreewaldpl. $ Entrees €2-5. ⏰ Open M-Th 11am-3am, F-Sa 11am-5am, Su 11am-3am.*

### 👍 MUSTAFAS
♿🍸 MIDDLE EASTERN ❶

Mehringdamm 32 🖥www.mustafas.de

Some say that this place serves up the best döner kebabs in the city—that's debatable, but what's not is that Mustafas has the best *durum (shawarma burrito with sauce; €4)* in the city. It tastes like the best thing in the world stuffed with the second-best thing in the world. Vegetarians who usually scrounge through various falafel options will rejoice over the delicious grilled vegetables in the veggie *durum (€3.10)*. If you want to check it out yourself, their website has a live webcam.

*🚇 U6 or U7: Mehringdamm. $ Entrees €2.50-5. ⏰ Open 24hr.*

### 👍 HENNE ALT-BERLINER WIRTSHAUS GASTSTÄTTEN
🍸☀ GERMAN ❷

Leuschnerdamm 25 ☎3061 477 30 🖥www.henne-berlin.de

Henne provides the most German experience imaginable. An antler-lined parlor crammed with plaid tablecloths, sturdy German damsels hauling mugs of beer, and a menu that consists of a single dinner: a piece of bread, creamy potato salad, and enormous, perfectly crispy, internationally renowned chicken that will forever redefine "fried food." The chicken skin whispers as you crunch it, "I'm better than the girls you'll miss out on by eating me and gaining weight." She only speaks the truth.

*🚇 U1 or U8: Kottbusser Tor. From the station, head northwest on Oranienstr. Take a right at Oranienpl. **i** Reservations needed for outdoor seating. $ Entrees from €8. ⏰ Open Tu-Sa 7pm-late, Su 5pm-late.*

### CURRY 36
♿🍸☀ CURRYWURST ❶

Mehringdamm 36 ☎0302 51 73 68 🖥www.curry36.de

The best currywurst in Berlin means the best currywurst in the world. Be brave: take it with ketchup, fries, and an enormous glob of mayo.

*🚇 U6 or U7: Mehringdamm. $ Currywurst €1.50. ⏰ Open M-F 9am-4am, Sa 10am-4am, Su 11am-3am.*

### SK KREUZBERG FOOD 24 GMBH
♿🍸 STREET FOOD ❶

Schlesischestr. 1-2 ☎0306 107 60 00

Home of the amazing €1.50 personal pizza and the €3 impersonal pizza (so cold), SK gets flooded by post-clubbers and pre-clubbers every evening. Heftier dishes come in the form of pastas and sandwiches *(€3-5)*. No need to look further; this is the cheapest drunk food in Kreuzberg.

*🚇 U1: Schlesisches Tor. $ Entrees €1-5. ⏰ Open 24hr.*

### SANTA MARIA
☀ MEXICAN ❷

Oranienstr. 170 ☎0309 221 00 27 🖥asmarias.de

A few bites of fare from this Mexican bistro will cause a riot in your mouth. *Choriqueso (€6.50)* is a pot of melted cheese and sausage...just think about that for a second. The standard issue grub like fat Mexican sandwiches *(€6)*, tacos *(€3-7)*, Coronas *(€2.50)*, and margaritas *(€5)* are also on hand. A popular evening

berlin

hangout for expats.

*🚏 U8: Moritzpl. From the U-bahn, head southeast on Oranienstr. $ Entrees €5-8. ⏰ Open daily noon-midnight.*

**AMAR** 💳♿🍸⛅ INDIAN [3]

Schloßstr. 50 ☎0306 956 66 73 💻www.amar-berlin.de

Always pleasant and always packed, Amar has classy, flashy Indian food, even if it's not the world's cheapest. For Indian in Kreuzberg, there isn't a better combination of taste and price. Curries come in separate metal pots to guests packed into every outdoor table. Vegetarians have a huge variety of cheese, vegetable, and curry dishes *(€5.70-8)* to choose from. Many guests use this place as a jumping-off point to the best nearby clubs in Berlin.

*🚏 U1: Schlesisches Tor. $ Entrees €4-10. ⏰ Open M-Th 11:30am-1am, F-Sa noon-2am, Su 11:30am-1am.*

# nightlife

## CHARLOTTENBURG

Charlottenburg's quiet cafes and music venues cater to the 30-something set. Great for a mellow evening, or a chance to hear the city's best jazz, but the real parties are eastward. The Ku'damm is best avoided after sunset, unless you enjoy fraternizing with drunk businessmen.

**👍 A TRANE** 🎵🍸 BAR AND CLUB

Bleibtreustr. 1 ☎030 313 25 50 💻www.a-trane.de

Small in size, big on talent. Hanging black and white photographs of jazz greats, some who even performed at A Trane (like legends Herbie Hancock and Wynton Marsalis), look down on crowded tables filled with jazz enthusiasts. First-class musicians still entertain guests on a quiet street corner.

*🚏 S3, S5, S7, S9, or S75: Savignypl. $ Cover €7-15, students €5-13. Sa from 12:30am no cover. ⏰ Open M-Th and Su 9pm-2am, F-Sa 9pm-late.*

**CASCADE** 🎵🚭🍸 CLUB

Fasanenstr. 81 ☎030 31 80 09 40 💻www.cascade-club.de

The walk down to the large basement club is bookended by steps flooded by flowing water, hence the name Cascade. With a high cover, this club might be a bit of a splurge, but in return travelers get a dance floor of underlit blocks (à la 👍**John Travolta**), a wall-to-wall bar, and a young crowd–there might even actually be dancing! There are ways to get around the high admission price; stop by on a Friday and pick up a voucher for free entry, good the next evening, or next weekend.

*🚏 U1: Uhlandstr. $ Cover €10. Beer €3.50, shots €4. ⏰ Open F-Sa 11am-late.*

**SALZ** 🎵🍸⛅ CLUB

Salzufer 20 ☎017 02 83 35 04 💻www.salz-club.de

You'll have to go a little out of your way to find more upbeat and youthful bunch in low-key Charlottenburg. And by that we mean a 20-minute walk from the nearest U-Bahn station. But if you're looking to stay "in the neighborhood" and see someone dancing under the age of 32, this is the place to go. Exposed brick walls keep the disco-ball-lit floor looking classy at this salt-warehouse turned techno club. Out front find a beautiful patio lit with multi-colored lights and tiki torches.

*🚏 U2: Ernst-Reuter-Pl. Walk down Str. des 17 Juni to Satzufer. Turn left and walk along the river to Salz. ℹ Check the website for music schedules. $ No cover. ⏰ Open F-Sa 8pm-late.*

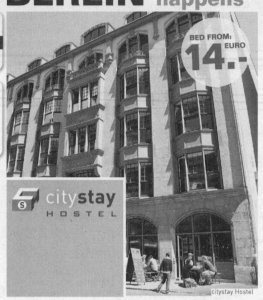

berlin

## QUASIMODO
⊗⊗♉ CLUB

Kantstr. 12A ☎030 312 80 86 ✉www.quasimodo.de

The upside is that Quasimodo showcases live music in a variety of genres, including soul, R and B, and jazz, nearly every night of the week. The downside is that the older crowd sometimes gives the club a kind of office-party energy. Spacious basement room with large bar and stage.

🍴 *U2, S5, S7, S9, or S75: Zoologischer Garten.* **i** *Check the website for music schedule.* ⓢ *Drinks €2.50-4.50. Cover for concerts €8-30, cheaper if reserved in advance.* ⌚ *Open daily 1pm-late.*

## ANDA LUCIA
✐♉⌂ BAR, RESTAURANT

Savignypl. 2 ☎030 54 02 71 ✉www.andalucia-berlin.de

So you're wandering around the streets of Berlin after hours, thinking, "Hey, you know what I'm in the mood for? A little Latin flavor! I wonder where I could nosh on tapas and show off my salsa at 2am!" Don't say we don't know our readers. And we've found the perfect place for you. Anda Lucia may not have a dance floor, but that doesn't keep the guests and staff from dancing around tables to salsa tunes blasting late into the heat of the night. Outdoor patio seating for those on a dance siesta and in the mood for a late night tapas (€3.70-4.10).

🍴 *S5, S7, or S75: Savignypl.* ⓢ *Wines from €4 a glass. Tequila €3.* ⌚ *Kitchen open 5pm-midnight. Tapas bar open 5pm-late.*

## SCHÖNEBERG AND WILMERSDORF

Schöneberg is still Berlin's unofficial gay district, full of GLBT nightlife. We've picked some of our favorites, but the neighborhood is full of outrageously popular bars and clubs that serve a vibrant gay community. From what we can tell, there aren't happier partiers in all of Berlin.

### [✓] HAFEN

🍸 GAY BAR

Motzstr. 19 ☎030 211 41 18 🖥www.hafen-berlin.de

Nearly 20 years old, this bar has become a landmark for Berlin's gay community. The sign outside may only specifically invite "drop dead gorgeous looking tourists," but you'll find plenty of locals all along the spectrum of attractiveness. The mostly male crowd spills out onto the streets during the summer. The weekly pub quiz, Monday at 8pm, is wildly popular (first Monday of the month in English), and every Wednesday features a new DJ. On April 30th, Hafen hosts their largest party of the year, in honor of the Queen of the Netherlands. They promise us that the "Queen" makes an appearance.

*🚇 U1, U3, U4 or U9: Nollendorfpl. $ No cover. ⏰ Open daily 8am-4am.*

### [✓] PRINZKNECHT

🍸 GAY BAR

Fuggerstr. 33 ☎030 23 62 74 44 🖥www.prinzknecht.de

Prinzknecht serves a mostly male clientele from a huge central wooden bar. Even with so many bar stools and couches, the bar fills up way past capacity on event nights, and people begin to resemble waves on the street. Check the website for upcoming events, including an incredibly popular [✓]**ABBA** night.

*🚇 U1 or U2: Wittenbergpl." $ No cover. ⏰ Open M-F 2pm-3am, Sa and Su 3pm-3am.*

### SLUMBERLAND

🍸 BAR

Goltstr. 24 ☎030 216 53 49

So normally we like a little more authenticity in our bars, but we're not going to pretend that we don't appreciate this island escape in the middle of land-locked Berlin, and the locals aren't either. So what if you didn't come to Germany for the reggae and palm trees? Try a mixed drink *(€5)* on a sandy floor, with rotating African art exhibits on the walls.

*🚇 U1 , U3, U4 or U9: Nollendorfpl. $ Most drinks €2-5. ⏰ Open M-Th and Su 6pm-2am, F 6pm-4am, Sa 11am-4pm.*

### BEGINE

🍸 LESBIAN BAR

Potsdamer Str. 139 ☎030 215 14 14 🖥www.begine.de

In a neighborhood dominated by male gay clubs, Begine is a welcome retreat for women. Named after a now-defunct Lesbian WC, Berlin's biggest lesbian community center has a popular, low-key cafe/bar with comfortable sofas, live music, and readings at night.

*🚇 U2: Bülowstr. $ No cover. ⏰ Open M-F 5pm-late, Sa 3pm-late, Su 7pm-late.*

### ALT BERLINER BIERSALON

🍸 BAR

Kufürstendamm 225 ☎030 884 39 90

The Alt Berliner Biersalon may cater to an older crowd on most nights, but from October to May, this is one of the best spots in Schöneberg to watch a German football match. For all its West Berlin wood-paneled opulence, the atmosphere is far from stuffy. With rowdy crowds and plenty of TV screens, you'll be right in the middle of the action, or just living vicariously through athletes while chugging down beer.

*🚇 U1 or U9: Kufüstendamm. $ Beer €3-4.50. ⏰ Open 24hr.*

### HELLE WELT

🍸 GAY BAR

Motzstr. 5 ☎030 21 91 75 05

Even with the addition of two enormous, quiet sitting rooms, the 20-something clientele still pack the bar and take over the street. The fur-covered wall, chandeliers, and well-directed mood lighting don't keep this sophisticated-looking club from being relaxed. Though it has a mostly male crowd during "prime time," more women show up in the early evening, on weekdays, and in the morning.

*🚇 U1, U3, U4, or U9: Nollendorfpl. [S] No cover. ⏰ Open daily 6pm-4am, sometimes later.*

**XARA CAFE AND LOUNGE** ◉🍸☁▼ HOOKAH BAR

Maaßenstr. 7 ☎030 30 10 47 77

In an area dominated by high energy nightlife, this bar offers up mellow with a hookah side. Serving inexpensive crepes and baguettes by day, this cafe turns into a relaxed lounge at night, with outdoor seating overlooking a popular street. Comfortable chairs are grouped around tables with hookah, popular with a younger crowd.

*🚇 U1, U3, U4 or U9: Nollendorfpl. [S] Crepes from €2, baguettes from €3.20. Hookah €8 per pipe. Cocktails €6.10-8.80. Beer €2.60-3.50. Shots €2.90-5.50. ⏰ Open daily from 9am-late. Happy hour Su-Th 7pm-10pm, cocktails €4.*

**MAXXX** ◉🍸▼ GAY BAR

Fuggerstr. 34 ☎030 21 00 52 89 💻www.maxxx-berlin.de

A smoky, dark-green interior with a simple bar draws a mostly male, leather-clad crowd for some unexpected chill-out conversation. Maxxx has inexpensive drinks and ready-to-talk bartenders. During the day, the bar doubles as a cafe.

*🚇 U1 or U2: Wittenbergpl. [S] Beer from €2.50. ⏰ Open daily noon-3am.*

## MITTE

**👍 BANG BANG CLUB** ◉🍸 CLUB

Neue Promenade 10 ☎030 604 053 10 💻www.bangbangclub.net

Hiding beneath the S-bahn tracks in groovy, smoky caverns of arched brick, the Bang Bang club plays it cool without being snooty. Weave through the tight hallways and dance the night away with Berliners.

*🚇 S5, S7, S9, S75: Hackescher Markt. U. [S] Admission free-€20. ⏰ Usually open F-Sa 10pm-late. Check website for details.*

**👍 COOKIES** 🎟🍸 CLUB

Friedrichstr. 158 ☎030 274 929 40 💻www.cookies-berlin.de

Hot, sweaty, sexy, and packed, Cookies jams in a former Stasi bunker that operates as a restaurant during the day. Locals claim that this party originally started in some guy's basement before moving to hip venues. The party don't start till 1am, so save your tears if you show up alone at midnight. Entrance can be a little exclusive—don't dress up, dress down—so it helps if you know the name of the DJ playing that night.

*🚇 U6: Französische Str. From the U-bahn, head north. [S] Admission €5-15. ⏰ Club open Tu 10:30pm-6am, Th 10:30pm-6am.*

**KAFFEE BURGER** ◉🍸 CLUB

Torstr. 58-60 ☎030 280 46 49 5 💻www.kaffeeburger.de

Those looking to groove can jam at this artsy dance club while those looking to chill can hop next door to the "Burger Bar." Despite looking a little like your grandma's living room, things get wild here later in the evenings. Weekly programs include poetry readings, film screenings, and drunken sloppiness.

*🚇 U6: Rosa-Luxemburg-Pl. [S] Cover M-Th €1, F-Sa €5, Su €1. ⏰ Open M-F 8pm-late, Sa 9pm-late, Su 7pm-late.*

**CLARCHENS BALLHAUS** 🎟🍸☁ CLUB

Auguststr. 24 ☎030 282 92 95 💻www.ballhaus.de

For travelers who enjoy the type of dancing that gets worse as the night wears on, this 1930s-style ballroom has cha cha, salsa, and other programs Mondays through Thursdays and Sundays. Friday and Saturday see DJs playing "hipper" music. Come early for a drink in the beautiful patio garden.

❦ *U8: Rosenthaler Pl.* ⑤ *M-Tu, Su programs €8, students €6, F-Sa €3.* ⚱ *Open daily 10am-late. Dance programs start at 8pm.*

### WEEK-END ♥&♿♀ CLUB
Alexanderpl. 5                          ◼www.week-end-berlin.de

Not the cheapest place in the world, but the only experience of its kind in Berlin. Come for good music and the chance to see the sun rise over the city from Berlin's only real skyscraper. A night you'll remember.

❦ *U6: Alexandr Pl.* ⑤ *Admission €10-20.* ⚱ *Open F-Su 11pm-late.*

### 8MM BAR ⑧&♿♀ BAR
Schönhauser Allee 177              ☎030 405 006 24 ◼www.8mmbar.com

A dimly lit, low-key hipster bar where you can chat about how ironic you are or just play a round of pool, just 'cause. Crowd levels vary randomly, but when it's bustling, it's bustling.

❦ *U2: Senefelderpl.* ⑤ *Beer €2.50-6. Mixed drinks €4-7.* ⚱ *Open M-Th 8pm-late. F-Su 9pm-late.*

### KIT KAT CLUB ⑧⑧♀ CLUB
Köpenicker Str. 76                    ☎030 7871896 ◼www.kitkatclub.org

A visit here is an unforgettable experience. Everyone is decked out in straps, chaps, and leather. If you're scared of penises, don't come.

❦ *U8: Heinrich Heinestr.* ❢ *Fetish dress code strictly enforced.* ⑤ *Admission €5-10.* ⚱ *Open F-Sa (sometimes Su) 11pm-late.*

### ZAPATA ⑧&♿♀ BAR
Oranienburger Str. 54                ☎030 281 6109 ◼www.cafe-zapata.de

The hippest of the bars at Tacheles, Zapata has parties every night of the week with some of the biggest DJs in town. Anyone trying to keep it "clean" and "tame" should definitely stay home, as Zapata's crowd spills into the attached faux-beach, and dirt and broken glass become as much a part of the experience as the music and the dancing. The outdoor sculpture garden bores images into your mind that may never leave. Guests willing to climb can enjoy cocktails from on top of a forklift.

❦ *U6: Oranienburger Tor.* ⑤ *Admission €5-10.* ⚱ *Club open daily 10pm-late.*

### DELICIOUS DOUGHNUTS ♥⑧♀ CLUB
Rosenthaler Straße 9              ☎0302 809 92 74 ◼www.delicious-doughnuts.de

No, it's not a donut shop. Yes, it's a hip backpacker hangout. Not tons of room to dance here, but plenty of room to relax, talk, drink, and smoke. If your friends are boring, you can escape to the pinball machine. A small steel ball is friend enough for anyone.

❦ *U8: Roenthaler Pl.* ⑤ *Cover €5-10.* ⚱ *Open daily 10pm-late.*

### TAPE ⑧⑧♀ CLUB
Heidestr. 14                          ☎0308 48 48 73 ◼www.tapeberlin.de

The huge open spaces of this converted warehouse keep it cool when the party gets hot. And it does frequently. Party starts (and goes) very late.

❦ *U8: Rosenthaler Pl.* ⑤ *Admission varies.* ⚱ *Open F-Sa 11pm-late.*

### CCCP KLUB ⑧⑧♀ CLUB
Torstr. 136                          ☎030 99194904 ◼www.cojito.de/cccpclubbar.5653.htm

This Soviet-themed bar shows off a bunch of communist relics including flags, maps, and a stuffed badger, undoubtedly of the communist persuasion. Down drinks at the perfect bar and show Richard Nixon who's boss. Unfortunately, the drinks are not provided free according to need, but the downstairs club does feel unpretentious and of the people.

🚇 *U8: Rosenthaler Pl.* [$] *Cover varies with party.* ⏰ *Open Tu-Th 6pm-late, F-Sa 10pm-late.*

## PRENZLAUER BERG

Far less techno and far more laid-back than other parts of Berlin, Prenzlauer Berg's trendy cafes and late-night restaurants each have a devoted local following. Opt for bars over clubs in this part of town.

### 👍 THE WEINEREI: FORUM ⊛🍸☁ BAR

Veterenenstr. 14 ☎030 440 6983

This unmarked wine bar has gone from a local secret to a local legend, catapulted by its comfortable elegance and unique paying system. Pay €2 for a glass, sample all the wines, and then sample again, and again, and before leaving, pay what you think you owe. Enjoy your vintage at an outdoor table, on an indoor sofa, or in the downstairs wine cellar (by request).

🚇 *U2: Senefelderpl.* [$] *Depends on how drunk you get.* ⏰ *Open M-Sa 10am-late, Su 11am-late.*

### 👍 SOLSI E MORSI ⊛🍸☁ BAR

Marienburger Str. 10

It's not often that an owner becomes as loved as his bar, but Johnny Petrongolo is that rare exception. Buzzing about tables, opening wine bottles, and handing out plates of free parma ham, cheese, bread and olives, Johnny and his familial staff have won over the hearts of their young regulars, and ours as well. If you're not sure where to start, let the Petrongolos help you pick your wine.

🚇 *U2: Senefelderpl.* [$] *Wine from €3 a glass.* ⏰ *Open daily 6pm-late.*

### 👍 KLUB DER REPUBLIC (KDR) ⊛🍸☁ CLUB

Pappelallee 81

There are few museums that have as many authentic Soviet artifacts as KDR has hanging on its walls. Once the showroom of the DDR carpet and linoleum supplier, KDR kept the old formica bar and leaded glass, and added lamps from the original Palast Republik, collected as the building was being torn down. The furniture is from the DDR landmark Cafe Moscow. DJs play every night to a mixed crowd attracted by the club's no cover policy.

🚇 *U2: Eberswalder Str. Turn into what looks like a deserted parking lot and climb the metal stairs.* [$] *Drinks €5, beer €4.* ⏰ *Open from "dark to light." In more definite terms, that's around 9pm in the summer, in the winter 8pm-late.*

### INTERSOUP ⊛🍸☁ BAR

Schliemannstr. 31 ☎030 23 27 30 45 💻www.intersoup.de

With worn '70s furniture, retro floral wallpaper, and soup specials, this is your East-Berlin Soviet-era grandmother's living room turned ironic. Named after the DDR-era general store Intershop, Intersoup has been keeping things quintessentially Prenzlauer Berg-esque and getting quite the local following doing it. The upper level always has a DJ, but the real highlight is the downstairs **undersoup,** where international bands perform every night at 10pm, in genres from folk to rock, to an audience seated in comfortable mix-matched chairs covered in lurid orange and olive patterns. There's almost never a cover.

🚇 *U2: Eberswalder Str.* [$] *Soup €4.50-5.* ⏰ *Open M-Sa 6pm-3am, Su.*

### WOHNZIMMER ⊛🍸☁ BAR

Lettestr. 6 ☎030 445 5458

Wohnzimmer means "living room," and it's not hard to see why this bar goes by that name, given its wide wood-planked floors, and glassware cabinets along the walls of the bar. Settle into a velvety Victorian sofa with a mixed drink among a diverse crowd. Wohnzimmer is a favorite of hip 20-somethings and an older crowd who could have furnished the bar with relics from their garage sales.

*🚇 U2: Eberswalder Str. $ Cocktails €4-5. Beer €2.50-3. ⏰ Open daily 9am-4am.*

**DR. PONG** 🔞🍸 BAR

Eberswalder Str. 21

In the middle of a concrete room with peeling paint, and under falling fluorescent lights, stands a single ping-pong table, the centerpiece of this minimalist bar. Intense hipsters ring the table, gripping their paddles. All are welcome, including beginners and the severely intoxicated.

*🚇 U2: Eberswalder Str. $ Drinks €2-5.50. ⏰ Open M-Sa 8pm-late, Su 6pm-late.*

**PRATER GARTEN** 🔞🍸⛅ BEER GARDEN

Kastanienallee 7-9 ☎030 448 5688 💻www.pratergarten.de

Locals and travelers of all ages eat and drink at sprawling picnic tables under a canopy of chestnut trees. Set just off a busy street, the peaceful ambiance of the hundreds of small hung lights is perfect as either a stop-off between clubs, or as the setting for a whole evening of relaxed conversation and good beer. Prater Garten, arguably the prettiest beer garden in Berlin, also has an outdoor theater and television.

*🚇 U2: Eberswalder Str. $ Bratwurst €2.50. Beer €2.50-3.50. ⏰ Open in good weather Apr-Sept daily noon-late.*

**WHITE TRASH FAST FOOD** 🔞🍸 BAR

Schönehauser Allee 6-7 ☎030 50 34 86 67 💻www.whitetrash-fastfood.com

Guarded by two gilded lions out front, four levels of kitsch at White Trash Fast Food provide endless visual entertainment. Fish tanks, rabbit skins, rocking horses, and movie memorabilia cover the bar. Drinks come with honest, English explanations: the Zombie will "blast your head into 1000 pieces!" International rock bands play to a packed crowd in this I-Spy paradise.

*🚇 U2: Senefelderpl. $ Specialty drinks from €8. ⏰ Open M-F 12pm-late, Sa-Su 6pm-late.*

**SCOTCH AND SOFA** 🔞🍸⛅ BAR

Kollwitzstr. 18 ☎030 44 04 23 71

Exactly what the name promises. This bar channels gold-foiled '70s glamour in the Sean-Connery-as-James-Bond tradition, and serves up classic drinks on vintage sofas. Far from stuffy, Scotch and Sofa relaxes to some mellow, big-band tunes, and grand French doors open up to a quiet street lined with patio seating.

*🚇 U2: Senefelderpl. $ Scotch from €5. Happy hour daily 6pm-7pm, when the cocktail of the day is €3.80. ⏰ Open daily 6pm-very late.*

**MORGENROT** 🔞🍸⛅ BAR

Kastanienallee 85 ☎030 44 31 78 44 💻www.cafe-morgenrot.de

This little cafe is trying to save the world, and they're having a great time doing it. Owned by a five person work collective, Morganrot makes vegan, organic, fair-trade food by day *(including a weekend brunch buffet where guests pay only what they can afford from €4)*, and serves up frosty vodka shots at night. Deep teal walls and climbing plants on the outside pull in crowds off Kastanienallee.

*🚇 U2: Eberswalder Str. $ Shots €2. ⏰ Open Tu-Th noon-1am, F-Sa 11am-3am, Su 11am-1am.*

**DUNCKER** 🔞🍸⛅ CLUB

Dunckerstr. 64 ☎030 445 9509 💻www.dunckerclub.de

Suits of armor, chainmail, and retro bead curtains hang from the high ceilings of this horse-stable-turned-club. Trees and climbing ivy cover the outside of the building, and form a canopy over the back patio. Duncker heats up at about 1am, when it draws an intense crowds with its insider vibe. Ring the bell for entry.

*🚇 S8, S41, or S85: Prenzlauer Allee. ℹ M-Tu goth, Th live bands. $ Cover M €2.50, F €4, Sa €4.50, Su €2.50. Th free. F-Sa all drinks max €2. ⏰ Open M-Tu, Th-Su 8pm-late.*

## FISHING FOR COMPLIMENTS

◉♥⌂ BAR

Kastanienallee 23

☎030 51 05 76 86

By day, Fishing for Compliments eagerly seeks your compliments with its fish and chips. But on weekend nights, this becomes one of the coolest fried food places around. The staff opens the front wall up to the street, and sets up a stereosystem that blasts music onto Kastanienallee.

✠ *U2: Eberswalder Str.* ⑤ *Fish and chips €3.50. Beer €2-3.* ⌚ *Open M-F noon-11pm, Sa-Su noon-late.*

## CAFE NEMO

◉♥⌂ BAR

Oderberger Str. 46

☎030 4 48 19 59

Woven reed mats line the walls of this south-of-the-border bar, and model ships hang from corners of the ceiling. With some quirky murals of inexplicably blue men on the walls, Cafe Nemo manages to avoid being kitschy while still creating a Central American vibe. The outside patio gets crowded early, as does the back room pool and foosball table.

✠ *U2: Eberswalder Str.* ⑤ *Beer €1.80-3. Mixed drinks €4-5.* ⌚ *Open M-Sa 6pm-late, Su 4pm-late.*

# FRIEDRICHSHAIN

When people think of Berlin techno clubs, they're picturing Friedrichshain. You won't find more legendary converted factory or warehouse clubs in any other neighborhood in Germany, and maybe even all of Europe. Most of these raging dance venues are spread out along the river and railroad tracks, between the car dealerships and empty lots on **Mühlenstrasse.** More low-key, but equally popular bars are clustered around **Simon-Dach-Strasse.** In fact, even as we've recommended our favorite laid-back and hoppin' bars below, you really can't go wrong with any place along **Simon-Dach.**

## ◈ ASTRO-BAR

◉♥⌂ BAR

Simon-Dach-Str. 40

▣www.astro-bar.de

This popular bar gets back to the basics with cheap prices and generously poured alcohol. A DJ plays vinyl records every night starting at 10pm, featuring classics like the Stones and the Beatles, along with some newer indie tracks. Run by a bunch of guys who like their music, love their whiskey *(€4)*, and decorate the back of their bar with Transformers nailed to the wall.

✠ *U5: Frankfurter Tor.* ⑤ *Beer from €2.50. Mixed drinks from €5.* ⌚ *Open 6pm-late.*

## ABGEDREHT

◉♥⌂ BAR

Karl-Marx-Allee 150

☎030 29 38 19 11 ▣www.abgedreht.net

This no-frills bar is located right next to Frankfurter Tor, so you can soak up Soviet ambiance while you practically sit on the laps of locals. Sheet music papers the walls, and leather couches are clumped around antique sewing tables. This bar caters to the 30+ crowd, and is a little removed from most of the action on Simon-Dach, but if you're looking to drink a beer with a view of the DDR main street, this is the place to go.

✠ *U5: Frankfurter Tor.* ⑤ *0.5L beer €3-4.* ⌚ *Open daily 5pm-late. Happy hour 7-9pm, cocktails from €5.*

## SANITORIUM 23

◉♥⌂ BAR

Frankfurter Allee 23

☎030 42 02 11 93 ▣www.sanitorium23.de

If you're looking to experience the techno scene, but don't know if you're ready for the Mühlenstr. madness, get your feet wet at Sanitorium 23. This bar plays relaxed tunes to guests that lounge on sleek couches and chaises. With globe lights suspended from the ceiling, Sanatorium 23 still manages to be a laid-back hangout.

✠ *U5: Frankfurter Tors.* ⑤ *Cocktails €6-8. Beer €3.20.* ⌚ *Open M-Th 4pm-2am, F-Sa 4pm-4am, Su 4pm-2am.*

## RED ROOSTER

🍴🍸🎵 BAR

Grünbergerstr. 23 ☎030 29 00 33 10 🖥www.redrooster.de

This bar is a favorite of locals and travelers alike. The Red Rooster is linked to the hostel next door, and an international crowd of backpackers lounge on the outdoor patio and porch swing. From behind an old wood countertop and under exposed brick ceilings and pipelines, bartenders serve up cider and Czech beers from the tap. For the particularly outgoing or desperate backpacker, "perform 4 stay" events invite you to sing for a free beer—or even a free bed!

*🚇 U5: Frankfurter Tor. $ Beer from €2.50-3. ⏰ Open M-Th 5pm-1am, F-Sa 5pm-3am, Su 5pm-1am.*

## JÄGERKLAUSE

🍴🍸🎵 BAR, BEER GARDEN

Grünbergerstr. 1 ☎0176 222 86 892 🖥www.jaegerklause-berlin.de

Jägerklause is frequented by pin-up stylers, leather-clad bikers, and the old-T-shirt, ripped-jeans crowd. Hence the mounted antlers with disco ball combo. This bar is known for its large beer garden lined with tall shrubs, where guests can lounge in canvas chairs under strands of outdoor lights, while bratwurst and steaks are grilled on a barbeque. The connected pub has a dance floor, and usually features live bands on Wednesdays.

*🚇 U5: Frankfurter Tor. ⏰ Biergarten open 3pm-late. Pub open 6pm-late.*

## PAUL'S METAL ECK

🍴🍸🎵 BAR

Krossener Str. 15/Simon-Dach-Str. ☎030 201 16 24 🖥www.paules-metal-eck.de

Metal hits from the last 50 years are blasted on speakers with videos showing performances of all the best bands. A pierced and tattooed staff serves over 12 varieties of beer from 10 different countries to an international crowd of hard-core fans in this bar outfitted with dart boards and pool tables.

*🚇 U5: Frankfurter Tor. $ Beer €2.50-4.50. ⏰ Open daily 1pm-late, usually around 5am-8am.*

## HABERMEYER

🍴🍸🎵 BAR

Gärtnerstr. 6 ☎030 29 77 18 87

Habermeyer's retro stylings, and soft red lighting from funky lamps compliment New Wave DJ sessions. The foosball table in the back lends a competitive edge to an otherwise relaxed bar. The young regulars enjoy conversation on low, loungy chairs.

*🚇 U5: Samariterstr. $ Mixed drinks €6-7.40. ⏰ Open daily 7pm late.*

## ROSI'S

🍴🍸🎵 CLUB

Revaler Str. 29 🖥www.rosis-berlin.de

This always crowded, outdoor club is blocked from the street with bamboo matting. A series of buildings "decorated" with graffiti frame a courtyard full of picnic tables and strung lights. This laid-back river club plays mostly techno and rock music.

*🚇 U1 or S3, S5, S7, S9, or S75: Warschauer Str. $ Cover €3-7. ⏰ Open Th-Sa 11pm-late.*

## CASSIOPIA

🍴🍸🎵 CLUB, BEER GARDEN, RESTAURANT, MUSIC VENUE

Revaler Str. 99 ☎0302 936 29 66

A sprawling nightlife oasis in an abandoned train factory, this all-in-one entertainment complex is its own self-sufficient entertainment community. Outdoor couches and a climbing wall let you take a break from the indoor dance floor. The multiple bars in the beer garden cater to a mostly student crowd. Occasionally, the club hosts concerts, usually starting around 8pm.

*🚇 U1 or S3, S5, S7, S9, or S75: Warschauer Str. $ Cover €5-7. Beer €2.50-3. Vodka €2.50. ⏰ Open W-Sa 11pm-late.*

## K-17

🍴🍸🎵 CLUB

Pettenkoferstr. 17 🖥www.k-17.de

This towering club has a dance floor and bar for each of its four floors. Students crowd the courtyard of this out-of-the-way, underground techno club, and colored lights shine on the graffitied exterior walls. Concerts are usually hosted once a week; keep an eye on the website for dates and prices.

*🚇U5: Frankfurter Allee. Once you're on Pettenkoferstr., keep an eye out for signs; the club is off the road, on your right. $ Cover €6. Beer €2.50. Vodka and coke €3.50. ⏰ Open F-Sa 10pm-late.*

**ASTRA** ⊛🍸⛅ CLUB

Revaler Str. 99 ☎0302 005 67 67 💻www.astra-berlin.de

This converted warehouse by the train tracks is now home to one of the largest dance floors on Revaler. Themed parties draw in big crowds of mixed-age clubbers, from 20-somethings to 40-year-olds, depending on the night, and keep the mood relaxed even while the music blasts. Live bands perform almost weekly. Check the website for performance schedules.

*🚇U1, S3, S5, S7, S9, or S75: Warschauer Str. $ Cover €4-7. ⏰ Open 11:30pm-late.*

## KREUZBERG

**👍 CLUB DER VISIONAERE** ⊛⊘🍸⛅ CLUB

Am Flutgraben 1 ☎030 695 189 44 💻www.clubdervisionaere.com

Though this river-front cabana/bar/club/boat is packed, the experience is worth the sweaty armpits. A mini-indoor club has a DJ spinning, but the fun is outside with rum-based drinks, feet dipped in the river, and large pizzas *(€8)*. This club is like a mix of the Bayou, New York, and Cancun. One of the best experiences you will have anywhere. So relaxing, so engaging, so Berlin.

*🚇 U1: Schlesisches Tor. From the U-bahn head southeast on Schleissichestr. $ Admission €4-15. ⏰ Open daily 10pm-late.*

**👍 WATERGATE** ⊛⊘⛅🍸 CLUB

Falckensteinstr. 49 ☎030 61 28 03 96 💻www.water-gate.de

This ultra-exclusive club lights up the river with an eye-popping display of lights, but from the street, not even a sign marks its entrance. You'll have to rely on the enormous line of partiers who've come for a club that lives up to its reputation. Tired guests can "chill out" on the floating dock, while raging rhinos can tear up one of two dance floors. The place won't get packed until 2am—but then it roars until the sun shushes it down. Groups of more than two should pretend like they're separate, and couples should pretend like they're single—seriously.

*🚇 U1: Schlesisches Tor. Head toward the bridge. It's the unmarked door at the top of those stairs immediately before the river. $ Cover €8-20. Mixed drinks €6.50. ⏰ Open W 11-late. F and Sa midnight-late.*

**LUZIA** ⊛⊘⛅🍸 BAR, CAFE

Oranienstr. 34 ☎030 611 074 69 💻www.luzia.tc

An artsy cafe and bar full of slightly older chums. The patio is most popular in the summer. Try inside for a little privacy, say, inside this place's person-sized doll-house, or in one of the lofts that you climb a ladder to get to.

*🚇U1, U8: Kotbusser Tor. From the U-bahn head northeast up AldabertStraße and turn left on Oranienstr. $ Beer €3-6. Mixed drinks €6-8. ⏰ Open daily noon-late.*

**FARBFERNSEHER** ⊛⊘🍸 BAR

Skalitzer Str. 114

During the day, you wouldn't think twice about this abandoned office building, but when the sun goes down, this ultra-chill, miniature night club goes up. The whole place has a more relaxed feel than nearly most in Berlin, and its small size means the parties feel both active and intimate without ever being overpowering. Young locals sway to DJs, smoke out front, or talk in the back with friends. They're trying to keep it super-local here, so avoid wearing your fanny pack.

*🚇U1, U8 to Kotbusser Tor. From the U-bahn head east down Skalitzer Str. $ Cover €1 (or free with drink purchase). ⏰ Open Sept to mid-July W-Su 10pm-late.*

**CLUB TRESOR** CLUB

Köpenicker Str. 70 ☎0306 290 87 50 💻www.tresorberlin.com

Tresor has an act that starts at 7am. Starts. At. 7am. Multiple DJs spin nightly in this enormous converted warehouse that now houses Berlin's first official Techno Club. The downstairs houses a store, mini-cafe, and men's and women's bathrooms that are literally just cubbles in one long wall. A huge outdoor garden makes space for breaks, while inside, projectors shoot images on every wall, an advanced lighting system disorients and intoxicates, and a killer sound system makes aural magic.

*U8: Heinrich Heinestr. $ Admission €8-15. ⏰ Usually open W, F, Sa 10pm-late.*

**MAGNET CLUB** CLUB, MUSIC VENUE

Falckensteinstr. 48 ☎030 44008140 💻www.magnet-club.de

This club's guests break down into two groups: cool locals who come for the DJs and frequent live bands, and angry tourists who got rejected from Watergate Club next door. Bands play on a short, shallow stage that makes them seem like they're dancing in the crowd. An additional dance floor with separately spinning DJ, and an outdoor chillspace that feels like a converted construction sight, allow guests choose their own experience.

*U1: Schlesisches Tor. Head toward the bridge. An "M" hangs above the door. $ Admission €5-10. ⏰ Usually open Tu-Su from 8pm. Check online for exact schedule.*

**HEINZ MINKI** BEER GARDEN

Vor dem Schlesischen Tor 3 ☎030 6953-3766 💻www.heinzminki.de

A beautiful garden large enough for your group to have some privacy even in a very full, very public place. Lanterns and outdoor music make nights here feel like a drawn-out Fitzgerald novel, without the deep-seated ambiguities and obligatory death. Various booths around the garden serve pizza *(€3)*, bratwurst *(€2.50)* and other snacks *(€1-7)*. Stealthier guests can steal a bite from the fruit trees spread throughout the garden.

*U1: Schlesisches Tor. $ Beer €2-5. Mixed drinks €5-9. ⏰ Open daily 10pm-late.*

**ARENA CLUB** CLUB

Eichenstr. 4 ☎030 533 20 30 💻www.arena-club.de

This awesome indoor/outdoor complex has a swimming pool in the river during the summer, a faux beach that sells drinks, and dance floors ranging from epic to legendary. A ticket into one of the clubs gets you access to the pool-and-beach bar.

*U1: Schlesisches Tor. From the U-bahn head south on Schlesischestr. across both canal bridges. The Arena complex is the large industrial set of buildings on your left after the 2nd bridge. $ Vary. ⏰ Party hours vary but usually Th-Su from 10pm.*

**SO36** BAR, CLUB, MUSIC VENUE

Oranienstr. 190 ☎030 61 40 13 06 💻www.so36.de

SO36 sees itself less as a club, though it's a great club, and more as an organization with an attitude. The various parties, live bands, and cultural presentations that go on here attract a mixed gay/straight clientele whose common demoninator is that they like to party hardy. Gayhane, a gay cabaret that performs the last Saturday of every month, has become a staple of the Berlin gay scene, and can get pretty epic. Remember how *Cabaret* takes place in Berlin? Well, this lives up to that reputation.

*U1, U8: Kottbusser Tor. $ Vary. ⏰ Opening times vary, but usually open F-Sa 10pm-late.*

**ROSES** GAY BAR

Oranienstr. 187 ☎030 6156570

Mostly gay men and a few lesbians hang out in this little bar that has fuzzy pink walls and a fuzzy pink ceiling. The bar's small size keeps the energy level high, and the endless assortment of wall trinkets (glowing mounted antlers, glowing hearts) will keep you curious.

*🚇 U1, U8: Kottbusser Tor. $ Beer €3. Mixed drinks €4-6. ⏰ Open daily 9pm-late.*

### FESTAAL KREUZBERG

🚫♿🍸⛅ CLUB, MUSIC VENUE

Skalitzerstr. 130 ☎030 611013-13 💻www.festsaal-kreuzberg.de

Live bands play regularly in this punkish old-school former movie theater. The type of place that feels perfectly worn-in but not yet old or dirty. After the concerts, local partygoers spill into the courtyard for more drinks, smokes, and some good ol' post-production chatting. Some nights feature poetry readings, screenings, or art performances.

*🚇 U1, U8: Kotbusser Tor. From the U-bahn, head east on Stalitzerstr. $ Tickets €5-20. ⏰ Hours vary. Usually open F-Sa from 9pm. Check website for details.*

### BIERHIMMEL

🚫♿🍸⛅▼ CAFE, BAR

Oranienstr. 183 ☎030 6153122

A relaxing gay-friendly cafe that draws a good mix of gays, lesbians, and straight people. Many have a drink or two here before heading out to more wild adventures like Roses and SO36 next door. The barstaff requests that only nice people who understand tipping stop by.

*🚇 U1, U6: Kotbusser Tor. $ Mixed drinks €4-6. Coffee €1-4. ⏰ Open daily 1pm-late.*

### CLUB MONARCH

🚫⊘🍸 BAR, CLUB

Skalitzerstr. 134

Few clubs fit the word "fun" as well as Club Monarch. A great mixture of old and young, gay and straight, creepers and guys you'll hook up with fill out this small bar above Kaiser's supermarket. A large window gives you a nice view of the U-Bahn and solid DJs keep the party pumping. Smaller crowds are made of regulars and a few foreigners. Parties won't shake out your molars, but they might loosen your bicuspids.

*🚇 U1, U8: Kotbusser Tor. Go through the door into the staircase next to Kaiser's. $ Cover €1. Mixed drinks €4-7. ⏰ Open Tu-Sa 10pm-late.*

### KLEINE REISE

🚫⊘🍸 CLUB

Spreewaldpl. 8

This little underground club, which looks like a bombed-out middle school locker room, spins from the basement of a hostel. Not a place to rage your ass off, but a fantastically hip hangout where you can meet future friends, chat with current friends, or get "friendly" in one of the natural dark spaces in this crumbling basement. The €2 Jager shots are nice, and the robots marching on the window sill are special, indeed.

*🚇 U1: Görlitzer Bahnhof. $ Admission €3. ⏰ Open Th-Sa from 10pm.*

# arts and culture ♫

## MUSIC AND OPERA

### BERLINER PHILHARMONIKER

MITTE

Herbert-von-Karajan-Str. 1 ☎030 25 48 89 99 💻www.berlin-philharmonic.com

It may look strange from the outside, but acoustically, this yellow building is pitch-perfect; all audience members hear the music exactly as it's intended to reach their ears. The Berliner Philharmoniker, led by the eminent Sir Simon Rattle, is one of the world's finest orchestras. It's tough to get a seat; check 1hr. before concert time or e-mail at least 8 weeks in advance.

*#* S1, S2, or S25 or U2: Potsdamer Pl. Ⓢ Tickets from €7 for standing room, from €13 for seats. 🗓
Open July-early Sept. Box office open M-F 3-6pm, Sa-Su 11am-2pm.

### DEUTSCHE STAATSOPER                                                     MITTE
Unter den Linden 7                        ☎030 203 545 55 🖥www.staatsoper-berlin.de
The Deutsche Staatsoper is East Berlin's leading opera theater. Though it suffered during the years of separation, this opera house is rebuilding its reputation and its repertoire of classical Baroque opera and contemporary pieces.
*#* U6: Französische Str. Or bus #100, 157, or 348: Deutsche Staatsoper. Ⓢ Tickets €50-160; students €12, if purchased 30min. before shows and ½-price on cheaper seats for certain performances. 🗓 Open Aug to mid-July. Box office open daily noon-7pm, and 1hr. before performances.

### DEUTSCHE OPER BERLIN                                                    MITTE
Bismarckstr. 35                          ☎030 34 38 43 43 🖥www.deutscheoperberlin.de
The Deutsche Oper is Berlin's newest opera house. If you have the chance, don't pass on a cheap ticket to go see one of Berlin's best performances.
*#* U2: Deutsche Oper. Ⓢ Tickets €12-118. 25% student discounts. 🗓 Open Sept-June. Box office open M-Sa 11am until beginning of the performance, or 11am-7pm on days without performances; Su 10am 2pm. Evening tickets available 1hr. before performances.

## FILM

Finding English films in Berlin is anything but difficult. On any night, choose from over 150 different films, marked **O.F.** or **O.V.** for the original version (meaning not dubbed in German), **O.m.U** for original version with German subtitles, or **O.m.u.E.** for original film with English subtitles.

### KINO BABYLON                                              ⊗⊛⅌ MITTE
Rosa-Luxemburg-Str. 30                   ☎030 242 59 69 🖥www.babylonberlin.de
A spunky little independent film house with a commitment to quality films, Kino Americans and Berliners alike who flock here for pure film culture. Occasional summer screenings happen outdoors on the beautiful Rosa-Luxemburg-and an epic screening of Rocky Horror Picture Show goes down regularly here.
*#* U2: Rosa-Luxemburg-Pl. Ⓢ Tickets €4-8. 🗓 Schedules change daily. Check website for details.

### IMAX 3D SONY CENTER                                       ✦よ⅌ MITTE
Potsdamer Str. 4                         ☎030 230 979 50 🖥www.cinestar-imax.de
A big, commercial theater that shows new releases as early as you'll find them anywhere in Berlin. 3D costs extra, but can you really put a price on a dimension?
*#* U2: Potsdamer Pl. Ⓢ Tickets €7-13. 🗓 1st showing at noon. Last showing at 11pm.

### CENTRAL KINO                                              ⊛よ⅌❀ MITTE
Rosenthaler Str. 39                      ☎030 28599973 ◼kino-central.de
A small theater right in the middle of hip Mitte, this place shows indie American, German and international films, mostly in their original format with German subtitles. While the screens aren't huge, the theater makes up for it with style. One of the theaters is even outside.
*#* U8: Weinmeisterstr. Ⓢ €6.50, students €6. 🗓 Open daily before the 1st movie, noon-3pm.

### ARSENAL                                                            KREUZBERG
In the Filmhaus at Potsdamer Pl.         ☎030 26 95 51 00 🖥www.fdk-berlin.de
Run by the founders of Berlinale, Arsenal showcases indie films and some classics (€6.50). Frequent appearances by guest directors make the theater a popular meeting place for Berlin's filmmakers.
*#* U2, S1, S2, or S25: Potsdamer Pl.

### FILMKUNSTHAUS BABYLON                                                   MITTE
Rosa-Luxemburg-Str. 30                   ☎030 242 59 69 🖥www.babylon-berlin.de
This *haus* shows classics like *Goodfellas* in the main theater and global art films in

the intellectual Studiokino. Most English-language films not dubbed in German.
*🚇 U2: Rosa-Luxemburg-Pl. Entrance on Hirtenstr. $ Main theater M-W €5.50, Th-Su €6.50.*

## THEATER

### ENGLISH THEATER BERLIN
💳♿🍸 KREUZBERG

Fidicinstr. 40 ☎030 693 56 92 💻www.etberlin.de

For over 20 years Berlin's only all English-language theater has been defying German-language totalitarianism with everything from 10-minute short festivals to full length productions. Leave your *umlauts* at home.

*🚇 U6: Pl. der Luftbrücke. $ €14, students €8. ⏰ Box office opens 1hr. before show time. Shows are at 8pm unless otherwise noted.*

### DEUTSCHES THEATER
💳♿🍸 MITTE

Schumann Straße 13a ☎030 28 44 10 💻www.deutschestheater.de

Built in 1850, this world-famous theater that legendary director Max Reinhardt once controlled is still a cultural heavy hitter in Berlin. Performances tend to be in German, and they tend to change frequently, so check the website for details.

*🚇 U6: Oranienburger Tor. From the U-bahn, head south on Friederichstraße, take a right on Reinhartße and another right on Albrecthstr. $ €5-30. ⏰ Box office open M-Sa 11am-6:30pm, Su 3-6:30pm. Shows are at 8pm unless otherwise noted.*

### VOLKS BÜHNE
💳♿ MITTE

Linienstraße 227 ☎030 24 06 55 💻www.volksbuehne-berlin.de

Recently re-opened after a renovation, this imposing theater that looks straight from a Utopian sci-fi thriller delivers on its promise of "art for the people." While the enormous stage goes quiet during the summer, from September to May it is alive with concerts, theatrical shows in German and English, and touring performances and festivals. Before and after the shows, crowds gather in the beautiful plaza to smoke and talk.

*🚇 U2: Rosa-Luxemburg-Pl. $ Tickets €6-30. Students get 50% discount. ⏰ Box office open daily noon-6pm and 1hr. before performances. Shows are at 8pm unless otherwise noted.*



### BERLINER ENSEMBLE
MITTE

Bertolt-Brecht-Pl. 1 ☎030 28 40 81 55 💻www.berliner-ensemble.de

The theater, established by Brecht, is enjoying a renaissance under the leadership of Claus Peymann. Hip repertoire with the like of Heiner Müller, young playwrights, and Brecht. Some of the plays are in English.

*🚇 U6 or S1, S2, S5, S7, S9, S25, or S75: Friedrichstr. $ Tickets €2-30; students €7. ⏰ Box office open M-F 8am-6pm, Sa-Su 11am-6pm, and 1hr. before shows.*

# shopping

## CLOTHING

### Department Stores

#### KADEWE
💳 CHARLOTTENBURG

Tauentzienstr. 21-24 ☎030 212 10

You'll find a thousand things you can't live without, and absolutely nothing you can afford. But you'll have a great time looking. KaDeWe is Berlin's Harrod's, with the stylish extavagance of Chanel, Prada, and Cartier flashing out from every window display. And even if most of us will never actually shop in the KaDeWe, watching the people who do is almost as fun as window shopping.

*🚇 U1, U2, or U3: Wittenbergpl. ⏰ Open M-Th 10am-8pm, F 10am-9pm, Sa 9:30am-8pm.*

## Secondhand

### MACY'Z
**WILMERSDORF**

Mommsenstr. 2
☎030 881 13 63

Mommenstr. is Berlin's secondhand designer-label mecca, and Macy'z may have the best collection around. Everything the store carries is less than two years old, and designed by the biggest names in the industry: It's 🅶Gucci bags and Prada shoes, for half the original price or less. Just to clarify, half-price on a Burburry coat might still set you back €500. But for the truly devoted, a (very relative) deal can be found.

⌗ U1: Uhlandstr. ⌚ Open M-Sa noon-6:30pm, Su noon-4pm.

### CACHE-COEUR
**PRENZLAUER BERG**

Schönehauser Allee 174
☎030 44 35 49 62

Prenzlauer Berg is full of costly vintage clothing shops, but dedicated shoppers can still find a deal. Cache-Coeur is a women's vintage clothing store that specializes in clothing from the 1950s-70s, but carries pieces from the '20s-'40s as well. All clothing is tailored before it goes on the rack, so no rips or tears. The owner has painstakingly selected only the most beautiful pieces, and sells at very reasonable prices. Most dresses, for example, fall between €50-125.

⌗ U2: Senefeldcrpl.

### GARAGE
**SCHÖNEBERG**

Ahornstraße 2
☎302 11 27 60

The Garage is one of Berlin's cheapest secondhand clothing stores, and with one of the biggest selections. About a third of the items are fix-priced, but the rest is sold by the kilo, for €15 per kg. Über cheap deals like that mean mostly basic items; but, as always, shoppers with a little more time and energy might be able to find something out of the ordinary.

⌗ U1, U2, U3, U4, or U9: Nollendorfpl.

## JEWELRY

### MICHAELA BINDER
👓♿ MITTE

Gipsstr. 13
☎030 2838 4869 🖥www.michaelabinder.de

There's plenty of great street jewelry all over the city; most of it can be found near the cash registers at T-shirt stores. But for the big spenders who need real valuables to boost their self esteems, this Mitte jeweler does beautiful rings, bracelets, and necklaces with textbook Berlin understatement.

⌗ U8: Weinmeisterstr. Ⓢ Pieces from €60. ⌚ Open Tu-F noon-7pm, Sa noon-4pm.

## FLEA MARKETS

### 🏪 ARKONAPLATZ
🌐♿🍴♻ PRENZLAUER BERG

Arkonapl.
☎786 9764

Craftsmen sell jewelry. Farmers juice oranges. That guy down the street hawks his CDs from a towel. Arkonaplatz brings out the weird, the old, the desperate, and everyone who wants their stuff. The market's enormous size makes the junk spread incredible: DDR relics, massive rolls of fabric, pictures of vendors' babies, antique space hats? Stick around in the afternoons when the unnamed Irish man comes by with a karaoke machine on his bike. He's been doing it for years now.

⌗ U8: Bernaurstr. ⌚ Open Su 9am-6pm.

### 🏪 TURKISH MARKET
🌐♿🍴♻ KREUZBERG

Along the south bank of the Landwehrkanal

Fruit vendors shout to passersby about their fruit, bakers shout about their baking, clothing dealers shout about their clothing. The Turkish Market is not just an amazing place to find great deals on fruit and clothing, it's one of the best

*shopping · flea markets*

experiences of the entire city. The fruit stands have fruits you've never seen, and they only cost €1. The clothing stands have deals like three pairs of socks for the price of one. On top of this, musicians play at the ends of the market. Not exactly a "flea" market, but an incredible market, and one you won't forget.

⚐ *U1: Kottbusser Tor. From the U-bahn, head south toward the canal.* ⏰ *Open Tu and F noon-6pm.*

## ⊠ MAUERPARK FLEA MARKET                    PRENZLAUER BERG
On Eberswalderstr.

The Mauerpark Flea Market is the biggest and best-known in all of Berlin. A labyrinth of booths and stalls sells everything from hand-ground spices to used clothing to enamel jewelry to potted plants. Hordes of bargain hunters, hipsters, and gawking tourists crowd the park, drinking fresh-squeezed orange juice and listening to the street musicians who swarm the market. Like all secondhand stores in Prenzlauer Berg, Mauerpark is rarely dirt-cheap. You can still find good values, but expect slightly higher prices.

⚐ *U2: Eberswalderstr.*

## STRASSE DES 17 JUNI                          ⊛க♥♨ MITTE
Str. des 17 Juni

A large but touristy market, Straße des 17 Juni gets a lot of people looking for the "authentic Berlin flea market experience." But it's a little like tasting a McDonalds cause you heard Americans made good hamburgers. Check it out if you're in the area, but if you don't want to experience trashy, unpredictable flea markets of Berlin, steer clear.

⚐ *Take the S-Bahn to Tiergarten.* ⏰ *Open Sa-Su 11am-5pm.*

## PREUSSENPARK FLEA MARKET                    ⊛ WILMERSDORF
On the corner of Brandenburgische Str. and Hohenzollerndamm

The Preußenpark flea market is smaller and less varied than the Mauerpark one to the east, but the prices are a lot cheaper. Clothing is rarely more than €10, and usually less. Some handmade crafts and original paintings, and a large selection of antique maps and prints. Preußenpark is a great place to find vintage jewelry and woodblock prints.

⚐ *U3 or U7: Fehrbelliner Pl.* ⏰ *Open Sa-Su 10am-4pm.*

## AM KUPFERGRABEN                             ⊛ OUTSKIRTS
On Am Kupfergraben, across from the Bodemuseum

Stroll along Museum Island while you shop at secondhand tents. For the location, there may be no better flea market in Berlin. Though the selection is relatively small, Am Kupfergraben's flea market has a wide variety of antique and old books and maps, as well as some works by new, young artists. A requisite collection of *steins* rounds out this quintessentially Berlin market.

⚐ *S3, S5, S7, or S75: Hackeshire Markt.* ⏰ *Open Sa-Su 10am-5pm.*

# BOOKS

## ⊠ ST. GEORGE'S BOOKSTORE                    ⊛ PRENZLAUER BERG
Wörtherstr. 27                                 ☎0308 179 83 33

You'll be hard-pressed to find a better English-language bookstore on the continent. St. George's owner makes frequent trips to the UK and US to buy up loads of titles so that his customers can find any book they're looking for, and then some. Over half of the books are used and extremely well-priced *(paperbacks €4-6)*, with a number of books for just €1. This shop also carries new books and can order absolutely any title they don't already carry. If you're looking for travel reading material, there's absolutely no better place to go in Berlin. Pay in euros, British pounds, or American dollars (oh my!).

⚐ *U2: Senefelderpl.* ⏰ *Open M-F 11am-7pm, Sa 10am-4pm.*

**HUNDTHAMMERSTEIN** PRENZLAUER BERG

Alte Schoenhauser Str. 23/24 ☎0302 345 76 69 🖥www.hundthammerstein.de

This medium-sized book store has a large English section of literature, poetry, non-fiction, and trash literature. Almost half the books are in English, which is rare for Berlin. Racy books like *The Giant Book of Penises* sit behind the counter. If you ask, they'll let you take a peek.

*U8: Winmeisstr. Open M-Sa 11am-8pm.*

## MUSIC

### SPACE HALL KREUZBERG

Zossenerstr. 33, 35 ☎306947664 🖥www.spacehall.de

They don't make them like this in the States no more. The CD store is two doors down from the vinyl store. The vinyl store just keeps going, with a "bunker" vibe and a courtyard where DJs sometimes spin and sample turntables. They also have an inspiring collection of rubber duckies.

*U7: Gneisenaustr. Open M-W 11am-8pm, Th-F 11am-10pm, Sa 11-8pm.*

### MELTING POINT PRENZLAUER BERG

Kastanienallee 55 ☎030 44047131 🖥www.meltingpoint-berlin.de

An unassuming little pod with vinyl and CD collections, this little joint gets frequented by Berliner DJs and other members of Berlin's popping club scene. Don't come here for the White Album.

*U8: Rosenthaler Pl. From the U-bahn walk nort east up Weinbergsweg, which will turn into Kastanienallee. $ Records €5-30. Open M-Sa noon-8pm.*

### HARDWAX KREUZBERG

Paul-Lincke-Ufer 44a ☎030 611 301 11 🖥www.hardwax.com

This record shop lies hidden, pushed back from the street, up a graffiti-covered stairwell to the third floor of a space that could as easily be a garage or a storage shed. Instead, records that set the latest trends in Berlin line the walls, and a staff that lives and breathes this music stands by to (if they must) help out clueless tourists.

*U1 or U8: Kottbusser Tor. From the U-bahn, head south on Kottbusserstr. Take a left just before the canal. $ Records €5-30. Open M-Sa noon-8pm.*

### FRANZ AND JOSEF SCHEIBEN PRENZLAUER BERG

Kastanienallee 48 ☎030 417 146 82

This is secondhand vinyl at its best. With a huge collection of used records that spills out of the shop and onto the street outside, Franz and Josef may specialize in '80s rock and punk, but they carry much more. Records sell for as low as €1, but prices vary in a store that sells some true antiques; the owner will tell you to expect to pay somewhere between €1 and €1000 for your vinyl. Thankfully, almost all the records fall pretty close to that first marker.

*U2: Senefelderpl. Open M-Sa 1pm-8pm.*

### FIDELIO SCHÖNEBERG

Akazienstr. 30 ☎030 781 97 36

For those looking to get in touch with their classier side, Fidelio is the place to go. An extensive selection of classical, jazz, and world music lines the walls and spills out of low bookcases. If you've only just recently been inspired to give Wagner a listen, the staff here are more than happy to point newcomers in the right direction. Fidelio sells primarily CDs, with some vintage vinyl on the side. Prices are generally standard; there's a wide range, but albums usually fall in at about €12.

*U7: Eisenacherstr. Open M-F 11am-7pm, Sa 10am-3pm.*

# essentials

## baby, you called?

The phone code for Berlin is ☎030.

## PRACTICALITIES

- **TOURIST OFFICES:** Now privately owned, tourist offices provide far fewer free services than they once did. ◼www.berlin.de has quality information on all aspects of the city. **EurAide** sells rail tickets, maps, phone cards, and walking-tour tickets. *(☎1781 828 2488 ✠ In the Hauptbahnhof, across from the McDonald's.)* **Tourist Info Centers.** *(Berlin Tourismus Marketing GmbH, Am Karlsbad 11, 10785. Office located on the ground floor of the Hauptbahnhof. The entrance is on Europl.* ☎030 25 00 25 ◼www.berlin-tourist-information.de ℹ Service in English. Siegessäule, Sergej, and Gay-Yellowpages have gay and lesbian event and club listings. ⑤ Reserve rooms for a €3-6 fee. Transit maps free; city maps €1. The monthly Berlin Programm lists museums, sights, restaurants, and hotels, as well as opera, theater, and classical music performances, €1.75. Full listings of film, theater, concerts, and clubs in German Tip, €2.70, or Zitty, €2.70. English-language movie and theater reviews are in Ex-Berliner €2. 🕐 Open daily 8am-10pm.)* **Alternate location.** *(Brandenburger Tor ✠ S1, S2, or S25 or bus #100: Unter dne Linden. On your left as you face the pillars from the Unter den Linden side.* 🕐 Open daily 10am-6pm.)*

- **TOURS:** **Terry Brewer's Best of Berlin** is legendary for vast knowledge and engaging personalities, making the over 6hr. walk well worth it. *(Tours leave daily from in front of the Bandy Brooks shop on Friedrichstr.* ☎0177 388 1537 ◼www.berwersberlintours. com. ✠ S1, S7, S9, S75, or U6: Friedrichstr. 🕐 10:30am.⑤ €12.)* **Sinful Berlin** tour meets for some good (not so clean) fun and includes entrance to Europ's largest erotic museum. *(🕐 Th and Sa 8pm.)* **Insider Tour** offers a variety of fun, informative tours that hit all the major sights. More importantly, the guide's enthusiasm for Berlin is contagious, and their accents span the English-speaking world (we'll be honest, we always fall for a good accent). *(☎030 692 3149 ◼www.insidertour.com ℹ Offers tours of Nazi Berlin, Cold War Berlin, Potsdam, and a Berlin Pub Crawl as well as daytrip tours to Dresden. ⑤ €12, under 26 or with a WelcomeCard or ISIC €10. Bike tours €20/18.)* 🕐 Picks up daily Apr-Oct 10am, 2:30pm at the McDonald's outside the Zoo Station, 30min. later at the Coffeemamas at "Hackescher Markt"; Nov-Mar 10am from the Zoo Station and 10:30am at "Hackescher Markt" only. Bike tours meet by the Coffee Mamas at "Hackescher Markt." June-Sept 10:30am and 3pm. Tours last 4hr. **Original Berlin Walks** offers a range of English language walking tours, including "Infamous Third Reich Sites," "Jewish Life in Berlin," "Nest of Spies," and "Discover Potsdam." *(☎030 301 9194 ◼www.berlinwalks.de ⑤ Discover Berlin Walk €12, under 26 €10, WelcomeCard and ISIC €9. 🕐 Tours meet Apr-Oct 10am, 2:30pm at the taxi stand in front of Bahnhof Zoo and at the Hackescher Markt Häagen-Datz 10:30am, 3pm; Nov-Mar 10am at the taxi stand and 1-:30am at Hackescher Markt).* **New Berlin** offers free tours on a tip-only basis, which means some pandering from the guides, of Berlin's biggest sights, and special tours (Sachsenhausen, Third Reich tour, pub crawl, etc.) for a fee. Backpackers with little cash are encouraged to take the tour but occasionally dislike the cursory nature of the set-up. *(☎030 51 05 00 30 ◼www.newberlintours.com ℹ A new bike tour daily at 11am, 2pm in front of the Postfurhramat, on the corner of Oranienburgerstr. and Tucholskystr., S-Bahn:*

*berlin*

*Oranienberger Str.* Ⓢ *With bike rental €15, without bike rental €12.* 🕐 *Tours leave daily from the Brandenburg Gate Starbucks at 11am, 1, 4pm, and the Zoologischer Garten Dunkin' Donuts at 10:30am, 12:30, 3:30pm.)*

- **STUDENT TRAVEL OFFICES:** STA books flights and hotels and sells ISICs. *(Dorotheen-str. 30* ☎030 20 16 50 63 ✠ *S3, S5, S7, S9, S75, or U6 to Friedrichstr.* 🕐 *Open M-F 10am-7pm, Sa 11am-3pm.)* **Second location.** *(Sleimstr. 28 ✠ S4, S8, S85, or U2: Schönhauser Allee.* 🕐 *Open M-F 10am-7pm, Sa 11am-4pm.)* **Third location.** *(Hardenbergerstr. 9 ✠ U2: Ernst-Reuter-Pl.* 🕐 *Open M-F 10am-7pm, Sa 11am-3pm.)* **Fourth location.** *(Takustr. 47* 🕐 *Open M-F 10am-7pm, Sa 10am-2pm.)*

- **CURRENCY EXCHANGE AND MONEY WIRES:** The best rates are usually found at exchange offices with *Wechselstrube* signs outside, at most major trainstations, and in large squares. For money wires through Western Union, use **ReiseBank.** *(Haupt bahnhof* ☎030 20 45 37 61 🕐 *M-Sa 8am-10pm)* **Second location.** *(Bahnhof Zoo* ☎030 881 7117)* **Third location.** *(Ostbahnhof* ☎030 296 4393.)*

- **LUGGAGE STORAGE:** *(✠In the Hauptbahnhof, in "DB Gepack Center," 1st fl., East side.* Ⓢ *€4 per day.)* Lockers also in Bahnhof Zoo, Ostbahnhof, and Alexanderpl.

- **INTERNET ACCESS:** Free Internet with admission to the **Staatsbibliothek.** During their renovation, Staatsbibliothek requires a €10 week-long pass to their library. *(Potsdamer Str. 33* ☎030 26 60 🕐 *Open M-F 9am-9pm, Sa 9am-7pm.)* **Net-lounge** *(Auguststr. 89* ☎030 24 34 25 97 🖥*www.netlounge-berlin.de* ✠ *U-Bahn: Oranienburger Str.* Ⓢ *€2.50 per hr.* 🕐 *Open daily noon-midnight).* **Easy Internet** has several locations throughout Berlin *(Unter den Linden 24, Rosenstraße 16, Frankfurter Allee 32, Rykestraße 29, and Kurfürstendamm 18).* Many cafes through-out Berlin offer free Wi-Fi.

- **POST OFFICES: Main branch** *(Joachimstaler Str. 7* ☎030 88 70 86 11 ✠ *Down Joachimstaler Str. from Bahnhof Zoo and near Kantstr.* 🕐 *Open M-Sa 9am-8pm).* **Tegel Airport** *(🕐 Open M-F 8am-6pm, Sa 8am noon).* **Ostbahnhof** *(🕐 Open M-F 8am-8pm, Sa-Su 10am-6pm).*

- **POSTAL CODE:** 10706.

# EMERGENCY!

- **POLICE:** *(Pl. der Luftbrucke 6. ✠ U6: Pl. der Luftbrüche.)*

- **EMERGENCY NUMBERS:** ☎110. **Ambulance and Fire** ☎112. **Non-emergency advice hotline:** ☎030 46 64 46 64.

- **MEDICAL SERVICES:** The American and British embassies list English-speaking doc-tors. The **emergency doctor** *(☎030 31 00 31 or ☎01804 2255 2362)* service helps travelers find English-speaking doctors. **Emergency dentist.** *(☎030 89 00 43 33)*

- **CRISIS LINES:** English spoken at most crisis lines. **American Hotline** has crisis and referral services. *(☎0177 814 15 10)* **Poison Control.** *(☎030 192 40)* **Berliner Behindertenverband** has advice for the handicapped. *(Jägerstr. 63d* ☎030 204 38 48 🖥*www.bbv-ev.de* 🕐 *Open W noon-5pm and by appointment.)* **Deutsche AIDS-Hilfe.** *(Wilhelmstr. 138* ☎030 690 0870 🖥*www.aidshilfe.de)* **Drug Cri-sis.** *(☎030 192 37*🕐 *24hr.)* **Women's Resources.** Frauenkrisentelefon Women's crisis line. *(☎030 615 4243* 🖥*www.frauenkrisentelefon.de* 🕐 *Open M and Th 10am-noon, Tu-W, F 7pm-9pm, Sa-Su 5pm-7pm)* **Lesbenberatung** offers lesbian counseling. *(Kulmer Str. 20* ☎030 215 2000 🖥*www.lesbenberatung-berlin.de)* **Schwulenberatung** offers gay men's counseling. *(Mommenstr. 45* ☎030 194 46 🖥*www.schwulenberatungberlin.de)* **Maneo.** Legal help for gay violence victims. *(☎030 216 3336* 🖥*www.maneo.de* 🕐 *Open daily 5pm-7pm)* **LARA.** Sexual as-

*essentials • emergency!*

sault help. *(Fuggerstr. 19 ☎030 216 88 88 🖳www.lara-berlin.de ⏰ Open M-F 9am-6pm.)* **Children's emergency helpline.** *(☎030 610 061)*

## GETTING THERE

### By Plane

**Capital Airport Berlin Brandenburg International (BBI)** will open in the southeast Berlin in 2012. Until then, **Tegel Airport** will continue to serve travelers. *(Take express bus #X9 or #109 from Jakob-Kaiser Pl. on U7, bus #128 from Kurt-Schumacher-Pl. on U6, or bus TXL from Beusselstr on S42 and S41. Follow signs in the airport for ground transportation. ☎49 30 6091 2055 🖳www.berlin-airport.de)*

### By Train

International trains *(☎972 226 150)* pass through Berlin's **Hauptbahnhof**and run to: **Amsterdam, NTH** *($ €130. ⏰ 6½hr., 16 per day.);* **Brussels, BEL** *($ €165 ⏰ 7hr., 14 per day.);* **Budapest, HUN** *($ €165 ⏰ 13hr., 4 per day.);* **Copenhagen, DNK** *($ €155 ⏰ 7hr., 7 per day.);* **Paris, FRA** *($ €200 ⏰ 9hr., 9 per day.);* **Prague, CZR;** *($ €80 ⏰ 5hr., 12 per day.)* **Vienna, AUT.** *($ €155 ⏰ 10hr., 12 per day.)*

### By Bus

**ZOB** is the central bus station. *(Masurenallee 4. 🚇 U2: Kaiserdamm. Alternatively, S4, S45, or S46: Messe Nord/ICC. ☎030 301 30 80 ⏰ Open M-F 6am-9pm, Sa-Su and holidays 6am-8pm.)*

## GETTING AROUND

### By Bike

The best way to see Berlin is by bike. Unless your hostel's out in the boonies, few trips will be out of cycling reach, and given that U-Bahn tickets verge on €3 and that the average long-term bike rental costs €8 per day, pedaling your way is just a better deal.

**FAT TIRE BIKE RENTAL** MITTE

Alexanderpl. ☎030 24 04 79 91 🖳www.berlinfahrradverleih.com

Rents bikes for half- and full-days.

*🚇 East location U2: Alexanderpl. Directly under the TV Tower. West location U2 or U9: Zoological Garten. $ €7 per ½-day (up to 4hr.), €12 per day. ⏰ Open May-Oct 15 daily 9:30am-8pm; Oct 16-Nov and Mar-Apr daily 9:30am-6pm.*

### The BVG

The heart of Berlin's public transportation system is the U-Bahn and S-Bahn Metro trains, which cover the city in a spidery and circular patterns, respectively. Trams *(Straßenbahn)* and buses (both part of the U-Bahn system) scuttle around the remaining city corners. *(BVG's 24hr. hotline ☎030 194 49 🖳www.bvg.de)* Berlin is divided into three transit zones. Zone A has central Berlin, including Tempelhof Airport. The rest of Berlin is in Zone B; Zone C consists of outlying areas, including Potsdam and Oranienburg. An AB ticket is the best deal, since you can later buy extension tickets for the outlying areas. A one-way ticket is good for 2hr. after validation. *($ Zones AB €2.10, BC €2.50, ABC €2.80, under 14 reduced fare, under 6 free.)* Within the validation period, the ticket may be used on any S-Bahn, U-Bahn, bus, or tram.

Most train lines don't run Monday through Friday 1-4am. S-Bahn and U-Bahn lines do run Friday and Saturday nights, but less frequently. When trains stop, 70 night buses take over, running every 20-30min. and tending to follow major transit lines; pick up the free Nachtliniennetz map of bus routes at a **Fahrscheine und Mehr** office. The letter "N" precedes night bus numbers. Trams also continue to run at night.

Buy tickets, including monthly passes, from machines or ticket windows in Metro stations or from bus drivers. **Be warned:** machines don't give more than €10 change, and many machines don't take bills, though some accept credit cards. Validate your ticket by inserting it into the stamp machines before boarding. Failure to validate becomes a big deal when plainclothes policemen bust you and charge you €40 for freeloading. If you bring a bike on the U-Bahn or S-Bahn, you must buy it a child's ticket. Bikes are forbidden on buses and trams.

Single-ride tickets are a waste of money. A **Day Ticket** (Ⓢ *AB €6.10, ABC €6.50*) is good from the time it's stamped until 3am the next day. The BVG also sells **7-day tickets** (Ⓢ *AB €26.20, ABC €32.30*) and **month-long tickets** (Ⓢ *AB €72, ABC €88.50*). Another option are the popular tourist cards: the **WelcomeCard** (sold at tourist offices) buys unlimited travel. (Ⓢ *AB 48hr. €17, ABC €19; 72hr. €23/26*) and includes discounts on 130 city sights. The **CityTourCard** is good within zones AB (Ⓢ *48hr. €16, 72hr. €22*) and offers discounts at over 50 attractions.

### By Taxi

**Taxis:** Call 15min. in advance. Women can request female drivers. Trips within the city cost up to €30. (☎*030 26 10 26*, ☎*0800 263 0000 toll-free*)

# berlin 101

## facts and figures

- **POPULATION:** 3,406,000
- **AREA:** 892 sq. kilometers
- **DISTRICTS:** 23
- **NUMBER OF SUCCESSFUL ESCAPES OVER THE BERLIN WALL:** Approx. 500
- **NUMBER OF SUCCESSFUL ESCAPES VIA HOT AIR BALLOON:** 1
- **ANNUAL VISITORS TO PERGAMON MUSEUM:** 1,000,000+

## HISTORY

### Brandenburg Boomtown

Berlin dates its founding to 1237, the first recorded mention of its sister settlement Cölln. These fledgling cities were just a couple of trading posts on either side of the Spree river, with only a church (the **Nikolaikirke**, or St. Nicholas' church, built around 1230) to brag about. Things got cooking when Berlin joined the Hanseatic League of regional cities in 1360. In 1435, local stud **Frederick I** became the elector of the Margraviate of Brandenburg, and in 1451 Fred's steely successor Frederick Irontooth established the city as the royal residence of the Brandenburg Electors, upping its regional profile. The city hit a rough patch during the Thirty Years War of 1618-1648, losing over half its population. A more peace-loving regime acceded in 1640 with Frederick William, who promoted religious toleration and welcomed thousands of displaced French Huguenots after the **Edict of Potsdam** in 1685. By 1700 more than 20% of the city was French, a minority that had a lasting influence on Berlin culture. Perhaps approving of his countrymen's foothold, Napoleon granted the city self-rule after invading in 1806, and in 1815 Berlin became part of the new Province of Brandenburg.

## War: What is it Good for?

The 19th century industrial revolution made Berlin Prussia's economic center, and when **Bismarck** got busy it became the capital of the new German Empire in 1871. In 1918 the Weimar Republic was created and centered in Berlin. In 1920 the Berlin Expansion Act drew various suburbs under the city's umbrella, ballooning Berlin's population to around four million and cementing its position as an international cultural center. The situation changed dramatically in 1933 with the Nazi regime. Thousands of Jewish residents were sent to concentration and death camps after the **Kristallnacht pogrom** of 1938; much of the city was decimated during the 1943-1945 air raids and the 1945 **Battle of Berlin.**

## Another Brick in the Wall

After the war, the city was split into four sectors to mirror Germany's four zones of occupation: the Western Allies' sectors (the US, UK and France) formed **West Berlin**, while the Soviet sector was **East Berlin.** This awkward situation turned nasty when Russia protested currency reform in West Berlin by blockading all access routes; in response, the Allies flew in supplies from 24 June 1948 to 11 May 1949, in what is known as the **Berlin Airlift.** Eventually the Soviets admitted they couldn't rule the skies, but tension only increased when West Germany became the Federal Republic of Germany in 1949, and many of East Germany's best and brightest began fleeing to the Republic through West Berlin. To stop the brain drain, the Soviets erected the big ol' **Berlin Wall** in 1961, which effectively stopped emigration (with a few spectacular exceptions…enter hot air balloons). The West tolerated the restrictions, but proclaimed solidarity with Berliners…or, in President Kennedy's case, with a delectable jelly-filled pastry of the same name.

### 1157
Albert the Bear becomes the First Margrave of Brandenburg.

### 1435
There's a new sheriff in town, Frederick I.

### 1812
Berlin brothers Wilhelm and Jacob Grimm publish their Fairy Tales, leading to spikes in nightmares nationwide.

### 1905
Kaufuaus des Western, the biggest department store in Continental Europe, opens.

### 1936
Hitler allows only "Aryans" to compete for Germany in the Berlin Olympics, which makes for bad PR when Jesse Owens becomes the Games' star. Hitler didn't learn his lesson.

## gnome home

An unusual first that Germany can claim for itself is the production of the first garden gnome. This little lawn ornaments were developed in the mid-1800s by a man named Philip Griebel. He chose the gnome for its kindly reputation among German gardeners: it was said in German myth that gnomes often could help with gardening during the nighttime. The gnomes were a huge hit and spread across all of Germany and into the rest of Europe, until World War II began and discouraged people from buying things like lawn ornamentation. Today, only a few gnome-makers remain in Germany, and Griebel's descendants are one of them. Even still, there are estimated to be around 25 million garden gnomes still residing in Germany!

## Come Together

In 1989, citizens who saw the Iron Curtain beginning to fall started spontaneous protests along the Berlin Wall, until East and West Berliners alike began to destroy it themselves. Pickaxes and enthusiasm almost brought the entire structure down; only a small section is left today along with a museum built around the infamous **Checkpoint Charlie.** In 1990, the two halves of Germany were reunited as one republic, with Berlin as the capital. East Berlin, once a poorer, industrial shadow of its Western neighbor, has prospered under democracy and is the focus of much new development today.

## The City Today

At 892km square and a population of 3.406 million, Berlin is big. Located about 70 miles from the western Polish border, in the relatively flat, marshy valley of the Spree River; Berlin's only hills are the wimpy Teufelsberg and the Müggelberge (the first an artificial hill constructed from WWII rubble). The Spree and Havel rivers meet in Western Berlin, which connects a chain of lakes, including the Tegeler See and Großer Wannsee. Though Berlin is a highly developed, modern city, room is made for green space—most notably the city's expansive main park, the **Tiergarten.**

The city has technically been the German capital since the reunification treaty of 1990, but the national government only finished setting up shop in 1999 (there were a lot of filing cabinets to move from the old West German capital, Bonn). The local government sounds suspiciously derivative: the city and state parliament translates as the House of Representatives (*Abgeordnetenhaus*), while Berlin's executive body is known as the Senate (*Senat von Berlin*). The governing mayor is also prime minister of the state, or Ministerpräsident des Bundeslandes, following the German rule that more syllables equals a more important title.

# FOOD AND DRINK

Berlin's most popular culinary specialties follow the three B's of German eats: Bread, Brats and Beer. Nothing is a more quintessential gastronomic experience than a pretzel, a wurst, a full stein, and a seat in one of the city's **biergartens** (beer gardens), such as the **Prater Garten.** For an authentically local brew, try the **Berliner Weiße,** a sour wheat beer made only in the region. The city is not known for its haute cuisine; traditional Berlin dishes include *currywurst* (a pork sausage, curry and ketchup combo), *eisbein* (pickled ham hock), *boulette* (fried meatballs), and, of course, *Berliners*, the jelly doughnuts made famous by JFK when he accidentally declared he was one (although they're called *Pfannkuchen* in the city, so Kennedy's Berlin audience caught his real drift...but not before the press ran away with it). If your palate doesn't range to the carnivorous, fear not: alternatives to Berlin's meat-and-potatoes staples do exist, mostly in the form of foreign cuisine. Thanks to the influential French minority extant since the 17th century, French cuisine options are particularly abundant.

**1938**
Berlin engineer Konrad Zuse invents the first programmable computer, finally giving us a way to add single-digit numbers.

**1943**
The first Allied bomb drops on Berlin, killing the Berlin Zoo's only elephant.

**1964**
57 East Berliners tunnel under the Wall and reach the West successfully. They dig it.

**1989**
The Iron Curtain comes a-tumblin' down.

**1990**
East and West Germany get together again, with Berlin as the capital.

berlin

# SPORTS AND RECREATION

## International Competition

Berlin has long been a prominent host of international sporting events. These include the 1936 Olympics, the FIFA World Cup in 2006,the World Track and Field Championships in 2009, and the famed annual Berlin Marathon.

## Football

As in much of Europe, football (call it soccer and you might as well get TOURIST tattooed somewhere visible) is the most popular spectator sport, and Berlin has made itself a mecca for enthusiasts with a biannual event known as the **"fan mile."** Whenever the UEFA European Championship or the World Cup is contested, Berlin turns this 1.2 km stretch of *straße* into a open air theater, drawing hundreds of thousands of fans to watch soccer on jumbo screens, including a 60 sq. m screen right above the Brandenburg Gate. Berlin's home team, **Hertha BSC,** draws plenty of cheers on a more regular basis while playing in the city's 74,000 seater Olympiastadion.

## Other Spectator Sports

Professional basketball, ice hockey, handball and volleyball leagues all have teams based in Berlin. The multi-purpose O2 World Arena plays host to many of Berlin's more indoorsy squads, including the ALBA Berlin basketball team (also known as "Berlin's Albatrosses," mostly for their large wingspans) and the Eisenbären ice hockey club.

## Recreation

Besides a stock of gyms and fitness centers to suit any iron pumper, Berlin has 16 golf courses and the popular Rotweiss Tennis Club. For aquatic activities Berlin has several public pools, beaches on Wannsee, Tegeler See, and Grosser Müggelsee lakes with sailing and windsurfing opportunities. The Tiergarten trails are also hard to beat when the weather permits.

# MEDIA

## Newspapers

For international news, the newspaper of record is the *Frankfurter Allgemeine Zeitung.* If business is your thing, the *Financial Times Deutschland* and *Handelsblatt* are solid news sources as well, or for more in-depth political coverage, try *Die Tageszeitung* or *Die Welt.* If you'd rather keep up with celebrity splits than stock listings, look for *BILD*, Germany's premier tabloid. For English speakers, the Munich-based *Sueddeutsche Zeitung* carries a *New York Times* International Supplement on Mondays, and various international papers (the *Times of London, the NY Times*, etc.) are available at any good newsstand. For local coverage, the best bets for English speakers are actually virtual, on websites such as *The Berlin Paper* (🖳www.theberlinpaper.com) and *The Local* (🖳www.thelocal. de).

## Magazines

For news, culture and pretty pictures, magazines such as *Focus*, *Der Spiegel*, and *Stern* are popular throughout Germany. *Spiegel* publishes many stories in English on its website (■*www.spiegel.de/international*). *The Ex-Berliner* is also a great English source for events listings and local buzz.

## Radio and Television

Those who find German offerings hard to follow (or just boring) can surf for English options such as BBC, ITV, Channel 4, Channel 5 and Sky. These channels are provided by the Astra 2 satellite system, so opt for this in an apartment or hotel if possible. The ubiquitous BBC World Service can be received on digital FM 90.2 and Satellite Hot Bird 2-13° East, while Rock Star FM 87.9 features American news bulletins. Fritz FM 102.6 sometimes broadcasts in English after 6pm, Jazz Radio FM 101.9 goes English from 6pm-midnight, and the news station Deutsche Welle occasionally broadcasts in English. US National Public Radio (87.9) has also made it over, so you can hear pledge drives from another continent. For more options, try online radio—all of the BBC stations can be heard online from links at ■www. bbc.co.uk/radio.

# ART AND ARCHITECTURE

## Mitte

This central district of Berlin is home to many of its architectural showpieces and fine arts resources. The **Unter den Linden Boulevard** is at the district's heart, anchored by the colossal **Brandenburg Gate**. Along the boulevard you'll find the tantalizingly named Lustgarten park, the stately Berliner Dom cathedral, the Crown Prince's Palace, and the State Opera House. Modern architectural feats in the neighborhood include the postmodern Volkswagon Showroom and the glass-walled department store Galeries Lafayette (no stone throwing). Nearby stand Berlin's oldest landmarks, the **Marienkirche** and **Nikolaikirche**—both in the ancient Nikolaiviertel. **Museum Island** sits in the middle of the Spree River, creatively named for the five big-time museums on its northern end. All must-sees for art and history buffs, the list includes the **Pergamon** (named for the famous Grecian altar housed there), the

## festivals

- **BERLINALE INTERNATIONAL FILM FESTIVAL (FEBRUARY).** 19,000 film professionals from 136 countries make this event a truly global affair, as Berlin screens more than 400 films throughout the city and hosts the world's most watched film awards show, which dispenses small golden bears (in honor of the bear on Berlin's seal) as trophies. Americans may care more about Oscar, but Berlinale's bear could probably eat that guy up.

- **CARNIVAL OF CULTURES (MAY-JUNE).** Around half a million people converge on the Kreuzberg district for free concerts and performances, funky costumes and exotic food.

- **BERLINER FESTSPIELE.** Not an event, but an arts center which hosts a number of annual cultural festivals in Berlin. Its productions include Musikfest Berlin, the Berlin Jazz Festival, the International Literature Festival, MaerzMusik, Theatertreffen, and various other performing arts celebrations. They don't sleep.

**Bode Museum** (Hellenic and Byzantine sculpture), the **Alte Nationalgalerie** ('Old National Gallery,' oddly exhibiting newer art than the Bode), and the Altes and Neues (old and new) Museums. More architectural notables cluster around **Tiergarten Park.** The Schloβ Bellevue (palatial residence of the German president—like the White House on steroids) sits on the park's north edge, near the Reichstag, which houses the German parliament. Originally built in 1894 and severely damaged in WWII, the Reichstag was not fully refurbished until 1994, with the controversial addition of a huge glass dome—a literal interpretation of transparency of government. Nearby stands the **Berlin Victory Column**, or Goldelse (Golden Lizzy) as the locals affectionately call their favorite giant metal person.

## The Wall

No tour of Berlin is complete without a visit to this onetime monolith, though only the eastern corner remains. This last vestige has been converted into a gallery of politically charged graffiti by artists from all over the world. Complete your wall experience with a trip to the small museum set up at the former Checkpoint Charlie. Don't worry, it's not as tough to get in as it used to be.

## hair i am

When I popped from my mother, she said, "I can't love this, it needs hair." It's true, Mother lacked a basic understanding of human growth patterns, but her message about the importance of hair was not lost on me.

Nor was it lost on Berliners who regard locks and waves as something more than just a poof of hair follicles. The head is a temple, and the hair is that temple's grass; and wouldn't you want your temple's grass to be novel and well groomed?

Outside of this city, hair is too often the crud we pull from our shower drains as we convince ourselves it was worth it to let our girlfriend live with us.

But Berliners know better, and never live with their girlfriends.

They also know better on the hair front. It's not uncommon to see 70-year-old women waiting in line at the supermarket with pink blotches in their hair, or businessmen in suits with uneven segments shaved from their heads.

The head challenges the Berliner—what will you do with me? The answers can be pretty novel.

*Nelson Greaves*

# PRAGUE

Since the Commies got the boot 20 years ago, Prague has worked overtime to shape up its act. And shape up it has: this former crumbling communist puppet has become a prime tourist Metropolis that showcases the history of a former center of the Western world. And we're talking grade-A top choice history here. Take **Jan Hus**—who kind of invented Protestantism. Jan got into some hot water here back in 1413; it only got hotter on the stake.

**Holy Roman Emperor Charles IV** ruled one of Europe's largest kingdoms from Prague and built a city of medieval wonders in the process: towers, castles, statues of himself, bridges with his name on it, universities named "Charles," more Charles statues. Real charmer, that Charles.

And let's not forget Prague's defenestration, that classy tradition of tossing politicians from windows, which happened thrice from Prague's various towers. Thanks to the renovations, these towers now shimmer like new, as if calling you to enact a defenstration of your own—maybe of that irritating chatterbox couple in your hostel. Either way, the city will be sparkling clean and a pleasure for the eye.

However, beautification has come at the price of a general Disney-fication of Prague. But don't let this be an excuse to miss out on its more compelling flavors; it's a small town with tourist districts that rub buns and elbows with the areas containing the real Czech Kahunas. And even if the reality is that in the summer the tourist-to-local ratio reaches nine to one, they've come for a a set of reasons: it's cheap, cheery, and delicious. The only thing Prague won't deliver is disappointment.

## greatest hits

- **UNDERGROUND AND UNDER THE INFLUENCE.** Get lost in the subterranean labyrinth of U Sudu bar and club (p. 141).
- **SNACK HOURS.** Support a family business by pigging out on baked goods at Café Šlagr (p. 134).
- **FAST FOOD.** Walk your hot dog through Wenceslas Square before heading to the National Museum (p. 105).
- **SAMPLE (S)ALE.** Muster up some liquid courage with an 8-beer sampler at Pivovarský Dům (p. 119).

Chock full of amazing hostels, Nové Město is the perfect place for penny pinchers to meet frugal friends. But there's more to life than Wi-Fi and luggage lockers, so plan some sightseeing for a steal and venture out into Prague's other neighborhoods. Get your culture on in Malá Strana with some state-sanctioned public art, or admire the graffiti in the bohemian paradise of Žižkov. Drop some Banksy knowledge on the students walking to lectures at the University of Economics, and convince them to cut class for a cold one at Vinohrady's amazing biergartens. Did your pregame turn into a game? Work off your beer belly by busting a move with some dancing queens in the nearby gay district.

# orientation

### NOVÉ MĚSTO *New Town*

At 650 years of age, Nové Město (New Town) would hardly feel at home at the kiddie table. Sure, founded by Charles IV in 1348, this town might be "comparatively new." And sure, it's got a tradition of childishly chucking its leaders from top floor windows (see **New Town Hall**) but you'll always find the new esconced with the old. Just look at the booming commercial center of Wenceslas Square where KFC and McDonalds share grill space with sausage vendors, the descendants of medieval butchers who hawked weiners when this square was a horse market.

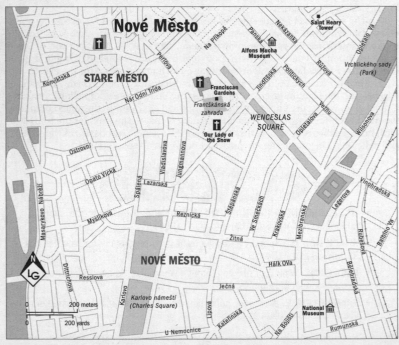

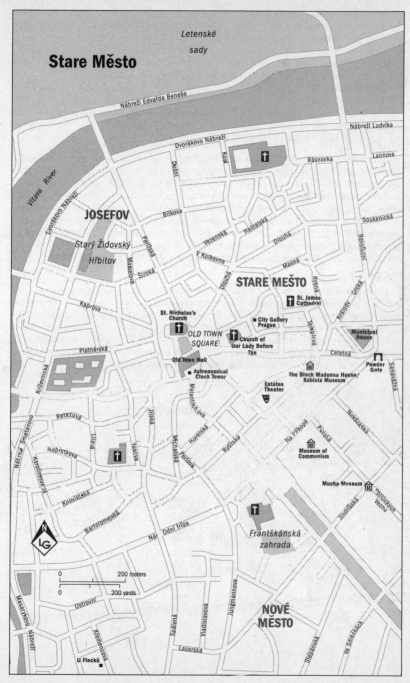

Stare Město

Letenské sady

JOSEFOV

Starý Židovský Hřbitov

STARE MEŠTO

St. Nicholas's Church

OLD TOWN SQUARE

City Gallery Prague

Church of Our Lady Before Týn

Old Town Hall

Astronomical Clock Tower

Estates Theater

St. James Cathedral

Municipal House

Powder Gate

The Black Madonna House/ Kubista Museum

Celetná

Museum of Communism

Mucha Museum

Frantškánská zahrada

NOVÉ MĚSTO

U Flecků

Nábřeží Edvařda Beneše

Dvořákovo Nábřeží

Nábřeží Ludvíka

Lannova

Rásnovka

Soukenická

Vltava River

Dvořákovo Nábřeží

Bílkova

Vezeňská

Haštalská

Dlouhá

V Kolkovne

Masná

Rybná

Dlouhá

Pařížská

Maiselova

Široká

Kaprova

Platnérská

Křížovnická

Retězová

Smetanovo Nábřeží

Karolínmysvje.

Nábřstkova

Jilská

Melantrichova

Michalská

Perlová

Hožejská

Ryřřská

Na Výhopě

Panská

Nekázatká

Revoluční

Orská

Karloz

Templová

Senovážná

Jindřišská

Toušických Vezriu

Konviklská

Bartolomejská

Nár Odní Trída

Ostrovní

Masarykovo Nábřeží

Kremenicová

Spálená

Vladislavova

Jungmannova

Lazarská

Štěpánská

Ve Smečkách

Košl

Dušní

Uhlo-a

Husova

0   200 meters

0   200 yards

N LG

It's the same story at the beautiful Franciscan Gardens at Our Lady of the Snow. The impressive chapel still holds services 650 years after the first bricks were laid, but its abbey now serves as gallery space for local artists. Then there's Saint Henry's Tower, whose 700-year-old bell still tolls the time, though the tower now houses a *whiskeria*, restaurant, museum, and several galleries. Frank Gehry's "Dancing House" sways next to baroque tenement buildings like a hipster skanking at a masquerade.

But ultimately Nové Město's old outcharms its new. Having escaped the facelifts that plasticized much of Old Town, Nové Město still offers travelers some authentic Czech experiences: getting lost on a crumbling street, sharing beers at an exclusively Czech-speaking bar, or eating like a king for just a few dollars.

## STARE MĚSTO

Despite being overrun with tourists and dog dung while distinctly lacking in authentic Czech culture, Old Town still enchants like a princess doped on charm pills. There's **Old Town Hall,** or what's left of it after sore-loser Nazis bombed it on the war's last day. Then there's the **Astronomical Clock Tower,** a mathematical wonder tracking the planet's motions. **Our Lady Before Tyn** keeps the bones of the guy who first described those motions. Last but not least, there's **Estates Theater** where Mozart "premiered" Don Giovanni. You'll have to read this history between the lines (well, between the crystal shops and marionette stores), but even though wiser travelers will eat and sleep in Prague's less besieged quarters, no one—not even he who passes through Prague for a mere hour—should miss the Old Town.

## JOSEFOV

Josefov is the Jewish district of Prague whose main attractions are the six synagogues and the old cemetery. It may seem surprising that such a large, clearly marked Jewish district survives in post-World War II Europe; in fact, during the Nazi occupation Hitler demarcated the area as a future glorified museum of a soon-to-be extinct race and stored pillaged Jewish artifacts there. Because much of the area was demolished in the late 19th century and never restored, the 20th century Art Nouveau architecture is tinged by the the district's lingering medieval quality. While it is certainly worth a

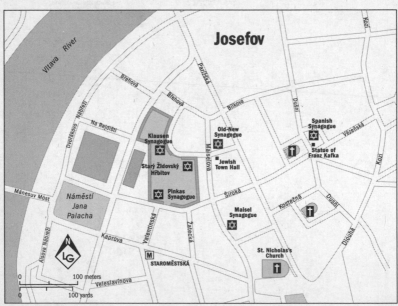

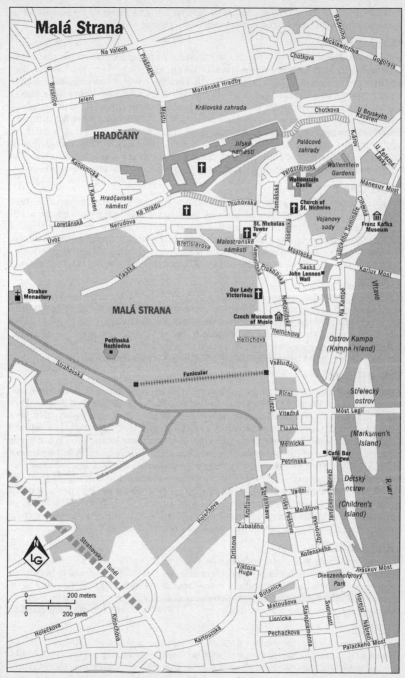

# Malá Strana

Na Valech
U Prašného
Jeleni
U Brusnice
U Brusnice
Mariánské Hradby
Mostu
Chotkova
Mickiewiczova
Gogolova

Královská zahrada

Chotkova
U Bruských
Kasáren

**HRADČANY**

Jiřské
náměstí
Palácové
zahrady
Karlov

Kanovnická
U Kasáren
Valdštejnská
Wallenstein
Gardens
U železné
Lávky

Hradčanské
náměstí
Ke Hradu
Thunovská
Tomásská
**Wallenstein
Castle**
Mánesův Most

Loretánská
Nerudova
Mánesuv Most
**Church of
St. Nicholas**
Cihelná
Ciheina

Úvoz
**St. Nicholas
Tower**
Vojanovy
sady
**Franz Kafka
Museum**

Břetislavova
Malostranské
náměstí
Kamenická
Lužického Semináře

Vlašská
Prokopská
Mostecká

Saská
**John Lennon
Wall**
**Karluv Most**

**Strahov
Monastery**
**Our Lady
Victorious**
Nebovidská
Na Kampě
Vltava

**MALÁ STRANA**
**Czech Museum
of Music**

Hellichova
Hellichova
Ostrov Kampa
*(Kampa Island)*

Petřínská
Rozhledna

Všehrdova
Říční
Střelecký
ostrov

Strahovská
**Funicular**
Újezd
Viteżná
Most Legii

Nosák
*(Marksmen's
Island)*

Mělnická
■ **Café Bar
Wigwa**

Petřínská
Vedni
Dětský
ostrov

Šeřfantkova
Elišky Peškove
Janáčkovo Nábreži
Malátova
*(Children's
Island)*

Strahovský Tunél
Drtinova
Zubatého
Kořenského
Jiráskuv Most

Holečkova
Kmochova
Viktora
Huga
V Botanice
Dienzenhoferovy
Park

Matoušova
Zborovská
Svornosti
Hořejší Nábřeži
Palackého Most

Holečkova
Kmochova
Kartouzská
Lisnicka
Pechackova
Staropramenná

N
LG

0          200 meters
0          200 yards

visit to the synagogues, it must also be noted that the area has become somewhat of a tourist trap, with over-priced restaurants and souvenir peddlers.

## MALÁ STRANA

Malá Strana, literally "Lesser Town," is so-called for its placement below the castle, but geographically Malá Strana continues past the Castle, all the way down to what would be **Vinohrady** on the East side. Malá Strana's length, combined with its assortment of yuppie artistic types, make it something of a hodge-podge district. Crowds storm the castle in the northern area of the district, but the sparser southern regions host some of the trendiest digs in the city. The other ace in Malá Strana's hole is **Petřín Hill,** Prague's "Olympus." Petřín has the highest point in Prague and is so full of flower gardens that you'll think you've tripped into one of your sister's dumb romance books. Finally, if your doctor ordered you to see a lot of public art, you can "fill" that prescription in Malá Strana. If he ordered you to avoid unnecessary metaphors, then don't read the previous sentence.

## HRADČANY

Prague's castle district is located above the rest of the city, providing some of the best panoramas and the biggest crowds. While a trip to the top is obligatory, it might be worth keeping an open mind and a resistance to the magnetic force of the crowds, as some of the quaintest architecture and most serene streets in the city are found several meters in the opposite direction of the cathedral on **Novy Svet.** A grassy knoll hidden by trees above Novy Svet also offers an angle of the gothic cathedral that few tourists have witnessed.

## ŽIŽKOV

Žižkov is a bohemian paradise with enough graffiti (or "street art") murals sprayed on abandoned garage doors and bars to make even the happy-go-lucky feel a little emo. Perhaps the biggest draw for average tourists is the freaky TV tower that looks like a needle in a stack of crumbs. Home to one of Prague's universities, the quiet, hilly streets are reminiscent of Paris's Latin Quarter and parts of San Francisco, but Žižkov's are set apart from them by the cobblestones on every path.

## VINOHRADY

Legend has it that in days of yore, Princess Libuse, a probably-fictional-princess, stood on a hill at Vinohrady's Vyšehrad fortress and foresaw the glory of Prague. Fact has it that the first King of Bohemia landed here in the 11th century and ruled here until Charles IV moved across the river. Let's Go has it that Vinhorady is a relaxed neighborhood with the best green spaces and *biergartens* in the city, a lively gay district, and some of the best and cheapest eats. The Vyšehrad cultural monument should really not be missed since it contains the **Church of Saint Peter and Saint Paul,** visible from nearly any point in Prague, and the **Vyšehrad cemetery,** which houses Dvorak's bones and the oldest Roman chapel in the city. Additionally the neighborhood is a great setting for a beautiful afternoon walk with a great view of the river and a better view of Czech kiddies swapping tongues along the fortress wall. For the best sweets in the entire city—maybe the entire world—try out Vinohrady's **Café Šlagr.**

## HOLEŠOVICE

Without question, the most underappreciated neighborhood in all of Prague is Holešovice, which has some of the coolest sites that aren't just enjoyable because a guidebook tells you they're important. From **Cross Club,** which might be the best club in Europe, to **Křižík's Fountain,** an incredible water and light show accompanied by ballet, to Prague's biggest open air market, these sites are alive, fresh and full of Czech youth.

## DEJVICE

Dejvice is mostly for the old and tired or the middle-aged and child-bearing. It's no surprise that one can barely find a tourist on the streets of Dejvice, because unlike the undiscovered parts behind Prague Castle, this district simply has little to offer

prague

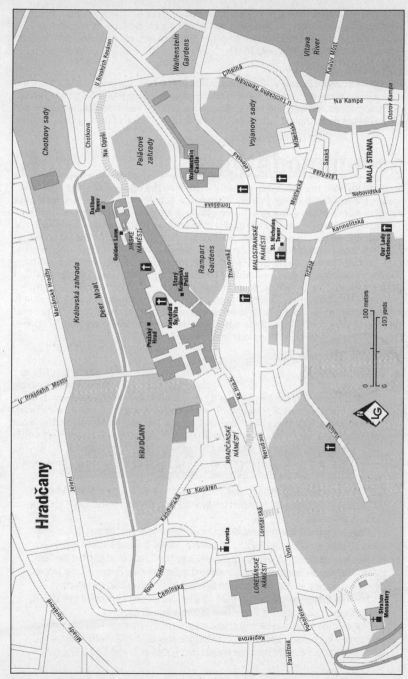

# Hradčany

Chotkovy sady

Wallenstein Gardens

Vltava River

Karlův Most

U Brusských Kasáren

Chotkova

Na Opyši

Cihelná

U Lužického Semináře

Na Kampě

Ostrov Kampa

Palácové zahrady

Wallenstein Castle

Vojanovy sady

MALÁ STRANA

Mariánské Hradby

Královská zahrada

Deer Moat

Dalibor Tower

Golden Lane

JIŘSKÉ NÁMĚSTÍ

Rampart Gardens

Tomášská

Letenská

Mostecká

Míšenská

Saská

Lázeňská

Nebovidská

Karmelitská

Our Lady Victorious

Starý Královský Palác

St. Nicholas Tower

MALOSTRANSKÉ NÁMĚSTÍ

Tržiště

Thunovská

Jelení

Katedrála Sv. Víta

Pražský Hrad

HRADČANY

HRADČANSKÉ NÁMĚSTÍ

Ke Hradu

Vlašská

U Prašného Mostu

Kanovnická

U Kasáren

Nerudova

Loretánská

Loreta

Nový Svět

Černínská

LORETÁNSKÉ NÁMĚSTÍ

Úvoz

Pohořelec

Parléřová

Keplerova

Mlady Hořákové

Strahov Monastery

100 meters

100 yards

orientation . dejvice

the foreigner. Apart from a few good restaurants, most of which are light-years beyond a backpacker's budget, a cool fountain, and a gigantic flowery roundabout, the neighborhood is best left for those to come: the area is under construction, so who knows what the future will hold for Dejvice.

## SMICHOV

Smichov is a area of Prague's fifth district that boasts a giant shopping complex, several quality restaurants that are far less expensive than anything found in central Prague, the Staropramen brewery, and lush greenery that provide visitors with a welcome and off-the-beaten path respite from the main attractions and noise of the Old Town streets.

# accommodations

Accommodations in Prague differ greatly. Thanks to the opening of some new "chic" hostels throughout the city (Mosaic House, Sir Toby's, Miss Sophie's, Czech Inn), travelers willing to pay a bit extra (or sometimes, even not) can find digs with full bedding, in-house restaurants and top quality Wi-Fi. Those who want that hostel-specific thrill of wondering if your roommate's going to kill you won't be disappointed, as there are many "earthy" options throughout the city. In general, Stare Město costs more and offers less, while Nové Město costs less and offers more. Several large hostels in Holešovice start resembling hotels (or fantastic, cushy communes) but require a Metro ride to visit sites, and might be a bit out of the way for most travelers, especially lazy ones. Finally, a note on prices. The prices included are simply approximates. Most Prague hostels price with an algorithm that takes into account the time of year, the fullness of the hostel and the current rate of demand for rooms. This system rewards those who book in advance.

## NOVÉ MĚSTO *New Town*

### MOSAIC HOUSE
Odborů 4

🚶♿ HOSTEL, HOTEL ❷
☎725 84 67 73 📧www.mosaichouse.com

Mosaic House, Prague's newest and most luxurious hostel, understands what makes hostels great: a restaurant/bar/stage-venue with live music, a carpeted lounge space with bean bags, and Wi-Fi that's fast and omnipresent. But what makes Mosaic the (pre-hooker) Tiger Woods of Prague hostels is how it improves

---

## prague didn't get the memo

You know, the one for buildings that goes something like "brown, black, white or tan, please!" All over this cramped and faded city, the story—the more colorful story—is the same.

Prague just didn't feel the need to bow down to the social norms that dictate which colors a legitimate office building can be painted. Maybe it was a reaction to the communist-era repression of expression, or maybe it's just the Czech effort to offset the Slavic gloom. Whatever the reason, a randomly chosen Prague street wears mostly pinks, yellows, greens and purples, leaving earth tones to its less-daring Metropolitan colleagues.

The real shame is that the city hasn't had a decent paint job since the 1960s, and back then, photographs were taken in black and white.

However, the future may be bright! Tourist boom profits have already done wonders for Prague's impeccably refurbished cobblestone streets, and if tourist swarms continue to descend, we might soon see Prague returned to its former Easter Egg glory.

prague

the tiny annoyances of hostels. Bunks in large dorms have privacy curtains, lighting is indirect instead of overpowering, and the rooms have soft beds and bountiful power outlets. Even Mosaic's few faults come in pursuit of noble goals, like lights over-eagerly shut off to save power. Still, you gotta respect that this hostel has the only greywater heat recycling system in the Czech Republic. Hotel rooms are 4 star, which bodes well for hostel rooms, which are basically the same with bunks.

⚑ *B: Karlovo namesti. From the station, head north along the west edge of the park. At the north-west corner of the park, take a left at Odborů.* *i* *Netbooks 40-50Kč per hr. Women-only room available. Non-smoking. 4 computers available 1Kč per minute. Breakfast 150Kč. Towel 100Kč deposit, free for hotel guests. Lockers included. Safe box at desk.* Ⓢ *Dorms 250-550Kč. Doubles (hotel room) 1700-1900/room.* Ⓠ *Reception 24hr. Check in 3pm. Check-out 11am.*

### MISS SOPHIE'S                    ⮕⊘❄(ᵂ) HOSTEL ❶
Melounová 3                          ☎293 303 0530 🖳www.miss-sophies.com

A bit out of the way and a bit more expensive than the cheapest hostel, Miss Sophie's is nevertheless the best bang for your buck in Nové Město. Genuinely cool modern designs including mural-sized original artwork line the newly-painted walls. Steel and glass showers are classier than what you'll find in most hotels. With polished wood floors, comfortable leather couches, flatscreen TV, and DVD library, it's easy to forget this is an accomodation for budget travelers.

⚑ *C: IP Pavlova. Take 1st left from platform, then follow Katerinska to 1st right, onto Melounová.* *i* *Wi-Fi included and 2 computers with Internet available. Kitchens in some rooms. Most staff members are students.* Ⓢ *Dorms 410Kč; singles 1150Kč. Apartment 1390Kč. Towels 30Kč. 5% discount with ISIC student card if booked online. 4% additional charge if you pay with a credit card.* Ⓠ *Reception 24hr. No curfew. Check-in 3pm. Check-out 11am.*

### CHILI HOSTEL

HOSTEL ❶

Pštrossova 7, 110 00 Praha 1 ☎60 311 9113 💻www.chili.dj

Chili Hostel can't be beat when it comes to price and community. Large, comfortable common rooms, kitchens, and dining areas play host to nightly multi-national pregames, supported by the front desk's ample beverage service. Rooms are bunk-heavy and lack adornment besides the occasional chair, but bathrooms are kept very clean and well-stocked.

*🚇 B: Národní trida. From the station, walk south on Spálená, make a right on Myslíkova, and then another right on Pštrossova. i Non-smoking. Wi-Fi included and is reliable on most floors. Very large breakfast 89Kč. Linens, towels, and lockers included; laundry available for stays of 5 days or more. [$] Dorms from 200Kč; singles 400Kč. Key deposit 200Kč. ⏰ Reception 24hr. Quiet time starts at 2:30am. Check-in 2pm. Check-out 10am.*

### HOSTEL U BUBENÍČKŮ

HOSTEL ❶

Myslikova 258/8, 120 00 Praha 2 ☎22 492 2357 💻Ububenicku.hotel.cz

Located both inside and on top of a restaurant, this 65-bed hostel doesn't charge extra for the smells of roast pork and sauerkraut, and will give you a 10% discount should you choose to investigate the source of those smells. Pastel-walled rooms are very comfortable thanks to free bedding more generous than the traditional sleep sack. Lucky visitors stay in rooms with polished wooden floors.

*🚇 B: Karlovo náměstí. From the station, take Resslova toward the river and then right on Na Zderaze and then left on Myslíková, the hostel will be on your right; it looks like a restaurant. i Towels and lockers included. Breakfast available at the attached restaurant 65-100Kč. [$] Dorms 290Kč; doubles 960Kč. Discount available for large groups; ask the receptionist for more details. ⏰ Reception 9am-midnight. No curfew. Check-out 10am. Check-in 2pm.*

### AZ HOSTEL

HOSTEL ❶

Jindřišské 5, 110 Praha 1 ☎22 424 1664 💻www.hostel-az.cz

With large rooms at reasonable prices, AZ Hostel is especially ideal for travelers looking to keep to themselves. Full linens come with every room, and no rooms have bunk beds. All the rooms have wood floors and free lockers. No private showers available. Passably comfortable common room has a small TV and free coffee and tea.

*🚇 A or B: Mustek. From the station, walk up the square toward the National Museum, then make a left on Jindřišské; the hostel will be on your left. i Laundry service 190Kč per load. Computer use 20Kč per 10min. Wi-Fi and lockers included. Power adapters available upon request. [$] Dorms 320Kč; singles 950Kč. ⏰ Reception 24hr. Check-in noon. Check-out 10:30am.*

### HOSTEL PRAGUE LION

HOSTEL ❷

Na Zbořenci 6, 120 00 Praha ☎73 148 7936 💻www.prague-lion.com

This little hostel may be called the lion, but roaring won't be tolerated; it's ideal for couples or cranks who want things quiet. Drinking games not welcome. One computer is available with free Internet. Breakfast free when booked through 💻hostelbooker.com; otherwise 90Kč. Hostel is small and tends to fill up; book at least a week in advance. No common spaces. Visitors must knock to enter.

*🚇 B: Karlovo náměstí. From the station, head down Resslova street, then take your first right on Na Zderaze and another right on Na Zbořenci i Reservations recomended 1 month in advance.Wi-Fi included. [$] Dorms 620Kč; singles 2050Kč; doubles 1200Kč. ⏰ Reception 24hr. Check-in 2-8pm. Check-out 10am.*

### HOSTEL EMMA

HOSTEL ❶

Na Zderaze 267/10, 12000 Praha ☎774 807 787 💻www.hostel-emma.com

Hidden behind a raised bend in the road, Hotel Emma suffers from an identity crisis, torn between bare-bones dorm rooms with wireframe beds and opulent private rooms with TVs and full kitchens. The large, clean common room with a foosball table makes up for having to pay 30Kč for a towel and a 300Kč deposit for keys. One computer with Internet is available.

*🚇 B: Karlovo náměstí. From the station, head down Resslova street, then take your first right on*

*Na Zderaze . i Wi-Fi and lockers included. Beer, soda and baguettes available at reception. Ⓢ 8-bed dorms 240Kč; 6-bed dorms 330Kč; singles 1700Kč; double 2000Kč. ⏰ Reception 24hr.*

### THE WELCOME PRAGUECENTER HOSTEL

HOSTEL ❶

Žitna 17, 11000 Prague 1 ☎22 432 0202 🖥www.bed.cz

Possibly the worst-named hostel in the city, Welcome Praguecenter provides some impressively luxurious private rooms for, in some cases, dormitory prices. Located on the second floor of an apartment building, its rooms resemble apartments with glass tables and king-sized beds. Refrigerators and safe boxes are available in each room. Small bathrooms, and the lack of common spaces and a kitchen are the only downfalls of this hostel...except for the name, of course.

*🚇 B: Karlovo náměstí. From the station, head away from the river down Žitna. i Reservations 1-2 weeks in advance recommended. Sheets and towels included. No breakfast. Ⓢ All private rooms. 400Kč for bed with shared facilites. 500Kč for bed with private facilties. ⏰ Check-in 9am-9pm (call ahead if you'll be later). Check-out by 11:30am. No parties after 10pm.*

### CENTRAL HOSTEL

HOSTEL ❶

Sokolská 29, 120 00 Praha 2 ☎22 424 7412 🖥www.hostel-centre.eu

Heroically living up to its name, Central Hostel offers forgettable but acceptable accommodations at a very central location and workable prices. By no means a bargain, Central does have carpets that add a level of "hominess" rare in any hostel. Additionally the rooms are very clean and each comes with free lockers. Common room has kitchen, refrigerator, laundry and TV. Definitely try elsewhere first, but given the recent closing of several hostels in the area, this is a valuable cheap—if not ideal—option.

*🚇 C: I.P. Pavlava. From the station, head towards the river on Jugoslávská 1 block, then turn left on Sokolská. Hostel will be on your right. i Wi-Fi included. 1 computer with Internet access. €5 deposit for key. Very basic breakfast 56Kč. Ⓢ Dorms 400Kč; apartments 750Kč. ⏰ Check-in whenever. Check-out 11am.*

### ADVANTAGE

HOSTEL ❶

Sokolská 11, 120 00 Praha 2 ☎22 491 4062 🖥www.advantagehostel.cz

The only real "advantage" offered by this low-frills hostel (with no kitchen!) is that it's closer to the train station than some of its competitors. That and free breakfast, towels, linens, Wi-Fi, and lockers. So there are a couple advantages, but there are much nicer places available for the same price. No central common area to speak of; lounge up front has three computers where you can pay to surf the Internet (is that still a thing people say?). The paint job in the rooms is a little loud, but they are very spacious and clean.

*🚇 C: I.P. Pavlava. From the station, head towards the river on Jugoslávská 1 block, then turn left on Sokolská. Hostel will be on your right after a short block. i 20min. on comptuers free. 1Kč per min after. Ⓢ Dorms 400Kč, with private toilet 450Kč; singles 1000/1400Kč; doubles 550/700Kč. ⏰ Check-in 8am-10pm (call if later). Check-out 10am.*

## STARE MĚSTO

### OLD PRAGUE HOSTEL

HOSTEL ❷

Benedikstská 2 ☎224 829 058 🖥www.oldpraguehostel.com

Run by the same guys as Prague Square hostel, Old Prague just has a homier, more welcoming feeling to it. Perhaps because an old-school, exposed elevator services the hostel's five stories, but either way, Old Prague does a few things better than its sister hostel. Perhaps most importantly, its desk sells beer in addition to soft drinks. Common areas also have flatscreen TVs and comfortable couches. Rooms are nice and roomy. Beds sit a little close to the ground, and some of the rooms have mental-asylum padded doors, but the brightly colored artwork keeps the experience interesting.

*🚇 B: Náměstí Republiky. From the station, walk north on Revoluční. Take a left on Dlouhá and another quick left onto Benedikstská. i Non-smoking. Breakfast, towels, linens, lockers, adapters, irons, and hair dryers included. Wi-Fi available on the mezzanine and in the common area. Key*

*deposit 100Kč.* $ *8-bed dorms 295-430Kč; 4-bed dorms 431-539Kč; doubles 539-700Kč.* ⏰ *Reception 24hr. Check-in 2pm. Check-out 10am.*

**PRAGUE SQUARE HOSTEL** ♿ HOSTEL 2

Melantrichova 10 ☎224 240 859 💻www.praguesquarehostel.com

A well-kept joint in a well-frequented part of town, Prague Square Hostel is uncommonly generous with travel amenities. Unfortunately, it also suffers from some typical Old Town maladies. No laundry service and a sparsely stocked desk store mean travelers are on their own. The rooms are clean, if at times a bit small and the sheets are strangely, but cheerfully, colorful.

*A or B: Můstek. From the station, head north on na Můstku and continue on it as it turns into Melantrichova. The hostel will be on your right.* ℹ *Non-smoking. Hair dryers, irons, adapters, towels, linens, lockers, and breakfast (8am-10am) included. Free computer access and Wi-Fi in common spaces.* $ *8-bed dorms 300-450Kč; 4-bed 300-530Kč. Singles 645-750Kč; doubles 950-1250Kč.* ⏰ *Reception 24hr. Check-in 2pm. Check-out 10am.*

**TRAVELLER'S HOSTEL** ♿ HOSTEL 3

Dlouhá 33 ☎224 826 662 💻www.travellers.cz

Travelers staying in Prague for more than a week should consider this slightly dated hostel, where every seventh night comes free of charge. Rooms can be small and it gets oppressively hot on the top floor. The hostel has a cheap 24hr. laundry service *(150Kč)*, though no self service.

*C: Náměstí Republiky. From the station, walk north along Revoluční. Take a left at Dlouhá. The hostel will be on your right.* ℹ *Smoking only permitted in dining room. Breakfast included. Third floor absinthe bar; beer and soft drinks can be purchased from the front desk. Computer access available in the front lobby. Free Wi-Fi accessible on the 3rd fl. Key deposit 200Kč.* $ *Dorms 350Kč; 4-bed rooms 500Kč; singles 1190-1390Kč; doubles 690-800Kč; apartments 2250-2550Kč (2-4 beds). ISIC/IYHF card holders recieve 40Kč discount.* ⏰ *Reception 24hr. Check-in 1pm. Check-out 10am.*

**HOSTEL TÝN** 🍸 HOSTEL 2

Týnská 19 ☎224 828 519 💻www.hosteltyn.com

Hostel Týn's digs grow some some fine deals, even if they are sometimes rough around the hedges. The downstairs common and kitchen spaces seem like they might have been designed by your grandpa, but they're kept very clean. Bad news is the downstairs closes at 2am; good news is depending on how charming you are, this time is negotiable. Týn's perks (no bunks and large rooms) offset Týn's faults (no breakfast or laundry).

*B: Náměstí Republiky. From the station, head south to U Prašná Brány and follow it as it becomes Celetná. Continue towards the river, then take a right at Štupartská and a left onto Týnská. Follow Týnská as it winds around. The hotel will be on your right.* ℹ *Non-smoking. Wi-Fi accessible in common spaces. Towels and lockers included.* $ *Dorms 300-400Kč; doubles 1000Kč; triples 1200Kč.* ⏰ *Reception 24hr. Check-out 10am.*

**RITCHIE'S HOTEL AND HOSTEL** 🍸 HOSTEL 2

12 Karlova ☎222 221 229 💻www.ritchieshostel.cz

Ritchie's excellent location and reasonable prices come at the expense of luxury. Untidy carpets that pay tribute to the '80s match the age of the computers in the lobby. The general gloom of the place isn't helped by the photos of drifters plastered on the walls. But if you're okay with a little grit, some torn carpets, and a warm top floor, Ritchie's can be a deal. The reception desk carries soap, toothpaste, and other essentials like beer and candy. Kichen proves to be the only good hangout spot.

*A: Staroméstka. From the station, head down Křižovnická directly along the river. At the Charles bridge, turn left at Karlova. The hostel will be on your left, through a gallery.* ℹ *Linens and towels included. Breakfast 90Kč. Lockers 30Kč per day. Luggage room 100Kč deposit. Self-service laundry 140Kč; no dryer. Women dorms available.* $ *Dorms 330-420Kč. Singles 1380-1200Kč; doubles 1200-900Kč. ISIC holders get a 5% discount. Credit card users charged a 3% fee.* ⏰ *Reception 24hr. Check-in 1pm. Check-out 11am. Kitchen access 8am-1am.*

**HOSTEL APPLE** 💳⊗ HOSTEL [3]

Králodvorská 16 ☎224 231 050 💻www.applehostel.cz

While very few Old Town hostels would satisfy the Queen of England, Hostel Apple is dubious even for commoners. Several doors—most notably in bathrooms—have holes in them, and some of the beds have wire frames with only flimsy mattresses. Paint peels from many a dirty wall, but none of this really detracts from the hostel experience. More heinous is the information set up: Apple offers no Wi-Fi, and the only computer available *(1Kč per min)* is as archaic as an original Apple. Clean bathrooms, a hearty breakfast, plus the spacious rooms might make up for the common area and kitchen closing at midnight.

*🚶 B: Náměstí Republiky. From the station, walk north on Revoluční then loop around onto Králodvorská. The hostel is on the 2nd floor of the building. ℹ Breakfast, linens, and towels included. Full-service laundry 150Kč. Safety deposit boxes 200Kč deposit. Free luggage storage. $ Dorms 330-380Kč. Singles 890-990Kč; doubles 1200Kč; quads around 2000Kč per bed. ISIC Card holders receive a 10% discount. Key requires 200Kč deposit or some item of value. ⏰ Reception 24hr. Check-in 2pm. Check-out 10am.*

## HRADČANY

### ★ ROMANTIK HOTEL U RAKA 💳♿📶🍸❄☁ HOTEL [5]

Černínská 10 ☎220 511 100 💻www.romantikhotel-uraka.cz

Housed in the only timbered building in Prague, this romantic little hotel is nestled in a quiet corner of Hradčany. This is a giant splurge for a backpacker, but perfect for a couple in search of a magical stay, providing the best of both worlds: a forest escape from all that is the tourist influx of Prague, while being just a skip down the cobblestone street from it. The hotel is run by a family of genial artists who are only too excited to make your visit to Prague better than the movies.

*🚶 Tram 22: Brusnice. From the tram, walk across the street and onto the path that leads towards the trees. Walk down the giant staircase and the hotel will be on the left directly at the base of the stairs. ℹ Breakfast included. $ Singles 2280Kč; doubles from 3074Kč. ⏰ Reception 8am-10pm. Check-in 2pm. Check-out 11am.*

### THE GOLDEN HORSE HOUSE 💳♿📶❄ HOTEL [4]

Úvoz 8 ☎603 841 790 💻www.goldenhorse.cz

Modern apartments in a pretty, antique building are located near the castle. Simple, clean rooms are juxtaposed with ornate bathrooms. The satellite TV, and a fully stocked kitchen might make you want to spend your vacation indoors.

*🚶 Trams 12, 20, 22, 91: Malostranské náměstí. From the tram, head west on Malostranské náměstí, which becomes Nerudova, and then eventually Úvoz. ℹ Huge breakfast buffet 125Kč. TV in every room. Wi-Fi included. $ Singles from 1050Kč; doubles from 1290Kč. ⏰ Reception 8am-4pm.*

### THE GREEN LOBSTER 💳♿📶🍸❄ HOTEL [5]

Nerudova 43 ☎257 532 158 💻www.garzottohotels.cz

Best for a romantic evening or a truly decadent splurge, this hotel near the base of Prague Castle offers three levels of luxury. Some rooms make you think you've stepped into the queen's chambers. If you're already doling out more than usual, keep the experimentation going with a quick douse in the bidet, available in the most expensive rooms.

*🚶 Trams 12, 20, 22, 91: Malostranské náměstí. From the tram, head west on Malostranské náměstí, which becomes Nerudova; the hotel will be on your left. ℹ Breakfast and Wi-Fi included. You can often score a better deal if you book online. Pickup from airport 650Kč. $ Rooms 1400-3150Kč. ⏰ Reception 24hr. Check-in 2pm. Check-out noon.*

# ŽIŽKOV

### HOSTEL ELF
Husitská 11

♦ ♿ (ŋ) ⚲ ⚇  HOSTEL ❷

☎222 540 963 🖥www.hostelelf.com

The perfect place to stay for those who wouldn't mind crashing on a couch in a friend's apartment that's covered (intentionally) in graffiti. The common room is the center of hostel life, with seven enormous, thoroughly lived-in couches and a communal kitchen nearby. Clean and simply furnished dorms with shared hall baths.

🚋 *Trams 5, 9, or 26: Husinecká Tram stop. From the tram stop, follow Husinecká until you reach the square and then make a left at Orebitská, which will run into Husinecká right in front of the hostel.* ⓘ *Bike storage available. Breakfast included.* Ⓢ *6-to-9 bed dorms 370Kč; 11-bed dorm 340Kč; singles with bath 1230Kč. Prices go down in low season. 5% discounts in dorms for students.* ⓩ *Reception 24hr. Check-in 2pm. Check-out 10am.*

### PENSION PRAGUE CITY
Štítného 363/13

♦ ♿ (ŋ)  HOTEL ❹

☎222 782 483 🖥www.praguecity.cz

Relatively cheap rooms in an unassuming building on a hilly, quiet street. Beautiful black iron beds are simple yet comfortable and the white-washed rooms are sleek and tasteful.

🚋 *Tram 5, 9, or 26: Husinecká. From the stop, walk east on Seifertova 3 blocks and turn left on Cimburkova, then 1st right on Štítného.* ⓘ *Breakfast sometimes included, 100Kč in high season. Computers and TVs in rooms. Parking 150Kč. Mobile phones available with 1000Kč deposit.* Ⓢ *Singles 850-1400Kč; doubles 1000-1400Kč.* ⓩ *Reception 8am-10pm. Check-in 2pm. Check-out 11am.*

# VINOHRADY

### CZECH INN
Francouská 76

♦ ♿ (ŋ) ⚲  HOSTEL ❶

☎267 26 76 00 🖥www.czech-inn.com

Justifiably billing itself as a "designer hostel," Czech Inn takes pains to distinguish itself from the rest of the humdrum hostel world. The lobby and bar areas serve double duty as an art gallery, and every six weeks the hostel changes the art and throws a "gallery opening," complete with wine and snacks. That appreciation for detail extends into the rooms, which have sleek single-sheet glass showers with polished concrete floors.

🚋 *A: Náměstí Míru. From the station, walk southeast along Francouská. The hostel will be on your right.* ⓘ *Wi-Fi and lockers included. 8 computers available; 1Kč per min. Towels 30Kč with a 100Kč deposit. Breakfast 120Kč at check-in, 140Kč the morning of. Dinner 120-180Kč. Beer 33-55Kč. The entire hostel is smoke-free.* Ⓢ *Dorms 295-472Kč. Singles 1540-2282Kč; doubles 1320-1694Kč. Apartments 1650-2544Kč.* ⓩ *Reception 24hr.*

### ADVANTAGE
Sokolská 11

⊛⊛(ŋ)  HOTEL ❶

☎224 91 40 62 🖥www.advantagehostel.cz

The only real "advantage" to this no-frills hostel is that it's closer to the subway than some of its competitors. That said, much nicer places are available at this same price. No central common area or kitchen to speak of. The paint job in the rooms is a little loud, but rooms are spacious enough and clean.

🚋 *C: I.P. Pavlava. From the station, head toward the river on Jugoslávská 1 block, then turn left on Sokolská. Hostel will be on your right after a short block.* ⓘ *20min. on computers free, 1 Kč per min. thereafter. Breakfast, Wi-Fi, towels, linens, and lockers included.* Ⓢ *Dorms 400Kč, with private toilet 450Kč; singles 1000 Kč/1400Kč; doubles 550Kč/700Kč.*

# HOLEŠOVICE

### SIR TOBY'S HOSTEL
Dělnická 24

♦⊛(ŋ)⚲  HOSTEL ❶

☎246 032 610 🖥www.sirtobys.com

A quirky, comfortable, feels-like-your-mom-was-involved-in-preparing-your-room kind of hostel where details matter, Sir Toby's combines the efficiency and cleanliness of a large hostel with the intimacy and community of a small one. To start, Sir

Toby's room's are identified by respective theme rather than numbers, and they're decorated accordingly. The quirks continue into the grill-equipped back garden where the tables are all old sewing machines. The pub downstiars *(Beer 20-35Kč)* hosts subtitled Czech movie screenings, live concerts, and DJs on a regular basis. There's a hot, all-you-can-shove-down-your-pie-hole breakfast *(100Kč)* from 8:30-11:30am, while Afghani or Czech homemade dinner plates are available nightly *(100-120Kč)*. Guests can also use the modern communal kitchen. Brochures, signs, and homemade guidebooks in the lobby will keep you informed, since you, like Steve Tyler during the filming of Armageddon, "Don't Want To Miss a Thing." But best of all, Sir Toby's is that rarest of things: a hostel without any of the classic hostel musk.

*🚋 C: Vltavská. From the station, take any tram that departs to the left. Ride it 2 stops to Dělnická. Walk to the traffic lights and turn left onto Dělnická. ℹ Lockers included. Towels 15Kč with a 200Kč deposit. Laundry service costs 200Kč, self-serve 100Kč. Wi-Fi is free, and 5 computers are available at 1 Kč per min. $ Dorm 220-400Kč, women's dorm 400-560Kč. Singles 950Kč; doubles 1200Kč. ⏰ Reception 24hr. Buzz to enter.*

### PRAGUE PLUS
🎫♿📶🍸 HOSTEL [1]

Prívozní 1, 170 00 Praha 7 ☎22 051 0046 💻www.plusprague.com

A large and tightly-run establishment, Prague Plus feels a bit like foreign summer camp for students. Excitement revolves around the "restaurant," which is secret talk for "enormous effing dining hall" that includes a nightly DJ, a full service bar *(beer 40Kč, mixed drinks 80-120Kč)*, a full service grill *(85-150Kč)*, 5 flatscreen TVs, two tricked out with Nintendo Wiis, a pool and foosball tables, and plenty of horizontal surfaces for getting friendly (wink!). Back at the hotel, a swimming pool and nightly movie screenings let the quiet folk interact quietly. Women-only rooms include hairdryers and vanity sets. The breakfast buffet *(100Kč)* consists of meats, beans, eggs, and cheeses. Prague Plus is one of the best handicap-accessible accommodations in Prague. Before you leave the lobby, say hello to Boris the turtle, who is not dead, but "just sleeping."

*🚋 C: Nadraži Holešovice. From the station, go 1 stop on any tram heading north, or just walk down Ortenovo Namesti in the direciton of the Hotel Plaza Alta. ℹ Laundry 170 Kč. Breakfast 100 Kč. Linens and lockers included. Free Wi-Fi in lobby and restaurant plus a few free-to-use computers in the lobby and restaurant. Non-smoking. $ Sept-June mixed dorms 260-380Kč, women only 300-420Kč; singles 1000Kč; doubles 500Kč. July-Aug 1400Kč/700Kč/380-570Kč/400-590Kč. ⏰ Reception 24hr. Check in 3pm. Check out 10am.*

### HOTEL EXTOL INN
🎫♿📶🍸 HOTEL [4]

Přístavní 340/2 ☎+22 087 6541 💻www.extolinn.cz

Though this is not actually a hostel, travelers looking for single or double rooms can find hotel amenties here at hostel-like prices. Hotel Extol Inn offers two levels of service. Full sevice includes gym, spa, and sauna access—but the hostel-esque deal doesn't. Who cares? It's still a hotel room with free breakfast. And get this—it's the same hot breakfast buffet that the sauna-enjoying full service humans will be eating. Rooms share facilities but never between more than 6 people. Wi-Fi is available in the lobby; computers are also available *(2 Kč/min)*. Although the hotel has full service handicap rooms, no budget rooms are handicap-accessible.

*🚋 C: Vltavská. From the station, take any tram that departs to the left. Ride it 2 stops to Dělnická. Keep walking an additional block and take a left onto Přístavní. ℹ Discount available for HI Card holders. Check-in 2pm. Check-out 10am. $ Singles 820Kč; doubles 1400Kč; triples 1990Kč. ⏰ Reception 24hr.*

### A AND O HOSTEL
🎫📶🍸 HOSTEL [2]

U Vystaviste 1/262, 170 00 Praha 7 ☎22 087 0252 💻www.aohostels.com

A and O Hostel could be better located, or worse located—there's a strip club behind the hostel—but it's a 5min. walk to the train station. The rooms are relatively bare-bones and pretty small. None of the rooms have lockers, but a safebox is available at the front desk. A spiral stone staircase leads down to what feels like a dungeon, but instead is a bar and hangout area, equipped with a big screen and a Wii!

*🚏 C: Nadraží Holešovice. From the station, head right (west) onto Vrbenského, then Partyzánská; keep going around to the left to get onto the raised street. ℹ Non-smoking rooms available. A very large breakfast is available for 120Kč. Wi-Fi 60Kč per hr. Check-in 4pm. Check-out 10am. $ Prices vary daily. Prviate rooms around 450Kč. Dorms around 270Kč. ISIC card holders get a 10% discount. ⏰ Reception 24hr. No curfew.*

## SMICHOV 🏠

### ARPACAY HOSTEL
💳🚭📶☕ HOSTEL [2]

Radlická 76 ☎251 552 297 💻www.arpacayhostel.com

This hostel—a little ways from central Prague, but a pleasant escape from the throngs of tourist shops—will provide you with a quiet evening for well-rested repose. The hostel has two buildings across from each other and boasts giant breakfast rooms, as well as guest kitchens on each floor. The red building has a terrace on the roof where you can take in the view of Prague and beyond.

*🚏 Trams 12, 14, 20: Plzeňka. From the tram, walk toward the park and up the stairs, across the train tracks. At the intersection, keep walking straight up the hill on Radlická and look for the Arpacay sign on the right. ℹ Breakfast, linens, and towels included. Computers available. Smoking deck that overlooks much of the city. $ 3- to 5-bed dorms from 300Kč. ⏰ Reception open 7am-midnight. Check-in flexible. Check-out 10am.*

### HOSTEL 5
💳🚭📶 HOSTEL [1]

Plzeňská 540/23 ☎257 324 908 💻http://hostel5.pl

A low-key, simple, clean hostel where the selling point is no bunks. Other than that, the place is cheap and has a tiny "terrace" with basically one plastic table and a few chairs. A good option for groups because it offers highly discounted deals, as well as breakfast, for over 15 people.

*🚏 C: Andel. Walk up Plzeňská about 300m. ℹ Terrace, kitchen, and linens included. $ 2- to 5-bed dorms 290-320Kč; singles 250-535Kč. ⏰ Reception open 10am-noon and 1pm-11pm.*

### HOSTEL KLAMOVKA
📶 HOSTEL [1]

Vrchlického 647/78 ☎257 210 698 💻www.hostel-klamovka.com

This bright, pink building of a hostel provides simple wooden bunks in pink-themed rooms. Quite a trek from central Prague; we only recommend it if you're looking for a little adventure that leads you into residential territory and away from the tourist attractions and willing to pay for trams. While it might be the cheapest option in Prague, the tram fare adds up. Friendly staff will make you feel right at home.

*🚏 Trams 4, 7, 9, 10 Klamovka. Across from the stop. ℹ Breakfast, linens, towel, iron, and hair dryer included. $ 5- to 8-bed person dorms 230Kč; singles 440Kč; doubles 330Kč. ⏰ Reception 24hr. Check-in 2pm. Check-out 10am.*

# sights 👁

## NOVÉ MĚSTO

### 👍 SAINT HENRY TOWER
♿ BELFRY

Jindřišské ulice, Praha 1 ☎22 223 2429 💻www.jindrisskavez.cz

Originally built from wood in 1475, then again from stone in 1599, the 67.7m tower was designed as a belfry for the nearby Saint Henry's Church. At one time 10 bells rang out from the tower, but neglect and damage over the years has left just one. The remaining 723kg, 101cm diameter bell rings on the hour and half hour. In recent years, the middle portions of the tower have been ingeniously returned to public use as a restaurant, museum, whiskey bar, and several galleries. Admission gets you into the museum and galleries, but it's worth taking the stairs to peek at the tiny restaurant's tables, which are built around the tower's scaffolding system.

*⚑* A or B: Můstek: follow Jindřišské to the end of the street. *i* Elevator access to all but the last 14 steps. *Ⓢ* Adult 80Kč. Student 55Kč. *Ⓣ* Open M-F 9am-7pm, Sa-Su 10am-7pm.

## ▦ NEW TOWN HALL                                          ◉⊗ TOWN HALL

Karlovo náměstí 1/23, 120 00 Praha 2          ☎22 494 8225▤www.nrpraha.cz

A building whose history far outsexes its architecture, the New Town Hall served as the administrative headquarters of New Town for nearly 400 years. The Hall's foundations were laid by Charles IV, the granddaddy of Czech modernity. In 1419, a bunch of angry Hussites threw the town counselors out the top story windows in the first Defenestration. While the hall has a few furnished parlors open for viewing, the building's real thrill comes in climbing the seemingly endless series of wooden platforms leading to the lookout tower. Besides the amazing views of of Prague, the top platforms hold a giant bell, which was described as being "currently broken." It was later discovered that this meant it had been broken for the past 200 years.

*⚑* B: Karlovo náměstí. Exit the station and find the giant tower at the north end of the park. *Ⓢ* Admission 30Kč. Cash only. *Ⓣ* Open Tu-Su 10am-6pm.

## WENCESLAS SQUARE                          ◈Ġ ⦅•⦆Ψ CITY SQUARE

Originally built by its namesake as a horse market, Václavské náměstí (Wenceslas Square) now sells everything but. American-style commercial department stores and historic hotels compete for attention with the true stars of the walk— the hot dog and sauerkraut vendors selling up to six different types of sausage. In the olden days, butchers would come selling their wares, and that tradition of sausage excellence has held to the present. Up at the top of the boulevard, check out the ▦**National Museum**, which in addition to being one of the more beautiful buildings in Prague—especially at night—also contains some impressive zoological and paleological exhibits, mostly in Czech. Also noteworthy are the displayed medals of former president Václav Havel.

*⚑* A or B: Můstek or Můsem. *Ⓢ* Students 100-150Kč.

## ALFONS MUCHA MUSEUM                              ◈Ġ MUSEUM

Panská 7, 110 00 Praha          ☎22 421 6415 ▤www.mucha.cz

This medium-sized exhibit focuses on Mucha's works, and is a good introduction for those unfamiliar with the Art Nouveau pioneer and all-around Czech hero. The exhibit pays particular attention to Mucha's time in Paris (1887-1904) during which he painted the famous portraits of Sarah Bernhardt that Americans will likely recognize. For the student price, anyone even remotely interested should check it out. Without the student discount, pre-existing appreciation for Mucha is recommended. Don't miss the hilariously over-the-top video about Mucha's construction of the "Slav Epic."

*⚑* A or B: Můstek. Walk up Václavské náměstí toward the St. Wenceslas statue. Go left on Jindřišské and left again on Panská. *Ⓢ* Admission 160Kč. Students and seniors 80Kč. Guide sheet 30Kč. *Ⓣ* Open daily 10am-6pm.

## OUR LADY OF THE SNOW                              Ġ CHURCH

Jungmannovo náměstí 18, 110 00 Praha 1

Kostel Panny Marie Sněžně (Our Lady of the Snow) remains one of the most oddly-shaped churches in Central Europe. When commissioned by Charles IV in 1347, the church was intended to be the largest in Prague, with three naves and 30m tall ceilings. When the Franciscans arrived to repair the building in 1603, damage from the Hussite Wars prevented them from carrying out the original plan, and only one nave remained along with the impressively large ceilings. Check the chapel door for a schedule of services in order to listen in on incredible organ music against the sweet the voices of the regular parishioners. While you listen to the music, let yourself wonder how they painted such intricate stars on the ceiling. Don't go without checking the miniature chapel on the church's right side, and the exhibits from local artists displayed in the abbey.

**sights · nové město**

*A or B: Můstek. From the station, walk up Wenceslas Sq. and then turn left on Jungmannovo náměstí; the entrance to the church is behind the statue. ⏰ Open daily 6am-7:30pm. Su services at 9am, 10:15am, 11:30am and 6:30pm.*

**U FLECKŮ** ♿ 🍸 MUSEUM AND BREWERY

Křemencova 11, 110 00 Praha 1 ☎ 22 49 340 1920 💻www.efleku.eu

Skip the tacky, overpriced restaurant if you can help it, and take a guided walk of the museum or an hour-long tour of the brewery. Both are obnoxiously designed to convince guests how important the U Flecků Brewery actually is, but the over-aggrandized tales and obsession over uninteresting U Flecků details more persuasively argue the opposite. Still, it's worth visiting if you want to see old brewing techniques without trecking out to to the brewery at Pilsen.

*B: Národní trida. From the station, walk south on Spálená, make a right on Myslíkova, and then another right on Opatovická. Follow it as it cuves around. When it hits Křemencova, take the second left. $ Museum tour 100Kč. Brewery tour 160 Kč. Groups of 10 or more get a 30% discount. Credit cards discouraged, and no discounts will apply if used. ⏰ Tours available by reservation only M-F 10am-4pm. Sa and Su tours must be accompanied by a meal at the restaurant. Restaurant open daily 9am-11pm.*

**FRANCISCAN GARDENS** ♿ GARDEN

A beautiful couple of acres of land, this little oasis between Our Lady of the Snow and the bustling St. Wenceslas square offers a serene escape from the howl of the city. Massive strange light-bulb-like street lamps line the walk, but unfortunately the park closes before we can ever see them in their full glory. Street performers grab spaces in the shade. The picturesque cottage in the middle of the roses is actually a second-hand clothing store, but don't let that stop you from appreciating its tranquility.

*A or B: Můstek. Enter through the arch to the left of Jungmannova and Národní, behind the statue. ⏰ Open daily dawn-dusk.*

**UNIVERSITY OF CHARLES BOTANICAL GARDENS** ♿ 🎟 GARDEN

Na Slupi 16, 120 00 Praha 2 💻www.web.natur.cuni.cz/www/en/data/faculty/botanicalgarden.html

Adding greenery to the Charles University campus since 1898, the Charles University Botanical Gardens contain thousands of species of plants in a several acre garden and accompanying green house. The Garden isn't free but some patrons report not being charged admission. Rotating exhibits roll through the greenhouse regularly, but the garden is best enjoyed by just laying out in the sun. Among the plants in the garden is the giant water lily, *Victoria cruziana*, whose beautiful summer flowers last for only a single day.

*B: Karlovo náměstí. From the Metro, follow Vyšehradská south until it becomes Na Slupi. $ Adults 50Kč; students 25Kč. ⏰ Open Feb-Mar 10am-5pm, Apr-Aug 10am-7:30pm, Sept-Oct 10am-6pm, Nov-Jan 10am-4pm. Greenhouses close 1hr. before close.*

**DANCING HOUSE** MONUMENT

Rasinovo Nabrezi 80 120 00 Praha 2

Now approaching its 15th birthday, the Tančící dům (Dancing House) has comfortably become a national icon after being the source of fierce controversy during its inception and construction. Designed by Vlado Milunic and Frank Gehry (of Guggenheim-Bilbao fame), the eight-story office building allegedly resembles an image of Fred Astaire and Ginger Rogers, earning it the early moniker "Fred and Ginger." The building was known as "Drunken House" for years by Czech traditionalists who felt that it had no place amid the neo-Baroque and Art Noveau architecture of the neighborhood. Through the help of supporters like Václav Havel, however, the building has become one of Prague's most recognizable landmarks. While the top floor is occupied by Céleste, one of Prague's top French restaurants *(entrées 450-900Kč)*, budget travelers can visit the upstairs patio M-Sa 4-6pm for the price of a drink *(150-200Kč)*.

*B: Karlovo náměstí. From the station, walk down Resslova toward the river. The building is on your left.*

**EMAUZY** ♿ MONASTERY

Vyšehradská 49/320, Prague 2 ☎221-979-211 💻www.emauzy.cz/en/index.php

Walking through the poorly-maintained cloister of Emauzy is a haunting experience. This cloister, which once served as abode to Jan Hus, the theological martyr and revolutionary, and Johannes Kepler, that dude who explained planetary motion, now sits silent. A train museum for children now occupies part of the old abbey, and the frighteningly empty chapel can be toured for the price of a train admission.

*🚇 B: Karlovo náměstí. From the park, follow the brown signs to the monastery down Vyšehradská. $ 50kč. 🕐 Mass daily 10am. Open M-F 11am-3pm.*

**CHURCH OF SAINT IGNATIUS** CHURCH

Ječná 2, 120 00 Praha 2 ☎221 990 200 💻www.jesuit.cz

This Jesuit church is one of the oldest Baroque buildings in Prague and is the third largest Jesuit complex in all of Europe. Built in the second half of the 17th century, this amazing chapel stands out for its brilliant slabs of green, red and yellow marble. The sculpture work on the altar was done by Matěj Václav Jäckel, who is best known for his work on the statues on the Charles Bridge. The figure of St. Ignatius on the church peak was considered semi-heretical in its day, as clerical rules stated that a full-body halo could only be administered to Christ himself.

*🚇 B: Karlovo náměstí. From the station, head away from the river toward Ječná. The church will be on the corner. 🕐 Open daily 6:15am-5:30pm. Daily mass 5:30pm.*

## STARE MĚSTO

**👍 CHURCH OF OUR LADY BEFORE TÝN** ⊗ CHURCH

Staroměstské náměstí 💻tynska.farnost.cz

Our Lady Before Týn dominates the skyline of Old Town Square with two enormous spires sticking out among the surrounding Baroque buildings. Dating back to the 14th century, the church has seen some bizzare happenings and accumulated some colorful residents in its time. For instance, the church contains the remains of the astronomer **Tycho Brahe**, whose notable achievements include helping to describe planetary motion and peeing himself to death or, more accurately, "unpeeing" himself to death. In 1601, Brahe was at Emperor Rudolf's for dinner, and since it was taboo to leave the table before the Emperor did, Tycho just held it until his bladder burst. But on the bright side, he kept decorum. The church's towers reach a staggering 80m into the air; in traditional Gothic style, one of the spires is just a bit smaller than the other. The church's exterior construction is expected to be finished in 2011.

*🚇 A: Staroměstká. Just walk towards the giant twin towers. $ Free. 🕐 Open Tu-Sa 10am-1pm, 3pm-5pm. Su Mass 9:30am and 9pm.*

**👍 CHARLES BRIDGE** ♿ BRIDGE

Probably the most famous site in all of Prague, the Charles Bridge is also the bridge Mr. Phelps falls from in the brilliant movie with mediocre sequels, *Mission Impossible*. Charles IV commissioned the bridge to cross the Vltava River in 1357—if you haven't figured it out already, Charles IV is responsible for everything cool in Prague—but the actual design and construction of the crossing was done by the famous architect Peter Parléř. Although the bridge was originally decorated only by a crucifix, the church commissioned 32 statutes for the bridge between 1600 and 1800, featuring shady characters like St. Augustine, St. Anne, and Lamenting Christ. Weather damage forced the city to remove the original statues, which are now on display at the National Gallery. The bridge also features the Old Town Bridge Tower *(Staroměstská mostecká věž)*, which offers an Ethan Hunt's eye view of the city below. Cross the bridge after sundown for an especially titillating experience.

*🚇 A: Malonstranská or Staroměstká. $ Tower 70 Kč, students 50 Kč. 🕐 Open daily Nov-Feb 10am-8pm, Mar-Oct 10am-10pm.*

## ASTRONOMICAL CLOCK TOWER AND OLD TOWN HALL     &#x267F;&#x24B8; BELFRY

Old Town Square 1/3   &#x260E;724 911 556 &#x25A0;www.prazskeveze.cz/staromestska-radnice-a-vez.html

Here's a free lesson: if you build an amazing clock that tells the position of the sun, the moon, and the planets, people will never stop fabricating legends about it. It's said that after the city council hired the famous clockmaker Mikulas of Kadan to build the clock, they gouged out his eyes so he could never repeat his work (talk about worker's comp issues). In reality, the clock was a collaboration between Kadan and Jan Ondrejuv, a professor of mathematics and astronomy, and Kadan built several clocks after this one. The clock also features another clock that moves once a day and has 365 names on it; Czech tradition "requires" parents to name their children one of said names. The day on which the clock points to your name is your "name day," a kind of bastardized birthday. On the hour, the 12 apostles poke their heads out to the crowd, and a rooster crows. Climb or take the elevator to the top of the tower for amazing views of the city. Also available is a not-that-worth-it tour of the Old Town's halls, highlights of which include the back view of the "apostle clock mechanism" and a walk through the the original romanesque basement. This basement served as the original ground floor before the king raised the level of Old Town by 6m or so.

&#x2720; *A: Staroměstská or A or B: Mustek.* &#x24C8; *Halls 100 Kč, students 80 Kč. Tower 100 Kč, students 50 Kč.* &#x24D8; *Halls open M 11am-6pm, Tu-Su 9-6pm (last tour starts at 5). Towers open M 11am-10pm, Tu-Su 9am-10pm.*

## ST. NICHOLAS'S CHURCH       CHURCH

Parízská Str     &#x260E;224 190 994

St. Nicholas might not be one of the "cool cathedrals" that gets slapped on the cover of every guide book, but the chandelier hanging in its center might be the coolest in the city. Given as a gift to Prague in 1787 by Tsar Nicholas II, this crown is an enormous replica of the royal hat that Russian czars wore. The church contains a succinct but impressive exhibit on the history of the church and of Czech Christianity in general. The church was under the control of Benedictine monks for most of its existence, and a plaque on the former Benedictine monastery attached to the building marks the site where Franz Kafka was born.

&#x2720; *A: Staroměstská. A or B: Mustek. Directly behind the Astronomical Clock Tower.* &#x24C8; *Free.* &#x24D8; *Open M noon-4pm, Tu-Sa 10am-4pm. Su Mass 10:30am, noon, and 3pm.*

## MUNICIPAL HOUSE     &#x24B8;&#x267F;&#x270F; GOVERNMENT BUILDING, CONCERT HALL

Naměstí Republiky 5     &#x260E;222 002 101 &#x25A0;www.obecnidum.cz

It might feel a little uncomfortable to get really excited about a state house and a concert hall, but if you visit the Municipal House, this is what will happen to you. Just go with it. Designed in 1911 by Antonin Balšánek and Osvald Polívka in classic Art Nouveau style, this publicly-commissioned state house features specifically-comissionend works from over 20 of the country's top artists. Every detail, from the shape of the door handles to the doors themselves to the patterns on the banisters, are the careful work of some art Noveau master. Daily guided tours take visitors through Smetana Hall, where the Czech Philharmonic plays, and the Mayor's Hall, decorated by the Czech painter, Alfons Mucha. For a trip to the past, stop by Kavárna Obecní Dům located on the ground floor. This incredible Art Noveau cafe features an oh-so-classic fountain by Josef Pekárek and eight enormous chandeliers hanging overhead.

&#x2720; *B: Naměstí Republiky. Walk across the square; Municipal House is the gigantic building on your left.* &#x2139; *Tours in Czech and English. Tickets must be purchased on the day of your visit in the ticket office located in the basement of the Municipal House.* &#x24C8; *270Kč, students 220Kč.* &#x24D8; *Open daily 10am-7pm. Tour times vary by week and month; check the calendar for details.*

## THE BLACK MADONNA HOUSE/KUBISTA MUSEUM  ♨⊗❄  MUSEUM

Ovocný trh 19 ☎222 321 459 ▣www.ngprague.cz

The Black Madonna House is the best living example of Cubist architecture—a uniquely Bohemian trend that tried to extract the rules of Cubism into the third dimension. Designed by Gočar, one of 3D Cubism's godfathers, the building now contains a gallery and permanent exhibit analyzing this Bohemian movement. While the exhibit's paintings deliver the whacked-out perspective we expect from cubist masters, what's more bizarre is the Cubist furniture. Chairs, cabinets, and armoires out of an M.C. Escher painting will make you lament that this genuinely awesome movement never became mainstream. Finally, check out the fully-restored "Cubist Cafe" located on the second floor of the building, and if you've got a rich uncle, check out the Kubista Museum store downstairs to pick up some replicas of Cubist jewelry and furniture.

⚑ B: Náměstí Republiky. Walk south through Náměstí Republiky and through Powder Gate, then continue west down Celetná, the museum is right at the fork in the road. Ⓢ 100Kč, after 4pm 50Kč. Students 50Kč/30Kč. 1st W of every month free. ☼ Tu-Su 10am-6pm.

## POWDER GATE  ⊗◉  MONUMENT

Na Příkopě ▣www.prazskeveze.cz/prasna-brana.html

Six hundred years ago, Horská brán, or "Mountain Tower," which once stood on this site, actually served a purpose: it protected the city from bad guys and marked the starting point of royal coronation ceremonies. When New Town become a part of the city proper, the tower lost its function and they tore it down to build Powder Gate, an essentially cosmetic and purely symbolic monument. While the tower served as a gundpowder storage center for awhile, now it just kind of chills and lets cars tickle its belly as they drive under it. Climb up to the top for a view of the city and a small rotating exhibition.

⚑ B: Náměstí Republiky. From the Metro, walk south down náměstí Republicky. It's the giant tower in front of you. Ⓢ 70Kč, students 15Kč. ☼ Open daily Mar and Oct 10am-8pm, Nov-Feb 10am-6pm, Apr-Sept 10am-10pm.

## ESTATES THEATER  ♨⊗☕  THEATER

Ovocný trh 1, Praha 1, 110 00 ☎224 228 503 ▣www.estatestheatre.cz

The Estates Theater, the legendary stage were Mozart "premiered" *Don Giovonni* in 1787, now has a haunting statue out front commemorating the event. Just one problem: the opera premiered—and bombed—in Vienna. Prague was the back-up premiere. To make a long story short, Prague loved it and it's one of the greatest operas ever written. The film *Amadeus* features a scene with Mozart directing inside the Estates Theater. Popular ballets, dramas, and operas, including *Don Giovonni*, still play nightly in the Estates, and since the theater offers no public tours, the moderate ticket price is definitely worth the experience.

⚑ A or B: Můstek. From the station, head towards Old Town down Na Můstku and take the second right at Rytířská. The theater and box office will be ahead on your right. Ⓢ Tickets 100-1200 Kč. ☼ Performances at 7pm unless otherwise listed.

## ST. JAMES CATHEDRAL  ⊗  CHURCH

Malá Štupartsá 6, Old Town

According to legend, a thief once tried to steal a necklace from a Virgin Mary statue in Saint James. Well, as you can imagine, the statue came to life, grabbed the thief's arm, and refused to let go. Anyway, he had to cut his arm off and to this day, a mummified arm still hangs in the church. But this church doesn't need legends to be exciting, because you know what else is exciting? Eleven murals painted on the church ceiling, which are seriously cool. In fact, the entirety of the church is intricately decorated. No kidding, it's beautiful. And finally, here's a true story. When Count Vratislav died, he was placed in one of the most beautiful tombs in all of Prague. But for days after he was buried, terrible noises kept coming from the tomb. Finally the noises stopped when the priests sprinkled holy water on the tomb. Years later, the tomb was opened and scratch marks were found on the inside; this is why you always check that someone's dead before burying him. This church is not to be missed.

*➤ From starostka naměstí, take Týnska east, continuing straight through the courtyards as it turns into Týn. The courtyard lets out at Malá Štupartsá where you should take a left. $ Free. ⏰ Open M-Th and Sa-Su 9:30am-noon and 2-4pm; F 9:30am-noon and 2pm-3:30pm. Su Mass 8:30am and 10:30am.*

## JOSEFOV

The sights of Josefov, mostly syngagogues, are all located within close proximity. *(➤ A: Staroměstská. $ Admission to all synagogues except Staronová 300Kč, students 200Kč. Staronová 200/140Kč. Combined tickets 480/320Kč. ⏰ Synagogues open Apr-Oct M-F and Su 9am-6pm; Nov-Mar M-F and Su 9am-4:30pm. Closed Jewish holidays.)* While ambling through the Jewish district, take note of the beautiful early 20th-century Art Nouveau architecture. While walking down Široká street—"Wide Street" in Czech—take a moment to realize the sheer gravity of the ghetto.

### 👍 OLD JEWISH CEMETERY (STARÝ ŽIDOVSKÝ HŘBITOV)
📷♿ CEMETERY

U starého hřbitova 243/3a ☎222 317 191

The Old Jewish Cemetery stretches between the Pinkas Synagogue and the Ceremonial Hall. A winding path snakes through the uneven mounds covered with eroded and broken tombstones jutting out of the ground at unexpected angles. Between the 14th and 18th centuries, the graves were dug in layers, and over time the earth settled so that the stones from the lower layers were pushed to the surface, forcing many of the newer stones out of position and creating an indistinguishable mass of graves. Rabbi Loew is buried by the wall opposite the entrance.

*➤ To the right of Pinkasova Synagogue. $ Camera fee 40Kč.*

### 👍 SPANISH SYNAGOGUE (ŠPANĚLSKÁ SYNAGOGA)
🎟♿ SYNAGOGUE

Vězeňská 141/1 ☎221 711 511

The Spanish Synagogue is the most richly decorated of the Josefov synagogues. Built in the Moorish-Byzantine style, the synagogue is covered from floor to ceiling with elaborate geometric patterns in beautiful reds, greens, and golds, and a cupola to top it all. The interior of the synagogue overshadows the exhibit within, which details the history of the Czech Jews from the Jewish Enlightenment to the decades after WWII, and contains an impressive set of silver Torah pointers. The synagogue also hosts classical concerts throughout the year.

*➤ On the corner of Široká and Dušní. $ Concerts about 700Kč.*

### PINKAS SYNAGOGUE (PINKASOVA SYNAGOGA)
🎟♿ SYNAGOGUE

Široká 23/3 ☎221 711 511

At the time of the Nazi takeover, 118,310 Jews lived in the Prague ghetto, many of them refugees from the conquered territories. While a few managed to flee before the terror began, more than 92,000 remained in Prague. Of these remaining Jews, about 80,000 were deported to their deaths at Terezín or other concentration camps. The names of these victims are recorded on the otherwise bare walls of the nearly 500-year-old Pinkas Synagogue. The names were originally added in the 1950s, but under the Communist regime they were whitewashed as part of ongoing efforts to reframe the victims of the Holocaust as anti-fascists. When Václav Havel was elected president in 1989, his first act was to have the names reinscribed onto the synagogue walls. The second floor contains the haunting drawings of children from their time in Terezín.

*➤ Between Žatecká and 17. Listopadu $ Yarmulkes 5Kč.*

### KLAUSEN SYNAGOGUE (KLAUSOVÁ SYNAGOGA)
♿ SYNAGOGUE

U starého hřbitova 243/3a ☎222 317 191

The Klausen Synagogue was originally built in 1573, burned down a while later, rebuilt in 1604, and then reconstructed in the 1880s. The inside is dedicated to the role of the synagogue in Jewish life and exhibits various artifacts. Next door, the Ceremonial Hall, maintained by the Prague Burial Society, showcases an exhibit on disease and death in Judaism.

❀ *Adjacent to the Cemetery.*

## MAISEL SYNAGOGUE (MAISELOVA SYNAGOGA)

⬧ SYNAGOGUE

Maiselova 63/10 ☎221 711 511

Like most old things in Prague, the Maisel Synagogue has been partially destroyed and subsequently rebuilt several times. While originally built in the Renaissance style, the synagogue is now a hodgepodge of Baroque and Gothic elements. It contains artifacts from the history of Jews in Bohemia and Moravia up until the Jewish enlightenment. Some of the more interesting artifacts include the oldest tombstone from the Old Jewish Cemetery, as well as the robes of a 16th-century Jewish martyr who was burned at the stake by the Inquisition.

❀ *Between Široká and Jáchymova.*

## OLD-NEW SYNAGOGUE (STARONOVÁ SYNAGOGA)

⬧ SYNAGOGUE

Červená

The oldest operating synagogue in Europe and one of the earliest Gothic structures in Prague, the relatively small Old-New Synagogue is still the center of Prague's Jewish community. The usual explanation for its oxymoronic name is that it was called the "New" synagogue when it was built in 1270 and took its present name when newer synagogues were built in the 16th century. However, a rumor persists that the synagogue was built with stones from the Temple in Jerusalem and that the name "Old-New" (*Alt-Neu*) is a mistranslation of the Hebrew "Al-Tnai," meaning "on condition"; the stones would be returned when the Temple in Jerusalem was rebuilt. Inside are the remains of a flag flown by the congregation in 1357, when Charles IV first allowed the Jews to fly their own city flag.

❀ *At the corner of Široká and Žatecká.* ℹ *Men must cover their heads. Yarmulkes free.* Ⓞ *Open May-Aug M-F and Su 9:30am-6pm. Services F and Sa at 8pm reserved for practicing members of the Jewish community.*

## STATUE OF FRANZ KAFKA

STATUE

Dušní

The statue of Franz Kafka stands astride an enormous figure that appears to be nothing more than a suit of clothes, as depicted in his story, "Description of a Struggle." At about 12 ft. tall, the statue is nowhere near the height of many of the city's other notable statues (perhaps fittingly so for this short-story writer), but has earned the attention of tourists and locals alike.

❀ *At the corner of Žatecká, between the Spanish Synagogue and the Catholic church.*

## JEWISH TOWN HALL

TOWN HALL

Židovská radnice, Maiselova 18

Though closed to the public, the Jewish Town Hall is notable, if not for its standard Renaissance architecture, then for its clock tower. The top clock displays the time in standard Roman numerals, while the lower face is marked with Hebrew numerals and ticks counter-clockwise, according to Hebrew convention.

❀ *Adjacent to the Old-New Synagogue.*

# MALÁ STRANA

## ▨ CHURCH OF SAINT NICHOLAS

⊕ CHURCH

Malostranské náměstí 272/1 ☎257 534 215

If you've spent any time in Europe by now, you've likely seen a church or two, or 50. But this ain't no ordinary house of the Lord. Boldly colored celestial scenes play out on an enormous fresco that spans the entire length of the towering ceilings, and floating above it all, like a magical cherry on a holy sundae (see what we did there?), sits the behemoth, effortless dome. Built by a father-son team in the 17th century, St. Nicholas is considered to be the most beautiful example of high Baroque architecture in central Europe, and was influential in defining the style throughout the continent. Music fans can stay after hours for a concert on an organ that Mozart played.

*A: Malostranská. Follow Letenská to Malostranské náměstí. i Concerts held daily at 6pm. $ 70Kč, students 30Kč. ⏰ Open daily Apr-Oct 9am-4:45pm, Nov-Mar 9am-3:45pm.*

### PETŘÍNSKÁ ROZHLEDNA — LOOKOUT TOWER

Petřín Hill

If the Petřín lookout tower seems like a shameless knockoff of the Eiffel Tower, it's because it is. The Eiffel Tower debuted at the 1889 World's Fair, and this shorter, fatter cousin popped up two years later at the Czech Jubilee Exposition. So what if it's only 60m tall; it's built at the peak of **Petřín Hill,** and from the lookout 299 steps up, you can see a 360-degree panorama of the entire Czech countryside. If you're a lazier breed, take the lift *(50Kč),* big enough for one fat man or five uncomfortable skinny men. The basement has an impressively blasé exhibit on the tower's history.

*It's the giant tower on the hill visible from anywhere in the city. Just walk towards it. $ 100Kč, students 50Kč. ⏰ Open daily 10am-10pm.*

### THE TOP OF PETŘÍN — 🍸 GARDEN, OBSERVATORY, MAZE

Petřín Hill

The hilltop has a number of sites worth briefly checking out, like the medieval **Hunger Wall,** Charles IV's purposeless welfare project to provide jobs to Prague's starving citizens. For a somewhat more purposeful, or at least aethestic, sight, go see the gardens with hundreds of varieties of roses; Czech lovers like to take up residence on benches there and remind the world how much they love each other. If canoodling Czechs don't do it for you, retreat to the observatory, where guides will help you view sunspots on a clear day, and creep on tourists on the ground when it's shady. There's also an underwhelming mirror labyrinth from the 1891 Jubile Exposition. The maze boasts a mural of the 30 Years' War in the middle of a mirror labyrinth. Go ahead, check it out, since you've already walked all the way up the mountain. When you get back down, see the **Memorial to the Victims of Communism,** a haunting monument near the funicular station that will give you the heebie jeebies at night.

*A: Malostranská. Walk southwest towards the hill. If you don't want to take the semi-strenuous 30min. mini-hike to the top of Petřín Hill, take the funicular, which leaves from a station in the middle of Malá Strana at Újezd and U tanové drahá. The alpine tram runs daily from 9am-11:30pm, accepts normal 26 Metro tickets, and takes 10min. of your time. $ Observatory 55Kč, students 40Kč. Mirror labriynth 70/50Kč. ⏰ Observatory open Nov-Feb Tu-F 6-8pm, Sa-Su 11am-8pm; Apr-Aug Tu-F 2-7pm abd 9-11pm, Sa-Su 11am-7pm and 9pm-11pm; Mar and Oct Tu-F 9-11pm, Sa-Su 11am-6pm and 8pm-10pm. Mirror labyrinth open daily 10am-9:30pm.*

### STRAHOV MONASTERY — 🍸 MONASTERY

Strahovské nádvoří 1 ☎233 107 711 www.strahovskyklaster.cz

This 17th-century monastic compound confuses as much as it entertains; just enjoy the beauty and question the craziness later. The compound's principal attraction, the monastic libraries, have some of the most beautiful interiors in Prague: gilded bookshelves flow endlessly under a fresco depicting the story of human progress, while the floor brims with relics like globes that lack Australia or models of an Earth-centered universe. The library's "Hall of Wonders" has everything from a dried whale penis to an eighth century Bible to a set of 68 "tree box/books," bound in a species' bark and filled with its leaves, fruits or cones. Oh, yeah—and a narwal horn, a 12th century spear, and buckets of very ordinary sea shells. Additional non-essentials here include the cloister and attached gallery of 14th-19th century pieces, the church (open only during services), and the cloister's microbrewery *(☎233 353 155 💻www.klasterni-pivovar.cz).*

*🚶 From Petřín Hill, take the paved asphalt road that leads away from the funicular station. Follow it along the left side of the Hunger Wall for about 10min. **i** A free guided tour can be arranged by calling ahead (☎233 107 749). $ Monastery admission free. Library 80Kč, students 50Kč. Cloister 30/15Kč. Gallery 30/15Kč. ⏰ Monastery open 10am-9:30pm. Library open daily 9am noon and 1-5pm. Cloister and gallery open daily 9am-noon and 12:30pm-5pm. Microbrewery open daily 10am-10pm.*

### OUR LADY VICTORIOUS
🚫 CHURCH

Karmelitská 382/14 ☎257 537 345

This place might be small potatoes next to St. Nicholas down the street, but for the faithful, it's a must-see. The church houses a wax Christ figurine that's supposed to have protected the city during the 30 Years' War and now posseses healing powers. A museum in the back shows off the more than 80 outfits of this figurine. The church also deserves some attention in its own right, as the oldest Baroque church in Prague, dating back to 1613.

*🚶 Follow Letecká through Malostranské náměstí and continue onto Karmelitská. $ Free. ⏰ Open daily 8:30am-7pm. Su Mass (in English) noon.*

### WALLENSTEIN CASTLE AND GARDENS
🚫 CASTLE

Valdštejnské náměstí 17/4 ☎257 075 707 💻www.senat.cz

Originally built from 1623-1626 as a castle for nobleman Albrecht Wallenstein, this immaculate and detail-rich compound now serves as the seat of the Czech Senate. Keep your eyes peeled for live peacocks wandering between the hedge rows and reflecting pools. And don't worry, that albino peacock isn't possessed by Satan, he was just born that way. Some sad-looking owls fill out the aviary next to the "stalagtite wall" with a disorienting concrete array affecting the interior of a cavern. If the statues of Hercules killing all manner of mythical beasts don't impress you, come back on the weekends, when tourists can snoop around the castle's interior.

*🚶 A: Malostranská. $ Free. ⏰ Gardens open daily June-Sept 10am-6pm, Oct-May 10am-4:30pm. Interiors open Sa and Su 10am-4:30pm.*

### FRANZ KAFKA MUSEUM
🚫 MUSEUM

Cihelná 2b ☎257 535 507 💻www.kafkamuseum.cz

In an attempt to be as "disillusioning" as Kafka's writing, this museum goes a bit overboard with the shadowy video projections and dramatic lighting effects. Walking through this exhibit feels like riding through Slugworth's evil tunnel from *Willy Wonka and the Chocolate Factory*. Histrionics aside, the facsimiles of Kafka's letters and the images from Kafka's life warrant at least the student admission price. Best thing: Kafka's cartoon drawings of depression and madness, but you could technically also just see these in an anthology in the gift shop.

*🚶 A: Malostranská. Go down Klárov toward the river, turn right on U. Luzické Semináre and left on Cilhená. $160Kč, students 80Kč. ⏰ Open daily 10am-6pm.*

### JOHN LENNON WALL
♿ MURAL

Velkopřevorské náměstí

After John Lennon got shot, someone painted his face here and then everyone went crazy on it. A lot of mumbo jumbo graffiti decorates it now. Don't get your hopes up, it's just a wall. But it's in a garden, and worth a five-minute walk-by.

*🚶 From Charles Bridge, take a left on Lázeňská soon after the bridge ends. Stay on it as it curves around into Velkopřevorské náměstí. $ Free. ⏰ Open as long as walls are open.*

### ST. NICHOLAS TOWER
🚫 TOWER

Malostranská náměstí 556/29 ☎724 323 375 💻www.abl.cz

Not one of Prague's best towers, but a cool vantage point in the middle of Lesser Town, St. Nicholas Tower has something of a sordid history. During Communist rule, the secret police used the belfry to spy on suspicious Czechs and Western diplomats. A mildly interesting exhibit on said spy work now lines the last of the 299 steps that lead 65m up to the tower's peak. At one point, they rang this bell on cloudy days—it was thought that the sound made clouds disappear.

*➔ A: Malostranská. Follow Letenská to Malostranské náměstí. $ 70Kč, with exhibition 100Kč, students 50Kč. ⏰ Open Apr-Sept 10am-10pm, Nov-Feb 10am-6pm, Oct and Mar 10am-8pm.*

# HRADČANY

## Around Prague Castle

### 👍 PRAŽSKÝ HRAD (PRAGUE CASTLE)

☎224 373 368 💻www.hrad.cz

One of the largest castles in the world, Prague Castle has been the seat of the Bohemian government since its construction over a millennium ago. After WWI, Czechoslovakia's first president, Tomáš Masaryk, invited Slovenian architect Josip Plečnik to rebuild his new residence after centuries of Hapsburg neglect. Plečnik not only restored the castle to its former majesty, but also added his own fountains and columns. During WWII, Reinhard Heydrich, the Nazi-appointed governor and notorious "Hangman of Prague," used the castle as his headquarters. An inspiration for *Raiders of the Lost Ark*, Heydrich wore the crown jewels that only rightful Bohemian kings were meant to wear. Though Heydrich's face didn't melt off, he was assassinated less than a year later, as per the film's legend. Arrive on the hour to catch the changing of the guard, complete with fanfare, and stay afterward to take a picture with one of them or try to get them to break their iron stares.

*➔ Tram 22 or 23: Pražský hrad. From the stop, go down U Prašného Mostu past the Royal Gardens and into the Second Courtyard. Alternatively, hike up Nerudova. ℹ Ticket office and info located opposite St. Vitus's Cathedral, inside the castle walls. Long tour covers everything, short tour covers the main rooms. Tickets valid for 2 consecutive days. $ Long Tour 350Kč, students 175Kč. Short Tour 250/125Kč. ⏰ Open daily Apr-Oct 9am-5pm; Nov-Mar 9am-4pm. Castle grounds open daily Apr-Oct 5am-midnight; Nov-Mar daily 9am-midnight. Changing of the guard daily on the hr. 5am-midnight.*



### 👍 KATEDRÁLA SV. VÍTA (SAINT VITUS'S CATHEDRAL) ♿ CHURCH

The centerpiece of the castle complex St. Vitus's Cathedral is an architectural masterpiece, complete with three magnificent towers and more flying buttresses than it knows what to do with (no wonder it took 600 years to complete). The cathedral, not surprisingly, is also the most popular attraction at Prague Castle. During tourist season, expect waits of 20-30min. just to get inside. Once you make it in, though, there's plenty to see. In the main church, precious stones and paintings telling the saint's story line the walls of Saint Wenceslas Chapel (*Svatováclavská kaple*). Don't miss the gorgeous Mucha Window, perhaps the cathedral's most beautiful. For a great view and a healthy hike, climb the 287 steps of the Great South Tower. Many of Prague's most important religious and political figures are buried here. To the right of the altar stands the silver tomb of Saint Jan Nepomuck, of Charles Bridge fame. The Bohemian crown jewels are kept in a room with seven locks, the keys to which are kept in the hands of seven different Czech leaders, both secular and religious.

### STARÝ KRÁLOVSKÝ PALÁC (OLD ROYAL PALACE) ♿ PALACE

The Old Royal Palace, to the right of the cathedral, is one of the few Czech castles where visitors can wander largely unattended—probably because its mostly empty. The lengthy Vladislav Hall is the largest Gothic hall in the Czech Republic; it once hosted coronations and indoor jousting competitions. Upstairs in the Chancellery of Bohemia, a Protestant assembly found two Catholic governors guilty of religious persecution and threw them out the window in the 1618 Second Defenestration of Prague, though without paying for an audio tour you would have no way of knowing this; what little information available is kindly written in Czech.

## ROYAL SUMMER PALACE AND ROYAL GARDENS      ♿ PALACE, GARDENS

The Italian-designed Royal Summer Palace was built in the 16th century to provide entertainment for royals until it fell into the hands of Austrian army, whose stay necessitated extensive rebuilding. Near the entrance, the Singing Fountain uses a vibrating bronze plate to create its rhythmic, enchanting sound, though you have to squat down awkwardly to actually hear it. The surrounding Royal Gardens contain dozens of species of trees and shrubbery, and make for a relaxing stroll at any time of day. The garden is also home to an assortment of birds of prey that a falconer displays daily noon-5pm.

## GOLDEN LANE AND DALIBOR TOWER      ⊗ TOWER

The small dwellings that line crowded Golden Lane once housed the castle's alchemists. At other times it's been home to the castle's artillerymen and artisans. Franz Kafka worked for a time at a workspace at #22, a small blue house marked with a plaque. At the end of the street you'll come to the base of Dalibor Tower, a cannon tower converted into a prison after a fire. Its most famous resident was the knight Dalibor, the subject of the old Czech adage "Necessity taught Dalibor how to play the fiddle" even though the actual fiddle was a torture—not musical—instrument designed to make the knight change his tune. The tower exhibits a variety of torture and execution implements, including cages, racks, stocks, "Spanish boots," and a headsman's axe.

✴ *To the right of the Basilica, follow Jiřská halfway down and take a right on Zlatá ulička, or "Golden Lane."*

## NOVÝ SVĚT      STREET

Meaning "New World," this small street seems to be completely ignored by tourists coming to the castle hill in Hradčany. While not necessarily a sight you can ogle for hours, this little cobblestone side street might just give you some of the most charming—and probably the only people-less—photographs in the district. If for nothing else, it's a nice respite from the hordes of people gazing skyward around the cathedral.

✴ *Head away from the church and keep right for about 400m.*

## Other Sights

## STRAHOVSKÝ KLÁŠTER (STRAHOV MONASTERY)      ⊛♿ MONASTERY

Strahovské nádvoří 1      ☎233 107 711 ▪www.strahovskyklaster.cz

Part pilgrimage site, part library, and part gallery, the Strahov Monastery has had a rough history; it was built in 1120, burned down in 1258, rebuilt, and then plundered in turn by the Hussites, Swedes, and French. Since the fall of communism, things have quieted down. The renowned library contains thousands of volumes of philosophical, astronomical, mathematical, and historical knowledge, though your admission only entitles you to look from behind a barrier. In the anterior chamber, an 18th-century cabinet of curiosities contains the remains of dozens of crustacean species and other sea fauna, including a crocodile, octopus, and hammerhead shark, as well as various shells, ceramics, and Hussite weaponry. Its most-prized artifact, however, is what is left of a ▪**dodo bird.** If you want a great view that you don't have to pay for, walk down the dirt path at the foot of the monastery to a sign that reads "Grand Panorama." The view from the top of the hill gives you a postcard panorama of Prague.

✴ *Tram 22: Pohořelec. From the tram, walk south and make a right on Dlabačov, then take a sharp left onto Strahovské nádvoří.* Ⓢ *Library 80Kč, students 50Kč. Gallery 60/30Kč. Audio tour 90/75Kč.* Ⓞ *Open Tu-Su 9am-noon and 1-5pm. Last entry 15min. before closing.*

## LORETA      ⊛♿ CHAPEL

Loretánské námesti 7      ☎220 516 740 ▪www.loreta.cz

Loreta knows the magic of twos. The Loreta complex consists of two chapels and a two-story, arcaded courtyard. The central Santa Casa contains a statue of the Lady of Loreta, holding what is purported to be a piece of Mary's house at Bethlehem. The site is considered the holiest place in the Czech Republic and is the traditional starting point of pilgrimages from the area. On the second floor, a small treasury contains several jewel-encrusted religious texts and an impressive collection of chalices.

*Tram 22: Pohořelec tram stop. From the tram stop, walk south, turn left on Pohořelec, then left on Loretánské námesti. $ 110Kč, students 90Kč. Open Tu-Su 9am-12:15pm and 1-4:30pm.*

## ŽIŽKOV

### CHURCH OF SAINT PROCOPIUS — ♿ CHURCH

Čajkovského 36 ☎775 609 952

In 1881, Žižkov became a city independent of Prague. Amidst jubilations over their newfound autonomy, the residents of Žižkov realized that they did not have a Catholic place of worship big enough to accommodate the population within the new city's limits. Eight years after Žižkov's independence, Archbishop Cardinal Frantisek Schonborn ceremonially laid the foundation stone, and the neo-Gothic style church was completed five years later. Of note inside is the side altar adorned by a statue of Madonna with Jesus, an artifact protected during the 30 Years' War in a house in Nové Město.

*Trams 5, 9, or 26: Lipanská. Head west 2 blocks on Seifertova. Confession M-W 8:30-11:30am, Th 8:30-11:30m and 1:30-4:30pm.*

### ŽIŽKOV TELEVISION TOWER — TOWER

Mahlerovy sady 1 ☎242 418 778 www.tower.cz

From a distance, the Žižkov TV Tower looks like a Soviet launch missile that never left Earth. Like the Dancing House and other strikingly modern structures in Prague, the tower was initially met with great hostility during its construction in the mid-1980s, in part because some feared that the tower would hurt infants living around the area with its radio transmissions. After more than 20 years, however, people have grown to at least accept, if not totally embrace, its unusual architecture. In 2000, controversial Czech artist David Černý cast nine figures of babies—perhaps in reference to that earlier paranoia—and attached them to the tower, where they have been suspended ever since. The tower hosts an overpriced restaurant and three observation decks, allowing for impressive views of the city minus the hassle of walking up hundreds of stairs.

*A: Jiřího z Poděbrad. From the Metro, cross diagonally through the park and then take Milešovská toward the enormous tower (duh). i Relative level of physical fitness required to reach observation deck. $ 150Kč, students 120Kč. Observation deck open daily 10am-11:30pm.*

### JAN ŽIŽKA STATUE AND VITKOV HILL — ♿ STATUE, HILL

In June 1420, Hussite general Jan Žižka repulsed an attack from King Sigismund of Germany and Hungary on Vítkov Hill, breaking the siege of Prague. The grateful citizens named the area after their savior, and in 1950, an enormous statue by Bohumil Kafka was erected on the hill to commemorate his great leadership. At more than 30 ft. high, the statue remains the largest equestrian statue in the world. Though you can't get very close, the statue is still impressive and worth making the trip uphill. Once there, you can join dogwalkers and picnickers in the surrounding park.

*Tram 5, 9, or 26: Husinecká. From the tram stop, follow Husinecká, then turn left on Jeronýmova and walk up the hill.*

## VINOHRADY

Vinohrady may not contain the most amazing assortment of historical treasures, but its collection of small parks and beautiful grassy squares is unrivaled. **Riegrovy sady** on the northside of Vinohrady is a set of amazing grassy hills with views of the river—the perfect place for an impromptu picnic. And remember, no open-container laws means your picnic can get as fun as it wants to. For a more romantic setting, try the vine-covered **Havlíčkovy sady** on Prague 2's southern end and enjoy a glass from over 100 varieties of wine *(33-550Kč)* at **Vinični Altán,** the wine bar at the top of the park *(Open dawn to dusk.).*

### VYŠEHRAD NATIONAL CULTURAL MONUMENT ⊛&℧ MONUMENT
V Pevnosti 5B ☎241 41 03 48 🖳www.praha-vysehrad.cz

Overlooking the beautiful Vltava River, the Vyšehrad monument plays host to scores of Czech couples getting busy on park benches, though **Princess Libuše** spent her time foreseeing the future glory of Prague. See, back then when you claimed to see crazy things, it made you famous instead of, well, crazy. An English guidebook can be purchased from any of the exhibitions *(35Kč),* a worthy investment to understand the signifcance of an afternoon spent here. Historical highlights include the **Church of Saint Peter and Saint Paul** built by Charles IV in the 14th century and the adjoining graveyard featuring some of the wildest and most provocative headstones you'll ever come across, as well as the remains of **Antonin Dvořak** and **Alfons Mucha.** Check out the Gothic Cellar for an archaeological look at the prehistoric inhabitants of the garrison.

🏵 *C: Vyšehrad.* Ⓢ *Park admission free. Vyšehrad Gallery 20Kč. The Brick Gate 20Kč. Casemate including guide 50Kč. Church of St. Peter and St. Paul 30Kč, students 10Kč.* Ⓩ *Exhibitions open daily Nov-Mar 9:30am-5pm; Apr-Oct 9:30am-6pm. St Peter and St. Paul open Tu-Th 9am-noon and 1-5pm, F 9am-noon.*

# HOLEŠOVICE

### LEVETSKÉ SADY &(ᵗᵖ)℧ PARK
A stroll through this enormous, luscious park with unconquerable views of the Vltava river can brighten your entire day. Meander along its densely forested trails, spectate at its organically-constructed Tony Hawk Skater Pro-style impromptu skate park (unless you're wicked cool and actually join in on the ollies and kick-flips), question the validity of art as you czech out the strange pieces of its sculpture garden, or just get kind of wasted at one of several beer gardens *(shots 30Kč).* In 1955 the Communists built the largest statue of Stalin ever constructed at the top of the park, but it was torn down in 1962. Now a giant Metronome stands in its place because what says reform like a maintained rhythm? The park also has an array of tennis courts and children's playgrounds, as well as a sometimes-functioning carousel, the oldest in Europe. For a snack you'll never forget, stop at the pricey-but-worth-it **Restaurant Hanavský Pavilon** *(Letensky Sady 173, 170 00 Praha 7* ☎*23 332 3641* 🖳*www.anavskypavilon.cz).* Over 100 years ago, this Art Nouveau Jubile Exposition pavilion was moved to its current perfect location overlooking the city below. It boasts the best dining atmosphere of the city.

🏵 *B: Hradčansky. From the station, walk to the other side of the building, and head anywhere in the general south eastern direction—Levetské sady is the enormous park you'll run into.* Ⓩ *Open daily dawn-dusk.*

### PRAGUE EXHIBITION GROUND PARK
Built on the easternmost section of Stromovka for the 1891 Jubilee Exhibition, this park offers some unique wonders of modern Prague. Coolest among them is the **Křižík's Fountain** *(U Výstaviště 1/20, 170 05* ☎*723 665 6941* 🖳*www.krizikovafontana.cz/en),* a Bellagio-style fountain and lights show that during the summer months is accompanied by live ballet, singers, and musicians *(200Kč).* Great for a date; if you're single, the fountain will take your mind off of that—sorry, btw. Other stops include the still-used-but-now-ghostly **Industrial Palace,** whose Art Nouveau exterior provides a phantom glimpse at the industrial "newness" of the past. There are also several beer gardens, skate rental shops, an enormous pyramid-shaped performance hall, and the **Lapidary of the National Musuem,** which holds major statue structures in their collection—including the original statues on the Charles Bridge. Finally, check out **Marold's Panorama,** an impressive circu-

lar mural depicting the Czech Battle of Lipany.

🚇 *C: Nádraží Holešovice. From the station, don't cross the street; instead, take tram 5, 12, or 15 to the next stop, Výstaviště.*

### PRAGUE MARKET — MARKET

Bubenské nábřeží, 170 00 Praha 7 ☎22 080 0592 💻www.holesovickatrznice.cz

A hundred or more street vendors, food peddlers, furniture salesman, and general bargain-gents call Pražská Tržnice (Prague Market), the city's largest market, their home. Sprawled out over an enormous campus of once-abandoned warehouses on the banks of the Vlatava river, flea market junkies, or heck, regular junkies can find hot deals on a variety of mainly manufactured goods. Deals won't walk into your lap, though: bargain hunters need haggling skills in English, Chinese, or Czech. Here's some advice for haggling: decide the honest price at which you value an item before approaching a vendor; then, stick to it. Don't be unreasonable, but don't let yourself get pushed around. Insist on your price, and if you don't get it, no loss. You can still enjoy the haggle-free bargains like ice cream and pastries *(10 Kč)*. Typical merchandise includes clothes, bags, and toys. Check out the smokeless cigarettes, full-sized swords, and the cheapest porno DVDs you'll ever find *(40Kč)*. If you object to pornography, these stands will be the perfect place to try out your jeering skills.

🚇 *C: Vltavská. From the station, walk to the left along the river. Be careful crossing large lanes of traffic. The market is on your left.* 🕒 *Open M-Sa 7am-8pm (prime time 9am-2pm).*

## DEJVICE

### ROUNDABOUT

Having found no decipherable history on this strangely enchanting giant roundabout, we have nothing more to say than, look! The thing is huge and has a colorful garden in the center; it's perhaps the only thing that would draw tourists to Dejvice.

🚇 *A: Dejvická.*

prague

### BRONZE HORSE FOUNTAIN

Between Kafkova and Wuchterlova Streets

Three bronze horses, created by Czech sculptor Michal Gabriel, wade in the waters of the fountain. It's a sight (and bath) for sore eyes on a boiling summer day, and the 24 trees surrounding the fountain will gladly offer shade.

🚇 *A: Dejvická. Keep right after the round about and turn right at Kafkova.*

## SMICHOV

### SANTOŠKA PARK — ♿ PARK

A little park atop a hill overlooking Smichov and parts of downtown Prague. Frequented by locals, many people come here to sunbathe in the summer or read a book and picnic in the grass.

🚇 *Walk up the stairs at the intersection of Radlicka and Za Zenskymi domovy (the street leading away from the bus station). Head left toward the path.*

### STAROPRAMEN BREWERY — 🚭♿🍸 BREWERY

Nadrazni 84 ☎257 191 402

Staropramen is the second largest beer producer in the Czech Republic and this venue alone pumps out half a million bottles per day. The tour guides you through a few of the giant copper vats that process malt and provides information on the brewing process, closing with a tasting of the liquid you've drooled over for the past hour. While it might be worth a trek if you've exhausted your options in Prague, the tour itself is quite small for the price.

🚇 *B: Andel.* ℹ *Tour takes 1hr.* $ *Tour and tasting 120Kč.* 🕒 *Open Tu-Su 11am-5pm.*

## VYŠEHRAD CASTLE

V Pevnosti 159/5b

●※ CASTLE
☎241 410 348

A 10th-century castle overlooking the Vltava river and adorned by beautiful black Gothic spires, at Vyšehrad one can find the Basilica of Saint Peter and Paul and a cemetery containing the remains of several Czech notables. The castle was once a royal home, as well as a training center for the Austrian army after the 30 Years' War. The castle itself is quite beautiful and goes under the radar of most tourists, giving it a serenely untouched feel. Its location high above the city provides a prime angle to capture Prague Castle in the distance.

⚑ C: Vysehrad. Or Tram 7, 8, or 24: Albertov. ⑤ Grounds free. Gallery 20Kč. ☒ Open daily 9:30am-6pm.

# food

If Czech food speaks to you, it will sing to you. Simple, hearty, rich and pork-filled, Czech meals carry weight. Must tries are the fried cheese (both hermelin or eidam), the pork knees, the goulash with dumplings and the schnitzel (think chicken fried steak). Consistent deliciousness, however, comes at the price of variety. Of the thousand or so restaurants in Prague, 800 of them easily share the exact same or nearly the exact same menu, so don't feel bad if you're tempted by the city's mostly-delicious Thai food or it's mostly awful but nevertheless omnipresent Chinese food. The best thing about Prague, however, is the sausages. Whether you're digging a stand at Wenceslas Square or relaxing at a pub along the river, sausages are served slightly charred in chewy rolls with hearty portions of mustard and a mug of beer. Which brings us to beer, achem, water, achem, the only liquid substance most Czech drink. It comes with every meal (even breakfast), it comes in vending machines (seriously) and it usually costs between 15-40Kč. Beer gets more treatment in Nightlife, but it's also key for food matters since half the Czech cuisine only exists for beer. Pickled sausages, pickled cheese, head cheese (brains), deep-fried bread (which is amazing), pickled onions, pickled cabbage and toasts of cheese and ketchup all serve to supplement drinking and usually won't cost more than 30-40Kč.

In fact, most Czech food is disproportionally cheap. Many restaurants will have a daily lunch menu which offers a lunch with soup (usually a simple garlic, noodle and beef soup) and some entree for 80-110Kč, but be warned, the menus are usually Czech only, and you'll have to ask to see them. The Czech eat small breakfasts, usually just some cheese and hearty bread, but the abundance of tourists has made English and American breakfasts a standard option. Dinner with a mug of beer should come in at below 200Kč, though some items, steaks, pork knees, though available at these prices in some locations, will generally cost you more.

A note about cafes. Hundreds of locations across Prague describe themselves as Cafe Bars. These small-to-large establishments serve both extensive coffee options (including a favorite, Czech rum with coffee) as well as a full bar and usually a small food menu of beer pairings.

Finally, a note about service and customs. When you enter a Czech restaurant, you are expected to seat yourself, and can even do so at a table already containing other guests. Although Czech service has a bad reputation, things have improved greatly as of late. Bread, pretzels or peanuts at the table are not free, and if you don't want them, don't touch them. Tipping is standard at 10%.

## NOVÉ MĚSTO

▧ **PIVOVARSKÝ DŮM**

Jecná 15, 120 00 Praha 2

●※※ CZECH ❷
☎29 621 6666 ▤www.gastroinfo.cz/pivodum

Packed with Czech locals and a few wandering randos, this stellar microbrewery does Prague's beer proud. Start off with an 8-beer sampler that includes flavors like coffee, sour cherry, nettle, and banana *(130Kč)*. But make sure you finish it—you'll need the liquid courage to tackle the football-sized roast pork knuckle with mustard and horseradish *(205Kč)*, or the Brewmaster's Pocket *(205Kč)*—deep fried pork stuffed with cheese and more pork. If beer isn't your thing, you should probably leave Prague, but for now, try settling for some red or white wine served hot *(50Kc)*. If pork isn't your thing, fear not: vegetarian choices abound.

*B: Karlovo náměstí. From the station, take Ječná east away from the river; it's on your right at the corner of Ječná and Stěpánská.* $ *Entrees 140-300Kč. Beer 25-80Kč.* ⏰ *Open daily 11am-11pm.*

## spread 'em

Spread your cheeses.

Prague-side, the story is sweeter and softer, unlike what we're used to: cheese that rhymes with macho made from 1 part milk and 3 parts industrial plastic. For starters, Praguers spread soft cheese on rolls or toasted bread, not just corn tortilla chips; what's more, soft cheese can comprise a meal in its own right, or be a featured component of a successful larger meal.

Soft, spreadable cheese usually comes as a wheel or as individually-wrapped wedges. If you're thinking, "I've SEEN cheese like this," it's because fortunately, one brand of spreadable cheese has found its way to the colonies. Copyright disputes prevent me from naming the brand, but the image of a "chuckling bovine" may come to mind.

But any Praguer would laugh at the idea that this brand could cover the spectrum of soft cheese. Praguers spread the love by adding flavors to the basic creamy base. *Se žampiony* adds mushrooms to the mix, *se šunko* ups the stakes with ham, and other styles add herbs, spices and just about anything else your heart can dream up.



### GLOBE BOOKSTORE — AMERICAN [1]

Pštrossova 1925/6, 110 00 Praha 1-Nové Město ☎22 252 0236 www.globebookstore.cz

Americans craving the type of culture that doesn't involve the Czech obsession with pasteurization will find a friend in the Globe. Great American fare like chicken wings *(5Kč)* during happy hour *(M-W 5-7pm)* and one of the best burgers you'll have this side of the pond *(180Kč)* both go well with excellent refillable drip coffee *(40Kč)*, a rarity in Prague. Don't miss brunch *(Sa-Su 9:30am-3pm)* with brilliantly Western dishes like scrambled chorizo *(180Kč)*. The cafe and attached bookstore host ex-pat book readings, movie screenings, or some kind of event most nights of the week. The bookstore itself has the largest collection of English books in the city.

*B: Karlovo náměstí. From the station, take Resslova toward the river and then turn right on Na Zderaze, which becomes Pštrossova; the cafe is on your right.* **i** *Make reservations if you have a big party. Three computers have Internet access for 1Kč per min.* $ *Entrees 100-250Kč. Beer 20-35Kč. Coffee 25-50Kč.* ⏰ *Open M-Th 9:30am-midnight, F-Sa 9:30am-1am (or later). Attached bookstore keeps the same hours.*

### PIZZERIA KMOTRA — AMERICAN [1]

V Jirchářích 12, Praha 1 ☎224 930 100 www.kmotra.cz

Tucked downstairs in a little Czech basement, Kmotra's puts most American pizzerias to shame at a quarter of the price. Just one of their 36 pizzas *(110-170Kc)* will fill up two people, but main dishes like gnocchi *(125-145Kč)* or entree salalds *(125-145 Kč)* will appease the pizza skeptic. Try the popular Don Corleone—it's literally soaking in pork fat—or get wild with the Spenatora II, which is cooked with spinach, bacon, and a cracked egg that fries as the pizza bakes. This is serious pizza.

*B: Národní třída. From the Metro, head down Ostrovni towards the river. After 2 blocks, take a left at Vorsilska. $ Entrees 100-200Kč. Open daily 11am-midnight.*

**RESTAURACE U ZALUDO** CZECH 1

Na Zbořenci 261/5, Praha 2, ☎77 632 7118

Don't look for this place in other guidebooks or at the top of any "Best of Prague" lists. Instead, U Zaludo is the tiniest, salt-of-the-earthiest, most authentic Prague pub experience the city has to offer. This recommendation however comes with a warning: some customers have reported that no one would speak English to them or even present them with a menu. Fear not: simply learn the Czech for a few common food items: fried cheese, *smažený sýr (40Kč)*, smoked pork, *uzená krkovice (55 Kč)*, beer cheese, *pivní sýr (40Kč)*, and grilled sausage, *opečená klobása(40 Kč)*. This will be the cheapest meal you have in Prague, or **Let's Go** will eat its hat. And if no one stops to serve you, at least watch old Praguers come in at noon, down five beers and a shot, then return to work. Worth the experience, even if you chicken out.

*B: Karlovo náměstí. From the station, head towards the Resslova. Take the first right, then another immediate right at Na Zbořenci. i Cash only. $ Beer 10-30Kč. Food 40-80Kč. Open M-F 10:30am-11pm, Sa-Su 11am-11pm.*

**LIBEŘSKÉ LAHŮDKY** BAKERY 1

Vodičkova 9, Praha 1 ☎22 254 0828 www.liberskelahudky.cz

Technically this place is a Czech chain store, with 3 other locations in the Prague area, but given the home-cooked love that goes into its food, you'd never know the difference. Mouth-watering pastries for pennies *(10-23Kč)* will take you to pleasure town. For a light snack, check out one of many *chlebiceks (16-19Kč)*. These open-faced sandwiches feature some assortment of caviar, salmon, pickles, tomatoes, eggs, ham, lettuce, or turkey. One croquette isn't completely filling, but two might do the trick—affordable at roughly 80 American cents a pop. Don't escape without rescuing the twice-stuffed donut from drowning in its glaze *(19.50Kč)*.

*B: Karlovo náměstí. From the station, head north past the New Town Hall staying to the right on Vodičkova when it forks; the restaurant will be on your right. i Takeout only. $ Everything 10-40Kč. Open M-F 7am-7pm, Sa-Su 8am-6pm.*

**LEICA GALLERY PRAGUE** CAFE 1

Školská 28, 110 00 Praha 1 ☎60 228 7820 www.lgp.cz

More Brooklyn than beer-soaked Prague, this little cafe/gallery is better enjoyed for its exhibitions and sleek mod interior than for its food. Coffees are on the pricer side *(39-60Kč)*, but they include a free entrance to the monthly-rotating exhibits, which are suprisingly large and elaborate. A must for arsty travelers looking to meet like-minded locals. Bond over your similar opinions on deconstruction while enjoying a Kafka sandwich (all of the sandwiches are named after Czech authors). At the very least, browse the immense collection of nude photography books. Don't worry, you're appreciating art.

*B: Karlovo náměstí. From Karlovo, head away from the river down Žitná. Školská is the second left. $ Sandwiches 65-99Kč. Hot drinks 40-90Kč. Open daily 2:30-10pm.*

**UNIVERSAL** INTERNATIONAL 3

V jirchářích 149/6, 110 00 Praha 1 ☎22 491 8182 www.universalrestaurant.cz

Despite being burdened with a menu that tries too hard to live up to its name, Universal manages to deliver a solid variety of cuisines. While pondering the giant elephant head on the wall, order a Chinese fondue for two *(219Kč per person)* or a French grilled tuna steak with ratatouille *(279Kč)*. Hodge-podge, international decorations make the place look like a high class Applebees, but the great espresso *(38Kč)*

and desserts *(12-min. chocolate mellow cake; 65Kč)* genuinely class up the experience.
*🚇 B: Národní třída. From the station, walk south on Spálená turning right towards the the river down Purkyňova and continuing down as it turns into Ostrovní. Take a left on Voršilská then a quick right onto V jirchářích. $ Entrees 175-299Kč. Mixed drinks 105-145Kč. Carafe of wine 100Kč. ⏰ Open M-Sa 11:30am-1am, Su 11am-midnight.*

**DYNAMO** 💳♿📶🍸 AMERICAN FUSION ❶

Pštrossova 220/29 Praha 1 ☎224 932 020 💻www.dynamorestaurace.cz

With a 50s retro interior and an international menu, Dynamo is among the hipper joints in New Town. Fortunately, it doesn't take itself too seriously, offering quirky international flavors like Burgundy snails *(125Kč)* next to trashy American favorites like cheese-stuffed jalapenos *(75Kč)*. Dynamo also boasts great drinks; its homemade lemonade *(40Kč)* comes in ginger or mint. Entrees, including great vegetarian options, err on the exotic side: there's grilled boned rabbit saddle with cream sauce *(210Kč)* or Red and Black—a grilled chicken steak with olive puree and spicy tomato salsa *(150 Kč)*.
*🚇 B: Národní třída. From the station, walk down Osrovní toward the river and then turn left on Pštrossova; Dynamo is on the right. $ Main dishes 100-150Kč. Salads 50-150Kč. ⏰ Open M-F 11:30am-midnight, Sa-Su 11am-midnight.*

**CAFÉ ROYAL** 🚭♿🍸☀ CAFE ❶

Myslíkově 1343/24 ☎22 491 3037 💻www.lunchtime.cz/royal-cafe/

Though Café Royal has a full English menu, the real deals here are the lunch specials *(84-89Kč)*. There's just the little problem of the Czech-only specials menu, but just ask the waitress to translate. Three different specials are offered daily, and the menus change every week. In fact, Café Royal keeps its menu so fresh that more than a few patrons report eating there nearly every business day of the week. For regulars, traditional "Beef Tea" soup arrives before you even order *(25Kč)*. Czech staples like fried cheese are also unbelieveably cheap *(69Kč)*, and traditional entrees still drive a hard bargain *(99-130Kč)*. Add apple strudel and coffee *(55Kč)* to any lunch special.
*🚇 B: Karlovo náměstí. From Karlovo take Odborů until it runs into Myslíkově. The cafe will be on your right. $ Entrees 90-175Kč. ⏰ Open M-F 11am-midnight, Sa-Su noon-midnight.*

**LEMON LEAF** 💳♿📶🍸❄ THAI ❷

Myslíkově 14 Praha 2 ☎22 491 9656 💻www.lemon.cz

Besides having great Thai food at reasonable prices *(lunch specials 99-129Kč)*, Lemon Leaf has one of the best happy hours in the city with discounts of 25% on meals *(M-F 3:30-6pm)*. Plenty of tastes reward the daring eater, like cream of artichoke heart soup with saffron and edible flowers *(49Kč)*, but traditional Thai staples are also well executed. Lemon Leaf is at its strongest when Czech and Thai forces work together, as in the milked corn soup with fresh horseradish *(49Kč)*.The weekend lunch buffet is suprisingly elaborate *(240Kč)*, as are the Thai murals and sculptures around the dining room.
*🚇 B: Karlovo náměstí. From Karlovo, take Rasslova toward the river and then make a right on Na Zderaze. Although the address says Myslíkově, the entrance is on Na Zderaze. $ Curry 149-169Kč. Noodle dishes 150-200Kč. Wine 240-800Kč. ⏰ M-Th 11am-11pm, F-Sa 11am-12:30am, Su 12:30pm-11pm.*

**CAFÉ AND RESTAURANT SLAVIA** 💳📶🍸 CAFE ❷

Smetanovo nábřeží 2, Prague 1 ☎22 421 8493 💻www.cafeslavia.cz

Café Slavia's food, which is deserving of its reputation, is only one reason to visit this historic Czech café. During communist rule, this bustling cafe was home base for political dissidents like Václav Havel, and, thanks to a recent renovation, you can now experience it as they did in its full 1930s Art Deco glory. The menu, though somewhat pricey, sets Czech standards like beef fillet with cream sauce *(189Kč)* against more revolutionary fare, like the asparagus-only menu *(70-190Kč)*. Or, skip the meal entirely and join well-dressed pre-theater Praguers for a pre-show "ice cup" *(109Kč)*. The Hot Love cup features vanilla ice cream, warm raspberries and mint.

☞ B: Národní třída. *From the station, walk north on Spálená and then turn left on Národní. The restaurant is at the end of the street, across from the National Theater.* ⑤ *Entrees 89-300Kč.* ☒ *M-F 8am-midnight, Sa-Su 9am midnight.*

## CAFÉ LOUVRE
♥✌ CAFE ❷

Národní 116/20 110 00 Praha 1      ☎22 493 0949 ▣www.cafelouvre.cz

A smart Parisian bistro with the most attractive waitstaff in town—maybe the world—Café Louvre brings welcome French snootiness to the Czech kitchen. Famous for serving minds like Einstein, Kafka, and Czech writer Karel Čapek, Louvre is a great stop for late breakfast with French favorites like quiche *(129Kč)*, an omelette *(109Kč)* or pea cream soup with mint potato and bacon *(60Kč)*. Vegetarian options like the tortilla with curry *(129Kč)* are also available. All go great with Café Louvre's excellent coffee. Check out the view of busy Národní from the café's second floor terrace and enjoy Czech specialites like *Mrkvový Jablk-* —a carrot salad with apples *(49Kč)*. The back of the cafe also has a smoky billiard room, open during restaurant hours.

☞ B: Národní třída. *From the station, walk north on Spálená and then turn left on Národní.* ⑤ *Entrees 100-200Kč. Coffee 40Kč.* ☒ *Open M-F 8am-11:30pm, Sa-Su 9am-11:30pm.*

## ZVONICE
♥♿❀ ROMANTIC ❺

Jindřišská věž 110 00 Praha 1      ☎22 422 0009 ▣www.restaurantzvonice.cz

Visitors to this intimate dining spot located on the seventh and eighth floors of the historic Saint Henry's Tower will literally have to compete with tower scaffolding for dining space, but the experience is truly one of a kind. Feel the building shake as the bells in the belfry chime every half hour. Definitely a splurge; a coke will cost you what an entire meal might elsewhere *(99Kč)*, but remember that it's paired with an unbeatable setting. Fancy, exotic main dishes like grilled deer medallions with sour cherry sauce *(730Kč)* or wild boar with coriander and potatoes *(790Kč)* ensure you won't soon forget your meal. There's technically no dress code, but you'll feel rather out of place without a tie, or at least a sweet hat!

☞ *From Wenceslas Square, walk down Jindřišská. It's the giant tower at the end of the street.* ℹ *Reservations recommended.* ⑤ *Expect to pay 1000 Kč for the full dinner experience.* ☒ *Open 11:30am-midnight.*

## RESTAURACE U JINDŘIŠSKÁ VĚŽE
♥♿ CZECH ❷

Jindřišská 26, 110 00 Praha      ☎22 423 0226 ▣u-veze.cz

Maybe the most accessible traditional Prague experience in the city, this old-world pub has decorated with dozens of antique clocks and Alfons Mucha paintings. Filled with smoke and boisterous Praguers having debates and drinking, Věže is the perfect place to try the strange Prague specialites you've been avoiding. Pig brains *(called head cheese; 53Kč)* and sausage come pickled with onions and vinegar *(53Kč)*. Main courses, like steak loaded with garlic and bacon, can only be described as "solid." If you're brave enough, try out the Kettle of Strong Mettle, made from chicken chili, onions, leaks, and mushrooms.

☞ A or B: Můstek. *From the station, head down Jindřišská street towards the tower. The restaurant will be on the right before you reach the tower.* ⑤ *Entrees 100-200Kč.* ☒ *M-F 10am-11pm, Sa-Su 11am-11pm.*

## CAFÉ RYBKA
▣⊗(ᵖ) CAFE ❶

Opatovická 7, 110 00 Praha 1      ☎22 493 1265 ▣rybkapub.cz

Antique typewriters hang on book-lined walls in this smoky cafe where cheap beer, espresso, and cigarettes flow freely. You'll have to fight Czech hipsters enjoying toasts with toppings like ham and cheese *(25Kč)* or pickled Camembert *(45Kč)* for table space. Things can get pretty rowdy at this wee cafe, so don't come here expecting peaceful reading space.

*🚇 B: Národní třída. From the station, walk south on Spálená, turning right towards the the river down Purkyňova, and continuing down as it turns into Ostrovní. Take a left at Opatovická and follow it around the curve (it remains Opatovická). $ Coffee 28-40Kč. Beer 20-35Kč. Food 20-60Kč. ⏰ Open daily 9:15am-10:15pm.*

### POD KŘÍDLEM NOCI
💳♿❄ CZECH ❶

Národní 10, 110 00 Praha 1 ☎22 495 1741 💻www.podkridlemnoci.cz

Dine under enormous portraits of rich people having a good time at a joint straight out of a 1970s space movie. Main courses like chicken schnitzel with cucumber salad *(129Kč)* are Czech with a modern spin, though that mostly just means fancier plates and smaller portions. Lunch specials like Hungarian goulash or chicken lasagna are well-priced *(90Kč)*, but you'll have to ask for a translation. Find an excuse to go to the bathroom, like having to go to the bathroom, for the full futuristic experience, or just get a drink from their hanging bar, suspended over the restaurant with a mess of wire. Desserts are incredible here, like chocolate cake with apricot puree *(59Kč)*.

*🚇 B: Národní třída. From the station, walk north on Spálená and then turn left on Národní towards the river. Take the third left, Voršilská, and the restaurant will be on your left (despite its Národní street address). $ Entrees 129-245Kč. ⏰ M-W 11am-4pm, Th-F 11am-11pm.*

### RESTAURACE U ZPĚVÁČKŮ
💳♿🍸☀ CZECH-ITALIAN ❷

Na struze 1740/7, 110 00 Praha 1 ☎22 493 0493 💻www.restauraceuzpevacku.com

Imagine a fried mozerella stick armed with the strength of 20 mozzarella sticks. That would almost be as good as this Czech-Itallian cookery's fried cheese *(62Kč)*, which is probably the best in Nové Město. In addition to serving beer in liters *(50-62Kč)*, this eatery earns points with more than 20 types of hearty, no-frills pasta *(90-135Kč)*. Also has all the Czech favorites, even grub like Pork Grimm *(164Kč)* made with baked apples and raisins, or the spicier Chili Goulash served with Italian pepperoni. Top it off with some Italian wine in their well-lit spacious dining room.

*🚇 B: Národní třída. Head towards the river down Purkyňova, continuing as it turns into Ostrovní. Turn left onto Pštrossova then take the first slight right. The restaurant will be on your right. $ Entrees 80-250Kč. Beer 19-62Kč. ⏰ Open daily 8am-2pm.*



### U MATĚJÍČKŮ
♿🍸❄☀ CZECH ❷

Náplavni 5, 120 00 Praha 2 ☎22 491 7136

U Matějíčků does solid Czech favorites very right. Start off with the comically enormous "Big Board full of Goodies" *(229Kč)*, which is an all-star sampling of Czech beer pairings: spicy sausage, smoked pork neck, Hermelin and Edam cheeses, *Olomoucke Tvaruzky*, hot peppers and pickled onions. Enjoy main dishes *(90-229Kč)*, like old bohemian roast duck or Czech cheese wrapped in English bacon and fried in beer dough, in the dining room decorated to look like the Czech countryside. For the truly brave, try their homemade "Devils' sauce" *(20Kč)* and wash it down with some dirt cheap wine *(18Kč)*.

*🚇 B: Karlovo náměstí. From the station, head towards the Resslova. Take 2nd right (Dittrichova) and the restaurant will be on your left at the fork. $ Entrees 90-229Kč. Beer 34-40Kč. ⏰ Open daily 11am-10pm.*

### CAFÉ CÉLESTE
💳♿🍸❄☀ CAFE ❺

Rasinovo Nabrezi 80, Prague 2 ☎22 198 4160 💻www.celesterestaurant.cz

Great food and a better view if you've got the green for it. Lunch comes in two or three courses M-F *(450/550 Kč)* and dinner means exotic dishes prepared exotically. If you don't believe us, try the Moravian suckling pig with black pudding and jus with rasberries *(555Kč)*, fresh crab meat in a seaweed jelly lagoon *(405Kč)*, or rhubarb *clafouti* with jelly and dark beer milkshake *(205Kč)*. If you just want a peek from the terrace without busting your bank, visit M-F 4-6pm when Céleste opens its roof to mere mortals who order a cocktail *(100-150Kč)*.

*🚇 B: Karlovo náměstí. From the station, walk down Resslova toward the river. The building is on your left. ℹ Lounge is on street level. Restaurant is through the elevator in the lounge. $ 500-1000 Kč ⏰ Bar open M-Sa 9am-midnight. Kitchen open noon-2:30pm and 6:30-10:30pm.*

### JÁMA (THE HOLLOW) 💳🚭🍸❄ AMERICAN ❷

V Jame 7, 110 00 Praha 1 ☎22 422 2383 🖥www.jamapub.cz

Positioning itself on an American outpost in the badlands of Prague, Jáma has actually very little to offer. Sure, it's probably got one of the biggest Mexican menus in Prague, with items like jalepenos stuffed with cheddar *(95Kč)* and meat-stuffed tortillas with veggies and sour cream *(95Kč)*, but these unfortunately resemble meat-stuffed tortillas more than they do actual fajitas. Obnoxious posters from American pop culture won't let you forget what cuisine is nonplussing you. Czech lunch specials like fried mushrooms *(85Kč)* are satisfying but a little on the meager side. Better to wait until evening and try to get lucky with English-speaking men and women at the bar, or come early for their impressively massive, delicious brunch.

*🚇 A and C: Muzeum. From the station, walk down Vaclavste Namesti and then turn left on Stepanska and then a right on V jámě; Jáma will be on your right. $ Entrees 100-200Kč. Beer 34-44Kč. ⏰ Open daily 11am-1am.*

### JÍDELNA 🚫🚭🍸 CHINESE ❶

Na Slupi 5, 120 00 Praha 2

If you're on a quest to find excellent Chinese food in Prague, you should cut your losses and go find the Holy Grail. Instead, here's the grungiest, cheapest, most perfectly bad Chinese food in the city. No one here speaks English, so bone up on your pointing skills before you come. An English menu is available, simplifying the process considerably. Large portions of Chicken Kung Pao are almost comically cheap *(49Kč)*, which is also the rule for oddly named-but-vaguely familiar dishes like Piquant Pork *(51Kč)* and gems like chicken chest in dough *(59Kč)*.

*🚇 B: Karlovo náměstí. From the station, follow Vyšehradská south until it becomes Na Slupio. Follow Na slupio about 1 block. The restaurant will be on your right. $ Entrees 35-75Kč. Beer 16-19Kč. ⏰ Open M-F 10am-9pm, Sa-Su 11-7pm.*

## STARE MĚSTO

### 👍 GRAND CAFE ORIENT ♿📶🍸 FRENCH, CAFE ❷

Ovocný trh 19 ☎224 224 240 🖥www.grandcafeorient.cz

In 1912, the Czech architect Gočar built the only ever "Cubist cafe" on the second story of the Lady of Black Madonna, the most famous "Cubist building" ever constructed. But at that time, Cubism was a fleeting trend and the cafe closed after just eight short years. After more than 80 years, the cafe was recently reopened with all of the original "Cubist" fixtures. A series of jarring angular lamp posts line the ceiling, and the little terrace out in the front is one of the cutest in the world. One doesn't expect great food out of a place like this, but that's where this little maverick surprises. The food, especially the *galettes*, savory crepes, are incredible. The spinach, ham, bacon, and cheese *galette* is the best experience you'll ever have with spinach—that's a promise.

*🚇 B: Náměstí Republiky. From the station, head south to U Prašná Brány and follow it as it becomes Celetná. The cafe is on the left at the fork. ℹ The cafe is on the 2nd fl., through the museum entrance. $ Galletes 95-135Kč. Coffee 40-60Kč, Desserts 25-60Kč. ⏰ Open M-F 9am-10pm, Sa-Su 10am-10pm.*

### 👍 APETIT 🚫♿🍸 CAFETERIA ❶

Dlouhá 23 ☎222 329 853 🖥www.apetitpraha.cz

Slum it like a real Praguer at this local cafeteria chain that might serve up the cheapest grub in Stare Město. Grab a tray, some silverware and select from one of several daily Czech entrees ranging from schnitzel to fried cheese to goulash *(67-78Kč)*. Individual entrees become a dinner with a choice of potatoes, dumplings, or vegetables, and a drink for just a few cents more *(89-92Kč)*. These cafeteria workers are no different from those you remember from grade school—very strict; they've even been known to shush policemen!

*➜ C: Republicky Náměstí. From the station, head north up Revoluční and turn left on Dlouhá. [$] Entrees 89-92Kč. 🕐 Open M-F 9am-8pm. Sa-Su 10am-8pm.*

### KAVÁRNA OBECNÍ DŮM — 💳♿🍸 CAFE [2]

Republicky Náměstí 5 ☎222 002 763

The price of a coffee and dessert *(30-90Kč)* or a light sandwich *(120Kč)* is worth 40 minutes resting under the eight hulking chandeliers in this Art Nouveau masterwork. Each detail, from the design of the chairs, to the Alfons Mucha decorated menus, has been specifically chosen to fit the era, and the fountain at the side of the dining room was built specifically for the cafe by the Czech master Josef Pekárek. So sit back, relax, have an oddly affordable breakfast *(90Kč)*.

*➜ C: Republicky Náměstí. ℹ Separate from restaurant across the hall. [$] Breakfasts 90-200Kč. Coffee 58-79Kč. Entrees 120-470Kč. 🕐 Open daily 7:30am-11pm.*

### LOKAL — 💳♿🍸 CZECH [2]

Dlouhá 33 ☎222 316 265 💻www.ambi.cz

Lokal brims with secrets. Take the serving area: it's not just the wee cafe in front; the left side corridor stretches an entire city block. Or take its beer: it comes from a spout, but it's not on tap. Rather, it's "on tank," a new system whereby beer skips pasteurization, proceeding directly from fermentation to your mouth, going down more smoothly with less of a bitter taste than traditional pasteurized beer. Try "the world's most tender beef with whipped cream and cranberry sauce" *(115Kč)* or the pork shoulder with spinach *(95Kč)*. For more surprises, check the daily menu that changes, well, daily. You might want to call ahead, as Lokal is packed with locals during peak hours.

*➜ C: Republicky Náměstí. From the station, head north up Revoluční and turn left on Dlouhá. [$] Entrees 99-242Kč. Beer 29-38Kč. 🕐 Open M-F 11am-1am, Sa noon-1am, Su noon-10pm. Kitchen closes daily at 9:45pm.*

### LEHKÁ HLAVA — 💳🚫♿🍸 VEGETARIAN [3]

Boršov 2 ☎222 220 665 💻www.lehkahlava.cz

This cozy vegetarian joint whose name means "Clear Mind" hides on a small, quiet street. But that's the genius of the place—its entire experience rests on relaxing its patrons, from the lightly glowing tables to the fish tank to the earthy, "paper bag" menus. And unlike most vegetarian joints whose portions are sized more for hipster toddlers than for hungry human beings, Clear Mind delivers actual quantities of food. The eggplant quesadilla *(145Kč)*, though blasphemous by Mexican standards, has sharp, crisp flavors and loads up on the cheese. The polenta gnocchi in sheep's milk *(175Kč)* takes you outside your comfort zone while comfortably filling you up. For dessert, the millet-based carrot cake is a slice of healthy heaven dipped in chocolate *(70Kč)*. At your meal's end, if you need a little "pep," try Brazilian Guaron juice, with triple the caffeine of coffee *(45-75Kč)*. Also, if you're a monk, ordained clergyman, or "enlightened person," you're in luck; you're saved for time and all eternity, *and* you eat free of charge.

*➜ A: Staroměstského. From the station, head towards the river then south on Křižovnické. Continue as it becomes Smetanovo nábřeží, then make a quick left fork onto Karoliny Světlé. Continue down, them make a left onto Boršov (it's a tiny street). ℹ Reservations recommended. [$] Entrees 90-185Kč. 🕐 Open M-F 11:30am-11:30pm, Sa-Su noon-11:30pm. Between 3:30-5pm, only drinks, cold starters, and desserts available. Brunch served 1st Su of the month 10:30am-2pm.*

**BOHEMIA BAGEL** CAFE ❶

Masná 2 ☎224 812 560 www.bohemiabagel.cz

Though it's become something of an institution, Bohemia Bagel still delivers solid breakfast and lunch options at bargain prices. If you've got a youngster, unleash him or her in the playpen while you enjoy bottomless filter coffee *(49Kč)* or a bagel sandwich *(60-90Kč)*. If a plump burger *(125-150Kč)* or American-style sandwich *(95-135Kč)* can't convince you, then maybe you'll be pleased with the ice-cream chipwich *(80Kč)*. Incredible breakfast special of any egg sandwich served with bottomless soft drink, tea or coffee *(89Kč)* offered M-F before noon.

*A: Staroměstského. From the station, take Kaprova away from the river and through Old Town Square. Stick to the left as you cross the square, and take Dlouhá on the opposite side. At the roundabout, take a right on Masná 2. $ Internet 1Kč per min. Bagels 30-50 Kč. Open daily 8am-11pm.*

**KLUB ARCHITEKTŮ** CZECH, ROMANTIC ❷

Betlémské náměstí 169/5A ☎224 248 878 www.klubarchitektu.com

Surprisingly sophisticated and reasonably cheap for Old Town, this little place makes good grounds for a classy evening. Low-vaulted ceilings and the lowest hanging lamps you've ever seen (ask and they'll raise them up for you) will make you feel out of place in shorts or flip flops, but nobody will tell you you can't be there. Don't stop by if you're in a hurry; the fractured and separated serving areas means you can go 10 minutes at a time without seeing heads or tails of a waiter. Food is Czech chic, but if you're not here mostly for the ambience, you'll be disappointed.

*B: Národní třída. From the station, head north on Spálená continuing as it turns into Na Perštýně. When it forks, take the left fork. Restaurant is down a somewhat unmarked staircase through a courtyard on your left. $ Entrees 130-280Kč. Desserts 80-105Kč. Open daily 11:30am-midnight.*

**LA CASA BLU** MEXICAN ❷

Kozi 15 ☎221 818 270 www.lacasablu.cz

A favorite among locals, La Casa Blu provides a meeting place for Latin culture in this city so often lacking thereof; the walls serve as gallery space and Latin musical artists regularly perform. Though it's hidden down a sketchball alley, the scene inside this casa is bright and happening as locals sip *cervezas* in this smoke-free environment. Suprisingly big for the small cafe vibe it maintains, the food here is not to be underestimated, with dishes like Prague's only non-embarrassing selection of nachos *(100-200Kč)* and loaded quesadillas *(128-148Kč)* La Casa Blu also stays hip late with tequila *(69-139Kč)*.

*C: Republicky Náměstí. From the station, head north up Revoluční and turn left on Dlouhá. At the roundabout, take a right on Kozí. $ Entrees 150-290Kč. M-F 10am-late, Sa 11am-late, Su 2pm-late.*

**U RUDOLFINA** CZECH ❶

Křižovnická 10 ☎222 328 758

You might have a bit of a struggle ordering here, but you've gotta give up something to eat at the cheapest, most authentic pun in Old Town. This locals-only favorite seems small on the first floor, but opens up downstairs to an impressively large restaurant, with antique photos and street lamps selling the 1930s effect. Staff speaks a wee bit of English, which should be enough to land you a *polévky (soup; 22Kč)* or a plate of *guláš (goulash; 98Kč)*. Even more elaborate dishes like *uzené koleno (smoked pork neck; 149Kč)* or *pečené koleno (sliced roast pork knee; 199Kč)* are incredible deals.

*A: Staroměstského. From the station, head towards the river then south on Křižovnické. $ Entrees 65-199Kč. Beer 18-35Kč. Open daily 10:30am-11pm.*

**ZAHRÁDKA U KRISTIÁNA** CZECH ❷

Smetanovo Nábřeží 6

The cheapest riverside dining in the city hides at this bare-bones assemblage of picnic tables and grills. The cafe has a well-stocked bar, but food is limited to what you could make in your backyard: sausages *(65Kč)*, potatoes *(50Kč)*, and steaks *(200Kč)*. Weekends sometimes see live acoustic musicians.

*➔ A: Staroměstského. From the station, head towards the river then south on Křižovnické. Continue as it becomes Smetanovo nábřeží. The cafe will be on your right down some stairs. $ Entrees 65-200Kč. Beer 25-45Kč. ⏰ Open daily 11am-midnight, weather permitting.*

**KAVÁRNA NÁPRSTKOVA** 💳🚭📶🍸 CAFE 2

Náprstkova 272/10 ☎775 755 142

Hip locals gather here under enormous murals of Vaclav Havel to chat, smoke, and have a light meal. Even though this cafe has solid food, like quesadillas *(95Kč)* and an array of well-priced sandwiches *(35-42Kč)*, it's better to come here for dessert *(14-49Kč)* and coffee *(39Kč)*. It's usually pretty tourist-free despite its proximity to Old Town.

*➔ A: Staroměstského. From the station, head towards the river then south on Křižovnické. Continue as it becomes Smetanovo nábřeží. At the Bellevue restaurant, take a left down the stairs and continue straight ahead onto Náprstkova. The cafe will be on your left. $ Coffee 39Kč. Breakfast 85Kč. ⏰ Open M-F 9am-1am. Sa-Su noon-1am.*

**CHOCO CAFE** 💳♿📶🍸☀ CHOCOLATE BAR 3

Liliová 4/250 ☎222 222 519 💻www.choco-cafe.cz

Let's Go highly reccommends a series of fantastic desserts in Choco Cafe's case. The tiramisu *(80Kč)* comes in loaf form and will make your stomach smile. The various hot chocolates might be a little overpriced *(59-95Kč)*, but the espresso *(35Kč)* is actually more of a bargain than you'll find elsewhere in Old Town, especially coming from Choco's ravishing waitresses.

*➔ A: Staroměstského. From the station, head towards the river then south on Křižovnické. At the bridge, head away from the river down Karlovo and take a left at Liliová. The cafe will be on your left. $ Toasts 85-93Kč. Desserts 50-100Kč. ⏰ Open M-F 9am-8pm Sa-Su 10am-8pm.*

**HAŠTALKSÝ DĚDEK** 💳🚭📶🍸 CZECH, PUB 1

Haštalksá 20 ☎224 827 196 💻www.hastalskydedek.cz

An uber-traditional Czech pub fantastically lodged in Old Town, this little joint lets you eat at Nové Město prices while grunting with a Stare Město crowd. The food is great, and at times, unreasonably cheap. A 400g steak of pork neck goes for a paltry 179Kč, while Grandpa's Sour Soup in a bread loaf does just 69Kč of damage. The delightful Old Man's goulash with horseradish *(129Kč)* comes in a pot with potato pancakes. Quiet, wooden interior makes for a good place to relax.

*➔ C: Republicky náměstí. From the station, head north up Revoluční and turn left on Dlouhá. Take a right at Rybá and then another quick right onto Haštalksá. The pub will be on your right. $ Entrees 50-200Kč. Beer 16-40Kč. ⏰Open daily 11am-11pm.*



## JOSEFOV

👍 **LA VERANDA** 💳♿🍸❄ INTERNATIONAL 3

Elišky Krásnohorské 2/10 ☎224 814 733💻laveranda.cz

While its pastel, flowery decor might make La Veranda appear a place for old, lunching ladies, the ingredients used are just as applicable to any man. The tagliolini with tiger prawns and sun-dried tomatoes will surprise both your tongue and your wallet *(295Kč)*.

*➔ Tram 17: Právnická fakulta. $ Soup 145Kč. Pasta 225-295Kč. Entrees 430-495Kč. ⏰ Open M-Sa noon-11:30pm.*

**LA BODEGUITA DEL MEDIO** 💳♿🍸☀ CUBAN 2

Kaprova 19/5 ☎224 813 922

It's always a party at this Cuban restaurant where Latin music flows almost as freely as the mojitos. While there are a few vegetarian options *(gorgonzola cheese and raspberry salad 180Kč)*, this is the place to go for beef with beef. Don't leave without trying the Mojo—grilled beef fillet served with Cuban baked potatoes *(485Kč)*. While most of the meatier entrees are a little pricey, it's certainly possible to keep within

budget with an equally hearty appetizer paired with a delicious soup *(85Kč).*
*🚏 A: Staroměstská. About 25m east on Kaprova from the Metro. ℹ Latin music and dancing most nights. $ Salads 155-190Kč. Entrees 98-485Kč. ⏰ Open daily 9am-2am.*

**PEPE NERO** 💳♿🍸❄☁ ITALIAN [2]
Bílkova 132/4 ☎222 315 543
Award-winning pizza is served up in this cheery pink building. Anything from a quick bite like focaccia bread *(60Kč)* to something more serious, like seafood pizza *(290Kč)* is catered to you on red-and-white checkered tablecloths. Pair this classic Italian dish with a classic Czech drink: beer *(from 29Kč)*, the country's old school.
*🚏 Tram 17: Právnická fakulta. $ Pizza 180-290Kč. ⏰ Open daily noon-midnight.*

**BOHEMIA BAGEL** 🚭♿☁ BAGELS [2]
Masná 2 ☎224 812 569 💻www.bohemiabagel.cz
Missin' that New York-style bagel while in Prague? This place—founded by expats and a frequented by English-speaking tourists looking to get their fill of chocolate-chip bagels and cream cheese—is only worth it if you're truly homesick. The gigantic "I Don't Wanna Go Anywhere After This Breakfast" dish will cure any longing you have for mom-made eggs, bacon, sausage, or biscuits *(169Kč).*
*🚏 B: Náměstí Republiky. From the Metro, walk north on Revoluční and then make a left on Dlouhá; follow it down to the sq. and make a hard left onto Masná. $ Bagels 11Kč-190Kč. ⏰ Open daily 8am-11pm.*

**PIVNICE U PIVRNCE** 💳♿🍸❄ CZECH [2]
Maiselova 60/3 ☎222 329 404
This restaurant serves up classic Czech cuisine in a cellar whose walls boast sexual cartoons, spicing up the otherwise bland food of the Bohemians. While the dumplings might not be the best in town, you can always opt for random odds-and-ends like gnocchi with spinach and cheese *(130Kč).*
*🚏 A: Staroměstská. 2 blocks from the Metro on Kaprova. $ Soups 35Kč. Entrees 115-490Kč. Salads 60-150Kč. ⏰ Open daily 11am-9:30pm.*

**PIZZERIE MODRÁ ZAHRADA** 💳♿🍸❄☁ ITALIAN [2]
Pařížská 14 ☎222 253 829
Delicious pizza served up by enthusiastic faux-Italian waiters in a no-frills setting. One of the better pizza deals around because, unlike around the Old Town, "mushroom pizza" means more than four mushrooms and you don't have to go searching for cheese with a magnifying glass.
*🚏 A: Staroměstská. On the corner of Pařížská and Široká. $ Pizza from 114Kč. ⏰ Open daily 11am-midnight.*

**ŠVEJK** 💳♿🍸❄ CZECH [2]
Široká 20 ☎224 813 964
Scrumptious Czech fare with an historically weighty name: Švejk, or Sweik, is a character in Jaroslav Hašek's famous satire from the earliest 20th century, *Good Soldier Švejk.* While the food might struggle to keep up with the namesake, it's still a decent place to go for dinner after a day of Synagoguing about town.
*🚏 Tram 17: Právnická fakulta. Head down Pařížská 3 blocks. $ Entrees 98-440Kč. ⏰ Open daily 11am-11pm.*

**LA VITA E BELLA** 💳♿🍸❄☁ ITALIAN [3]
Elišky Krásnohorské 12/5 ☎222 310 039 💻http://vitabella.cz
Fabulous Italian dishes in an equally fabulous setting. While the setting might appear posh, the price is relatively mild especially if you stick to one of the "first courses" or delicious desserts. Try the broccoli penne with chicken *(280Kč).*
*🚏 A: Staroměstská. $ Appetizers 220-310Kč. Seafood 330-650Kč. Entrees 350-590Kč. ⏰ Open daily 11:30am-midnight.*

**LES MOULES** 💳♿🍸❄☁ BELGIAN [2]

Pařížská 203/19 ☎222 315 022 💻www.lesmoules.cz

Enjoy buckets of mussels on the sunny terrace as you shield your shirt with a red checkered bib. This place is definitely the place to go if you're into mussels, but for the less adventurous, try "snails au gratin" *(295Kč).* If you're sick of mussels straight-up, add a twist with dark *Leffe* beer, white wine, or get them "Thai style."

*🚋 Tram 17: Právnická fakulta. ℹ Don't be afraid to get a little dirty. $ Mussels 295Kč per kg. ⏰ Open daily 11am-midnight.*

## MALÁ STRANA

**BAR BAR** 💳🚭📶🍸 PUB [2]

Všehrdova 17 ☎257 312 246 💻www.bar-bar.cz

Discovering Bar Bar anywhere would be an accomplishment, with its saturation of local flavor, infusion of exotic influences, and balance of excitement and hominess. However, this gem hides just off the main street in touristy Malá Strana. The pub's dishes resemble Mom's home cooking. If the thought of Mom's home cooking is too traumatizing, you can cook your own food on a stone grill *(490Kč).* Be warned: this vegetarian-friendly cellar restaurant is becoming more popular; come on the early side, because they don't accept reservations.

*🚋 A: Malostranská. From the station, take the tram to Újezd, walk north on Újezd, then turn right on Všehrdova. $ Entrees 139-325Kč. Tapas 175Kč. Beer 23-49Kč. Mixed drinks 90-160Kč. ⏰ Open Su-Th noon-midnight, F-Sa noon-2am.*

**RESTAURANT SOVOVY MLÝNY** 💳♿🍸☁ CAFE [4]

U Sovových Mlýnů 503/2 ☎257 220 121 💻www.restauracemlyny.cz

If you make it here by 4pm, you're in for an unforgettable treat—a classy, riverside feast for the price of a non-feast thanks to Sovovy Mlýny's ultra cheap "daily menu." Specials like beef over mushrooms and potato gnocchi *(124Kč)* change daily, but are always delicious and filling. To keep things even cheaper, come for the daily dessert menu *(20-85Kč)* for traditional Czech sweets like cottage cake *(75Kč)* or apple strudel *(60Kč).* But be warned, after 4pm this place comes to its senses and starts charging what it ought to. Sculptures from the attached modern art museum, like the enormous row of plastic yellow penguins, are great conversation pieces.

*🚋 A: Malostranská. From the station, head south past the Charles Bridge, sticking to the side of the river. When you reach the park, the restaurant will be in the middle, right long the water, behind the freaky baby statues and the art museum. $ Daily menu 100-150Kč. Entrees 255-455Kč. ⏰ Open daily 10am-11pm.*

**DOBŘÁ TRAFIKA** 🍴🚭🍸☁ CAFE, WINE BAR [1]

Újezd 37/400 ☎257 320 188 💻www.dobratrafika.cz

An excellent little cafe and wine bar popular with artists, musicians, and other tea-drinking types. Speaking of tea, this place has a four-page menu dedicated to it, and—the rarest sight in all of Prague—a *selection* of different coffees. Food pickings might be a little meager, but who can complain when there are seven different types of mead *(20Kč).*

*🚋 A: Malostranská. From the station, take the tram to Újezd, walk north on Újezd. Cafe is through the specialty store in front. $ Pitas 13-50Kč. Coffee 30-50Kč. ⏰ Open M-F 7:30am-11pm, Sa-Su 9am-11pm.*

**RESTAURACE TLUSTÁ MYŠ** 🍴🚭🍸 CZECH [2]

Všehrdova 19, 118 00 Praha 1 ☎605 282 506 💻www.tlustamys.cz

Tulstá Myš, "Fat Mouse" directly next door to its neighbor, Bar Bar, has a similar vibe, similarly awesome food, and similarly great prices. Adorable "fat mice" dance around the menu. Grilled sausages *(55Kč)* are cheaper than a street vendor's, and the daily menu has terriffic international samplings, like Mexican beans with beef *(99Kč).* The cozy pub is also a great place to spend an evening sipping "Fire Water," Czech liquors like *Bechorovka*, plum vodka and *Fernet* *(20-40Kč).*

*➜ A: Malostranská. From the station, take the tram to Újezd, walk north on Újezd, and then turn right on Všehrdova. $ Entrees 99-150Kč. Soup 24Kč. Beer 20-34Kč. Wine 32Kč. ⏰ Open M-F 11:30am-midnight, Sa noon-midnight, Su noon-10pm.*

### POD PETŘÍNEM
💵🚭🍸 CZECH ❶

Hellichova 5 ☎257 224 408 💻www.pivnicepodpetrinem.cz

This friendly, ultra-traditional Czech pub has just a few menu items: goulash *(99)*, schnitzel *(129Kč)*, and pork knee *(139Kč)* among them at medievally cheap prices. The older Czech crowd won't be speaking English, and won't even have an English menu for you, but the few staff members who speak English will happily translate.

*➜ A: Malostranská. From the station, take the tram to Hellichova and walk south to Hellichova on your left. $ Entrees 99-140Kč. Beer 18-26Kč. Mixed drinks 40-95Kč. ⏰ Open 11am-12:30am.*

### U MALÉHO GLENA
💳🚭📶🍸 AMERICAN ❸

Karmelitská 23 ☎257 531 717 💻www.malyglen.cz

Boasting solid servings of food, this little American bar (despite its Czech name) actually has quality American burgers *(145-185Kč)*. The best news is the great Tex-Mex *(95-150Kč)* in huge portions. Also, this is probably the only place in town with chili cheese fries *(150Kč)*.

*➜ A: Malostranská. From the Metro, take the tram to Újezd, walk north on Újezd. $ Entrees 95-250Kč. ⏰ Open M-Th 11am-2am, F-Su 11am-3am.*

### KAVÁRNA ČAS
💵♿📶🍸⛱ SNACKS ❶

Míšenská 92/2 ☎721 959 903

A delicious and cheap stop for a light lunch or dinner comprised entirely of snack food, the delights of this joint are all small, but magical. The snacks are made with recognizable ingredients, but are combined in a 100% foreign way. Toasted cheese sandwiches *(45Kč)* come with ketchup, and strudel pastries *(40-65Kč)* are filled with bologna, sausage, or cabbage. These magical bites won't fill you up, but they won't empty your wallet either.

*➜ A: Malostranská. Go down Klárov toward the river, turn right on U. Luzické Semináré. Take a right when you get to Míšenská. $ Toasts 45Kč. Beer 23-30Kč. Espresso 25Kč. ⏰ Open daily 10am-8pm.*

### CAFE BAR WIGWAM
💳🚭📶🍸 INTERNATIONAL ❶

Zborovská 54 ☎257 311 707 💻www.cafebarwigwam.cz

A meal at Wigwam will oscillate between Czech experiments, like the Pork Neck Burger *(145Kč)*, American non-experiments, like the classic hamburger *(145Kč)*, or dubious Asian dishes like *Mat Suman* Curry *(170Kč)*. The nachos with blue cheese *(95Kč)* is enough to start any party, as long as it's a cheese party.

*➜ A: Malostranská. From the station, take the tram to Újezd. Continue down Újezd, then take a left onto Petřínská and another left onto Zborovská $ Entrees 120-295Kč. Beer 20-35Kč. ⏰ Open daily 11am-1am.*

### ARTISAN
💳🚭📶🍸⛱ ITALIAN ❹

Rošických 4 ☎257 218 277 💻www.artisanrestaurant.cz

This new upscale Italian joint offers an impressively cheap "Business Lunch" menu of either two or three courses. Though the entrees change constantly, examples of fare include salmon, hamburgers, pasta, and chicken *(90-180Kč)*. The additional course can be either a dessert or a starter (soup or salad). The normal menu is pricier, but the penny-pinching traveler can grab an excellent cup of coffee *(39Kč)* on one of the most remote and relaxing patios in the city.

*➜ A: Malostranská. From the station, take the tram to Újezd. Continue down jezd and take a right on Rošických, curving around until you find the restaurant. $ Entrees 170-425Kč. ⏰ Open daily 11am-11pm.*

### CAFE KAFÍČKE
💵🚭 CAFE ❷

Míšenská 10 ☎724 151 795

A quiet stop for expats and other locals smack in the middle of tourist town, Cafe Kafíčke also has the distinction of being the first "non-smoking" cafe in all of Prague, when the American couple running this establishment had a child. You never know who'll be stopping by, from famous Czech film directors, to musicians to actresses. This small cafe's customers include some big names; maybe that's why they also accept euros.

*🚇 A: Malostranská. Go down Klárov toward the river, turn right on U. Luzické Semináré. Take a right when you get to Míšenská. Ⓢ Espresso 38Kč. Sweets 12-52Kč. 🕐 Open daily 10am-10pm.*

### LE BASTILLE
💳🍸❄☁ FRENCH [3]

Újezd 426/26 ☎257 312 830 💻www.labastille.cz

Nothing about this restaurant wins prizes, but it's reasonably priced and not bad for Malá Strana. Meat dishes tend to tiptoe on the pricey side *(255-355Kč)* with the exception of that miracle meat, chicken *(140-175Kč).* Fantastic Spanish and French wines *(54Kč)* make up for food that occasionally lacks flavor. Expect to add 30-40Kč to any meat dish for dumplings, or some perfectly-prepared boiled potatoes. Vegetarians will find comfort in a large list of inexpensive pastas *(129-139Kč)* or ratatouille *(139Kč).*

*🚇A: Malostranská. From the station, take the tram to Újezd. Ⓢ Entrees 120-355Kč. 🕐 Open daily 11am-midnight.*

### LA TRAITTOR
💳♿📶☁ ITALIAN [2]

Újezd 20 ☎257 312 451 💻www.trattoria-amedeo.euweb.cz

Well-priced if somewhat meager pizzas nevertheless make for a good, cheap meal in a neighborhood where those two factors together constitute a semi-miracle. Pizzas are large but thin. Stars on this list are the Four Cheese, with cream, mozzarella, blue, eidam and parmesan, or the Mexicana, which includes eggs and salami for some reason. Salads offer a healthier (and paradoxically, more filling) alternative. Staff is almost overly-nice; if you're not enjoying your food, they'll notice and ask why not. Space is tight—only one table fits more than five people, so don't show up with your entire JV football team.

*🚇 A: Malostranská. From the station, take the tram to Újezd. Ⓢ Pizza 79-129Kč. Meat entrees 99-329Kč. 🕐 Open daily 11:30am-11:30pm.*



### KLÁŠTERNÍ PIVOVAR A RESTAURACE SV. NORBERT
💳♿🍸☁ BREWERY [3]

Strahovské nádvoří 301 ☎233 353 155 💻www.klasterni-pivovar.cz

Only come here if you need to dine on Petřín Hill. On a nice day, most of the restaurant moves outside to large wooden tables in the sun. But sneak inside for a peek at the large copper tanks ,which are daily employed to make one of the brewery's six original St. Norbert beers. The only downside of this brewery is that the beer costs twice what it would elsewhere—but then again, you technically can't get this beer elsewhere. While the menu can be pricey, there are some affordable choices, like pork schnitzel *(160Kč)* or roast rabbit *(190Kč).* Vegetarians can choose from fried cheese, mushrooms, or spinach potatoes *(130-140Kč).* While your nose will be getting a beer tour the entire length of your stay, you can ask to be taken on an actual 30min. tour of the brewery at no extra charge with a purchase.

*🚇 From Petřín Hill, take the paved asphalt road that leads away from the funicular station. Follow it along the left side of the Hunger Wall for about 10min. ℹ Tour is free with medium-sized purchase. Ⓢ Entrees 160-390Kč. 🕐 Open daily 10am-10pm.*

### LE BISTROT KAMPA
💳♿📶🍸☁ BISTRO [1]

U Lužického semináře 23 ☎725 534 101 💻www.lebistrot.cz

Nicely-located and nicely-priced comparatively, the somewhat touristy Bistrot Kampa makes for a pleasant stop after a long day at the castle. The tuna *monsieurs (65Kč)* are made with real brioche and fill you up. The lasagna bolognese *(105Kč),* while somewhat unelegant, is incredibly tasty. Beer and sweets are overpriced *(30-80Kč),* so stick with the sandwiches.

*🚇A: Malostranská. From the Metro, take an immediate right down U Lužického semináře. Ⓢ Entrees 65-200. 🕐 Open daily 9am-8pm.*

### ŠVEJK RESTAURANT - MALOSTRANSKÁ PIVNICE
💳🚭⛱ CZECH [3]

Cihelná 3 ☎257 530 032 💻www.malostranskapivnice.cz

It's amazing what a difference context makes. On the other side of the river, this place would be a touristy, kitschy red flag to avoid, but over here in pricier Malá Strana, we can't be so picky, can we? Plus there are still some original experiences to be had. The pork knuckle *(259Kč)* feeds three people easily, but doesn't guarantee they won't all die from fat poisoning. The atmosphere, interrupted only by T-shirt and hat sales, is surprisingly more relaxed than other Švejk restaurants, and the clientele is almost exlcusively Czech locals.

*🚋 A: Malostranská. Go down Klárov toward the river. $ Entrees 139-400Kč. 🕘 Open M-Sa 11am-1am. Su 11am-midnight.*

### PIZZERIA FELICITA
💳🚭🍸 ITALIAN [2]

Říční 5, Praha 1 ☎257 312 565 💻pizzeria.felicita.sweb.cz

Like many of its Malá Strana peers, Pizzeria Felicita doesn't knock you out of the water, but with 41 types of relatively cheap pizza *(99-179Kč)*, the water's not so bad. Pizza style is completely European, so don't expect thick crust, dripping cheese or—one can dream—stuffed crust. Felicita also has a great selection of large salads *(129-149Kč)*. Interior feels a little cavernous, but fine for a light meal.

*🚋 A: Malostranská. From the station, take the tram to Újezd, walk north on Újezd, and then turn right on Říční. $ Pizzas 99-179Kč. 🕘 Open daily 11am-11pm.*

### STARÁ PRAHA
💳♿📶🍸⛱ CZECH [2]

Vítězná 11 ☎251 510 217

A forgettable, but adequate traditional Czech restaurant, Stará Praha has traditional Czech food at fair prices. You won't be finding any insane bargains, but the specialties, like minced beef in pita *(139Kč)* or grilled marinated pork neck *(159Kč)*, please the crowd. Famished travelers can benefit from the "Bohemian Square meal" composed of pork neck, smoked meat, sausage, cabbage and dumplings *(169Kč)*.

*🚋 A: Malostranská. From the station, take the tram to Újezd, then walk down Vítězná towards the river. [i] Only the patio is wheelchair-accessible. $ Entrees 130-400Kč. 🕘 Open daily 9am-11pm.*

## HRADČANY

### U ZLATÉ HRUŠKY SAVE
💳♿🍸❄⛱ INTERNATIONAL, CZECH [3]

Nový Svět 3 ☎220 514 778 💻www.restaurantuzlatehrusky.cz

Try the innovative goat cheese in a puff pastry, with arugula and bacon chips *(290Kč)* —and sail away to a far-off galaxy. The place has a terrace for every season, so even if you come in winter you can enjoy the crisp air and snowy landscape while noshing on beef carpaccio *(290Kč)*. Not for the faint of wallet.

*🚋 Tram 22 or 23: Brusnice. From the stop, walk across the street to the leafy pathway, down the stairs, turn left at the 1st street after the hotel and walk until you see the restaurant terrace on your right. $ Soup 190Kč. Entrees 290-690Kč. Dessert 190Kč. 🕘 Open daily 11am-1am.*

### RESTAURACE NAD ÚVOZEM
🚭♿🍸 CZECH [3]

Loretánská 15 ☎220 511 532

Tricky to find but worth the search—the view of Petřín Hill and the surrounding area is one of the best you can get. The atmosphere is friendly and casual, and you might even spot a real Czech person eating here on occasion. The menu majors in traditional Czech, with an emphasis in skewers *(169Kč)*.

*🚋 Tram 22 or 91: Brusnice. From the tram, take U Brusnice south and then turn left on Loretánská. Turn and go down the stairs toward Úvoz; the entrance will be on your left. $ Entrees 159-279Kč. Daily menu 179Kč. 🕘 Open daily 11am-11pm.*

### U CÍSAŘŮ
💳🚭 CZECH [5]

Loretánská 5 ☎220 518 484 💻www.ucisaru.cz

This 13th-century cellar, complete with crossed swords and a boar's head, has served the likes of George H.W. Bush, Margaret Thatcher, and Lech Wałęsa. Finally, a *goulash* worth splurging on *(340Kč)*. Other specialties include roast duck in honey and ginger *(420Kč)* and pork sirloin stuffed with carrots and celery *(440Kč)*.

*➜ Tram 22 or 91: Brusnice. From the tram, take U Brusnice south and then turn left on Loretánská. $ Appetizers 210-230Kč. Entrees 340-550Kč. ℹ No dress code per se, but you'd probably feel awkward in jeans and a T-shirt. Reservations recommended. ⏰ Open daily 9am-1am.*

## ŽIŽKOV

### AMORES PERROS
💳♿🍸 MEXICAN [1]

Kubelíkova 1123/33 ☎222 733 980 💻http://amoresperros.cz

The only Mexican food in the area, and one of a handful of Latin-style eateries in the city. Sizzling enchiladas smothered in heart-stopping sauce are the way to go. Come here for lunch, as the menu deals are superb, filling, and inexpensive.

*➜ Tram 5, 9, or 26: Olšanské náměstí. From the stop, walk west on Kubelíkova for 2 blocks. $ Salads 84-114Kč. Burritos 164-199Kč. Enchiladas 109Kč. ⏰ Open M-Th 11am-midnight, F 11am-1am, Sa 11am-midnight, Su 12:30pm-midnight.*

### ZELENÁ KUCHYNĚ
🚭♿☀ VEGETARIAN [2]

Milíčova 5 ☎222 220 114 💻www.zelenakuchyne.cz

Clean, fresh, wholesome ingredients combine to make any vegetarian orgasm. Check out the grilled tomatoes with goat cheese and blackberry dressing...do you want to get a room? Top off the pleasurable experience with a little dessert; savor the cinnamon pancakes made from oatmeal and apples and topped with ice cream and blueberry sauce.

*➜ Trams 5, 9, 26: Lipanská. From the stop, walk west on and turn right at Seifertova Milíčova. The restaurant is on your left. $ Menus from 90Kč. Entrees 110-290Kč. ⏰ Open M-F 11am-8pm.*

### SPICE INDIA
🚭♿ INDIAN [2]

Husitská 73/37 ☎776 293 320 💻www.spiceindia.cz

No fuss, no muss at this little Indian fast-food joint off the main street. Deliciously spicy cuisine is served up on metal plates by a genial counter staff. Don't forget to order water to wash down the burn.

*➜ Bus #133, 175, or 509: Tachovské náměstí. Keep walking in the direction the bus is going until you find the place on your right. $ Entrees 65-180Kč. ⏰ Open M-F 11am-11pm, Sa Noon-11pm, Su 5pm-11pm.*

### ČAJÍRNA NAD VOKEM
🚭🚫☀ CAFE [2]

Božích bojovníků 3 ☎721 837 553 💻www.cajirnanadvokem.cz

A gorgeous and meditative terrace cafe serves up tea from all over the world in equally beautiful china. Also sells leaves in bulk, as well as Japanese porcelain. Housed in a tiny corner off the main street, it's easy to miss this gem. Here's hoping you won't.

*➜ Bus #133, 175, or 509: Tachovské náměstí. Walk in the direction of the bus and turn into the little alley marked Božích Bojovníků. $ Tea from 35Kč. ⏰ Open M-F 3-10pm, Sa-Su 2-10pm.*

## VINOHRADY

### 👍 CAFÉ ŠLAGR
🚭♿🍸☀ CAFE [1]

Francouzská 72/563 ☎607 27 76 88 💻www.kavarnaslagr.cz

"Mind-blowing" is an appropriate word to describe Café Šlagr's baked goods. If they have it in stock, the *Pářvžký rohliček (29Kč)* will be one of your finest culinary experiences, while the *krernrole (17Kč)* will help you understand what the Italians were aiming for with cannoli. Be sure to get it with some coffee and milk—the milk comes from a little cow vessel who happily regurgitates into your espresso *(36Kč)*. The family behind this genius operation dressed their little cafe like 1930s Paris and plays cute little swing tunes to sell the effect.

*➜ A: Náměstí Míru. From the station, walk southeast along Francouská. The cafe will be on your right. $ Baked goods 17-40Kč. Breakfast 49-69Kč. ⏰ Open M-F 8am-10pm, Sa-Su 10am-10pm. Breakfast served 8-11am.*

## LAS ADELITAS
⊗(())ᵞ  MEXICAN ❷

Americká 8     ☎776 80 53 17 ▤www.lasadelitas.cz

Described by some locals as "the only real Mexican restaurant in Prague," this hole-in-the-wall taqueria serves up oddly authentic south-of-the-border fare. Enchiladas, burritos, and tacos all come with legit Mexican *queso*, pickled onions, and hearty refried black beans. Both come with pork and chicken, but pork is the specialty—and boy is it special. Vegetarians will enjoy any major dish served up with sauteed mushrooms, while parched *amigos* can sooth themselves with a cool glass of *horchata (25-69Kč)* or with one of 13 tequilas *(69-150Kč)*. Try the *Sopa Azteca (49Kč)* for a surprisingly filling soup packed with cheese, chicken, and onions.

🍴 A: *Náměstí Míru. From the station, walk down Americká. The restaurant is past the square with the dinosaur fountain on your left.* ⓢ *Entrees 99-179Kč. Margaritas 89-99Kč.* ☼ *Open M-F 11am-11pm, Sa-Su 2-11pm. Kitchen open until 10pm.*

## CAFE ZANZIBAR
⊗(())ᵞ⌂  CAFE ❷

Americká 15     ☎222 52 03 15 ▤www.kavarnazanzibar.cz

This relaxing French cafe has a strange power to improve your mood. Set breakfast menus with combinations of cheese, eggs, pastries, coffee, and baguettes come at great prices *(79-149Kč)*—and yes, some of them come with beer instead of coffee. Lunch includes 20 salad options *(59-149Kč)* and a mess of French and international favorites, like *croques monsieur (ham and cheese super-sandwiches; 65-95Kč)* and Mexican tube sandwiches *(burritos; 129-139Kč)*. Stick around and try a few "beer cocktails"—beers sloshed with things like lemon syrup, Coke, and Sprite *(46-59Kč)*. If you drink enough, you'll get to check out the strangely nautical bathrooms, where a net above the urinals threatens to trap the slow pisser!

🍴 A: *Náměstí Míru. From the station, walk down Americká. The cafe is on your right at the square with the dinosaur fountain.* 𝒊 *Only the porch is wheelchair-accessible.* ⓢ *Coffee 36-42Kč. Breakfast 79-149Kč.* ☼ *Open M-F 8am-11pm, Sa-Su 10am-11pm. Kitchen open 8am-10pm.*

## MEDUZA
⊗♿ᵞ⌂  CAFE ❷

Belgická 17     ☎222 51 51 07 ▤www.meduza.cz

Meduza boasts a darker, more Eastern European feel and charges more authentically Eastern European prices (read: it's cheap). Sweet and savory pancakes *(68-106Kč)* stuffed with prosciutto, spinach, cheese, ham, and tuna constitute most of the menu, but fruit and chocolate options promise to be a great dessert. Individuals who like consuming different parts of a pig will enjoy the meat plate, consisting of spicy sausage, ham, and prosciutto. Even if you're not hungry, there's at least one exposed female human breast on the wall of this cafe—reason enough for anyone to attend.

🍴 A: *Náměstí Míru. From the station, head down Belgická. The cafe will be on your right.* 𝒊 *Only patio is wheelchair-accessible.* ⓢ *Entrees 68-120Kč.* ☼ *Open M-F 10am-1am, Sa-Su noon-midnight.*

## PIZZERIA GROSSETO
♿⊗ᵞ  ITALIAN ❸

Francouzská 2     ☎224 25 27 78 ▤www.grosseto.cz

Don't dismiss Pizzeria Grosseto beause it's a chain restaurant. Most of the 29 pizzas *(135-195Kč)* shoot it straight, though occasional deviants slip through, like the *Carpaccio*, which has roast sirloin slices *(195Kč)*. Meat in general does a fine business on Grosseto's menu, with dishes like pork with bacon and cheese sauce *(220Kč)*. The enormous window overlooking the square and the murals of Florence on the wall give this place a posh edge over most Czech pizza joints.

🍴 A: *Náměstí Míru. Grosseto is directly across the street from the Metro exit.* ⓢ *Entrees 175-377Kč.* ☼ *Open daily 11:30am-11pm.*

## AMBIENTE
♿⊗ᵞ  AMERICAN ❹

Mánesova 59     ☎222 727 85 18 ▤www.ambi.cz

For a restaurant that dubs itself "the living restaurant," Ambiente spends a lot of time reminding you it serves dead cows. When you enter, there's a glass fridge showing your potential cuts of meat, and in the menu—SURPRISE!—there's a diagram of cow types and cow parts you'll be enjoying. But Ambiente rightfully takes pride in its extensive, if somewhat pricey, beef menu. Steaks *(348-645Kč)* from all corners of the world comprise two entire pages, while a third displays the rest of the menu, most of which changes seasonally. This short-life menu emboldens Ambiente to take risks along vaguely Southwestern lines, and entrees can range from buffalo wings *(178Kč)* to jambalaya creole with prawns *(268Kč)*. The permanent menu, conversely, plays more safely with items like spaghetti Ambiente with chicken and cheese *(245Kč)*. Vegetarians might find solace in an array of vegetable side dishes *(58-78Kč)*.

⚘ *A: Jiřího z Poděbrad. From the station, walk west on Vinohradská 2 blocks past the park, then turn right on Třebízského. The restaurant will be on your right.* ℹ *Reservations recommended.* Ⓢ *Entrees 178-425Kč.* ⏰ *Open daily 11am-midnight. Kitchen open until 11:15pm.*

## U PALEČKA
Nitranská 1625/22

●✱⊗Ⴤ⚐ CZECH ❸

☎224 25 06 26 🖳www.vinarnaupalecka.cz

U Palečka's simple, rustic interior does not do justice to its gastromically rich menu. One can enjoy its food best from the intimate outdoor porch-boxes in front of the restaurant. On a dry summer day, take in a strange starter like smoked tongue *(60Kč)* or even a well-priced dish of caviar *(110Kč)*. Beef dishes will cost you the most, maybe because of the thick whipped cream they're garnished with *(260Kč)*, but chicken dishes, including mind-blowers like the chicken pocket stuffed with ham and cheese *(155Kč)*, or the turkey stuffed with blue cheese and broccoli *(150Kč)* are more than reasonable.

⚘ *A: Jiřího z Poděbrad. From the station, head south on Nitranská, the restaurant will be on your right.* Ⓢ *Entrees 90-260Kč.* ⏰ *Open daily 11am-midnight.*

## U BULÍNŮ
Budečská 803/2

⊗✱Ⴤ CZECH ❷

☎224 25 46 76 🖳www.ubulinu.cz

Before you order from this amazing traditional Czech restaurant, read its legend printed in English on the first two pages of the menu. When you're done laughing at the most comprehensive piece of incomprehensible private history you've ever encountered, order anything you want from the large and exciting menu. In keeping with the "devilish" theme of the restaurant (according to legend, the original owners grew horns, a condition called bulinia), chicken dishes *(139-179Kč)* are served with Lucifer skewers and hellish hot sauce. Even vegetarians can get their kicks by ordering any of the several pastas *(89-159Kč)* without chicken, or geting some "traditional Mexican" fare like tortilla with red kidney beans, corn tomatoes, and sour cream.

⚘ *A: Náměstí Míru. From the station, walk southeast down Francouzská. The restaurant will be on the corner 3 blocks down.* Ⓢ *Entrees 119-200Kč.* ⏰ *Open daily 11am-11pm.*

## RADOST FX
Bělehradská 234/120

⊛⛫ VEGETARIAN ❸

☎603 19 37 11 🖳www.radostfx.cz

This little vegetarian cafe thrives inside the Radost FX "complex," comprising a dance club, bookstore, music store, and lounge. The cafe's funky decor—statues climbing through walls—make the menu items seem less outrageous, though The Hot Licker, a combination of dips and stuffed peppers *(330Kč)*, still seems a bit out there. The enormous menu features four different types of veggie burger patties *(180Kč)*; even if you hate vegetarians for being whiney, you gotta admit that's impressive. Other notable achievments include the "Mexican" nachos *(from 185Kč)* and the admirably realized Sloppy Joe *(195Kč)*, made from a mixture of grains, tofu, and sheer balls.

⚘ *C: IP Pavlova. From the station, walk east on Jugoslávská. Take a left on Bělehradská. The cafe will be on your right.* Ⓢ *Entrees 165-195Kč.* ⏰ *Open M-Th 11am-midnight, F-Sa 11am-1am, Su 10:30am-midnight.*

**BANDITOS** 💳🚭📶🍸 MEXICAN [3]

Melounová 2 ☎224 94 10 96 💻www.banditosrestaurant.cz

If you're willing to sacrifice Mexican authenticity for heartier portions, take Banditos over Las Adelitas. While Banditos is surprisingly Mexican for the Czech Republic, it smells more Baja Fresh than Tijuana kitchen. But Banditos has some pinch hitters of its own. A huge variety of Mexican breakfasts washes the floor with options elsewhere around town. Not feeling a Mexican Hat Dance? Banditos also serves burgers, including the Coronary Bypass *(255Kč)*, which has mayo, fried egg, double cheese, and double bacon.

*🚇 C: IP Pavlova. From the station, head left down Ječná. Fork left quickly at Kateřinská, then take the 1st right on Melounová. The restaurant will be on your right. $ Entrees 120-280Kč. ⏰ Open daily 9am-12:30am.*

## HOLEŠOVICE

**👍 LA CRĚPERIE** 🥗🚭📶🍸 FRENCH [1]

Janovského 4, Praha 7 ☎22 087 8040 💻www.lacreperie.cz

La Crěperie's jive is as hip and French as anyone could hope for. Decor details like a gold-star-striped walls, old photos, even those red bathroom doors Frenchies require for their bowels to work, win this place before we even get to the food. But the food's great too. Sharp "zappy" espresso *(32Kč)* comes *avec* biscuits, the crepes *(35-89Kč)* are perfectly drizzled with honey, and the tunes are hand-selected French grunge rocks and froggie ballads. Someone should film a movie here called, *Amélie II: Czech Out My Quirks!* French *galettes*—buckwheat crepes with savory innards like ham and cheese—are the VIPs of this menu...crunchy and flaky, they're the original Hot Pockets *(72-110Kč)*. Get them with a cup of traditional Brittany cider mixed with blackcurrant cream.

*🚇 C: Vltavská. From the station, head right down Bubenské nábřeží then loop around and cross in front of the giant church; the restaurant is on your left. $ Crepes 35-89Kč. ⏰ Daily 9am-11pm. Kitchen closes at 10pm.*

**MOLO 22** 💳🚭🍸☀ FUSION [3]

U Průhonu 22, Praha 7 ☎22 056 3348 💻www.molo22.cz

Full of annoyed-looking Czech businesswomen sharing bottles of wine, Molo 22 is a reasonably priced, semi-classy affair where Czech and Thai cuisnes blend with a splash of Italian charm. Main dishes combine cultures in innovative ways; try the Hot Thai Risotto *(179Kč)* or the pork tenderloin with sour cherry sauce and grilled grapes *(229Kč)*. Meals are suprisingly filling and well-prepared if not always smash hits flavor-wise. Maybe they'll film the next *Sex and the City* sequel here: *I Have Problems with Men and I'm in Prague.*

*🚇 C: Vltavská. From the station, take tram 5 or 12 to the 4th stop to your left, U Průhonu. Go to your left down U Průhonu; the restaurant will be on your right. $ Entrees 154-425Kč. Wine 200-500Kč. ⏰ Open M-F 8am-midnight, Sa-Su 9am-midnight.*

**KORBEL** 💳🚭🍸 CZECH [1]

Komunardů 1001/30, 170 00 Praha 7 ☎22 298 6095 💻www.restauracekorbel.cz

The building that held Holešovice's oldest restaurant now houses its youngest and hippest one. But don't let the fancy, vaguely-Cubist chairs or the free-form paintings of "sexy Pilsner bottles" give you the wrong idea; the prices and the fare are still solid and traditional. Czech specialties dominate the menu, with options of pork, duck, rabbit, beef, and chicken in a variety of goulashes, stews, and steaks. Vegetarians will also find a selection of vegetables and cheese dinners *(89-95Kč)*. Currently the menu is only available in Czech, but an English menu is in the works, and the staff is friendly and glad to translate.

*🚇 C: Vltavská. From the station, take any tram that departs to the left. Ride it 2 stops to Dělnická. $ Main dishes 89-175Kč. Beer 24-40Kč. ⏰ M-Sa 11am-2am, Su noon-midnight.*

### ZLATÁ KORADLNIA

CAFE, BOWLING ALLEY [3]

Komunardů 36, Praha 7 ☎24 600 5313 www.zlatakovadlina.com

Eating and bowling, the two recreations of the wise and lazy man, come together at this innovative little pub. In addition to the 4 lanes it packs in the nether regions of the restaurant, Zlatá has a small cafe in the front decorated with a checkout-worthy collection of antique snapshots of the old-school brewing process. Meals stick to the Czech palate and favor snack foods like globs of meat, fried cheese, mushrooms, and various other delicacies *(79Kč)*. Portions are solid enough to fill the serious bowler, while bowling—up to 6 people per lane—is fun enough to thrill the serious eater, who can nonchalantly choose to snack on a 1200g steak. Be warned: you may not ever find a reason to leave this restaurant.

*C: Vltavská. From the station, take any tram that departs to the left. Ride it 2 stops to Dělnická; the restaurant is on the right side of the street. $ Bowling 360Kč per hr. per person. Entrees 109-769Kč. Beer 15-28Kč. Restaurant open daily 11am-11pm. Lanes open 3pm-midnight.*

### LUCKY LUCIANO II

ITALIAN [2]

Dělnicbá 28, 170 00 Praha 7 ☎22 087 5900 Luckyluciano.cz

On a sunny day, not a soul sits in Lucky Luciano's—they're all outside under the giant covered patio. Pizzas are large enough for two people but delicious enough for more, so keep leftovers close enough to slap away would-be scavengers. While some pizzas roll with the standard flavors, others are yellow-bellied rats, like the Tom Buscetta with cream, spinach, eggs, mozzarella, and blue cheese, named after the famous *mafioso* traitor. Main dishes all live in the shadow of the 250g roast pork steaks that can be prepared several ways, including Caribbean, with cream, butter, and region-inspired spices. It's a beautiful slab of pork. Wash it down with a bottle from a great list of Italian wines.

*C: Vltavská. From the station, take any tram that departs to the left. Ride it 2 stops to Dělnická. Walk to the traffic lights and turn left onto Dělnická. i Only outdoor portion handicap-accessible. $ Pizza 105-180Kč. Pasta 115-145Kč. Entrees 240-330Kč. M-F 11am-11pm, Sa-Su 11:30am-11pm.*

### BOHEMIA BAGEL

CAFE [1]

Dukelských hrdinu 48, Praha 7 ☎22 080 6541 www.bohemiabagel.cz

Bohemia Bagel, the joint venture of an American and a Bohemian, successfully serves up authentic Yankee chow. But it does more, too. BB boasts giant, fat-sweating hamburgers *(135-185Kč)*, finger-licking chicken wings *(95Kč)* and best of all, refillable filter coffee *(40Kč)*. The good news continues with the frozen American fru-fru drinks, like frozen margaritas and daiquiris *(105-135Kč)*, which can save your life on a hot day in this city sans air conditioning. Decor is bold, red and vaguely jungle-themed—a nice environment in which to enjoy the free Wi-Fi. Also, use their Bohemian drink specials to ease yourself into some of the funky Czech alcohols you've been scared of. Fernet stock and tonic *(55Kč)*, in a delicious way, tastes like shoe polish and orange juice.

*C: Nádraží Holešovice. From the station, don't cross the street. Take tram 5 to your right 1 stop to Výstaviště. Head under the bridge down Dukelských Hrdinu; the cafe will be on your left. $ Entrees 80-200Kč. M-F 9am-11pm, Sa-Su 10pm-11pm.*

## DEJVICE

### VEGETKA

VEGETARIAN [1]

Kafkova 16 ☎776 343 462 www.volny.cz/vegetka

A Buddhist vegetarian restaurant that serves up the freshest of dishes with an Asian twist. It'll be hard not to like tofu after you've eaten here. The "special soup" is especially noteworthy and stocked with noodles, mushrooms, and coriander (among other secret ingredients).

*A: Dejvická. Keep right around the round about, and make a right on Kafkova from Dejvická. $ Entrees 25-120Kč. Open M-Sa 10:30am-9pm.*

## UNA BELLA CANZONE

🍴👥🍸♨ INTERNATIONAL ❸

Eliášova 331/7

☎224 325 226 🖥www.canzone.cz

A conglomeration of the best foods from different regions and nations found in an almost—but not entirely—affected interior, and a supremely casual terrace. Croatian food is highlighted, as is Italian, but you can also find the classic Caesar salad *(150Kč)*. You only live once though, so go ahead, try the octopus salad *(165Kč)*.
🌱 *A: Dejvická. From the Metro head up Dejvická and make a left on Eliášova. The restaurant is on the next corner.* Ⓢ *Pasta 130-175Kč. Meat entrees 130-395Kč.* ⏰ *Open daily 11am-11pm.*

## PIVNICE BRUSKA

🌐👥⑽🍸❄ INTERNATIONAL ❸

Dejvická 20

☎224 322 946 🖥 www.restaurace-bruska.com

Something of a neighborhood landmark that locals have largely managed to keep to themselves. The wooden furniture and ceiling beams and brick floor all signal a typical Czech pub, but the menu contains several surprises for those who can decipher it. Highlights include kangaroo with cranberry sauce and vegetables *(143Kč)* for those who hate adorable animals, and pork stuffed with bacon *(189Kč)* for those who hate themselves.
🌱 *A: Hradčanská. From the Metro, walk north on Bubenečská and then turn left on Dejvická.* Ⓢ *Salads 70-125Kč. Entrees 120-190Kč.* ⏰ *Open M-Sa 11am-11:30pm, Su 11:30am-10pm.*

## HAVELI

🍴✖🍸 INDIAN ❸

Dejvická 6

☎233 344 800 🖥www.haveli.cz

Authentic Indian food with a price to match. Dine in yet another brick cellar, albeit this time surrounded by portraits of Indian people rather than Czechs or Italians. Vegetarians with money to burn will appreciate the wealth of options, including Bharwan Aloo *(stuffed potatoes with cottage cheese, cashew nuts, and raisins cooked in tandoor; 145Kč)*. Carnivorous types may spring for the Raunaq-e-Seekh *(lamb with coriander, tomato, and onion; 325Kč)*.
🌱 *A: Hradčanská. From the Metro, walk north on Bubenečská and then turn left on Dejvická.* Ⓢ *Appetizers 70-160Kč. Vegetarian dishes 145-225Kč. Entrees 235-330Kč.* ⏰ *Open M-Sa 11am-11pm, Su noon-10pm.*

## ARGUMENT RESTAURANT-CAFE

🍴👥🍸 INTERNATIONAL ❷

Bubenečská 19

☎220 510 427 🖥www.argument-restaurant.cz

Yeah, we thought the name was cool, too. The best part about the place, apart from the dishes of unclassifiable food, are the decorative bookshelves (sans books) and the charts of insects strung on the walls. Regardless of the decor, the 🔳**chili goulash in a bread bowl** *(195Kč)* is the best.
🌱 *A: Hradčanská. From the Metro, walk up Bubenečská. The restaurant will be on your left.* Ⓢ *Appetizers 85-220Kč. Entrees 195-360Kč.* ⏰ *Open daily 11:30am-11:30pm.*

## PERPETUUM

🍴👥🍸 INTERNATIONAL ❸

Na Hutích 9

☎602 666 550 🖥www.restauraceperpetuum.cz

This high-end restaurant serves only home-bred duck and contains various duck effigies of the wooden and rubber variety scattered throughout. Specialties include duck with stuffing and apple *(280Kč)* and homemade duck ravioli with tomato sauce, cinnamon, and pumpernickel *(190Kč)*. For starters, try the strong duck broth with quail egg and celery *(85Kč)*.
🌱 *A: Dejvická. From the Metro, walk through the traffic circle and veer right onto Dejvická, then turn left on Na Hutích.* Ⓢ *Appetizers 130-180Kč. Entrees 260-420Kč.* ⏰ *Open M-Sa 11:30am-11pm.*

## U CEDRU

🍴👥🍸♨ MIDDLE EASTERN ❸

Národní obrany 27

☎224 312 386

On nice days, the outdoor seating offers a fantastic view of downtown Dejvice. Though usually only in the price range of well-to-do older residents, even the occasional student is willing to shell out for some shawarma *(265Kč)*; but be warned,

food · dejvice

whatever your definition of shawarma includes, they still charge for pita.

*🚇 A: Dejvická. From the Metro, walk through the traffic circle onto Československé armády and then make a right onto Národní obrany. $ Appetizers 85-150Kč. Entrees 265-295Kč. ⏰ Open daily 11am-11pm.*

## SMICHOV 🍎

### PIZZA COLOSEUM
🚫⊘📶🍸❄⛅ ITALIAN ❷

Nádražní 344/25 ☎257 322 622 💻 www.pizzacoloseum.cz/

This place is part fast-food dining and part refined cuisine. The decor might be simple and no-frills, but the food offerings include classic pizza and pork tenderloin stuffed with walnuts, raisins, and fresh sage *(260Kč)*.

*🚇 C: Andel. Down the street from the Metro towards the shopping complex. $ Pizza 105Kč. Soup 39Kč. Entrees 95-260Kč. ⏰ Open daily 10am-11:30pm.*

### ARSLAN KEBAP
🚫♿⛅ KEBAB ❶

Bozděchova 2246/3 ☎257 212 869

Hands-down some of the best kebab and gyros found in the city. The bread used to create the gyros sandwich is a fluffy, airy piece of heaven resembling something akin to ciabatta rather than the soggy pita that most places offer. Way cheaper than anything you'll find around the center and also gives you a giant bang for your tiny little buck.

*🚇 B: Anděl. Head away from the mall on Nadrazini and make a right on Bozděchova. $ Gyros from 59Kč. ⏰ Open M-Th 10:30am-10pm, F-Sa 10:30am-11pm.*

### CUKRÁRNA EVELÍNA
🚫♿ PASTRY SHOP, CAFE ❶

Bozděchova 5 ☎602 891 724

This adorable little pastry shop looks like some place you'd take your dolls out for tea and chocolate cake. Don't spend too long ogling the tiers behind the glass case—a long line waits behind you. Enjoy your find at a little white table and be amused by the drooling passersby.

*🚇 B: Anděl. Head away from the mall on Nadrazini and make a right on Bozděchova. $ Cake slices from 18Kč. ⏰ Open daily 9am-7pm.*



### LOKALBLOK
🚫♿📶🍸⛅ CAFE ❶

Náměstí 14 ☎251 511 490 💻www.lokalblok.cz

An adorable little cafe that serves up feasts for cheap by day and functions as a bar come nightfall. Locals love the joint for its leafy courtyard with comfortable armchairs and for the comprehensive lunch meals that will keep you going throughout the day without breaking the bank.

*🚇 Trams 4, 7, 10, 14: Zborovská. Walk in the direction of the tram ½-block to Náměstí, turn right. ℹ Separate smoking room. $ Lunch menus 75-260Kč. Sandwiches 95-135Kč. Salad 55-145Kč. Vegetarian 105-145Kč. ⏰ Open M-F 11am-1am, Sa 4pm-1am.*

### ASTON CAFE RESTAURANT
💳♿📶🍸⛅ ITALIAN ❷

Preslova 13 ☎257 326 483 💻aston-cafe.cz

Fantastic Italian dishes served up in a funky, colorful setting. The decor is modern, with a funky personality, and the food is divine. Try the "demon sandwich," hot toast with a spicy vegetable mix and topped with cheese *(49Kč)*.

*🚇 Trams 6, 9, 12, 20: Arbesovo náměstí. Walk on Kartouzska towards the river and make a right on Preslova. $ Sandwiches 49Kč. Pizza 119-139Kč. Pasta 119-139Kč. Salad 99-129Kč. ⏰ Open daily 11am-11pm.*

# nightlife

Although Prague has one of the greatest clubs in the world (Cross Club) and a few genuinely amazing bars (Chapeau Rouge), most of the nighlife centers on the pub scene. On a typical night, Praguers head out for dinner at a pub (sometimes called Bar Cafe) and just stay there the entire night, drinking beer, smoking cigarettes (indoors, it never gets old) and munching on cold snacks like pickled sausage and fried cheese. Pubs stay open late (12am Su-W, 2-4am Th-Sa) and clubs stay open to 4am or later most night of the week.

Booze across the Czech Republic comes at prices comparable to what you pay for air, but especially cheap and especially delicious are Prague's fire waters: Fernet tastes like a less-syrupy Jagermeister; Becherovka tastes like Christmas in your mouth, and Plum Vodka, tastes—well, the point isn't the taste with the plum vodka.

Nights out in Prague are especially incredible, given that some nights, you can come home completely wasted having spent seven or eight euro. But drink responsibly. Drunk Americans especially become the targets of pickpockets and puking tourists will piss off the tourist police. And then you'll have to sit in the van.

## NOVÉ MĚSTO

### 🞭 ZACHRAŇTE O2 BAR    ●⑂🈀🏍⚷ CHILLOUT BAR

Karlovo náměstí    ☎60 814 4344 🖳www.o2bar.cz

This tiny cabana in the middle of Charles Square Park fits just four cocktail tables. Space is so tight the nightly DJs set their decks on a foosball table in the corner. But it still packs such a huge punch that crowds spill out into the park onto the roof terrace. There's no drink service on the roof, so you'll just have to chill with the punks rolling their own cigarettes and enjoy the surreal view of the New Town Hall lookout tower. Somehow they also fit a kitchen in this place serving cowards a hot dog or some nuts *(15-35Kč)*, while the brave undertake the Delicate Stuffed Cheese with True Story *(55Kč)*. Tell your friends to check the bar's website to see you rocking out on a live web cam.

⚑ *B: Karlovo náměstí. Exit the station on the side closest to New Town Hall and walk 1 block to the north side of the park.* ⑤ *Beer 25-40Kč. Mixed drinks 35-80Kč.* ☼ *Open daily 10am-whenever the party stops.*

### U SUDU    🏍🌐 BAR, CLUB

Vodičkova 677/10    ☎222 23 22 07 🖳www.usudu.cz

From the street, U Sudu seems to be a low key five-table pub with a single bar. But if you take the strangely inviting stairway at the back of the club, you'll encounter a large underground pub space. And if you take the enormous brick tunnel leading out of there, you'll find yet another space. And it kind of keeps going like this—snaking below the street in labyrynthine tunnels. It would be easy to spend a night here and not visit all of the different rooms, each of which has a slightly different vibe. Just hope there isn't a fire. In addition to regular drinks, U Sudu has Master 18 proof *(38Kč)* on tap.

⚑ *B: Karlovo náměstí. From the station, head north towards New Town Tower along the eastern side of the park. Continue past New Town Hall along Vodičkova. The bar will be on your right.* ⑤ *Snacks 10-55Kč. Beer 23-55Kč.* ☼ *Open M-Th 9am-4am, F 9am-5am, Sa 10am-5am, Su 10am-3am.*

### CLUB PRDEL    ●⑂🏍⚷ DANCE CLUB

Žitná 4, 120 00 Praha 2    ☎22 223 0890 🖳www.prdelclub.cz

Like the milk bar of Kubrick's *A Clockwork Orange*, this sweaty young dance club serves wild nectars amid rather accurate busts of women's rumps, hips and etc. Older (lamer) patrons can chill upstairs sucking on the bitter "Cum of Cucumber" *(185Kč)* or the vanilla vodka-based "Orgasmus" *(120Kč)*, while others can head downtairs for a smoky, steamy romp in the juices of youth. Dress for the occasion: 'cause it's close quarters downstairs and when the second DJ gets spinning, this energetic young crowd makes the temp go up. When 6am rolls around, take five in the "special room" behind the curtains. What you do there is your choice–but there are no chairs, only pillows and bean bags.

✤ B: Karlovo náměstí. From the station, head away from the river down Zitna. The club is on your right. ⚡ No dress code, but you'll feel out of place in shorts. ⑨ Beer 40-80Kč. Mixed drinks 120-185Kč. ☼ M-Sa 5pm-7am, Su 5pm-5am.

## WHISKERIA V        ♿ ✿ WHISKEY BAR
Jindřišské Věž        ☎22 424 8645 █www.whiskeria.cz

Travelers who hate dancing, or who don't have legs, will love this brand new whiskey bar where a night can be spent sampling the fruits of rye's labor. Whiskeria offers over 450 varieties of the liquor at prices that are both student-friendly (100Kč) and billionaire-friendly (10,000Kč). If malts are all Greek to you, fret not. The bartenders have graduated from booze university and are eager to share their knowledge. You can check their website for classes and tastings. If whiskey's not your thing, they also have other drinks. Non-smoking seathing is available.

✤ A or B: Můstek. From the station, head away from the river down Jindřišské. It's in the giant tower at the end of the street. ⚡ Whiskey tastings F. ⑨ Drinks 100-10000Kč. ☼ Open daily 10am-midnight or later.

## KARA OK!        ⑨⊛⊗✿ KARAOKE BAR
Legerova 78, 120 00 Praha 2        ☎222 240 035 █www.bekaraok.cz

Like controlled substances in your bloodstream, cultures get more interesting when mixed. This principle makes a night at Kara OK!—Prague's first and only karaoke bar—a confusing, though provoking and generally hilarious concept. Night here starts with your crew renting an elegant private room (800Kč per hr.) and finishing after 12 shots of Jack and a couple carafes of Brittney. It doesn't hurt the fun that drinks and snacks are ordered on a touch screen menu and delivered to your room. Sushi service and sake tastings can be arranged with two days prior notice. Otherwise, just enjoy the bottles of sparkling sake in stock and groove to the song lists in Russian, German, Czech, Swedish, English, Japanese, and Chinese.

✤ C: I.P. Pavlova. From the station, head north on Legerova. The club is on your right. ⚡ Reservations needed for weekends. Bills must be paid for as a group. ⑨ 800Kč per hr. ☼ Half-price rooms 6pm-8pm.

## CLUB STŘELEC        ♿⊛✿▼ CLUB
Žitná 51, Praha 2        ☎60 694 7673

This low-key GLBT hangout is so happy with the small set of locals it serves, it almost refused to be listed. A night at this ace hole-in-the-wall where students mix with septuagenarians could end over beers and traded stories or on top of the tables with an impromptu elderly strip tease. Ask the one bartender who speaks English for authentic Czech drinks like the Bloody Back, a combo of cherry liqueur and vodka drunk simultaneously from two separate shot glasses. But be warned, this pub does cater to seniors as well as students, so don't go looking for too wild a time.

✤ C: I.P. Pavlova. From the station, head north on Legerova and make a left on Žitná. The club is on your right. ⑨ Beer 17-31Kč. Mixed drinks 25-50Kč. ☼ Happy hour daily 5-8pm.

## ROCKY O'REILLYS        ➳⊗✿ PUB
Štěpánská 32/620 Praha 1        ☎22 223 1060

Included more as a warning than as a recomendation, this "Irish" pub pegs itself as, and often ends up being, an obligatory stop for British and American tourists. It need not be so. While Rocky's does blast Prague's half liters for actual English "pints," the charm comes with a hefty price tag. Food, like nachos (145Kč) or ribs

prague

(*295Kč*) is solid enough, and the beer (*30-65Kč*) tastes like beer, but the best things about Rocky's happen on its walls. Sports events get projected onto a big screen, and a hanging poster, "Rocky's 10 Commandments of Travelers," delivers some very wise Prague-specific advice for staying safe and financially responsible while in the city.

*🚇 A and C: Muzeum. From the station, walk down Václavské náměstí and take a left on Štěpánská. The pub will be on your left. $ Entrees 155-300Kč. ⏰ Bar open daily 10am-1am. Kitchen open 10am-11pm. Happy hour M-F 5pm-8pm.*

### ROCK CAFÉ
⊘♿📶🍸 CLUB

Národní 20, Praha 1 ☎22 493 3947 🖥www.rockcafe.cz

Loud and raw, with as much beer in the plastic cups as there is on the floor, Rock Café will, ahem, rock you. Have a beer (*27-45Kč*) beneath the oval wall that's painted like fire, or take your wine (*32-220Kč*) to the tunnel-like dance floor where nightly DJs and occasional live acts rock the jams. No dress code; you could probably wear a burlap sack and it'd be fine, especially during happy hour (*M-F 10am-6pm*), when beer and espresso are a hobo-priced 19Kč. Tu is "Free Zone," which means a free concert and 15min. of free Internet.

*🚇 B: Národní třída. From the station, walk north on Spálená and then turn left on Národní. $ Beer 27-45Kč. Mixed drinks 40-100Kč ⏰ M-F 10am-3am, Sa 5pm-3am, Su 5pm-1am.*

### REDUTA JAZZ CLUB
⊘⊗ JAZZ CLUB

Národní 20 Praha 1 ☎22 493 3487 🖥www.redutajazzclub.cz

Serving up swings and sings since 1958, the Reduta Jazz Club has a different combo act every night of the month. Whether it's a local artist or an international jazz legend, visitors to the club pack sardine style into this one level club for a smoky intimate night of music that's the stuff of legend in the States. While an occasional waitress might show up for a drink order, count on getting them yourself.

*🚇 B: Národní třída. From the station, walk north on Spálená and then turn left on Národní. $ Mixed drinks 40-150Kč. Ticket prices vary, 100-500Kč. ⏰ Open 9pm-midnight, music starts at 9:30pm.*

## STARE MĚSTO

### CHAPEAU ROUGE
⊘⊗🍸 BAR, CLUB

Jakubská 2 ☎222 316 328 🖥www.chapeaurouge.cz

Chapeau Rouge is smarter—and hipper—than your average bar. Maybe it's the sprawling Optimus Prime flying over the bar's front room, or the smattering of penis drawings and condom machines around place, but Chapeau Rouge seems to be that quintessential club we all imagine exists in Europe. Downstairs, where the dancing happens, feels like an entirely different club: smokier and darker. Club has a DJ or a band every night of the week. On Friday and Saturday nights, it's hard to imagine a better bar.

*🚇 C: Republicky Náměstí. From the station, head directly west until you dead end at Rybná. Take Rybná head north up and take a left on Jakubská. $ Beer 25-40Kč. Mixed drinks 60-100Kč. ⏰ Open M-Th noon-4am, F noon-6am, Sa 4pm-6am, Su 4pm-3am. Dance club open daily from 9pm.*

### KARLOVY LÁZNĚ
⊘⊗🍸 CLUB

Smetanovo nábřeží 198 ☎222 220 502 🖥www.karlovylazne.cz

A colossal five-story club with some genuinely impressive lighting and dance floor effects, Karlovy Lázně also manages to be less trashy than you'd imagine from the outside. Each floor plays a particular decade's music, with the exception of one floor that proclaims it plays "black music." The variety of music means that one of the scenes will probably appease you. Drink selection is limited, but the point of this club is mostly to get as drunk as possible and makeout with people: most pub crawls end here. Other highlights include the psychedelic checkerboard dance floor, the Elvis and Marilyn Monroe statues, and the strange laser shooting torso. Huge crowds turn out on weekends, making this place buzz.

⚑ A: Staroměstského. From the station, head towards the river then south on Křižovnické. Club is directly past the Charles Bridge through the tunnel of tourist shops. *i* No dress code. Ⓢ Cover until 10pm 70Kč. After 10pm 120Kč. Drinks 40-160Kč. ⏰ Open daily 9pm-5am.

## ROXY
⊛⊗⌕ CLUB

Dlouhá 33
⬛www.roxy.cz

A large, vaguely industrial dance floor full of reveling Czech locals, the Roxy has a down-to-earth feel that comes from being one of the oldest clubs in liberated Prague. Chill-out sections on the side let you awkwardly watch what's happening below, while the shining circular bars in the middle of the club supply reasonably priced drinks.

⚑ C: Republicky Náměstí. From the station, head north up Revoluční and turn left on Dlouhá. Ⓢ Beer 35-50Kč. Mixed drinks 60-100Kč. Cover F-Sa 100-200Kč. ⏰ Open M, and F-Sa. Hours change, but usually 10pm-late.

## BUDHA BAR
⊛⊗⌕ BAR

Takubská 649/8
☎221 776 400 ⬛www.buddha-bar-hotel.cz

A classier bar with a more adult crowd, don't come here if saving dough is high on your list of priorities. But the experience is enjoyable. Low lights and intoxicating red decor keep the place from being stuffy, even if it is a little hoity-toity. A 12ft. Buddha statue holds court downstairs, rising high enough to peek at the yuppies reclining on the small red sofas. An enjoyable alternative to the beer beer beer that the rest of the city provides, Buddha Bar has an enormous list of sakes as well as over 30 original cocktails (140Kč) including a few large champagne cocktails (380Kč). Fruit smoothies (90Kč) and sushi (100-150Kč per piece) available for those wanting to fill their stomachs.

⚑ C: Republicky Náměstí. From the station, head directly west until you dead end at Rybná. Take Rybná head north up and take a left on Jakubská. Ⓢ Mixed drinks 140Kč. Sake 475-815Kč. ⏰ Open summer Tu-Sa 6pm-4am; winter daily 6pm-4am.

# MALÁ STRANA

**prague**

### ▨ JAZZ DOCK
⊛⊗(((•))⌕♫ MUSIC CLUB ❷

Janáčkovo nábřeží 2
☎774 058 838 ⬛www.jazzdock.cz

For a little over a year now, this newbie jazz club has been setting trends and making waves, and not just because it's by the water. Impressive when it's empty with laser neon stools, full wall windows ,and a black angular interior, Jazz Dock swings hard when it's full of live jazz every night of the week. The gig here is serious; five days of the week include double shows, with programs for children on Saturday and a Dixieland program on Sunday. Due to its genius design, live music can play until 4am without soliciting noise complaints, though on most nights a DJ takes over at 1am or 2am. The ambitious list of progressive cocktails (135Kč) is supplemented by a food menu with catches like Tunafish Snails (85Kč)—"a rolled surprise"—and the Jazz Hot Dock (75Kč)— a hotdog buried in onions and mustard.

⚑ B: Anděl. From the station, head north on Nádražní and take a right on Lidická. At the river, take a left on Janáčkovo nábřeží. *i* Guests who visit the club 3 times receive a card entitling them to a 20% discount on all future club transactions. Ⓢ Cover 190Kč. Under 26 or over 65 90Kč. Beer 29-35Kč. Mixed drinks 135Kč. ⏰ Open M-F 3pm-4am, Sa-Su 11am-4am. Th, F, and Sa shows at 7pm and 10pm. Food served until 4am.

### U MALÉHO GLENA JAZZ AND BLUES CLUB
⊛⊗⌕ MUSIC CLUB ❸

Karmelitská 23
☎257 531 717 ⬛www.malyglen.cz

This tiny jazz spot in the basement of the pub with the same name brings in big talent for intimate little audiences. The pleasurably cramped space has a New York underground sort of vibe and makes for an in-your-face evening. Food can be purchased from the pub usptairs in case you like to gnaw on burritos in swing time.

⚑ Trams 12, 20, 22, 91: Hellichova. From the stop, head north on Karmelitská. Ⓢ Cover 100-200Kč. Beer 30-95Kč. Mixed drinks 65-150Kč. ⏰ Open daily at 8pm. Jazz from 9:30pm-12:30am.

**DIVADLO NAPRÁDLE** CAFE, BAR [2]

3 Besedni ☎777 944 646 www.napradle.cz

Summertime means that the cafe at Divaldo Naprádle is merely the hangout for bougie, upper-class artsy types who come to suck wine in large amounts. During the year, however, the space doubles as a stage where theater students and professionals present wine-soaked mini shows. Wine plays a big role here, as it should with any assemblage of theater types, but you gotta give it to the Czechs for knowing how to up the ante. Divadlo Naprádle serves wine "on spout;" you can even buy wine from this fountain in 1L portions *(89Kč)*. Cafe gets even artsier, tripling as a monthly-rotating gallery.

*A: Malostranská. From the station, take the tram to Újezd, then head north on Ujezd, and take the 1st right at Říční an immediate left at Besedni. $ Wine 20Kč per glass, 189Kč per carafe. Beer 29-45Kč. Show tickets 150Kč, students 90Kč. Open M-F 11:30am-midnight. Sa-Su 3pm-midnight.*

**KLUB ÚJEZD** BAR [2]

Újezd 18 ☎251 510 873 www.klubujezd.cz

Klub Újezd attracts guests as wild as its decorations: bathroom doors show monsters taking dumps, a 20ft. long leviathan snaps above the bar, and corpse faces melt out of the walls. The clientele isn't exactly like that, but three floors do cater to three very different scenes. Upstairs is secluded and smoky, the basement is cold and dungeon-like with a DJ spinning on a mini-stage for the 20 people who can fit there, and the main bar is filled with artists—or posers.

*A: Malostranská. From the station, take the tram to the Újezd stop. $ Beer 25-60Kč. Mixed drinks 65-100Kč. Open daily 2pm-4am.*

**POPOCAFEPETL MUSIC CLUB** MUSIC CLUB [2]

Újezd 19 ☎602 277 226 popocafepetl.cz

A small music club that captures the essence of cool, PopoCafePetl hosts mini parties that are mega fun. A DJ spins from a dance space at the front of the bar most nights, which is nice since the club only has about 15 tables. Hoegaarden on tap also comes as a relief, if Pilsner has you craving another option.

*A: Malostranská. From the Metro, take the tram to Újezd. $ Beer 30-45Kč. Mixed drinks 50-100Kč. Open M-Su 6pm-2am.*

**ŠKABETKÁ BAR** BAR [2]

Zborovská 37 ☎724 032 167 www.skabetkahov.cz

A true Czech dive, this little family-run hideaway has cheap beer and a chill vibe, but it can be pretty quiet. On the bright side, you won't have to worry about handsome Czech locals swooping down on the Czech babes you're hitting on. On the down-side, there might not be any Czech babes. A stage in the front hosts occasional live music and theatrical performances, and the mosaic bar is worth a second look.

*Tram #6, 9, 12 or 20: Svandovo divadlp, then take Vodní towards the river. $ Beer 18-27Kč. Mixed drinks 30-90Kč. Open M-Sa 4pm-2am, and sometimes Su.*

# ŽIŽKOV

**PALÁC AKROPOLIS** CAFE, CLUB

Kubeliková 27 ☎296 330 912 www.palacakropolis.cz

Situated in a pre-WWII theater, this entertainment complex has become a landmark in the Žižkov area. The bar and cafe upstairs serve a mix of expats, local artists, and intellectuals, while the multi-level club downstairs has two bars, each with its own nightly DJ and a clientele that changes according to the music. Reggae night on Sunday is always well attended. The space also hosts concerts and regularly collaborates with a group of performance artists.

*A: Jiřího z Poděbrad. From the Metro, cross diagonally through the park and then take Milešovská; Kubelíkova is on the other side of the Žižkov tower park. i Cover F and Sa 30Kč. Some concerts cost money; check online before you go. $ Beer 25Kč. Open daily 11am-1am.*

## BAR ZNÁMÁ FIRMA
♿&(((·)))᷂⤒ BAR

Husitská 19        ☎222 540 066 █www.znamafirma.com

A trippy, bohemian bar with wild colors on the walls and perhaps the cleanest bathroom you will ever find in a place that serves more Pilsner than water. Nightly programs include live DJs and the occasional karaoke, complimented by an incessant loop of alternative jams in the background.

*Trams 5, 9, or 26: Husinecká. From the tram stop, follow Husinecká until you reach the sq. and then make a left at Orebitská, which will run into Husitská.* ⓢ *Beer 30Kč.* ⓓ *Open M-Th 4pm-2am, Th-Su 6pm-2am.*

## BUKOWSKI'S
♿&᷂ BAR

Bořivojova 86        ☎774 539 689

A designer bar with a literary flourish. Prides itself on using high quality beer and liquors for its signature mixed drinks like "the Naked Lunch" and "the Dorian Gray." A relaxed atmosphere and stylish crowd make this a good place to get respectably sauced. Those who find themselves slipping past respectability can slow down with a smoothie *(75Kč)*. If you hate waking up refreshed and rested on Monday mornings, head to "Sunday 7Kč beer night."

*Tram 5, 9, or 26: Husinecká. From the tram, take Seifertova east, make a right onto Víta Nejedlého and then another right onto Bořivojova.* ⓢ *Beer 30Kč. Mixed drinks 80-100Kč.* ⓓ *Open daily 7pm-3am.*

## LEGENDARIO
♿&᷂ BAR

Jeronýmova 577 / 2        ☎602 800 444 █www.barlegendario.ic.cz

Black leather cubes to sit on, zebra-print "paintings" and a glittery mosaic-tile trim welcomes locals and visitors alike for a night of steamy mingling in close quarters, but don't worry, it's not quite as Metro as it sounds. Mostly draws a relatively middle-aged and laid-back crowd, and is happening even on Sundays.

*Tram 5, 9, 6: Husinecká. Turn right on Husinecká then left onto Jeronýmova* ⓢ *Beer from 35Kč.* ⓓ *Open M-Th 6pm-1am, F-Sa 6pm-3am, Su 6pm-midnight.*

# VINOHRADY

## ▣ RADOST FX
♿᷂ CLUB

Bělehradská 2334/120        ☎60 319 37 11 █www.radostfx.cz

Open as a lounge and cafe every night of the week, Radost takes weekends to unleash its inner world-famous dance club on the city. Glowing rooms and zebra-print couches sell the disco effect, especially when coupled with the eight or so LCD screens flashing crazy images. One of the more advanced light rigs in Prague sexes up the dance floor. If you get tired downtairs, go up for the great but pricey quesadillas and other drunk food *(from 195Kč)* at the cafe. Vegetarians will particularly enjoy getting wasted on veggie and lentil burgers *(185Kc)*. You must try one of the following drinks: Cosmic Granny *(145Kč)*, Lesbian Joy *(110Kč)*, or Sex with an Alien *(145Kč)*.

*C: I.P. Pavlova. From the station, head east on Jugoslávská for a little more than 1 block. when you reach Bělehradská, the club will be on your left.* ⓘ *R and B on Th; house, 80s, and 90s on F; funky on Sa. Lounge is wheelchair-accessible; club is not.* ⓢ *Cover Th 100Kč, F 100-200Kč, Sa 100Kč.* ⓓ *Cafe open M-Th 11am-midnight, F-Sa 11am-1am, Su 10:30am-midnight. Club open Th-Sa 10pm-5am.*

## VALENTINO
♿⊗᷂⤒▼ CLUB ❶

Vinohradská 40        ☎222 51 34 91 █www.club-valentino.cz

On weekends, this caterpillar of a gay dance club blooms into a beautiful butterfly when it adds two additional dance floors to its always-open dance basement and ground-floor bar. In such a huge club, you can tailor weekend nights to your type: get down and d-d-d-dirty on one of the three "floors," bob yo' brain to the beat with a drink at the bar, or, like Chill Bones Bill Bones Baggins, veg out on the patio with a pipe full of the Shire's best tobacco weed. Heck—don't even wait for the weekend. The basement dance floor shakes even when the full club isn't open. Females regularly in attendance; straight gents, not so much.

*A: Náměstí Míru. From the station, walk east on Korunní, then turn left on Sázavská and left on*

*Vinohradská.* ***i*** *Full club only open F-Sa.* Ⓢ *No cover. Beer 19-80Kč. Mixed drinks 33-135Kč.* ⏰ *Open daily 11am-5am.*

### PIANO BAR
BAR

Milešovská 10 ☎775 72 74 96 🖥www.pianobar.sweb.cz

This low-key gay bar may have a piano in its center room, but "piano" could refer to the noise level, which stays soft thanks to the older crowd Piano Bar attracts. But they're not that old—don't let the sewing-machine table fool you.

*C: Jiřího z Poděbrad. From the station, head east on Vinohradská and take a left onto Milešovská.* Ⓢ *Beer 20-30Kč. Mixed drinks 40-70Kč.* ⏰ *Open daily 5pm-late.*

### VINÁRNA VINEČKO
WINE BAR

Lodynská 135/29 ☎222 51 10 35 🖥www.vineckopraha.cz

An upscale wine bar that errs on the side of adult, Vinárna Vinečko is the perfect place to spend a relaxed evening discussing how delightfully you boogie in a non-ironic way. On warm summer nights, the patio lets you decompress even further. Or, if you're lucky enough to be spending the evening with yourself, bring your laptop, use the free Wi-Fi, and treat yourself to a nice glass of *vino*—no buts—you deserve this.

*A: Náměstí Míru. From the station, head west down Rumunská, then take a left down Lodynská. The bar is actually to the right on Bruselská where it meets Lodynská.* Ⓢ *Snacks 68-105Kč. Wine 52-72Kč. Beer 23-60Kč.* ⏰ *Open M-F noon-midnight, Sa-Su 2pm-midnight.*

### SOKOOL
BAR

Polská 1a/2400 ☎222 21 05 28 🖥www.sokool.com

Calm down, nerd-bomber, this bar won't make you popular; it's not Jesus or a new smell, so just calm down. What this bar *can* do is supply a totally relaxed, locals-only experience for the willing traveler. The bartenders speak a bit of English, so it will help if you speak a bit of Czech. For an easy night that won't end on the dance floor but might end with jigging and Czech drinking songs, come on out where the beer flows freely (and comes in liters!). Caution: those old radios hanging around are harder to steal than it would appear.

*A: Náměstí Míru. From the station, walk east on Korunní, then turn left on Budečská.* Ⓢ *Beer 15-64Kč (because it comes in liters!). Shots 35-40Kč.* ⏰ *Open M-F 11am-midnight, Sa noon-midnight, Su noon-11pm.*

### LATIMERIE CLUB
BAR

Slezská 74 ☎224 25 20 49 🖥www.latimerieclub.cz

Watch out for floating fish at this vaguely nautical gay bar that brings together a group of hip locals with fun foreigners. Perfect for travelers looking for more well-lit evenings, Latimerie isn't a slutty, sweaty grind-fest; it's just as animate, but slightly less sinister. That's not to say the club doesn't get wild—no printed closing time means the party goes as late as it's bumping.

*A: Jiřího z Poděbrad. From the station, head south down Nidranská. Slezská will be on your left.* Ⓢ *Beer 30-50Kč. Mixed drinks 50-180Kč.* ⏰ *Open M-F 4pm-late, Sa-Su 6pm-late.*

## HOLEŠOVICE

### CROSS CLUB
CLUB

Plynární 1096/23 🖥www.crossclub.cz

Possibly the coolest club you will ever attend, Cross Club exists over five or six stories, including a five-level patio. The club works like this: half of the club is "pay to enter" and the other half, the cafe and restaurant, is free. But here's the rub—none of these places are connected. In other words, you get a stamp and then you wander between the rooms, all decorated with the most amazing assortment of industrial steel. The crowds err on the side of Czech, but internationals can be found about. The real treats are the various "themed rooms" that you discover making your way through the multi-level club. One room is only tall enough to sit in, and you have to crawl to your seat; another is lit only by narrow lamps made from car engines. The club also features several incredibly cheap food options, like hamburgers *(39Kč)* and fried cheese *(39Kč)*, at different stations. As if this wasn't enough, the upstairs has two speciality shops, one featuring a load of original, hip T-shirts, the other selling vinyl records.

*🚇 C: Nádraží Holešovice. From the station, head south through the bus station to Na zátorách. Head east on Na zátorách until it becomes Plynámí; the club is on your left. $ Cover 40-100Kč. Beer 25-40Kč. Mixed drinks 40-105Kč. ⏰ Cafe open daily 2pm-2am. Club open Su-Th 6pm-4am, F-Sa 6pm-6am.*

### CLUB MECA

🎟⊘🍸 CLUB

U Průlomu 3 ☎28 387 0522 💻www.mecca.cz

If a club's quality can be judged by the number of disco balls hanging above its dance floor, then Mecca's quality is 40. Overpriced drinks look good in the hands of the well-dressed clientele who sometimes boogy on the fancy glowing dance floor. Guest DJs from Vienna, Paris, London, and the States spin some quality tunes, but if the dance floor DJ isn't doing it for you, just follow the red-light runway downstairs to the "chill out" room where a different DJ spins a slightly more relaxed groove.

*🚇 C: Nádraží Holešovice. From the station, take tram 5 or 12 east (to the left) 2 stops to U Průlomu. Walk right half a block down U Průlomu; the club is on your right. **i** No shorts or sandals. $ Cover F-Sa 190-290Kč. No cover July-Aug. Beer 45-65Kč. Mixed drinks 60-185Kč. Champagne 500-12000Kč. VIP section available for 500-900Kč with the purchase of a bottle of some hard liquor. Accepts USD$. Credit cards only allowed in VIP area for bills over 500Kč. ⏰ Open W and F-Sa 11pm-4am (or later).*

### FRAKTAL

🍴⊘🍸⛱ PUB

Šmeralova 178/1 ☎77 779 4094 💻www.fraktalbar.cz

Also a great local restaurant of the neighborhood, Fraktal serves double duty as one of the liveliest and most colorful late night pubs. Has great American drunk food, like quesadillas *(135-155Kč)*. Funky bar features some artwork that may have been created by by children as well as some that definitely was. Seats come in all shapes and sizes; a raised leather bench serves as seating at the bar alongside regular stools, and an elevated table in one corner seems to be reserved for hobbits. Eclectic mix of locals and internationals, especially on the weekends.

*🚇 C: Vltavská. From the station, follow Bubenské nábřeží to the right. Once you pass the church, continue down Milady Horákové to Latenské náměstí; the bar is on your right. Wheelchair-accessible on patio only. $ Beer 22-50Kč. Wine 40-90Kč. Entrees 80-185. ⏰ Open daily 11am-midnight. Kitchen open M-F 11am-11pm, Sa-Su 4pm-11pm.*

## SMICHOV

### DOG'S BOLLOCKS

🎟 BAR, CLUB

Nádražní 42/82 ☎775 736 030 💻www.dogsbollocks.cz

If the giant, gaping hole of literally a fake dog's ass doesn't deter you, it is possible to have some fun in this triple-threat venue that hosts live DJs and boasts a large dance floor to get your boogie on. If you're looking for something more mellow, the restaurant menu offers a diverse array of fare from burgers to eco-friendly vegetarian munchies.

*🚇 Trams 6, 12, 14, or 20: Na Knížecí. Walk 1 block and the place will be on your left. **i** Check online for performance listings. $ Pasta 99-134Kč. Vegetarian 74-119Kč. Burgers 115Kč. ⏰ Open M 5pm-midnight, Tu-Th 5pm-3am, F-Sa 5pm-5am.*

### FUTURUM MUSIC BAR

🎟⊘📶🍸 BAR, CLUB

Zborovská 82/7 ☎257 328 571 💻www.futurum.musicbar.cz

Perhaps the most stylish bar you will find in Prague, Futurum boasts high ceilings with gorgeous mosaic formations on the floor and ceilings. Set in red low lighting and expansive with its many nooks, the place is perfect for both an intimate evening or a melodic, high-spun night on the town. Order your drink at the long, winding bar that looks like the brim of a tastefully tiled swimming pool and enjoy the live music happening almost every night.

*🚋 Trams 4, 7, 10, or 14: Zborovská. Head towards the river ½ block, turn left on Zborovská **i** Check online for event listings. $ Beer from 30Kč. 🕒 Open daily 9am-3am. Concerts begin at 9pm.*

# arts and culture

Travelers itching for some authentic artistic and cultural experiences are about to get scratched. By Prague. But anyone interested in seeing a show of any kind should be warned: while Prague has incredible art, music, and showmania, there also exist God-awful tourist shows that cost inexcusable sums. The best opera Prague has to offer is available to students for the cost of a sausage from a street vendor. The best music Prague has to offer comes at the cost of *two* said sausages. In other words, any show that costs more than 190Kč for a student ticket is probably going to suck. Prague has three symphonies, each of which is world-class: the **Czech Philharmonic,** the **Czech Radio Symphony Orchestra,** and the **Czech National Sympohny Orchestra.** Opera can be seen at the **State Opera House,** the **Estates Theater,** or the **National Theater.** Additionally, there are private galleries all about the city, even in portions of Old Town where many artists personally show their work. As with all crafts, more legitimate respected artists will sell their wares away from Old Town. The popular music scene can be good at various clubs, but for some awful reason, someone decided it would be a good thing for piano players to play the same five songs at cafes around the city and for cover artists to sing the same five whiney guitar songs ("Wonderwall" included).

While Prague does have a few theaters that consistently show English productions, these shows are mostly tourist traps and in no way reflect the incredible wealth of English theater that actually goes on here. Prague does, however, have a number of companies that more or less consistently put on shows in various venues. Travelers interested in seeing legitimate theater should check 💻www.expats.cz and 💻www.prague.tv for extensive theater listings. In recent years, **Prague Playhouse** (*💻www.prague-playhouse.com*) has produced the highest number of English language shows, while **Blood, Love, and Rhetoric** (*💻www.bloodloverhetoric.com*) is a great up-and-coming company. The **Prague Shakespeare Festival** (*💻www.pragueshakespeare.cz*) even produces a few English performances of Shakespeare plays each year. While most Czech theater plays are repertory, or one or two nights over a six-month period, most English language shows play in short runs or in five to six runs scattered over two weeks or so.

## THEATER

### NATIONAL THEATER

🎭♿🍸 Nové Město

Národní třída ☎224 90 14 87 💻www.narodni-divadlo.cz

Producing a program of dance, opera, and Czech-language drama, the National Theater is considered one of the most important cultural institutions in the Czech Republic. The theater itself dates back to 1881, though various fires and other setbacks have caused alterations since then. In addition to its regular schedule, during the summertime, smaller, open-air productions consistently grace the surrounding square.

*🚋 B: Národní třída. From the station, walk north to Národní and turn left toward the river. $ Tickets 300-1200Kč. 🕒 Open M-F 10am-5:30pm, Sa-Su 10am-12:30pm and 1-5:30pm. Evening box office opens 1hr. before curtain.*

### STATI OPERA PRAHA

🎭♿🍸 Nové Město

Wilsonova 4 ☎224 22 72 66 💻www.opera.cz

Thanks to the State Opera House's student-rush program, travelers can see a fully staged opera for less than the price of a sausage at nearby Wenceslas Sq. Presenting a dozen or so plays at a time, the State Opera sticks with favorites but paints with a bigger brush than the tourist-friendly Estates. Wagner, Mozart, Verdi, and Puccini operas are most frequently produced, with new productions interspersed more occasionally.

*🚇 A or C: Muzeum. From the station, head past the National Museum to the left. $ Tickets 100-1500Kč. Students 50-750Kč. ⏰ Open M-F 10am-5:30pm, Sa-Su 10am-12:30pm, 1pm-5:30pm. Evening box office opens 1hr. before curtain.*

**ESTATES THEATER** 💳♿🍸 STARE MĚSTO

Ovocný trh ☎224 90 14 48 💻www.estatestheatre.cz

If it's not enough for you to walk by the famous theater where Mozart conducted *Don Giovanni* or the legendary theater where movie Mozart conducted *The Magic Flute* in the movie *Amadeus*, then it'd better be enough for you to see a show here, because otherwise you're out of options. These days, the Estates plays mostly opera hits like *Carmen*, *The Marriage of Figaro*, and you guessed it, *Don Giovanni.*

*🚇 A or B: Můstek. From the station, head northwest up Na Můstku and turn right on Rytířská. $ Tickets 300-1200Kč. ⏰ Open M-F 10am-5:30pm, Sa-Su 10am-12:30pm and 1-5:30pm. Evening box office opens 1hr. before curtain.*

## FESTIVALS

👍 **PRAGUE SPRING MUSIC FESTIVAL** MALÁ STRANA

Hellichova 18 ☎257 31 25 47 💻www.prague-spring.net

An enormous, month-long festival featuring over 70 performances by the world's best soloists, small ensembles, symphony orchestras, and conductors. In addition to public exhibitions ranging in admission price from free to exorbitant, the festival also plays host to an extensive soloist competition. Founded in 1945, the fest survived the pressures of an oppressive communist regime and continues to bring music to the world in a truly unique way.

*$ Tickets 100-10,000Kč. ⏰ Early May-early June. Check website for specific dates.*



**PRAGUE WRITERS FESTIVAL** STARE MĚSTO

Platýz, Národní 37/416 ☎224 24 13 12 💻www.pwf.cz

An exciting five-day celebration of writers of all tongues, the Prague Writers Festival prides itself on bringing in the best of the craft. In 2010, the Festival honored Nobel Prize winner Gao Xingjian, among other top writers in the field. Events of the festival include readings, signings, galas, and question-and-answer sessions.

*$ Tickets 100-500Kč. ⏰ During the 1st 2 weeks of June. Check website for specific dates.*

# shopping

It'd be a bit of a stretch to call Prague a prime shopping destination. While rare items and great deals can be found, they are few and far between. Most of tourist Prague is overrun by Bohemian crystal dealers and marionette shops, but any traveler on a budget would do well to avoid these. Antique and secondhand stores offer the best shots for rare communist artifacts or snazzy, underappreciated clothing.

## CLOTHING

👍 **PARAZIT** 🚫💳🚫♿ STARE MĚSTO

Karlova 25 ☎603 56 17 76 💻www.parazit.cz

An amazing find in any city, Parazit has more unique fashion finds, outrageous wardrobe choices, and other pieces out of some Tim Burton nightmare. Dresses seem like passion projects from *Project Runway;* match one with a bag that looks like a human head. There are definitely more options for women, but men can find a few fiercely original T-shirts. Every item is handmade by Czech designers and Czech design students.

✠ A: Staroméstka. From the station, head down Křižovnická directly along the river. At the Charles Bridge, turn left at Karlova towards Old Town Sq. Keep following Karlova as it snakes around. The shop will be in a courtyard to the left. ⑤ Shirts 200-500Kč. Dresses from 1200Kč. Bags from 300Kč. ⌚ Open M-Sa 11am-8pm.

## ŠATNA (THE CLOAKROOM)
Konviktská 13

🕭🅧 STARE MĚSTO
☎444 03 04 15

A tiny little boutique with a large supply of secondhand leather jackets and men's jeans in good condition. A few men's shirts, shoes, some blouses, etc. Not exactly a bargain for secondhand, but definitely the pick of the litter.

✠ B: Národní třída. From the station, head north on Spálená and continue as it becomes Na Perštýně. Curve around to the left and move onto Konviktská. ⑤ Shirts 100-300Kč. Pants 150-400Kč. Jackets 240-400Kč. ⌚ Open M-F 11am-7pm, Sa 11am-6pm.

## LALY
Štupantská 3

🕭🅧 STARE MĚSTO
☎775 07 63 26 🔲www.laly.cz

Admittedly pricey for a secondhand store, Laly nevertheless does have a grip of nicely chosen retro thrift clothes in all shapes and sizes. Especially choice are the men's smoking jackets and crazy women's pants with floral designs. But what's coolest at Laly, strangely, are the tags, each of which is handmade, some which are miniature marker and collage masterpieces in and of themselves.

✠ A: Staroměstská. From the station, walk up to Kaprova and turn right continuing through Old Town Sq. Head around the right side of the church onto Celetná. ⑤ Shirts from 280Kč. Ties from 180Kč. Jackets from 400Kč. Dresses from 400Kč. ⌚ Open M-Sa 11am-8pm, Su noon-7pm.

## DUCCO SHOP
Spalená 21

🅐🅧 NOVÉ MĚSTO
☎602 81 80 29

A genuine little bargain clothing store full of Czech parents clothing their angsty teens, Ducco might not be the hippest stop for designer fashion, but it's a hard one to top for functional clothes at ridiculously low prices.

✠ B: Karlovo namesti. From the station, head south on Spalená. The store will be on your left. ⑤ Shirts 100-200Kč. Jeans 150-300Kč. Shoes 300-1000Kč. ⌚ Open M-F 9am-8pm, Sa 9am-7:30pm, Su 10am-7pm.

## EXCLUSIVE SECOND HAND
Revoluční 1201/18

🅐♿ NOVÉ MĚSTO

The aptly named Exclusive Second Hand sells a great selection of quality used clothing at genuinely secondhand prices. Locals fill up this little spot to poach great female blazers, like-new men's collared shirts, and pants of all sorts.

✠ C: Republicky Náměstí. From the Metro, head north up Revoluční. ⑤ Shirts 80-100Kč. Coats 200Kč. Pants 150-200Kč. ⌚ Open M-F 8:30am-6:30pm, Sa 8:30am-11:30am.

## NOVY SMICHOV (ANDEL)
Plzeňská 8

➔♿(¶)⛄✲ SMICHOV
☎251 511 151 🔲 novysmichov@segece.cz

This giant mall boasts a Tesco hyper-market, cinema with Czech-dubbed films, several coffee shops, clothing stores, an outdoor and sporting-goods shop and a food court with restaurants and fast-food. Much of downtown Smichov is organized around this area.

✠ C: Andel. Walk up Stroupeznickeho toward the giant complex. ⌚ Most shops open daily 10am-5pm. Tesco open daily 7am-midnight.

# BOOKS AND MUSIC

## 📓 GLOBE BOOKSTORE
Pštrossova 1925/6

🕭♿✲ NOVÉ MĚSTO
☎222 52 02 36 🔲www.globebookstore.cz

Attached to a cafe with the same name, the Globe caters specifically to American and British expats looking for literary enlightenment in Czech-speaking Prague. Featuring an impressive collection of literature, travel guides, and general-interest books, the Globe should definitely be a first stop for book-seeking travelers, and we're not just saying this because it sells 👍**Let's Go.**

*➤ B: Karlovo náměstí. From the station, take Resslova toward the river and then turn right on Na Zderaze, which becomes Pštrossova; the cafe is on your right. ℹ Attached cafe keeps the same hours. 🕰 Open M-Th 9:30am-midnight, F-Sa 9:30am-1am (or later).*

### BIG BEN BOOKSTORE
💳♿ STARE MĚSTO

Malá Štupartská 636/5 ☎224 82 65 59 💻www.bigbenbookshop.com

This cute little bookshop located just across from St. James Cathedral offers travelers a solid, authentic literary outlet in the middle of tourist-ridden Old Town. Although it doesn't have the most incredible variety of books, for its size, Big Ben has enough literature and travel guides to warrant a look. Stop by in May during the Prague Writers Festival for book signings by visiting authors.

*➤ From starestka naměstí, take Týnska east, continuing straight through the courtyards as it turns into Týn. The courtyard lets out at Malá Štupartsá, where you should take a left. 🕰 Open M-F 9am-8pm, Sa 10am-8pm, Su 11am-6pm.*

### RADOST CD-VIDEO
💳♿ VINOHRADY

Bělehradská 120 ☎224 25 27 41 💻www.radost-cdvideo.cz

The Oz of the Czech music scene, this 15-year-old shop offers not just music, but information and vibes like you can't get elsewhere. Maybe that's why many record producers and musicians like hanging out here.

*➤ C: I.P. Pavlova. 🕰 Open M-F 10am-8pm, Sa 11am-7pm, Su 1-7pm.*

### SHAKESPEARE AND SONS
💳🚫 MALÁ STRANA

U Luzické Semináře 10 ☎257 53 18 94 💻www.shakes.cz

Shakespeare and Sons offers an impressive collection of new and used books in English, Russian, Spanish, Czech, and German. So, whether you wanna be a Predictable Pauly and read Milan Kundera's *The Unbearable Lightness of Being* or an Impulsive Ike and read Jackson Pollack's unofficial biography, *Splattin' It*, you'll find it at a good price here. Note: *Splattin' It* is not an actual book.

*➤ A: Malostranská. From the station, go down Klárov toward the river, and turn right on U. Luzické Semináré. $ Prices vary. 🕰 Open daily 11am-8pm.*

### LUXOR PALACE OF BOOKS
💳🚫 NOVÉ MĚSTO

Václavské náměstí 41 ☎221 11 13 32 💻www.neoluxor.cz

This enormous Czech book warehouse also has a sizeable collection of English language volumes from travel guides to literature to children's books. The store also sells paper, pencils, and other stationery and has a cafe in the basement. But don't get lost; this cavernous bookery makes Barnes and Noble look cute.

*➤ A or C: Muzeum. 🕰 Open M-F 8am-8pm, Sa 9am-7pm, Su 10am-7pm.*

## SPECIALTY STORES

### 👍 VETEŠNICTVÍ
💳🚫 MALÁ STRANA

Vitězná 16 ☎257 31 06 11

Thrift-store shopping hasn't quite become as posh Prague-side as it has in the States, but one-of-a-kind treasures can still be found here—although at prices that are far from thrifty. Still, if you're looking to pick up a communist-era backpack or a secondhand bed pan, you'll find plenty here. Even if you know you intend to buy nothing, take a few minutes and appreciate the mildly pornographic glassware or the hundreds of strangely personal old photographs.

*➤ A: Malostranská. From the Metro, take the tram to Újezd then walk towards the river on Vitězná. $ Antiques 10-10,000Kč. 🕰 Open M-F 10am-5pm, Sa 10am-noon.*

**GOLD PRALINES** ♿🍸 NOVÉ MĚSTO

Rybná 668 ☎222 31 62 27 💻www.goldpralines.cz

This specialty store offers everything from truffles to miniature chocolate statues to intricately cut chocolate diamonds. With over 40 different types of truffles, each with a unique shape and flavor, Gold Pralines will please even the pickiest of travelers. Non-chocolate treats like marzipan figurines are also available.

*🚇 C: Republicka námestí. From the Metro, head west. $ Chocolate 30-300Kč. ⏰ Open daily 9am-8pm.*

**THE PRAGUE GALLERY** 🏷 MALÁ STRANA

Malostranske nabrezi 1/558 ☎602 32 69 83

Four local artists show and sell their work at this corner gallery. A nice place, since in addition to the 50,000Kč wallet-buster pieces, they offer plenty of prints for under 10 bucks *(200Kc)*. If you want to pick up something for mom or a girl—I guess your mom is also a girl—this isn't a bad place to kill a few minutes. Owners will help you package and ship any souvenirs you pick up.

*🚇 A: Malostranská. From the station, take the tram to Újezd, then walk toward the river on Vitězná. $ Art 200-50,000Kč. ⏰ Open daily 11am-7pm.*

# essentials 7

## communication breakdown

The phone code for Prague is ☎420.

## PRACTICALITIES

- **TOURIST OFFICES: Prague Information Services.** *(Arbesovo nám. 4, on the ground floor of Old Town Hall to the left of the Astronomical Clock. ☎221 714 133 💻www.pis.cz* ***i*** *Other branches at Na příkopě 20, Hlavní nádraží, and in the tower on the Malá Strana side of the Charles Bridge. Look for the green "i" signs throughout the city. ⏰ Open daily Apr-Oct 9am-7pm; Nov-Mar 9am-6pm.)*
- **LUGGAGE STORAGE:** Lockers in train and bus stations take 25Kč coins. For storage over 24hr., use the luggage offices in the basement of Hlavní nádraží. *($ 40Kč per day; bags over 15kg 60Kč. ⏰ Open daily 6-11am, 1:30am-5:30pm, and 6pm-5:30am.)*
- **POST OFFICE:** *(Jindřišská 14. ☎221 13 11 11 🚇 A or B: Můstek. ⏰ Open M-F 8am-6pm.)*
- **INTERNET CAFES:** Free Wi-Fi is available at countless cafes and restaurants across the city. Internet cafes are less frequent, but still extremely abundant.

## EMERGENCY!

- **EMERGENCY NUMBERS: Medical Emergency** ☎155. **Unified European Emergency Call (operator speaks Czech, English, German)** ☎112. **Fire Department** ☎150.
- **POLICE** ☎158. **City Police** ☎156.
- **PHARMACY:** *(Paleckeho 5. ☎224 946 982)*
- **MEDICAL SERVICES: Na Homolce (Hospital for Foreigners).** *(Roentgenova 2. 💻www.homolka.cz/en/ ⏰ Open M 8am-6pm, Tu 8am-8pm, W 8am-6pm, Th 8am-8pm, F 8am-6pm.)* **Doctor Prague Health Centre.** *(Vodickova 28. ☎603 433 833 💻www.doctor-prague.cz ⏰ Open 24hr.)*

# GETTING THERE

## By Plane

**Ruzyně Airport** is 20km northwest of the city. *(Take bus #119 to A: Dejvická.* ☎220 111 111 Ⓢ*12Kč, luggage 6Kč per bag. Buy tickets from kiosks or machines.)* Airport buses run by **Cedaz** *(*☎*220 114 296* Ⓣ*20-45 min., 2 per hr.)* collect travelers from náměstí Republiky *(*Ⓢ *120Kč);* try to settle on a price before departing.

## By Train

International trains *(*☎*972 226 150)* run to: **Berlin, DEU** *(*Ⓢ *1400Kč.* Ⓣ *5hr., 6 per day).* **Bratislava, SLK** *(*Ⓢ *650Kč.* Ⓣ *5hr., 6 per day).* **Budapest, HUN** *(*Ⓢ *1450Kč.* Ⓣ *7-9hr., 5 per day).* **Kraków, POL** *(*Ⓢ *950Kč.* Ⓣ *7-8hr., 3 per day).* **Moscow, RUS** *(*Ⓢ *3000Kč.* Ⓣ *31hr., 1 per day).* **Munich, DEU** *(*Ⓢ *1400Kč.* Ⓣ *7hr., 3 per day).* **Vienna, AUT** *(*Ⓢ *1000Kč.* Ⓣ *4-5hr., 7 per day).* **Warsaw, POL** *(*Ⓢ *1300Kč.* Ⓣ *9hr., 2 per day).*

## By Bus

**Eurolines** and airport shuttle tickets are sold at the terminal. *(*☎*224 218 680* 🖳www. eurolines.cz Ⓣ *Open M-F 7am-7pm, Sa 8am-7pm, Su 9am-7pm.)*

# GETTING AROUND

## walk it out

Let's Go recommends 🚶**walking.** Prague is a relatively small city; grab a pair of Nancy Sinatra's boots, and conquer it by foot.

## By Public Transportation

Prague's Metro system alone could sufficiently serve this fun-size city, but Prague also has a tram service (light rail), a bus service, a horde of angry taxis and something called a funicular.

An 18Kč public transportation ticket (there's just one type, regardless of the type of transportation) buys a 20min. non-transferable tram or bus ride or a five-station non-transferable Metro ride. A 26Kč ticket lasts 1¼hr. with unlimited transfers, and buys a ride on the funicular cable car that runs to the top of **Petřín Hill.** Tickets, which are available at stations and all convenience stores, must be validated at the start of each trip; unstamped tickets are invalid. Although ticket inspections are rare, a hefty fine awaits freeloaders, so pay up. One-, three-, and five-day passes cost 100Kč, 330Kč, and 500Kč, respectively; a monthly pass costs 550Kč. Metro trains run every 2-10min. on line A (green), B (yellow), and C (red) daily 5am-midnight. The dozens of tram lines keep different hours, and lines and routes change for late-night service.

Travelers should be mindful of pickpockets and remember that Praguers are big on respect. Persons under 30 should offer seats to seniors or prepare to be shunned like lepers.

# prague 101

## HISTORY

### Citadel on a Hill

Prague might not be the "mother of cities," as one nickname claims, but it certainly has been around long enough. The Celts settled the Vltava River basin as early as 200 BCE, but legend has it that the city was founded around the eighth century by a Slavic power couple named

## facts and figures

- **POPULATION:** 1.2 million (city), 1.9 million (metropolitan area)
- **TIME ZONE:** GMT +1
- **PHONE CODE:** 420
- **AVERAGE ANNUAL BEER CONSUMPTION:** 43 gallons per Czech, the highest per capita in the world. Now that's worth toasting.
- **LONGEST VOWEL-LESS WORD:** 8 letters. The distinction goes to *scvrnkls*, meaning "to flick one's finger."
- **AREA OF PRAGUE CASTLE:** 18 acres.
- **NUMBER OF TIMES YOU WILL HEAR THAT KAFKA LIVED IN PRAGUE:** Innumerable.
- **TIME IT TOOK TO BUILD ST. VITUS' CATHEDRAL:** Almost 600 years.
- **NUMBER OF SPIRES:** The "city of 100 spires" actually has around 500.
- **NUMBER OF MUSEUMS:** 53. Enjoy everything from the Museum of Medieval Torture to the Museum of Chocolate Paintings.

**Libuse and Přemysl.** This semi-mythical pair are the credited with founding the Přemyslid dynasty, which ruled the city until 1306. The oldest concrete (or rather stone) evidence of the Premyslids is Prague Castle, built on a hill overlooking the Vltava circa 870. Prague quickly became the seat of the Kings of Bohemia, a region of the Holy Roman Empire (not a hippie convention). In the 14th century **Charles IV (1316-1378)** stepped up city development, building institutions such as St. Vitus' Cathedral and Charles University and running such fantastic publicity that in 1355 Prague was made the capital of the whole HRE. Less fantastic was Charles IV's successor Wenceslas IV (1378-1419), whose reign saw a pogrom of 3000 Jews and the burning of notable religious reformer Jan Hus. His followers, the aptly-named Hussites, began a long civil war.

### Got your Defenestrate-on

The HRE joined the über-powerful Hapsburg empire in 1526 despite Prague's Protestantism not jiving with the Catholicism of the new rulers. This did not present a problem until 1618, when Prague's electors showed their disapproval of Emperor Ferdinand II (a hardline Catholic trying to impose religious uniformity) by shoving his cronies out a window of Prague Castle. Known as the **Defenestration of Prague,** this little tiff instigated the 30 Years' War, which included two foreign occupations and the loss of two-thirds of Prague's population before the Peace of Westphalia in 1648. Prague's bad luck continued with a conflagration in 1689, one last plague outbreak in 1713-1714, and damage from the **Battle of Prague** (an Austria-Prussia showdown) in 1757. The 18th and 19th centuries turned out better for Prague as it prospered as an industrialized trade center, courtesy of nearby coal mines and ironworks.

### Mightier than the Sword

Czech attempts to shake off Hapsburg rule began before the 20th century, but they remained part of Austria-Hungary until 1918, when A-H's big loss in WWI led to the creation of the Republic of Czechoslovakia with Prague as its capital. In 1939 the **Nazis** set up shop in Prague Castle, but this didn't stop heavy German bombing after a prominent Nazi (Reinhard Heydrich) was assassinated in 1942. Citizens finally revolted against German occupation on May 7, 1945, just two days before the Reich's surrender. The city did not savor freedom for long—the Soviets moved in four days later and Czechoslovakia fell behind the **Iron Curtain.**

**prague 101 . history**

In 1967 the Czechoslovakian Writers' Congress protested the Soviet regime, and the secretary of the Communist Party (a.k.a. leader of the country), **Alexander Dubcek**, listened. From 1967-1968, a brief attempt at democratic reform known as **Prague Spring** was spearheaded by Dubcek, but this garden party was decisively crashed when Soviet tanks rolled into Prague in August 1968. Prague bucked the system again in 1989, when riot police put down a peaceful student demonstration, which inspired a city-wide protest movement known as the **Velvet Revolution**. Using civil disobedience tactics, this bloodless revolution successfully dismantled Communist rule. Prague became the capital of the newly formed Czech Republic on Jan. 1, 1993. Since then Prague has flourished into a major tourist destination and the scene of rapid globalization—so rapid, in fact, that in 2000 more than 15,000 people gathered to protest the process. McDonalds executives steered clear of high windows.

### The City Today

Prague was founded as a literal city on a hill, its imposing castle overlooking the Vltava River from the high West bank. Today Prague spreads over nine hills in the Bohemian Basin, with the Vltava coursing through its center. The city has been the political capital of the Czech Republic since January 1, 1993, and houses the Czech parliament, president and prime minister. The city government is comprised of a mayor, a quadriennaly elected city council, and separate administrative offices for each of the city's 10 districts. Since 1990, city government efforts have focused on ameliorating situations neglected before the Soviet collapse, including industrial pollution and urban crime.

## FOOD AND DRINK

### Food

All the traditional central European staples make an appearance in Czech cuisine, including goulash, brats, and things ending in "kraut" and "schnitzel." Many dishes are served with a side of **knedlik**, i.e. gravy-laden flour dumplings. For vegetarians, **fried cheese** (*smazeny syr*), omelettes, and potato pancakes (*Bramborak)*, are local favorites. Other distinctly Czech specialties include *Beefsteak na Kyselo*, which is beef with a tartar sauce-like gravy, and *Kapr Peceny s Kyselou Omackou*, which is carp (the national fish). Soups such as *Cesnekovy Polevka* (garlic soup), *Drstkova Polevka* (tripe soup), and onion soup are also popular. Steer clear from these on date nights, though—unless you're packing industrial strength breath mints.

### Drink

With the world's highest per capita beer consumption, it's easy to guess the king of Prague's beverage world. It's actually tough to find a meal for which **beer** isn't an appropriate accompaniment—some Czechs even have it with soup for breakfast. Beer is also a lunch favorite, happy hour standard, and dinner is almost incomplete without this "liquid bread." It doesn't hurt that beer is cheaper than the average can of soda. For authentic local flavor, try brews like **Pilsner Urquell, Budvar, Staropramen** and **Branik**.

## SPORTS AND RECREATION

### Spectator Sports

Football (soccer) and ice hockey are Prague's biggest professional sports. Prague has not one but two hockey arenas: T-Mobile Arena (Za Elektrárnou 419, Praha 7) is home to the **Sparta Praha** squad, while the new Sazka Arena (Ocelárská 460, Praha 9), which hosted the 2004 World Championships, sponsors HC Slavia. The **AC Sparta Praha** football club has a fanatical following; if you're willing to handle some seriously rowdy Czechs, catch a match at the Toyota Arena (Milady Horákové 98, Praha 7).

## Recreation

Prague's parks are the star of the show; in 2006 the city spent $40 million renovating them, and upkeep remains a priority. Popular parks include Franciscan Garden, Petřín Hill, and Vrtba Garden all within the city center, and Havlickovy Sady, Letna Hill, and Riegrovy Sady just outside it. Prague also has a public tennis complex, Bedvik (Bedvik 1, 110 00 Prague 1, phone ☎+420 220 514 015), and public swimming pools at Podoli (Podolska 74, Prague 4, phone ☎+ 420 241433 952).

# MEDIA

Prague is home to all the premier Czech media sources, from the national daily *Právo* to *Frekvence 1* radio. For those used to taking a few more vowels with their consonants, however, there are plenty of English language options in this tourist-friendly capital.

## Publications

The weekly *Prague Post*, which proclaims itself "The Czech Republic's Only English Language Newspaper," is the only option in print, but not the only one available for local news in English. Online publications like the *Prague Daily Monitor* (🖳www. praguemonitor.com/), *Fleet Sheet* (🖳www.fleet.cz), and *The New Presence* (🖳www. new-presence.cz) all have English content (if you need a wireless hotspot, try the popular **Globe Bookstore**, Pstrossova 6). International English newspapers like the *Times of London* and the *New York Times* are also available at good newsstands. For listings of events, cinemas etc., free pamphlets such as *Think Again* and *Provokator* are available at many hotels and touristy restaurants.

## Radio and Television

*Radio Prague*, Prague's international station, has great coverage of national as well as international stories. Other options include *BBC World Service* (101.1 FM) and *Radio Free Europe* (1287 AM). If you want to czech out (sorry) the local happenings, talk options include Czech Radio, Frekvence 1, Radio Impuls, and Evropa 2. The Czechs have four nationally produced TV channels: Czech TV, CT 24 (public news channel), and the commercial stations TV Nova and Prima. English or other language options are limited to whatever your satellite provider picks up, but can include BBC and other European stations.

# ART AND ARCHITECTURE

Though relatively compact among European capitals, Prague boasts no small share of architectural wonders and cultural venues.

## Prague Castle

This hilltop fortress is Prague's oldest structure, dating back to c.870 CE, and boasts the largest castle area in the world, with about 18 acres of medieval nooks and crannies. Adjacent to the castle are two other historic structures: **St. Vitus' Cathedral**, perhaps the world's greatest testament to architectural OCD (it took the Czechs 600 years to pronounce it finished), and the Strahoy Monastery, a baroque confection from the late 17th-18th century. Also nearby are the well-manicured royal gardens.

## The Charles Bridge

Perhaps Prague's most recognizable monument, this bridge over the Vltava was built in 1357 and remained the primary route for crossing between the Old Town and the rest of the city until 1841. Cars were allowed until 1974, but now the cobblestoned length is for pedestrians and Monet wannabes only.

## The Old Town Square

If you have trouble wending your way through the Old Town's medieval streets, just follow fellow tourists and you'll end up at this square. Its landmarks come in a variety of architectural flavors, from the gothic Týn Cathedral to the baroque St. Nicholas Church. Climb the stairs of the Old Town Hall's towers to get a great view of the whole area, and make sure to get a staple tourist photo with the famous **astronomical clock** on the Hall's southern wall. Then catch your breath at the statue of Jan Hus in the square's center, which, along with Witches' Night, showcases Prague's historic affinity for burning people.

## Wenceslas Square

This second hub of the Old Town has two main landmarks: the National Museum, designed by Czech architect Josef Schulz in 1885-1891, and the monument to St. Wenceslas, whom the Czechs venerate as both a patron saint and a symbol of nationalism. He moonlights as a Christmas carol.

## Old New Synagogue

The paradoxically named Old New Synagogue is Europe's oldest active synagogue, built in 1270. Word isn't in on when it gets to be simply "old."

# HOLIDAYS AND FESTIVALS

Globalization or not, Prague continues to celebrate itself in distinctly Czech ways. Christmas carp, anyone?

## festivals

- **MIKULÁŠ (ST. NICHOLAS' DAY-DECEMBER 5TH).** It's reverse trick-or-treating: An elaborately costumed St. Nicholas roams around Old Town Square, asking children whether they've been good or bad, and doling out treats or coal accordingly. What gives this tradition its Czech flair is St. Nick's entourage: an angel and devil. Don't leave the neighborhood without checking out the Christmas markets loaded with handicrafts and goodies. Get your holiday treats while you can—the traditional Christmas dinner is carp.

- **EASTER.** Prague's Easter markets take over the Old Town Square, selling traditional handcrafts of all kinds. The stars of this show are the hand-decorated Easter eggs. A less commercial (and PC) Easter tradition entails men making bundles of willow twigs called *pomlaskás*, and going to see their favorite girls, who can either decorate the *pomlaská* or throw cold water on their suitors. Seems cute today, but some remember when Easter was still "let's beat women with *pomlaskás*" day.

- **LOVER'S DAY (MAY 1ST).** In Prague, the traditional thing to do is take your honey to the top of Petřín Hill, deposit flowers on the grave of romantic poet Karel Hynek Mácha, and smooch away—nothing like taking in the view and being a spectacle simultaneously. Of course, most participants are too busy to notice others' PDA.

- **ST. VÁCLAV DAY (WEEKEND OF SEPTEMBER 28).** Czechs put the fun in fungi the weekend of this feast day, when thousands travel to the forests around Prague in search of the elusive Václavky mushroom. If Czechs have a national sport, it might just be mushroom hunting—they get pretty competitive about it, so don't even think of honing in on someone else's fungi.

- **WITCHES' NIGHT (APRIL 30).** Another Petřín Hill extravaganza, this tradition involves taking the effigy of a witch up to the top of the hill and burning it. Because it would be a shame if witch burning went out of style entirely.

prague

# BUDAPEST

Perhaps the single most underrated city in Europe, Budapest is a city for lovers and dreamers, a place where the grocery store clerk will chat you up even if he can't understand a word you say, a land where ruins become hang-outs where hipsters drink beer and watch experimental films, where people flock to museums until three in the morning, where every building has its own character, its own name and color. Nowhere else can you play chess with half-naked men three generations above you in the warm waters of a Turkish bath. You might be hard-pressed to find a picture comparable to one taken at sunset from Fisherman's Bastion on the top of Buda Castle. Enjoy a stroll down Andrássy boulevard, with its tree-lined walkway where purple and yellow flowers bloom to tickle your feet as you pass. In the past few years since Hungary entered the European Union and Union money began to flow into the once severely impoverished nation, Budapest has become a city under constant repair and reconstruction; the result is a city of juxtaposition. Newly erected buildings stand hand-in-hand alongside ancient 18th century ones whose crumbling facades become endearing rather than appalling. Bridges seem to crumble into the waters below and then suddenly reemerge polished. Perhaps what makes the city most remarkable is that rather than discarding its scars from a bloody history, it scrambles to preserve them. What makes this city great is not that it seeks to distance itself from the brutality of what was, but instead to learn from and at times even embrace the past towards the nurture of a future through acts of filial affection.

## greatest hits

- **RUBBER DUCKIE, YOU'RE THE ONE.** Make out in the bathtub upstairs at Szimpla Kert (p. 198), Budapest's original ruin pub.
- **GET ICED.** In the winter, an area of Hősök tere (Heroes' Square, p. 175) functions as an ice rink.
- **FRESH TO DEATH.** Learn proper hummus-and-pita-eating techniques at Hummus Bar (p. 186)
- **NOTHING IS GIVEN SO FREELY AS ADVICE.** The staff at Aventura Boutique Hostel (p. 166) gladly doles out suggestions on the where and what.

# orientation

### THE BELVÁROS, DISTRICT V

You can't say you've conquered Budapest until the Belváros, Budapest's downtown, has been checked off your list. Keep in mind, though, that this is the most heavily touristed area of the city; restaurants will gladly strip you of all you've got and stores will sell you the cheapest, well, garbage at high prices. That being said, this neighborhood's hostels will give you a lot of bang for your buck in an unbeatable location. **Grand Market Hall** at the foot of the green **Szabadság Bridge** is a place for the faint of wallet; rows of freshly baked bread and spicy strung salami create a visceral experience—free of charge. Perhaps the greatest asset this part of town has to offer the penny-pinching backpacker is the walk along the **Danube,** one street over from Váci utca. Benches line the boardwalk, folk musicians play their accordions in the summmertime, kids run after balls and puppies, and you can experience one of the most beautiful views of Buda and **Castle Hill** this side of the city.

### LIPÓTVÁROS, DISTRICT V AND XIII

Lipótváros includes parts of District V and XIII, beginning after Arany János utca, adjacent to the Belváros, and continuing along the river past Margit Island. This neighborhood boasts the majestic **Parliament Building** with its Gothic spires, as well as St. Stephen's mummified hand carefully preserved in the Basilica. Lipótváros also extends into Budapest's former factory district. Now home to a few dozen giant apartment buildings, the area is one of the few places yet to be refurbished in the city. While not much attracts the average tourist past Margit bridge, the more adventurous will find a few hidden treasures nestled between the towering residential complexes.

### ERZSÉBETVÁROS, DISTRICT VII

Named for the beloved wife of **Emperor Franz Joseph,** Erzsébetváros has been the center of Jewish life in Budapest for over 150 years. Almost entirely destroyed during WWII, the area has been in a state of reconstruction since the late '80s. "Elizabeth Town" now boasts some of the city's most beautiful architecture and inviting streets, not to mention to her Great Synagogue and many kosher delis. While the Jewish label remains, unfortunately, many of the area's once flourishing kosher, family-style restaurants have closed due to economic hardship. Although the mealtime establishments have dwindled, Erzsébetváros still plays host to the city's greatest number of

budapest

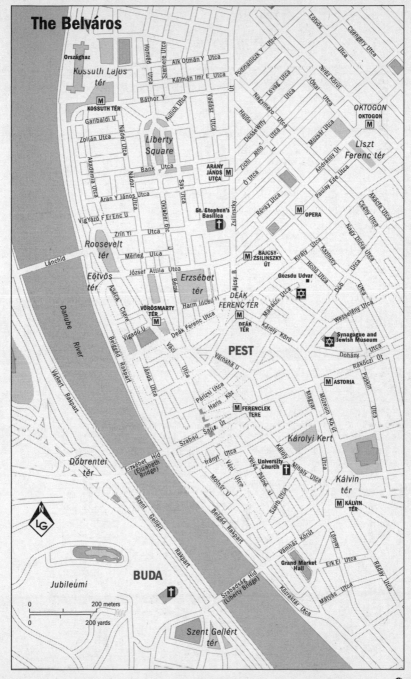

# The Belváros

Országhaz

Kossuth Lajos tér

**KOSSUTH TÉR** Ⓜ

Szemere Utca
Honvéd
Alk Otmán Y Utca
Kálmán Imr E Utca
Báthor Y
Garibaldi U
Nádor Utca
Vadasz. Utca
Alulich Utca
Aulich Utca

Zoltán Utca
Akademia Utca

*Liberty Square*

Bank Utca
Sás Utca
Oktober 6tc
Nádor

Aran Y János Utca
Vig Yázó F Er Enc U
Zrin Yi Utca

St. Stephen's Basilica ✝

*Roosevelt tér*

Lánchid
Mérleg Utca
József Attila Utca

*Eötvös tér*

*Erzsébet tér*
Bécsi

**VÖRÖSMARTY TÉR** Ⓜ

Harm Inced V

*DEÁK FERENC TÉR* Ⓜ

Deák Ferenc Utca
Deák Ferenc Utca

*Danube River*

Várkert Rakpart
Belgrád Rakpart
Vadágó U
Apáca Csere
Vigadó U
János Utca
Váci Utca

**PEST**

Varoshá U

Párizsi Utca
Haris Köz

**FERENCLEK TERE** Ⓜ

Szabad Sajtó Út

*Döbrentei tér*

Erzsébet Hid (Elizabeth Bridge)

Irányi Utca
Veres Palne U
Molnár U
Váci Utca

University Church ✝

Szent Gellért Rakpart

**BUDA** ✝

*Jubileumi*

0      200 meters
0      200 yards

Szabadság Hid (Liberty Bridge)

Belgrád Rakpart

*Szent Gellért tér*

Eötvös Utca
Csengery Utca
Perez Körút
Ókai Utca

Poczmaniczky Utca
Lovag Utca
Nagymezo Utca
DesseWffy Utca
Zicht Jeno
Ó Utca

*OKTOGON*
**OKTOGON** Ⓜ

*Liszt Ferenc tér*

Mózsár Utca
Andrássy Út
Paulay Ede Utca

ARANY JÁNOS UTCA Ⓜ

Zsilinszky
Révay Utca

Ⓜ **OPERA**

Akácta Utca
Cseny Utca
Nagy Dicfa Utca

Ⓜ **BAJCSY-ZSILINSZKY ÚT**

Gozsdu Udvar ✡

Király Utca
Kazmecy Utca
Holló Utca
Dob
Wesseleny Utca

Madáca Utca
Károly Körú

✡ Synagogue and Jewish Museum

Dohány Utca
Rákóczi Út

Ⓜ **ASTORIA**

Museum Kö Út
Puszim Utca

*Károlyi Kert*

Károly Mihaly Utca

*Kálvin tér*

Ⓜ **KÁLVIN TÉR**

Vámház Körút
Lónyay
Grand Market Hall
Erk E Utca
Ráday Utca
Köraktár Utca
Matyás Utca

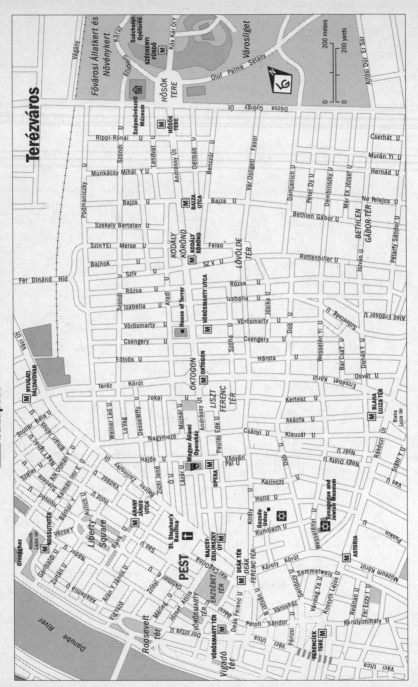

budapest

Terézváros

PEST

ruin pubs, keeping it a bustling and exciting climate during the late night and early morning hours.

## TERÉZVÁROS, DISTRICT VI

Perhaps the busiest district of Budapest, **Terézváros** hosts an international train station, corporate offices, giant supermarkets, import stores, and the most globally diverse selection of dining opportunities you'll find in the city. The district line begins at **Nyugati station** and extends eastward to **Erzsébet körút** and runs north-to-south along Andrássy út from **Heroes Square** to the **State Opera House.** The area to the south on and near Hajós utca boasts some of the city's coolest new ruin pubs, while **Liszt Ferenc tér,** a few blocks from the **Oktogon,** offers outstanding budget eateries from Hungarian canteen-style joints to fancier sit-down ordeals. As in most cases, a busier environment means more commotion, and while there's no reason to fret on an average day, heed the area around the train station for pickpockets, peddlers, and obnoxious drunks—especially at dawn.

## JÓZSEFVÁROS, DISTRICT VIII

Don't be discouraged from visiting Budapest's eighth district, an area that up until a few years ago was known for its homeless population and dicey sex shops. Józsefváros now has some of the city's friendliest little parks and squares, a fantastic artist community and the Budapest film school, and the gorgeous National Museum building. You will also be hard-pressed to find a young local who doesn't recommend the area for its newly polished charm and underground nightlife.

## FERENCVÁROS, DISTRICT IX

Similar to the eighth district, Ferencváros is an up-and-coming district with newly renovated Baroque buildings and winding cobblestone streets. The past few years of "city rehabilitation" projects have left the inner half-circle (the area contained between **Ferenc körút** and the Danube) of the district looking freshly polished, albeit a bit empty. As the renovated areas get prettier, they also become more expensive, forcing previous dwellers to move to communities outside of the boulevard, where delapidated buildings and streets with the homeless are still the norm. The main attraction for tourists in this part of town is **Ráday utca,** a small pedestrian street lined with restaurants and bars. While it can be an enjoyable place to dine in the evening hours, strict district codes forcing establishments to close their doors at midnight leave the nightlife seeker at a bit of a loss.

## THE VÁROSLIGET  *City Park*

The City Park is a lush respite from the heat and messy chaos of the city. It's located behind **Heroes' Square** and is the gateway to the freeway toward **Eger** and other parts in the northeastern corner of the country. While it's easy to stick to the parks and not spend any money here, it is also very easy to blow all your savings as the area is home to some of the most expensive restaurants in the city, namely the posh **Gundel,** a restaurant frequented by royalty. If you want to spend the whole day here and are too lazy to walk back toward the **Oktogon** on **Andrássy út** for cheaper fare, make great friends with the *lángos* makers, as fried dough is probably your only bet for budget-friendly gnawing.

## VÁRHEGY, CENTRAL BUDA, AND THE VIZIVAROS

These three adjacent districts are Buda's most attractive neighborhoods and include **Castle Hill,** the famous **Chain Bridge,** and some of the city's most authentic Hungarian restaurants. It's easy to spend a whole day perusing the cobblestone streets of Castle Hill, marveling at the view and learning about Hungarian art in the National Gallery. For the adventurous traveler with a day or month pass for city transportation, it is also recommended to take a bus from **Margit Bridge,** which winds through the Buda

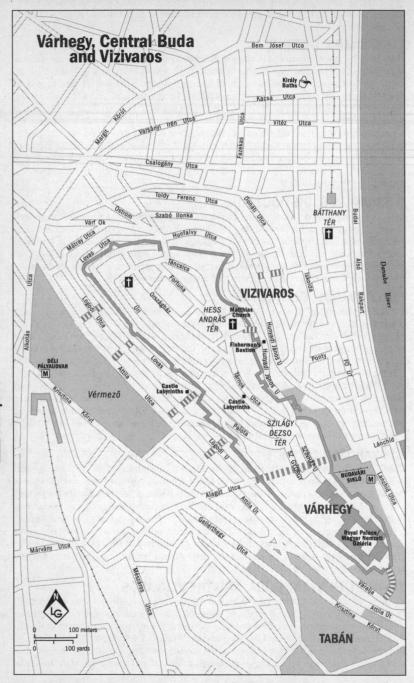

# Várhegy, Central Buda and Vizivaros

Bem Jósef Utca

Király Baths

Kacsa Utca

Vitéz Utca

Margit Körút

Varsányi Irén Utca

Csalogány Utca

Fazekas Utca

Budai

BÁTTHANY TÉR

Toldy Ferenc Utca

Donáti Utca

Ostrom

Szabó Ilonka

Várf Ok

Hunfalvy Utca

Mátray Utca

Lovas Utca

Táncsics

Islolda

Alsó Rakpart

Danube River

Fortuna

VIZIVAROS

Logodi Utca

Ország Ház

Uri

HESS ANDRÁS TÉR

Matthias Church

Fisherman's Bastion

Hunyadi János U

Alkotás

Utca

DÉLI PÁLYAUDVAR
M

Vérmező

Attila Utca

Lovas

Utca

Castle Labyrinths

Castle Labyrinths

Tárnok Utca

Hunyadi János U

Ponty

Fó Út

budapest

Krisztina Körut

Palota

SZILÁGY DEZSO TÉR

Logodi U

SZ GYÖRGY

SZÍNÚ U

Lánchíd

BUDAVÁRI SIKLÓ
M

Lánchíd Utca

Alagút Utca

Attila Út

Gellérthegy Utca

VÁRHEGY

Márvány Utca

Mészáros Utca

Royal Palace/ Magyar Nemzeti Galéria

Váralja

N
LG

0        100 meters

0        100 yards

Krisztina

Attila Út

Körut

TABÁN

hills and behind the castle, for some unofficial sightseeing from the window of the wealthy **Rózsadomb** neighborhood with its palatial abodes.

## GELLÉRT HEGY *Gellért Hill*

Gellért Hill offers the best view of **Pest** (and some peripheral views of **Buda**). If you're looking to capture impressive, heart-stopping photographs to flaunt, make the trek up here on foot, for a rewarding experience, or on bus, for a relaxed one. There are a few attractions on the hill itself, such as the **Liberty Monument** commemorating all who have risked their lives for the Hungarian state, but they fail to steal the show. If you're going to spend more than an hour or two up here, pack sandwiches before you go—anything being sold is triple the price found down the hill.

## ÓBUDA

Óbuda is a residential area north of downtown **Pest** and most attractions in **Central Buda**. If you're looking to witness how the layman lives in Budapest, it's worth a bus ride out and some open-minded wandering. Óbuda's most intriguing attraction, besides, of course, the magical Roman **Aquincum Ruins,** is the nation's largest communist-era apartment building called the **Panel** (for the panels of concrete with which they are assembled) at **Flórián tér.** A recent restoration project of this panel to make them a little more humane has left Flórián tér a giant block of apartments painted neon green.

## MARGIT-SZIGET *Margaret Island*

Margaret Island—an oasis of lush greens, expansive parks and a 5km running loop that wraps around the perimeter—is hands-down the most relaxing place in the city. Mostly a summer haunt for locals and tourists seeking respite from the blazing sun and dirty streets, this place offers something akin to Central Park in New York City, but even better as the river rushes past and building views are almost non-existent. It feels as if you've stumbled into a rain forest big enough to find your own secret nook.

# accommodations

## THE BELVÁROS

### ALL CENTRAL HOSTEL
Bécsi u. 2

⊷♿(ᵒⁱᵖ) HOSTEL ❷
☎01 328 0955 💻www.allcentral.hu

A no-frills hostel with friendly staff, sleek metal bunks, pristine bathrooms and unbeatable location and prices. An elevator whisks weary pack-toting travelers up to one of the four floors for a night of urban-style repose. While the place functions as a hostel during the summer months, foreign students might find this the cheapest deal in the city for term-time housing. A couple blocks away from the Parliament building, Danube River, Basilica and Váci utca, this place is a steal.

⚑ *M1, M2, or M3: Deák Ferenc Tér. Head down Bárczy István utca towards river and turn right on Bécsi utca.* *i* *Wi-Fi included. Laundry 800Ft. Kitchen. Luggage and safe included. Lockers available.* ⑤ *Dorms 3000-5000Ft; doubles 14,000Ft.* ⌚ *Reception 24hr. Check-out 10am.*

### THE LOFT HOSTEL
Veres Pálné u. 19

⊷♿(ᵒⁱᵖ) HOSTEL ❷
☎01 328 0916 💻www.lofthostel.hu

Gorgeous wood paneling, modern decor, tons of leisure activities to keep you occupied (if you choose to stay inside), and carefully-scrubbed bathrooms make this an oasis from tourism. The giant common room can keep the introverted busy and an energetic clientele will gladly team up for a night out. The helpful staff can point you in the right direction for excursions in and just outside of the city.

*➜ M3: Ferenciek Tere. Walk towards river, turn left on Veres Pálné. It's the 3rd street up, parallel to the river. i Wi-Fi included. Kitchen. Printing, DVDs, and games available. $ 3400-4400Ft. ⏰ Reception 24hr.*

**11TH HOUR CINEMA HOSTEL** 💳🚭📶 HOSTEL [2]

Magyar utca 11 ☎01 266 2153 💻www.11thhourcinemahostel.com

An eclectic decor welcomes the weary traveler at this fun-loving hostel. Although perhaps a bit noisier than some, this hostel's central location gives it an urban feel. Towering windows let in the morning light and illuminate the fresh, spacious dorms.

*➜ M2: Astoria. At Kossuth Lajos west, make a left on Magyar utca, just past the Danubius Hotel. i Towel, sleepsack, Wi-Fi, breakfast, coffee, and snacks included. Library. Kitchen. $ Dorms 2000-3500Ft; doubles 5100-7500Ft. ⏰ Reception 24hr.*

**GINKGO HOSTEL** 💳🚭📶 HOSTEL [2]

V, Szép utca 5 ☎01 266 6107 💻www.ginkgo.hu

Large dorms with graffiti-covered doors, chandeliers, and Alfons Mucha prints epitomize avant-garde. The common area provides plenty of space to relax even if the furniture is not the most luxurious.

*➜ M2: Astoria. From the Metro take Kossuth Lajos utca toward the river and turn left on Szép. i Continental breakfast, lockers, linens, Wi-Fi, domestic calls, towels, and linens included. Common room with TV and DVD. Kitchen. No bunks! $ Dorms 3500Ft; doubles 5500Ft. ⏰ Reception 24hr. Check-out 10am.*

**RED BUS HOSTEL** 💳🚭📶 HOSTEL [3]

V, Semmelweis utca 14 ☎01 266 0136 💻www.redbusbudapest.hu

A small hostel compensated by a large kitchen and clean dorms, not to mention a cool courtyard and staircase. The suites come with couches and storage cupboards. If you're in the area, check out the English-language bookstore next door.

*➜ M2: Astoria. From the Metro, take Kossuth Lajos utca toward the river and make a right onto Semmelweis. i Wi-Fi, breakfast, lockers, and linens included. $ Dorms 4100Ft; doubles 10,500Ft. ⏰ Reception 24hr. Check-out 10am.*

**7X24 CENTRAL HOSTEL** 💳🚭📶 HOSTEL [3]

Király utca 14 ☎20 999 9724 💻www.7x24central.com

This place explodes with color and an undeniable homey vibe with attic rooms and old-school furniture. While it's a great deal for traveling groups, beware that the prices go per bed and rooms must be filled entirely.

*➜ M1, 2, or 3: Deák Ferenc Tér. Head up away from river on Király utca i Wi-Fi, domestic calls, towels, and linens included. Common room with TV and DVD. Kitchen. No bunks. $ Quads 5000Ft per bed; doubles 7000Ft per bed. ⏰ Reception 24hr.*

## LIPÓTVÁROS

**👍 AVENTURA BOUTIQUE HOSTEL** 💳🚭📶 HOSTEL [2]

XIII, Visegrádi utca 12. ☎239 0782 💻www.aventurahostel.com

The lofted floors of this hostel feel like your neighborhood playground jungle gym. All the beds have locked storage compartments, and a super-friendly staff gladly doles out suggestions on the where- and what-to's. An amply-stocked kitchen offers free snacks, while a laid-back clientele keeps the ruckus at a low frequency.

*➜ M3: Nyugati. From the Metro head down Szent István körút toward the river and turn right onto Visegrádi. i Wi-Fi, food, spices, and cooking supplies included. Walking audio guide rental of the entire city 3000-5000Ft. $ Dorms from 3500Ft; doubles 11,000Ft. ⏰ Reception 24hr. Flexible check-out.*

budapest

## [pick] THE GROOVE HOSTEL

🚭(Wi-Fi) HOSTEL ❷

XIII, Szent István krt 16. ☎786 8038 🖳www.groovehostel.hu

This hostel has inviting hardwood floors, a cheery interior, plush cubes and beanbags scattered around, and views of downtown Budapest that leave other hostels in the dust. Check out the TV loft above the reception desk or head next door to the famous Comedy Theater for a night of laughs.

*# M3: Nyugati. From the Metro head down Szent István krt towards the river; the hostel will be on your right. i Wi-Fi, lockers, and linens included. $ Dorms from 2700Ft. ⏰ Reception 24hr.*

## CENTRAL BACKPACK KING

🚭(Wi-Fi) HOSTEL ❷

V, Október 6 utca 15. ☎ 200 7184 🖳www.centralbpk.hu

Located directly behind the Basilica, this hostel offers a welcome that rivals a college homecoming; the staff greets you with a shot of *palinka* from the owner's grandmother's village and loads of info on caving, pub-crawls, and baths. The interior boasts colorful rugs and a happening common room equipped with a widescreen TV and tons of movies, but wild kids won't have to look far for a clubbing partner.

*# M1: Bajcsy-Zsilinsky út. Take József Attila utca from the Metro going towards the river and make a right on Október 6. i Wi-Fi, lockers, and linens included. $ Dorms from 3600Ft; doubles 8000Ft. ⏰ Reception 24hr. Check-out 11am.*

## ADORO HOSTEL AND GARIBALDI GUESTHOUSE

🚭(Wi-Fi) HOSTEL ❷

V, Garibaldi utca 5. ☎302 3456 🖳www.adorohostelbudapest.com and www.garibaldiguesthouse.hu

The cheery owner, who speaks English, Italian, Russian, French and Bulgarian, will treat you like family as she shows you around the building and points you in the direction of eateries and sights in the area. One of the dorms features a terrace with a view of the Danube that would make five-star hotel suite guests seethe with envy. Private suites are decorated to emulate a typical Hungarian apartment and give the splurger something to remember.

*# M2: Kossuth Lajos tér. From the Metro take Akademia utca south and turn left on Garibaldi. i Linens and occasional breakfast included. Internet access and Wi-Fi available upon request. Skype the owner via the website if you have questions. $ Dorms from 3600Ft; doubles from 4400Ft. ⏰ Reception 24hr. Check-out 10am.*

## RIVERSIDE HOSTEL

🚭(Wi-Fi) HOSTEL ❷

V, Szent István krt 15. ☎302 6341 🖳www.riversidehostelbudapest.com

No frills here, but clean, fresh, sunny, and friendly. Riverside is within walking distance of all the downtown attractions. Some of the private rooms come with TVs and cable. Not a bad deal if you're looking for a cheap night. Several staff members lead and and organize wine and bike tours.

*# M3: Nyugati. Hostel is on your left as you walk down Szent István krt towards the river. i Lockers 1000Ft deposit. Wi-Fi, linens, and towels included. Laundry 1000Ft per load. Bike rental 1000Ft for 3hr. or 2000Ft for the day. $ Dorms from 3850Ft; doubles 11,000Ft. ⏰ Reception 8am-11pm. Check-out 10am.*

## EAST SIDE HOSTEL

🚭(Wi-Fi) HOSTEL ❶

V, Falk Miksa utca 24-26 ☎574 0224

A gold sneaker welcomes guests to this groovy joint, which offers a beautiful view of the Danube that can be enjoyed while eating breakfast or dinner occasionally cooked up by the staff. Within a pigeon dropping of the Parliament building and up the way from Váci utca, the hostel manages to maintain a level of peace in its niche on a side street.

*# M3: Nyugati. Head down Szent István krt from the Metro, towards the river, and turn left on Falk Miksa. i Wi-Fi, linens, and bike rental included. $ Dorms from 2000Ft; doubles 8000Ft. ⏰ Reception 9am-11pm.*

## ERZSÉBETVÁROS

### 10 BEDS
HOSTEL ❷

Erzsébet krt 15. ☎3620 933 59 65

Feels like you've stumbled into a long lost cousin's apartment. A happy and friendly hostel where long-term guests sometimes become quasi-staff members and welcome you to the city with a trip to a bath or a pub crawl. Eat your breakfast at the stylish new bar or take a bath in the relaxing tub.

*M2: Blaha Lujza tér. Head north on Erzsébet krt from the Metro for a block and a half; the hostel is on your right. i Laundry, lockers, linen, and Wi-Fi included. $ Dorms from 3000Ft. Reception 24hr.*

### THUMBS UP HOSTEL
HOSTEL ❷

Kertész utca 18. ☎3630 318 44 43 www.thumbsuphostel.com

A great deal in the center of town. Two giant common rooms give you something to do for a night and comfy beds at a low price will make you sleep like a baby. A giant flatscreen and loads of DVDs will make you feel right at home. Head to the kitchen to chat with a laid-back clientele.

*M2: Blaha Lujza tér. Head north on Erzsébet krt and veer left at the first intersection; the hostel is near the corner of Kertész and Wesselényi. i Breakfast, Wi-Fi, lockers, and linens included. Towels 300Ft. Laundry 2000Ft. Quiet after 10pm. $ Dorms from 2500Ft; doubles from 4500Ft. Reception 24hr. Check-out 11am.*

### ASTORIA CITY HOSTEL
HOSTEL ❶

Rákóczi út 4. ☎266 13 27 www.astoriacityhostel.com

A clean, basic hostel in a prime location. A beautiful balcony for hanging out, eating breakfast, and reading distinguishes it from other hostels. Friendly, young staff provides helpful information on tours, restaurants, and nightlife, and a mellow clientele enables a no-stress night. Truly unbeatable price, especially in the off-season.

*M2: Blaha Lujza. Head towards the river from the Metro on Rákóczi. i Breakfast included, served 8-10am. Lockers, linens, towels, Wi-Fi, and computer access included. TV and DVDs in common room. $ Dorms from 2820Ft; doubles 9000Ft. Reception 24hr. Check-out 11am.*

### YEP! HOSTEL
HOSTEL ❷

Wesselényi utca 13. ☎785 51 15 www.yephostel.com

An intimate common room invites guests for enjoyable conversation and the tipi-looking beds in the dorms offer a uniquely funky repose. A spacious kitchen stands ready to offer its supplies to top chef travelers. A welcome shot of *pálinka* helps you overcome any reservations you may have about getting close with your dormmates.

*M2: Astoria. Head east on Rákóczi út and turn left on Kazinczy utca and left again on Wesselényi. i Wi-Fi included. Laundry 1800Ft. $ Dorms 3000-3500Ft.; doubles from 8000Ft. Reception 24hr. Check-out noon.*

### LEANBACK HOSTEL
HOSTEL ❶

Erzsébet krt 20 1/4 ☎06 20 243 72 24

A no-frills hostel with a homey feel. Intimate dining room and welcoming owner make it a nice alternative to the rowdy frat-boy-type hostels scattered around the city. Simple bunks and clean showers are welcomed essentials. The hostel has its own bus tour taking guests on alternative routes around the city and just outside of it.

*M2: Blaha Lujza. Head north on Erzsébet krt. i Linens and Wi-Fi included. $ Dorms 2300-5000Ft. Reception 24hr. Check-in noon. Check-out 11am.*

### BIG FISH HOSTEL
HOSTEL ❷

Kertész utca 20. ☎786 2131 www.bigfishbudapest.hu

Take a shot of *pálinka*, but don't get too comfortable—the action is all happening outside. The gigantic bathtub makes up for the no-nonsense bunks and the staff is chill and knowledgeable. Don't worry if you've got nothing to write home about—the surrounding array of ruin pubs will keep the nights interesting and the stories fresh. Maybe you won't want to write home about those happenings either.

*➤ Tram 4 or 6: Wesselényi utca. Walk south from the tram stop one block until Wesselényi intersects with Kertész. ℹ Breakfast, linens, lockers, and Wi-Fi included. $ Dorms from 3000Ft; doubles from 10,000Ft. ⏰ Reception 24hr.*

## TERÉZVÁROS

### 👍 HOME-MADE HOSTEL — 💳🚭📶 HOSTEL [2]

Teréz Körút 22 — ☎302 21 03 💻www.homemadehostel.com

A happy, earthy, and surprisingly quiet little hostel in an apartment building on the main boulevard a block from the Oktogon. Extremely friendly staff cooks delicious food a few times per week to ease you into Hungarian living. Antique TVs, radios, rugs, and no bunks give a unique experience for the traveler looking for a safe and sound stay.

*➤ M1: Oktogon. From the Metro, take Teréz krt east from Oktogon; the hostel is on your left. ℹ Scooter rental. Towels, linens, and Wi-Fi included. Locker deposit 1000Ft. $ Dorms from 3600Ft; doubles from 12,000Ft. ⏰ Reception 24hr.*

### 👍 BROADWAY HOSTEL — 💳♿📶 HOSTEL [2]

Ó street 24-26 — ☎688 16 62 💻www.broadwayhostel.hu

Your name won't be in lights on Broadway, but you'll find a hammock in the courtyard to hang in and wonderfully comfortable beds upon which to sleep away your traveling hardships. Smaller rooms make the experience more personal and each bed has its own giant cupboard that locks. The location is perhaps one of the most happening streets in town and you can't miss the building covered in murals and colorful—intentional—graffiti.

*➤ M1: Opera. From the Metro head north on Hajós utca and take the first right; hostel is on the left and adorned by graffiti. $ 10 to 16-bed dorms from 3300Ft per person. ⏰ Reception 24hr.*

### CARPE NOCTEM — 💳🚭📶 HOSTEL [3]

Szobi utca 5 — ☎365 87 49 💻www.carpenoctemhostel.com

While the signs say "Silence on the Stairs, Shhh!," this hostel near-demands raucousness and energy. A half hour crash-course when you arrive introduces the places to party and drink in the city as well as the other kids you'll be shacking up with for the night. Relatively modest decor, bunks, and bean bags, make up for the extravagant atmosphere.

*➤ M1, M2, or M3: Nyugati. Head east on Teréz krt and left on Szobi. ℹ Linens, towel, and Wi-Fi included. Orthopedic mattresses. Laundry 1500Ft. $ Dorms 4200Ft ⏰ Reception 24hr.*

### ART GUEST HOUSE — 💳🚭📶 HOSTEL [3]

Podmaniczky utca 19 — ☎302 37 39

Nestled in a mellow little side street inside a gorgeous building with an inner courtyard, this respected hostel provides comfortable beds and pristine bathrooms. Great option if you want to escape the boozers without going to the boonies. Spacious kitchen stocked with spices and supplies bodes well for the cooking types.

*➤ M3: Nyugati. From the Metro, take Teréz körút east and turn right on Podmaniczky. ℹ Tea, coffee, and Wi-Fi included. $ Dorms 4400-5000Ft; doubles 12,200-12,800Ft. ⏰ Reception 24hr. Check-in 1pm. Check-out 10am.*

### UNITY HOSTEL — 💳🚭☀ HOSTEL [2]

Kiraly utca 60. 3rd floor. — ☎413 7377 💻www.unityhostel.com

Quirky cartoon drawings on the walls, a brick bar for eating breakfast or drinking tea and a stylish reception desk greet you at this roof-top hostel overlooking Király utca. The hostel's location offers a balcony view of the gorgeous Music Academy building where you can enjoy a complimentary breakfast after a peaceful night of rest.

*🚇 M1: Oktogon. Head west on Teréz krt and turn right on Király. ℹ Breakfast, linens, lockers, Wi-Fi, and goulash dinner first Su of each month included. Ⓢ Dorms from 3000Ft; doubles from 10,000Ft. ⏰ Late check out. Reception 24hr.*

### BEDS N ROSES
💳🚭 HOSTEL [1]

Zichy Jenõ utca 20 ☎332 632 2

A real Hungarian-type guesthouse. This place attracts a diverse clientele full of interesting things to say over meals in the intimate dining area. Simple and clean beds ensure a good night's sleep in what is an unbeatable location. Beds N Roses is really for the true backpacker looking for an authentic experience at probably the lowest price in the city.

*🚇 M1: Oktogon. Head west on Teréz krt and turn left on Zichy Jenő. Ⓢ Dorms from 1500Ft; doubles from 4400Ft. ⏰ Reception 9am-9pm.*

## JÓZSEFVÁROS

### 👍 MANDRAGORA BOUTIQUE HOSTEL
💳🚭🍸 HOSTEL [2]

Krúdy Gyula utca 12. ☎789 95 15 💻www.mandragorahostel.com

This phenomenal budget option doesn't offer dorm rooms, but there is no place in the city, especially with such a great location, that offers private singles and doubles for less. Its gorgeous interior decor looks like something out of a magazine and most of the rooms come with a bathtub. A kitchen and common dining room give the communality of a hostel, but the retreat into a private space gives you the comfort of home.

*🚇 M2: Blaha Lujza tér. Across from the Metro. ℹ Wi-Fi included. TV and DVDs available in the common area. Ⓢ Singles from 5500Ft; doubles from 8000Ft. ⏰ Reception 24hr. Check-out 11am.*

### BUDAPEST BUBBLE
💳🚭 HOSTEL [3]

Bródy Sándor utca 2. ☎266 95 32

Right by the National Museum in a beautiful building, this hostel welcomes guests with friendly service and a homey decor. Multiple common rooms decorated with Fritz Lang posters and the occasional hookah let you relax in sophistication. Ask the staff for expert tips on Budapest's undiscovered bars, clubs and hideouts.

*🚇 M3: Kálvin tér. From the station, head north on Múzeum krt from the Metro and turn right on Bródy Sándor. ℹ Computer access, Wi-Fi, and linens included. Ⓢ Dorms 4500Ft; doubles from 10,000Ft. ⏰ Reception 24hr.*

## FERENCVÁROS

### 👍 MAXIM HOSTEL
💳🍸🚭📶 HOSTEL [2]

Ráday utca 34 ☎2360 404 02 22 💻www.maximhostel.com

Maxim is a new hostel located on the main street of Ferencváros, Ráday. Amazing wooden beds will help you rest easy under crazy wall murals. A spacious bathtub will wash the city grime off your skin and help you relax from the energy of the street. Cool movie theater seats in the common area provide a fun repose and the staff is always on hand to give advice about the city. Occasional free Hungarian meals cooked by staff members cap off an unbeatable deal.

*🚇 M3: Ferenc körút. From the station, head west on Üllői and make a left at Kinizsi utca. The hostel is on the corner of Knizsi and Ráday. ℹ Wi-Fi, linens, towels, and breakfast included. Ⓢ Dorms from 2250Ft; doubles from 7000Ft. ⏰ Reception 24hr.*

**GRUND HOSTEL** 🛏🍸🚭📶 HOSTEL [2]

Tömő utca 6 ☎06 20 583 6712

Separating itself from other hostels in the area with a fabulous inner courtyard and a hopping bar that resembles the seventh district's ruin pubs, you will find a mixed clientele who will either accompany you to the clubs or sit and chat at home. Some savvy locals even flock to the hostel just to chill at the bar on the weekends, making for a uniquely international crowd. The rooms are clean and simple and most doubles have their own bathroom.

*➡ M3: Ferenc körút. From the station, head east on Üllői, left at Nagy Templom utca and first right on Tömö utca. **i** Breakfast, Wi-Fi, linen, and towel included. $ Dorms from 3000Ft. ⏰ Reception 24hr. Check-in 10am. Check-out noon.*

## GELLÉRT HEGY

✎ **BUDA BASE** 💻🚭 HOSTEL [2]

Döbrentei utca 16 ☎3620 543 74 81

Probably the coolest location to stay in this city. At the foot of Gellért Hill you can see the **Liberty Statue, Parliament, Chain Bridge,** and the beautiful buildings lining Pest's shore from your window. Two- and eight-bed dorms usually cost the same and depend on availability. A spacious living room that opens to the kitchen and dining room decorated with the owner's personal furniture give the place an inviting feel. Don't let the Buda location deter you: Pest's buzzing streets are only a 10min. walk away.

*➡ Tram 18 or 19: Döbrentei tér. From the tram stop, head south toward the square. **i** Lockers and linens included. Free Internet and Wi-Fi extends into the garden so you can surf the net in the cool breeze. $ 2- to 8-bed dorms 2000-3300Ft; doubles 8200-10,950Ft. ⏰ Reception 24hr.*

**BACKPACK GUESTHOUSE** 🛏🚭🍳 HOSTEL [2]

Takács Menyhért utca 33 ☎385 89 46 💻www.backpackersbudapest.hu

For those looking to branch out of the 3 sq. m that most tourists navigate in Budapest, this earthy hostel (15min. from central Pest)—where incense is always burning and people are always smiling—is the place to go. Laze in a hammock in the garden, smoke some fruity water pipe in the plush living room, or learn to cook up some sizzling goulash with a staff friendlier than Barney.

*➡ Bus #7 or #7a: Tétényi utca, then backtrack and turn left to go under the bridge. Take another left on Hamzsabégi út and continue to the 3rd right. The 49E night bus runs here after trams stop. **i** In-house yoga. Laundry 1800Ft. Cooking classes, group pub-crawls, and tours available. $ Yurts in garden 3000Ft; 7- to 12-bed dorms 3800Ft; 4- to 6-bed dorms 4500Ft. Doubles 11,000Ft. ⏰ Reception 24hr.*

**MARTOS HOSTEL** 💻♿ HOSTEL [2]

Stoczek utca 5-7 ☎209 4883

College-style dorms of various sizes here are ideal for students and people who wish they still were. Every suite comes with a sink and shower, though you'll have to walk down the hall to find the toilets. Decor is usually limited to whatever the previous semester's occupants left behind. Some have balconies with views of the other institutional-looking dorms. Only recommended if the summer crowds fill every other hostel in town and you're left to your last resort.

*➡ Trams 4 or 6: Petőfi híd, budai hídfő. From the tram stop, walk north along the river and turn left on Bertalan Lajos utca, then left on Stoczek utca. $ Rooms 3800-5600Ft. ⏰ Reception 24hr. Open July-Aug.*

# sights

## THE BELVÁROS

### GRAND MARKET HALL (NAGYCSARNOK)
●& MARKET

Váci utca and Vámház körút

While it looks more like the Nyugati train station, this hall was built in 1894 to emulate the trend of indoor markets in major Western European cities. If you are looking for legit local fruits and veggies, though, don't be fooled by this tourist trap, and head instead to the Buda side markets for a better value. Grand Market Hall *is* worth a trip to witness the infamous Hungarian assertiveness and to gawk at the arched windows, colorfully tiled roof, and Hungarian folk costume peddlers. If you do end up doling out some cash, be sure to haggle like crazy. Head downstairs for some fish and pickled delicacies like pearl onion, stuffed paprika, and cabbage.

✴ *M3: Kálvin Tér. From the Metro take Vámház toward the river.* ۩ *Open M 6am-5pm, Tu-F 6am-6pm, Sa 6am-2pm.*

### UNIVERSITY CHURCH
✪ CHURCH

Papnövelde utca 7

Once the site of a Turkish mosque, University Square is accented by the glowing orange Baroque architecture of University Church, built in 1725. Pauline monks spent 17 years building and then perfecting every nook and cranny of the church, while hiding valuable goblets and costumes in the cupboards lining the interior. This easy-to-miss chapel is between rows of tall buildings and several streets up from the main downtown tourist area, but is worth a gander if you like secret spots. Take it easy under one of the trees in front of the church, or head inside and marvel at its unsung glory.

✴ *M3: Ferenciek tere. From the Metro head east on Kecskeméti utca and turn right on Papnövelde.* ۩ *Services M-F 7am and 6pm, Su 8am, 9am, 11am, 12:30pm, 5pm, 7:30pm.*

### ERZSÉBET TÉR
&♨ CITY PARK

The largest green space in the downtown Pest area, this unassuming chunk of nature has undergone a series of name changes. Initially Queen Elizabeth Square, it became New Square, and then changed to simply Market Place. After WWII it became Stalin Square, then Engels Square from 1953, until its final christening as Elizabeth Square in 1990. An overeager administration planned to construct the new National Theatre Concert Hall at the site just over a decade ago—much to the dismay of the city—and even broke ground just before they were ousted from office. The beginnings of the dig were abandoned and residents began referring to the gaping hole in the middle of the downtown as *"gödör"* (pothole). Fortunately, an ambitious urban renewal project has turned the area into the city's most beloved park, equipped with rolling picnicking greens and a twinkling pool-fountain. The multi-function **Gödör Klub** hosts art shows and live music in what was once intended as a theater. Sit and enjoy the hum of melodies, the smell of *kolbász* grilling, and the grind of skate punks ripping past, with a cold brew and amiable company.

✴ *M1-3: Deák Tér.*

## LIPÓTVÁROS

### 📓 ORSZÁGHAZ (PARLIAMENT)
✎✪ GOVERNMENT BUILDING

Plaza Kossuth
☎01 441 4000 ▪www.parlament.hu

"The motherland does not have a house," lamented Hungarian poet Mihály Vörösmarty in 1846. In response to the growing sense of Hungarian nationalism during the period, the palatial Gothic building looks more like a cathedral than a seat of government. The building is the largest in Hungary and towers at 96m, a number symbolizing the date of Hungary's millennial anniversary. The building once required more electricity than the rest of the city combined to supply power to its 692 rooms! The gold and marble interior shines proudly on the original Holy Crown of Hungary.

*🚶 M2. Kossuth Tér. Head towards the river. ℹ Tours start at Gate XII. Tours last about 50min. $ Entrance and tour 2850Ft, students 1410Ft. Free with EU passport. Ask a guard for permission to buy a ticket at Gate X. ⏰ English-language tours daily 10am, noon, 2pm; buy tickets early especially in summer. Ticket office opens at 8am.*

**SAINT STEPHEN'S BASILICA (SZT. ISTVÁN BAZILIKA)** CHURCH

Hercegprímás utca 7

Completed in 1905 after 50 years of construction, this towering monument and its majestic cupola smile on Budapest's Wall Street. Built in the Neo-Renaissance style, the edifice was damaged during the siege of Budapest in WWII and has undergone a series of renovations. The red-green marble and gilded interior attracts both local worshippers and gaping tourists who come to see the Panorama Tower and the highest 360-degree view of the city. The Basilica's most prized treasure is St. Stephen's mummified right hand, removed from his body by a priest and hidden in the countryside until it was stolen during WWII and subsequently returned. A 100ft donation dropped in the box will illuminate the hand for two minutes!

*🚶 Metro to Deák Tér. Follow the signs. $ Church free. Entry to tower 500Ft, students 400Ft. ⏰ Church open daily 7am-7pm. Chapel May-Oct M-Sa 9am-5pm, Su 1-5pm; Nov-Apr M-Sa 10am-4pm. Mass M-Sa 8am and 6pm, Su 8, 9, 10am, noon, 6, 7:30pm. Tower open daily Apr-Oct. M-Sa 10am-6pm.*

**LIBERTY SQUARE** ♿ SQUARE

Szabadság Tér 8-9 ☎01 428 2752 💻www.english.mnb.hu

Built on the site of a former prison facility meant to tame rebellious Hungarians, the square is now a green space with benches and a cafe. It also contains the only remaining Soviet monument in Budapest proper, a massive obelisk commemorating the Russian soldiers who liberated the city from the Germans in WWII. Nearby, the Hungarian National Bank's elegant facade and the American Embassy ironically (or symbolically) stand face-to-face with the red star-topped obelisk.

*🚶 M3: Arany János. Directly diagonal from the Metro towards the river.*

## ERZSÉBETVÁROS

**GOZSDU UDVAR** WALKWAY

Between Király utca 13. and Dob utca 16.

A 200m stretch of six connected courtyards under six apartment and office buildings, the walkway feels like a secret little market with restaurants, cafes, shops and a stage for concerts, comedy and promo events in almost every courtyard. Perfect for a cool respite from the summer heat or a warm, friendly place in the winter to amble in the energy of Budapest's coolest locals.

*🚶 M1: Oktogon. Head east on Erzsébet krt and turn right on Király utca. ℹ Summer months bring open-air concerts and events. Check www.culture.hu for more information and event listings.*

**SYNAGOGUE AND JEWISH MUSEUM** ♿ MUSEUM, SYNAGOGUE

Corner of Dohány utca and Wesselényi utca. ☎3670 533 5696 💻www.greatsynagogue.hu

The largest synagogue in Europe and the second-largest in the world, Pest's Great Synagogue (Zsinagóga) was built in 1859 and heavily damaged during WWII when the Nazis used it as a radio base during the Siege of Budapest. The 20-year effort to restore the towering onion domes and Moorish Revival-style building is only now coming to a head. The enormous metal weeping willow called the Tree of Life stands in the courtyard as a beautiful Holocaust memorial. Next door, the Jewish Museum (Zsidó Múzeum), built at the birthplace of Zionist Theodor Herzel, displays Budapest's most prominent Jewish artifacts.

*🚇 M2: Astoria. ℹ Covered shoulders required. Men must cover their heads inside; yarmulkes available at the entrance. Admission to museum included with entrance to the synagogue. $ 1400Ft, students 750Ft. Tours 1900/1600Ft. ⏰ Open May-Oct M-Th 10am-5pm, F 10am-2pm, Su 10am-2pm; Nov-Apr M-Th 10am-3pm, F 10am-1pm, Su 10am-1pm. Services F 6pm. Admissions start at 10:30am. Tours M-Th 10:30am-3:30pm every 30min.; F and Su 10:30, 11:30am, 12:30pm.*

## TERÉZVÁROS

### ☑ ANDRÁSSY ÚT — BOULEVARD

Hungary's grandest boulevard, **Andrássy út** extends from **Erzsébet tér** northeast to **Heroes' Square** *(Hősök tér)*. Its elegant gardens and balconies, laid out in 1872 and renovated after the fall of the Iron Curtain in 1989, recall the grandeur of Budapest's Golden Age. While the Metro runs directly under the boulevard, it would be a shame to miss the walk, which takes you past rows of UNESCO-preserved buildings. At the intersection with **Felsőerdősor utca, Kodály körönd** is surrounded by beautifully painted buildings and statues of three of Hungary's greatest Ottoman-killers as well as a poet who celebrated the anti-Ottoman exploits of the other three when he wasn't celebrating more erotic exploits.

### ☑ NYUGATI PÁLYAUDVAR — GRASSY KNOLL

A brand-spanking new nook next to the train station, transformed from a parking lot to a grassy knoll for reading and lounging, along with a terrace for nightlife activities. Revel in the beautiful architecture of Nyugati as a backdrop for this secret little respite off the main boulevard. The venue boasts two cafes and bars and is an up-and-coming host to live concerts, plays, and broadcasts.

*🚇 M 1-3: Nyugati pályaudvar. At the intersection of Teréz körút, Szent István körút, Váci út, and Bajcsy-Zsilinszky út.*

### ☑ EIFFEL TÉR — 🎟♿📶🍸🍽 RAILWAY STATION

🖥www.eiffelter.hu

This railway station is smaller than its eastern cousin, though it has the advantage of being in a neighborhood you'll actually want to visit. The building was designed and built by the Eiffel Co., though its notably less phallic than the company's Parisian masterpiece. The station itself is a beautiful Baroque construction connected to the most lavish McDonald's you'll ever see.

*🚇 M 1-3: Nyugati pályaudvar. To the right of the station if you're looking at the big clock.*

### MAGYAR ÁLLAMI OPERAHÁZ — 🎟♿ OPERA HOUSE

Andrássy út 22 — ☎332 81 97 🖥www.opera.hu

This opera house was built between 1875 and 1884 and was largely funded by Austro-Hungarian Emperor Franz Joseph, who financed the building's construction on the condition that it would not be larger than Austria's own great opera house. The builders assented, though they arguably built a more beautiful opera house, which caused Franz Joseph to storm out of the inaugural performance in a rage. He never returned, and his box has remained empty to all but the most important guests. Not even Queen Elizabeth II was allowed to use it, though somehow Madonna and Antonio Banderas managed to snag the seats. The interior is built in a Neo-Renaissance style, complete with scenes from classical mythology. The informative guided tours are filled with amusing anecdotes about the building's history, including the smoking corridor that was once so thick with cigar smoke that aristocratic teens could make out in front of their hawk-eyed parents.

*🚇 M1: Opera. $ 2800Ft, students 1400Ft. ⏰ 1hr. tours daily in 6 languages 3 and 4pm.*

## THE VÁROSLIGET

### HŐSÖK TERE (HEROES' SQUARE) ♿ MONUMENT

At the Heroes' Square end of Andrássy út, the **Millennium Monument** commemorates Hungary's heroes. Built for the city's millennial celebration, the sweeping structure dominates the square. The pillar in the center is topped by the Archangel Gabriel, presenting the Hungarian crown to St. Stephen. At its base are equestrian statues of the seven chieftains said to be the leaders of the Magyar tribes that settled the Carpathian Basin. The pillar and the surrounding structures contain statues of other national heroes: it's a veritable hit parade of awesome hats through the ages from St. Stephen to King Matthias Corvinus. During the summer, concerts and other events are often held in the square and in the winter an area of the square functions as an ice rink. The square is flanked by the Museum of Fine Arts on the left and the Palace of Art on the right.

*M1:Hősök tere. You can't miss it!*

### SZÉCHENYI-GYÓGYFÜRDŐ (SZÉCHENYI BATHS) ♿ BATH, MONUMENT

Állatkerti körút 11 ☎363 32 10 www.szechenyibath.com

Statues and a fountain adorn the Neo-Baroque exterior of the biggest and one of the most luxurious bath complexes in Europe. A popular destination for locals and tourists alike, you could spend an entire day just relaxing in the swimming pool. Those looking to exercise their minds while their bodies unwind can challenge older intellectuals to a game of chess. Be warned that the games are often intense; don't be surprised if you find yourself surrounded by eager spectators. After your embarrassing defeat, swim away in shame and treat yourself to a consolation massage. The complex's 12 pools and three thermal baths mean you can probably avoid everyone who saw you lose.

*M1: Széchenyi Fürdő. i Bring your own bathing suit and towel. $ Swimming pool 2500Ft per 2hr., 2800Ft per day. Thermal tub tickets 1500Ft per day. Massages from 2000Ft. ⏰ Open daily 6am-10pm.*

### wet and wild

I took a bath for the first time since I've been in Budapest today. Today marks my one-month-and-one-week in this city. Now before you start scrunching up your pretty little noses in your primly scrubbed apartments, fully-equipped with hot showers and clean toilets, I'd like to clarify that this was a special type of bath—yes, I have showered and kept myself tidy since I've been here, thank you very much. What I am talking about here are the magnificent, magical, surreal, entrancing, phenomenally orgasmic Turkish baths where you can float around for hours in warm mineral water and rub elbows with sexy septuagenarians.

The bath I went to, **Széchenyi,** is housed in a beautiful building in the center of the City Park and is the only bath where you can witness said 70-year-old men playing chess on floating chess boards. I'm not sure if you've ever seen a cat play an accordion, but it's kind of like that. Anyway, I seriously recommend bathing when in Budapest. It will make you feel even more refreshed than half an hour of Bikram yoga and provide you with a tale you could never tell your grandchildren. It will be that wild.

*Vanda Gyuris*

### SZÉPMŰVÉSZETI MÚZEUM (MUSEUM OF FINE ARTS) ♿ MUSEUM

Hősök tere ☎469 71 00 💻www.szepmuveszeti.hu

Built to look like a worn temple from antiquity, this building's exterior is as much a work of art as the collections it houses. The museum's main focus is a large collection of Italian and Renaissance pieces. Many of Europe's artistic luminaries can be found here, from **Giotto** and **Bruegel** to **Monet** and **Rodin.** An excellent collection of Dutch work appears on the top floor. The basement juxtaposes the modern art collection with an awe-inspiring Egyptian collection focusing on all things mummified. Some of the striking pieces include mummified hawks, cats, and alligators. One of the museum's prized pieces, a magic wand that looks something like a boomerang, was once used to protect children and expectant mothers from harm.

*M1: Hősök tere. $ 1400Ft, students 700Ft. ⏰ Open Tu-Su 10am-6pm. Ticket booth open Tu-Su 10am-5pm.*

## VÁRHEGY, CENTRAL BUDA, AND THE VIZIVAROS

### ROYAL PALACE MUSEUM

Szent György tér 2

Towering above the Danube on Várhegy, the Castle District has had something of a rough history. Built between the 12th and 14th centuries, the original castle was occupied by the Ottoman invaders, who turned it into barracks and then left it to decay. During the campaign to retake Buda by the allied Christian forces, much of the palace was destroyed by heavy artillery bombardment. It wasn't until the middle of the 18th century that the palace was completely rebuilt, only to be destroyed again less than a century later, when the Hungarian revolutionary army laid siege to it during the 1848 revolution. In the last decades of the 19th century, the palace became one of the most lavish royal residences in the world. For the Hungarians, it was an emblem of national pride. For the Axis forces at the end of WWII, it was the best place to stage a last-ditch defense of the city against the advancing Red Army. Once again, heavy artillery reduced the palace to smoldering wreckage. The communists saw the ruined Royal Palace as a symbol of the old regime and completely gutted its interior. Today Buda Castle version 4.0 closely resembles its Hapsburg incarnation, with flowery courtyards, statues, and panoramic views of the rest of the city. The interior of the palace now houses the **National Széchényi Library** as well as some of the city's finest museums.

*M1, M2, or M3: Deák tér. From the Metro, take bus #16 across the Danube. Or, from 2: Moszkva tér, walk up to the hill on Várfok u. "Becsi kapu" marks the castle entrance.*

### FISHERMAN'S BASTION (HALÁSZBÁSTYA) MONUMENT

Szentháromság tér

Named for the fisherman's guild that was charged with defending this stretch of Castle Hill during the Middle Ages, Fisherman's Bastion is, despite its parapets and towers, a purely decorative structure. Frigyes Schulek, the same architect who restored Matthias Church, designed the bastion with a melange of Neo-Gothic and Neo-Romanesque elements that harmonize with the surrounding structures. The seven towers represent the seven Magyar chiefs who first settled Hungary in 896. The view of Parliament, St. Stephen, and downtown Pest is breathtaking, especially at sunset and at night.

*In front of Matthias Church, walk toward the river. $ Daytime 300Ft, nighttime free.*

### MATTHIAS CHURCH (MÁTYÁS TEMPLOM) ♿ CHURCH

Szentháromság tér 2 💻www.matyas-templom.hu

The colorful roof of Matthias Church on Castle Hill is one of Budapest's most photographed sights. The church was converted to a mosque in 1541, but 145 years later, the Hapsburgs defeated the Turks, sacked the city, and then reconverted the building, in that order. The church's decorations reflect its mixed heritage. Inside, intricate geometric patterns line the walls alongside murals by famed painter Károly Lotz, who also decorated the ceiling of the State Opera House. Facing the altar, turn left and you will find the tombs of **King Béla III** and his first wife, the only tombs in the church to survive the Ottoman occupation; in 1967, archeologists stripped the bodies of their royal jewelery to be included in the National Museum. Ascend the spiral steps to view the exhibits of the **Museum of Ecclesiastical Art,** where you'll find plenty of gold and a replica of the Hungarian crown, complete with a slanted cross.

*⇟ Bus 16, 16a and 116: Szentháromság tér. Or Morada: Estação acessível. Both take you right to the church. ℹ Because of extensive renovations that may extend into 2011, the church's normal hours of operation change daily. Check online prior to visit to confirm. $ Church and museum 750Ft, students 500Ft. ⏰ Open M-F 9am-5pm, Sa 9am-2:30pm, Su 1-5pm. High Mass M-Sa 7, 8:30am, 6pm, Su 7, 8:30, 10am, noon, 6pm.*

### 👍 SZÉCHENYI CHAIN BRIDGE (SZÉCHENYI LÁNCHÍD) BRIDGE

Built in 1849, the Széchenyi Chain Bridge was the first permanent bridge across the Danube in Budapest and one of the longest bridges in the world. At the time of its construction, it was a sensation in Budapest, its imperious structure symbolizing Hungary's national awakening. During WWII, the Chain Bridge (along with every other bridge in the city) was destroyed by the retreating Axis forces, and was later rebuilt with a pair of noble-looking lions flanks at either end of the abutments. A popular myth states that the sculptor forgot to give the lions tongues and that the public's merciless mocking caused him to throw himself into the Danube. In reality, the tongues are just hard to see from below. At the Buda end of the bridge you can see the Zero Kilometer Stone that marks the place from which all Hungarian highways are measured.

### MAGYAR NEMZETI GALÉRIA (HUNGARIAN NATIONAL GALLERY) 🎫♿ MUSEUM

Buda Palace, wings A, B, C, and D ☎356 0049 🖥www.mng.hu

The halls of Buda Castle now house the world's largest collection of Hungarian fine arts. Spread across three floors and divided by historical period, the permanent collection traces the development of Hungarian painting and sculpture from the Gothic period to the second half of the 20th century. The collections of painters like Gyárfás Jenő and Károly Lotz are some of the museum's best, though it's the sculptures that stop hearts and open minds. In the 20th century galleries, look for pieces by Impressionist 👍**Béla Czóbel.** The basement of the museum contains the crypt of the Hapsburg palantines, though admission can only be obtained through prior arrangement with a guide.

*⇟ Hike up or take the tram to Buda Castle. The museum is housed in the giant building that you couldn't possibly miss. $ 000Ft, Hapsburg crypt 600Ft. ⏰ Open Tu-Su 10am-6pm. Last entry 30min. before close.*

### KIRALY BATHS (KIRÁLY FÜRDŐ) 🚭♿ BATH

Fő utca 82-84 ☎202 3688 🖥www.spasbudapest.com

Tiny holes in the top of the giant cupola draw in delicately crafted lines of light, producing the sensation that you're bathing inside Heaven's gates. Construction began on the monumental Kiraly Baths by order of the Pasha of Buda in 1565. Unlike most of the area baths, the Kiraly Baths are not connected directly to the thermal springs, taking water from another nearby bath instead. The Pasha ordered them built far from the springs so that bathing could continue even during an inevitable siege by Christian forces. Renovated and rebuilt after damage from WWII, the Kiraly baths, perhaps more than any other in the city, evoke the spirit of the Turkish tradition with their crescent-topped domes and octagonal bath surrounded by pillars.

*🚏 Margit hid tram stop, trams 4, 6. From the tram stop, take south Frankel Leó utca; it will become Fő utca. i Bathing-suit rental available. $ 2100Ft. 🕐 Open daily M 8am-7pm (women only), Tu 9am-8pm (men only), W 8am-7pm (women only), Th-Sa 9am-8pm (men only), Su 9am-8pm.*

### CASTLE LABYRINTHS (BUDAVÁRI LABIRINTUS) ♿ LABYRINTH

Úri utca 9 or Lovas út 4/a. ☎212 0207 💻www.labirintus.com

Formed naturally by thermal springs that extend 1200m underground, the Castle Labyrinths were once home to Neanderthals. For a time, the caves served as personal wine cellars for the residents of Castle Hill. In the 1930s, the tunnels were connected and expanded to create a bomb shelter that housed up to 10,000 people. Nowadays, the caves have been converted into a series of chambers that toe the line between museum and haunted house. The caves are divided into several themed sections filled with decorations of dubious authenticity, including cave paintings and statues. Most memorable, perhaps, is a fountain of red wine that the wise are advised not to drink and the foolish are likely to splatter on their clothes. The final stretch of labyrinth, named the **Labyrinth of Another World,** is a bizarre mix of social and self-reflexive critique centered on "artifacts" like enormous stone Coke bottles from a species of man called "Homo Consumes."

*🚏 M1, M2, or M3: Deák tér. The labyrinths are toward the opposite end of Castle Hill from the Royal Palace. i Not the best place for those claustrophobic types. The best time to visit the labyrinths is between 6 and 7:30pm, when they turn out the lights and hand out woefully and comically ineffective oil lamps. Children under 14 and people with heart conditions are advised not to take part in the spooky festivities. $ 2000Ft, students 1500Ft. 🕐 Open daily 9:30am-7:30pm.*

## GELLÉRT HEGY

### 👍 LIBERTY MONUMENT (SZABADSÁG SZOBOR) ♿ MONUMENT

Gellért Hill

Visible from all over the city, Budapest's Liberty Monument has a complicated history. One story goes that the figure was originally designed to hold a propeller by the order of Regent Horthy, Hungary's right-wing leader during the interwar period. Before anyone got around to building the statue, however, the Soviets had "liberated" a then-grateful Budapest, which replaced the propeller with a palm leaf and dedicated the statue to their Soviet heroes. After half a century of communist rule, the citizens of Budapest no longer felt quite so liberated, and, in 1989, the statue of a Soviet soldier was relocated from the base of the monument to Memento Park. The monument was rededicated to everyone who has ever fought for Hungary's freedom and success. The steep hike up the mountain is worth the trek for an unparalleled panorama of the city and surrounding neighborhoods.

*🚏 The monument is at the top of the hill, near the Citadella. i Only wheelchair-accessible if you take bus #27 from Moricz Zsigmond.*

### HOTEL GELLÉRT AND GELLÉRT BATHS ♿ BATH

Szent Gellért tér 1 ☎466 61 66 💻www.spasbudapest.com

At the foot of Gellért Hill and directly facing the green Szabadság Bridge, the world-famous hotel was built in the Vienna Secession style and incorporates gorgeous elements of the then-emerging Art Nouveau. While the hotel itself is probably beyond most student budgets, the equally famous adjoining baths are certainly not. Probably the most popular of the Buda baths for tourists, the Gellért Baths feature a richly tiled interior with statues and columns surrounding the main bath. Outside, an enormous sitting bath is popular with visitors of all ages.

*🚏 Tram 49: Szent Gellért tér. i Bathing-suit and towel rental available. Check 💻www.danubiushotels.com for hotel details. $ Admission with locker 3500Ft. 🕐 Open M-F 6am-7pm, Sa 6am-10pm, Su 6am-8pm. Last entry 1hr. before close.*

## THE CITADELLA

●& VIEW

Citadella Sétány 1 ☎279 19 63 ■www.citadella.hu

This structure was originally built by the gloating Hapsburgs after the failed 1848 revolution to remind Hungarians who was in charge. The angled walls occupy most of the hill's plateau and must have provided the imperial soldiers garrisoned there with great views of the city that resented them. During WWII, the interior was converted into a massive, three-level air-raid shelter, which served as one of the strong points for the German and Hungarian forces during the bloody Siege of Budapest. Today, the Citadella is home to a luxury hotel and expensive restaurant. The former air-raid shelter contains an overpriced museum filled with wax figures depicting scenes from the war, ranging from not very to quite interesting. During the summer, the surrounding area is swamped with food vendors and souvenir stands. If you can, go at night to take in the view in relative peace.

⚜ *The citadella is at the top of the hill, near the Liberty Monument.* ⑤ *1200Ft.* ⌕ *Museum open daily May-Sept 9am-8pm; Oct-Apr 9am-5pm.*

## CAVE CHURCH (SZIKLATEMPLOM)

⊛ CHURCH

Gellért Hill

Certainly an eerie sight, this alleged abode of a holy and hermetic monk was expanded by the Paulite order in the '20s and '30s from the original cave into the modern complex. Under the communist regime, the entire order was arrested and imprisoned, and the church was walled up with concrete for nearly 40 years. Today, the church is an active site for tourists and pilgrims. The interior of the church is certainly interesting, but don't expect to be occupied for much more than a short while. While tourists aren't allowed inside the church during services, the music played inside takes on a strange but compelling echo.

⚜ *Szent Gellért tér tram stop. On the 1st level of the hill.* ℹ *Shoulders and midriffs must be covered.* ⑤ *Free.* ⌕ *Open daily 10-11am, noon-5pm, and 6:30-8pm.*

# ÓBUDA

◼ PÁL-VÖLGYI AND MÁTYÁS CAVES

●⊛ CAVES

☎325 95 05 ■www.caving.hu

Budapest is famous for its thermal baths, but few people know that the heated water that eats up entire afternoons has also spent hundreds of thousands of years eating through the limestone hills beneath the city. The result: over 100km of caves directly below many of Budapest's residential areas. The second longest of Hungary's cave systems, the Pál-völgyi and Mátyás Caves offer the unskilled numerous spelunking opportunities. The no-climbing walking tours are informative and interesting without asking you to do anything more stressful than climb a short ladder. These walks descend 30m below the surface, where you'll

## sandwich of death

The descent into the **Mátyás Caves** is met by overwhelming darkness and absolute silence. What brings travelers into the silent depths is the opportunity to partake in caving, the unforgettable experience of snaking through the underground labyrinthine caves. Yet what draws visitors to these particular caves is the "Sandwich of Death," the finale of the journey. Equipped only with a helmet and flashlight, spelunkers venture through the path that descends 220m to sea level and back up again, inching past heart-stopping 40m drops and squeezing through crevices barely large enough to fit your helmet. The climactic sandwich isn't quite as dangerous as it sounds—it's a 12m stomach-crawl through two slabs of limestone.

sights · óbuda

see many dripstones and even the occasional 40-million-year-old fossil. Many people bring a sweater, though during the hot summer nothing feels better than descending into the caves, which keep cool at 50°F all year long. Those looking for something a little more challenging should consider taking on The Sandwich of Death.

*Bus #86: Kolosy tér. From the stop, backtrack up the street and take the 1st right to reach the bus station. From there, catch bus #65 to get to the caves. i Bring warm clothing. English tours available; call ahead for times. $ 1050Ft, students 785Ft. Open Tu-Sa 10am-4pm. Tours every hr.*

### AQUINCUM RUINS

RUINS

Szentendrei út 135 ☎250 16 50 www.aquincum.hu

Long before the mighty Magyars settled the Carpathian basin, the Roman Empire had a thriving settlement of 40,000 inhabitants on this spot. The ruins of this ancient settlement can be seen all over northern Buda. The Military Amphitheater at the corner of Lajos utca and Pacsirtamező utca in Óbuda is especially awesome. The largest collection of ruins can be found at the **Aquincumi Múzeum,** just north of Budapest proper. The museum includes thousands of artifacts from the town like pottery, bricks, and jewelry. Upstairs, an exhibit recreates parts of the proconsul's palace as well as the famed Aquincum organ. Outside, you can explore more than an acre of ruins, including the workshops of various craft guilds. When in the former Roman Empire, do as the former Romans did and spend an afternoon hanging around the former thermal baths.

*From Batthyány tér, take the HÉV 7 stops to Aquincum, then get off and backtrack about 0.5km; the ruins and museum are on your left. $ 1300Ft, students 500Ft. Museum open Apr 16-30 Tu-Sa 10am-5pm, May-Sept daily 10am-6pm, Oct Tu-Sa 10am-5pm. Park open Apr 16-Oct 9am-dusk.*

## OUTER BUDA

### MEMENTO PARK (SZOBORPARK)

MONUMENT

On the corner of Balatoni út and Szabadkai utca. www.mementopark.hu

While in the rest of the former Soviet republics people were happily dismantling and demolishing the symbols of their hated regimes, the monument-loving people of Budapest decided it might be worthwhile to keep theirs around, even if they didn't want them anywhere near the city itself. Forty of these statues now reside a bus ride away in Memento Park *(25min.)* as a testament to a bygone political and artistic period. At the gates to the park you can see an authentic replica of the infamous Stalin statue that was torn down so thoroughly during the 1956 revolution that only the dictator's boots remained; the remains of the statue became a symbol of the revolution. Other notable statues include a striking metallic mass of bayonet-wielding soldiers charging past a podium as well as the deranged-looking Soviet soldier that used to stand at the base of the Liberty Monument, clutching his Soviet flag and machine gun. An indoor exhibition shows unnerving clips from old secret police training videos. If you pay attention, you may even learn a thing or two about how to hide secret messages in crushed soda cans.

*Express bus #7: Etele tér. From the stop, take the yellow Volán bus from terminal #7 bound for Diosd-Érd and get off at Memento Park. You'll need to buy a separate ticket from the Volánbusz ticket office. There is also a white direct bus from Deák tér (1, 2, or 3) Jan-June and Sept-Dec daily 11am, July-Aug daily 11am, 3pm for 3950Ft, students 2450Ft; includes price of admission and return ticket. $ 1500Ft, students 1000Ft. Open daily 10am-dusk.*

## MARGIT-SZIGET

### RUINS

RUINS

Margit Sziget

Though it may be hard to imagine now, there was once a time when the island was used for something besides outdoor drinking and sunbathing. For several centuries, Margaret Island was the place to be cloistered in Budapest. The Franciscans were the first on the scene, building their priory in the 13th century only to have it destroyed under the Ottomans in the 16th century. King Béla IV built a convent during the height of the Mongol invasion in the 13th century. At that time, he vowed to send his daughter, Margaret, to the convent if he ever had the chance to rebuild the country after the Mongol assault, though nobody seemed to have consulted Margaret on this arrangement. When the Mongols were finally beaten back, the king made good on his vow and sent his 11-year-old daughter to become a nun. While taking orders may not have done much for Margaret's social life, at least it guaranteed her a kind of immortality when the island was renamed after her death. Today, you can still see the ruins of both structures. Princess Margaret is buried at the site of the old nave.

⚑ *Take the main road from the Margit Bridge entrance. You'll pass the Franciscan priory 1st, on your left, between the Hajós Alfréd Swimming Pool and the Palatinus Baths. The convent is farther along, on your right near the water tower.*

### PALATINUS STRANDFÜRDŐ (PALATINUS BATHS)                    ◉⟳ BATH
Margit Sziget                                   ☎340 45 05 ▣www.spasbudapest.com
These baths opened in 1921 and immediately became a favorite of the city's residents. Since then, constant improvements and additions have turned the former stretch of beach into a sprawling complex with enormous fountains, waterslides, and jets across three large pools, all fed by the thermal springs underground. The thermal pools are a little less harrowing than their Turkish counterparts, staying at a manageable, less pruny 36°C. On summer weekends the pools are packed with local families and children.

⚑ *From the Árpád Bridge entrance, take Soó Rezső sétány south; the baths are on your right.* ⑨ *Admission with lockers M-F 9am-5pm 2100Ft, 5-8pm 1200Ft; Sa-Su 2400Ft.* ⌚ *Open in summer daily 9am-8pm.*

### ZENÉLŐ SZÖKŐKÚT (MUSIC FOUNTAIN)                    ⟳ FOUNTAIN
Margit Sziget
Built in 1936, the Musical Fountain consists of multiple waterjets choreographed to music from nearby speakers. Even if you can't make out the music, the sight of the jets pulsing and changing is mesmerizing. A favorite of local parkgoers, the Musical Fountain attracts visitors who love to set up picnics and hookahs in the shaded area nearby. At night, colorful lights add a whole new dimension to the show. While the sight of the enormous central jet is certainly impressive, perhaps someone should tell UNESCO that the island's beloved musical fountain is actually just a copy of an older fountain built by a Transylvanian handyman.

⚑ *From the Margit Bridge entrance, take the main road north; the fountain is just past the statue.*

# OUTSIDE BUDAPEST

## VISEGRÁD
Visegrád is a tiny town in Pest County home to the summer palace of King Matthias Corvinus of Hungary. Its main attraction is the two-part 13th century castle nearby. The center of the lower castle area is adorned by the giant Solomon Tower that was once a royal residence and now houses the **King Matthias Museum of Visegrád.** A trip to Visegrád would not be complete without a visit to the Royal Palace that was originally built in the early 14th century and later completely reconstructed by King Matthias Corvinus in the 15th century. Considering it was a vacation spot of one of the most powerful leaders in Hungary's history, the building is quite unassuming and looks more like a Mediterranean villa than a royal palace. Only limited rooms in the building's interior are open to the public,

but they're worth the visit to marvel at the king's jewels. Without a doubt the most fun to be had in the area is the summer bob-sledding course on **Mogyoró Hill.** Check the tourist office for information.

🪧 *Buses depart from Árpád híd bus station in Budapest every 30min. No trains go to Visegrád. The bus to the castle departs from the ferry boat pier (Nagymaros) at 9:26am, 12:26pm, and 3:26pm. The last bus from the castle back to the pier is at 4pm. Check with Budapest Tour Inform before you leave for maps and information, as there is no tourist office in Visegrád.*

### VÁC

The Vác cathedral is the main attraction of this tiny town. Built in the late 18th century and modeled after St. Peter's Basilica in Rome, the gorgeously restored columns invite visitors to meditate in holy peace. The **Stone Gate** built in 1764 for Empress Maria Theresa's visit to the town looks like Paris' Arc de Triomphe. Perhaps most intriguing, and also most overlooked, is the **Statue of the Holy Trinity** columns.

🪧 *Buses depart from Árpád híd station in Budapest every half-hour. The train departs from Nyugati toward Szob via Vác every 30min. The train station is at the northern end of Széchényi utca adjacent to the bus station. Follow Széchényi utca toward the river for 0.5km which will lead you toward the main square at Március 15 tér.* [S] *Prices vary depending on time of year.*

# food

## THE BELVÁROS

### 👍 CENTRAL KÁVÉHÁZ — 💳🚭🍸☀ CAFE [3]

V, Károlyi Mihály utca 9. ☎266 2110 💻www.centralkavehaz.hu

Doors and windows bust open to reveal local clientele, from cramming students to old men sucking on cigars to women gabbing about the latest he-said she-said at this larger-than-life coffee and sandwich shop. Don't let the marble tables and leather couches fool you; if you linger for long enough the laid-back waiters will find you and you'll begin to groove with the chill atmosphere.

🪧 *M2: Ferenciek Tere. From the Metro take Károly Mihály east.* [S] *Nosh 1800-2650Ft. Entrees 2300-3900Ft. Mixed drinks 500-1100Ft.* ⏰ *Open daily 7am-midnight.*

### 👍 CAFE ALIBI — 💳🚭🍸❄☀ CAFE [2]

V, Egyetem Tér 4 ☎01 317 4209 💻cafealibi.hu

An old-fashioned cash register and your grandmother's fine china will greet you at this little coffee shop in the center of student-city. Don't let the white tablecloths scare you--while the price is up there, you're unlikely to find a more tasteful cafe in this neighborhood away from all those foreign loudmouths.

🪧 *M3: Kálvin Tér. From the Metro take Kecskeméti utca west and turn left on Egyetem tér.* [S] *Salads 900-1600Ft. Coffee from 320Ft.* ⏰ *Open M-F 8am-2am, Sa 9am-1am.*

### KICSIMAMA KONYHÁJA — 💳🚭 HUNGARIAN, FAST FOOD [1]

Lónyay u. 7. ☎01 216 4178

A get-in-get-out kind of place perfect for backpackers on the run. Delectable Hungarian quick-eats for a tight budget. Not your grandma's kitchen, nor is it a five-star *resto*, but you get the idea. Try anything breaded or soaked in sauce.

🪧 *M3: Kálvin Tér. Head towards the river and make a left on Lónyay.ß.* [S] *Breaded cauliflower 580ft. Spinach ricotta pasta 280ft. Specials from 780ft.* ⏰ *Open M-F 10am-6pm, Sa 10am-3pm.*

### KÁRPÁTIA — 💳🚭🍸❄ HUNGARIAN [5]

V, Ferenciek Tere 7-8 ☎01 317 3596 💻www.karpatia.hu

The up-and-coming executive chef doles out revamped Hungarian cuisine, mix-

budapest

ing ancient spices and recipes with Mediterranean, Asian, and Latin flavors. An immaculate Baroque interior with red, gold, and green patterns cover a vaulted ceiling at one of the city's oldest restaurants. Dishes like venison filet with balsamic strawberries and maize polenta with black truffles (7050Ft) will blow your taste buds away. Your wallet will be crushed by debris from the explosion, so save it for a last-night-in-town-splurge.

✢ M3: Ferenciek Tere. *i* Reservation recommended. Ⓢ Appetizers 1900-3100Ft. Entrees 3300-7500Ft. ⏰ Open daily 11am-11pm.

## FATÁL
👆⊗💺❄ HUNGARIAN ❹

V, Váci utca 67 ☎01 266 2608 🖳www.fatalrestaurant.com

Gigantic portions served in pots and pans, hand-crafted stained glass, and kingly thrones attract the likes of Melanie Griffith and the occasional local at this traditional Hungarian restaurant that isn't afraid to put on a show for its tourist clientele.

✢ M3: Kálvin Tér. From the Metro take Vámház toward the river, turn right on Veres Palné and left on Só. Ⓢ Salads 750-1000Ft. Entrees 2100-2900Ft. ⏰ Open daily noon-midnight.

## BABEL
👆⊗💺❄ ROMANTIC ❺

V, Váci utca 83 ☎01 388 2143 🖳www.babeldelicate.hu

Fare like something out of the Food Network, clear wine coolers lining the walls, and sleek rectangular shades hanging from the ceiling make Babel truly a step toward heaven. Try the leg of goose confit with quince glaze and chestnut lentil (3090ft). The *kohlrabi* stew with herbed calf's brain and catfish (2650ft) is also a winner.

✢ M3: Kálvin Tér. From the Metro take Vámház toward the river and turn right on Váci. *i* Reservations recommended. Giant, artsy 4- and 5-course menus start at 11,000Ft. ⏰ Open M-Sa noon-midnight

## BIO GARDENS
👉⊗♨ MODERN ❷

V, Képíró u.3. ☎01 266 1497

Huge sunflowers adorning the walls hint at the earthy organic theme of this new urban oasis. Check out the daily specials deals, available weekdays noon-3pm (990ft). If you're looking for a clean-cut vegetarian meal with little spice but a healthful bite, this place won't disappoint.

✢ M: Kalvin Ter. Head up Kecskeméti utca from the Metro and turn left on Képíró. Ⓢ Pizza 1650-1750Ft. Pasta 1550-1890Ft. ⏰ M-F noon-10pm.

## 1000 TEA
👉⊗ TEA HOUSE ❸

Váci utca 65 ☎01 337 8217 🖳www.1000tea.hu

Take your shoes off and sip tea in one of the many arched alcoves of this Japanese-style tea house, located in a tranquil courtyard away from the buzz of Váci. With an impressive menu and worldly staff, you might receive a bit of knowledge along with your tea condiments. Couples can relish the tea samplers (from 1400ft). Get your Zen on, you're in tea land now.

✢ M3: Kálvin Tér. From the Metro take Vámház toward the river and turn right on Váci utca. Ⓢ Teas 420-1100Ft. ⏰ Open M-Sa noon-11pm, Su 1-11pm.

## GERBEAUD
👉⊗❈♨ FAMOUS ❸

V, Vörösmarty Tér ☎01 429 9000 🖳www.gerbeaud.hu

While no trip would be complete without a visit to this cafe and confectionary, don't be fooled. Take a peek, pose for a picture, but don't waste time pawning the family jewels for a subpar treat. Be the smart traveler that you are and go up the street or across the river for a more homemade experience.

✢ M1: Vörösmary Tér. Head down towards the river and Váci utca. Ⓢ Coffee 700Ft. Cake 780-850Ft. Fancy ice cream 1700-1900Ft. ⏰ Open daily 9am-9pm.

**food . the belváros**

## LIPÓTVÁROS

### 👍 SZERÁJ
💳🚭🍸☀ TURKISH, FAST FOOD ❶

V, Szent István krt.

Turkish fast food with a Hungarian touch. Perfect for a quick, delicious meal without the fuss of waiters and tips. If you've got more time on your hands, sit outside in the summer on the patio overlooking bustling Szent István krt or at one of the tables inside illuminated by massive windows. You can even smoke inside in the upstairs balconies. Try the Hungarian twists on Mediterranean classics like the kebab sandwich with red cabbage *(650Ft).*

*🚇 M3: Nyugati. Head down Szent István towards the river, the restaurant is on your left. $ Entrees from 400Ft. Desserts from 300Ft.*

### TRÓFEA GRILL ÉTTEREM
💳♿🍸☀ GOURMET, BUFFET ❸

XIII, Visegrádi utca 50A ☎01 270 0366 🖥www.trofeagrill.com

Gourmet meal and all-you-can-eat buffet don't usually hold hands on the playground, but somehow this place pulls it off. The large wooden dining area is lined with the skulls of the various species you'll be enjoying. An over 100-dish menu will leave you either unsurpassably satiated or slobbering indecisively. Stand-up and occasional folk dancing during the summer make for a somewhat bizarre (but entertaining) dining experience.

*🚇 M3: Nyugati. From the Metro take Szent István krt toward the river and turn right on Visegrádi. i Wi-Fi included. $ Buffet M-F lunch 3400Ft; M-Th dinner 3800Ft; F dinner and all day Sa-Su 4600Ft. ⏰ Open M-F noon-midnight, Sa 11:30am-midnight, Su 11:20am-8:30pm.*

### KASHMIR
💳🚭🍸❄ INDIAN ❸

V, Arany János utca 13 ☎01 354 1806 🖥www.kashmiretterem.hu

Stylish Indian cuisine if you're sick of paprika. House "special assortments" recommended *(meat 2990Ft, vegetarian 2590Ft).* The interior is classy and simple and you can enjoy the meal and company on plush white benches strewn with pilllows.

*🚇 M3: Arany János utca. i Reservation recommended. $ Appetizers 990-1390Ft. Curry 2190-2790Ft. ⏰ Open M-Sa noon-3pm, 5-11pm.*

### CSARNOK VENDÉGLŐ
💳🚭🍸 HUNGARIAN ❷

V, Hold utca 11. ☎01 269 4906

This archetypal, in a good way, Hungarian restaurant sports checkered tablecloths, wooden furniture, and meaty stews. The amiable staff caters to a local crowd with delicious and affordable Hungarian fare. Begin with a soup and quail egg *(480Ft)* and then move to a heartier course like the gypsy roast *(1250Ft).*

*🚇 M2: Arany János utca 9. $ Entrees 1150-2850Ft. ⏰ Open daily 11am-11pm.*

### CAFÉ KÖR
💳🚭🍸❄ CAFE ❸

V, Sas utca 17 ☎01 311 0053 🖥www.cafekor.com

Cool, classy dining caters mainly to professionals and tourists, though there are plenty of options that penny-pinching backpackers will relish. Elegant decor and starched waiters will fool you into thinking you've engaged in an upscale dining experience. Classy pairings like honeydew melon wrapped in prosciutto *(1690Ft)* set this place apart from the area's other boutique cafes.

*🚇 M1: Bajcsy-Zsilinszky út. From the Metro take József Attila west and turn right on Sas. $ Entrees 1990-4290Ft. Appetizers 950-2490Ft. ⏰ Open daily 10am-10pm.*

### MOMOTARO
⊛🚭🍸❄ ASIAN FUSION ❸

V, Széchényi utca 16 ☎01 269 3802

Learn about the famous Japanese hero, The Peach Boy, as you slurp simple yet scrumptious ramen noodles. Ideal for a quick lunch while sightseeing nearby Parliament or St. Stephen's Basilica. Puts some of the more beloved Asian-fusion restaurants in the States to shame. Don't forget to thank the gods as you leave this pagoda-inspired establishment for a refreshing respite from beef and paprika.

❦ *M2: Arany János. From the Metro take Bank utca west to find the restaurant on your right.* Ⓢ *Ramen 1500-3000Ft. Entrees 1500-3000Ft.* Ⓧ *Open daily 11am-10pm.*

## LUI AND LEI RISTORANTE
❦⊗❦❄❖❧ ITALIAN ❹

V, Széchényi utca 14
☎01 312 1405 ◼www.luiandlei.com

Upscale Italian wine bar and retaurant, catering mostly to tourists and uppercrust locals. If you're lucky, you'll grab the outdoor white leather bench when the weather is fine. Don't fret though; there are plenty more leather benches in the cool downstairs area. Specialties include roast duck breast *(2950Ft)* and monkfish in bisque sauce *(4700Ft).*

❦ *M3: Arany János. From the Metro take Bank utca west, the restaurant is on your right.* ❦ *Reservations recommended.* Ⓢ *Appetizers 1700-3700Ft. Entrees 2600-5900Ft. Pasta 1650-3600Ft.* Ⓧ *Open daily 11am-midnight.*

## GOVINDA VEGETARIAN RESTAURANT
⊛⊗⊗❄❈ INDIAN ❷

V, Vigyázó Ferenc utca 4
☎01 269 1625

Young, alternative, and health-conscious locals flock to this Indian buffet. The lazy can spring for the plated dishes while the cunning can mix and match *samosas* with *pakoras.* Plot a revolution or just enjoy your meal alone in the stone-walled basement.

❦ *M3: Arany János. From the Metro take Arany János toward the river and turn left on Nádor. Make a right onto Vigyázó Ferenc.* Ⓢ *Samosas from 230ft. Pakoras from 155ft. Rice from 180ft. Plates 1550-2000ft.* Ⓧ *Open M-Sa noon-9pm.*

## IGUANA BAR AND GRILL
❦⊗❦❈ MEXICAN ❸

V, Zoltán utca 16
☎01 331 4352 ◼www.iguana.hu

You don't have to cross the border...er, from the US...to get good Mexican food. Head to Iguana, where you can shed your skin in the summer on the outdoor patio while stocking up on spicy Latin ingredients. Great vegetarian options are available.

❦ *M2: Kossuth Lajos tér. From the Metro take KL east, right on Nádor and left on Zoltán.* Ⓢ *Appetizers 490-2250Ft. Burritos 1990-2190Ft. Entrees 1790-2395Ft.* Ⓧ *Open daily 11:30am-midnight.*

## FIRKÁSZ
❦⊗❦❈ HUNGARIAN ❹

XIII, Tátra utca 18
☎01 450 1118

The name refers to journalists who scribble in their notebooks, a motif echoed by the newspaper-covered walls and typewriters scattered around the interior. While it's a district XIII landmark, don't expect to be floored by the cuisine. Typical Hungarian dishes stock the menu, but locals usually wait for the lunch buffet while tourists gather on evenings and weekends. Try the chicken Kiev *(2200Ft)* or veal with paprika *(2485Ft).*

❦ *M3: Nyugati. From the Metro take Szent István krt toward the river and turn right on Tátra.* ❦ *Service charge included.* Ⓢ *Salads 1690-1990Ft. Vegetarian 990-1590Ft. Entrees 2190-4990Ft.* Ⓧ *Open M-Th noon-midnight, F-Sa noon-2am, Su noon-midnight.*

## CAFE KAFKA
❦⊗❦❈ CAFE ❶

V, Sas utca 9
☎01 266 1242 ◼www.kafkakavezo.hu

No, Kafka never ate here. But perhaps the loads of literary references adorning the walls and menu and the brooding intellectuals huddled in the corners will inspire you to write the next famous short story. If all else fails the cheap wine might just help you metamorphose. Bring your laptop or feather pen and get busy.

❦ *M1: Bajcsy-Zsilinszky. From the Metro take József Attila west and turn right on Sas.* ❦ *Wi-Fi included. Outdoor seating.* $ *Sandwiches from 890Ft. White wine 550Ft. Red wine 650Ft.* ⏰ *Open M-F 10am-11pm, Sa-Su 10:30am-11pm.*

**EURÓPA KÁVÉHÁZ** CAFE [1]

V, Szent István krt 7-9 ☎01 312 2362 💻www.europakavehaz.hu

Large, bustling cafe with fake marble counterops and red imitation-leather benches. Not the best place to have an intimate conversation or classy date, but an extensive cake and dessert menu encourages the clientele to sit, eat, and be merry.

*M3: Nyugati. From the Metro take Szent István krt toward the river and find the cafe on your left.* **i** *Wi-Fi included.* $ *Espresso from 350Ft. Tea from 300Ft. Canapés 1100-1350Ft. Cake from 450Ft.* ⏰ *Open daily 9am-11pm.*

## ERZSÉBETVÁROS

**CASTRO BISZTRÓ** BISTRO [1]

1075 Madách tér 3. ☎215 01 84 💻www.castrobistro.hu

An easy cafe where you can sit alone and read or chat with friends over an espresso. An eclectic decor boasts Buena Vista Social Club posters and a handsome bar serves a sizzling Illy roast and a selection of beer and wine. Windows bring in ample light and the summertime opens a whole new world and vibe with the outdoor terrace. Clientele ranges from artsy cafe regulars to the occasional tourist.

*M1, M2, or M3: Deák Ferenc tér. From the Metro head north on Király utca, right on Rumbach Sebestyén utca and right on Madách.* $ *Espresso 200Ft. Sandwiches from 700Ft.* ⏰ *Open M-Th 10am-midnight, F 10am-1am, Sa noon-1am, Su 2pm-midnight.*

**HUMMUS BÁR** ISRAELI [1]

Kertész utca 39 ☎321 74 77 💻www.hummusbar.hu

An explosion of olive oil, lemon zest, and chickpeas makes you feel like you're trotting the ancient limestone streets of Jerusalem. A young and modern decor (that's clientele included) rendez-vous with old recipes to birth some of the city's most delectable Jewish fare. Check out the "hummusology" posters for proper hummus-and-pita-eating technique. Don't leave without trying the *Laffa*, a giant flat bread stuffed with meat (or veggies), spices, and hummus.

*M1: Oktogon. Head east on Erzsébet krt, right on Király and left on Kertész.* $ *Falafel from 800Ft. Entrees 400-1800Ft.* ⏰ *Open daily noon-11pm.*

**KÖLEVES** RESTOBAR [2]

Kazinczy utca 35. ☎322 10 11 💻www.koleves.com

Wooden chairs and floors, funky paintings on the wall, three different basement areas each with a bar, and constant live music and shows. Köleves is a great place to go for a creepy "taste of Jewish Hungary"; try the "stone soups" *(from 470ft)*, during the day, but be sure to check it out before you hit the clubs to fill up on grub and a relaxing drink—or stay the night and head-bang with the rest of them.

*M1, M2, or M3: Deák Ference tér. From Metro head north on Király and turn right on Kazinczy.* **i** *Nightly entertainment.* $ *Soup from 470Ft. Entrees 1250-3350Ft.* ⏰ *Daily noon-midnight.*

**KÉK RÓZSA** HUNGARIAN [1]

Wesselényi utca 9. ☎342 8981

Accented by a view of the **Synagogue** in the backdrop, this very *kék* (blue) quick eatery is the haunt of many local professionals and dwellers looking for a wholesome and cheap Hungarian lunch. The lovingly placed World Cup paraphernalia and TV dating back to the early '90s make you feel like you've gone back in time to your childhood bedroom. The owners and staff are just as doting as your parents when you're home for the holidays.

🚇 *M2: Astoria. From the Metro head east on Rákóczi út, make a left on Sip utca which runs into Wesselényi; the restaurant is on the corner.* ℹ *Smoking and non-smoking sections. Kitchen starts slowing down at 9:15pm.* $ *Changing daily menu from 800Ft.* ⏰ *Open daily 11am-11pm.*

**SHALIMAR** 💳🚭🍸❄ INDIAN [3]

Dob utca 50. ☎352 02 97 💻www.shalimar.hu

One of Budapest's best Indian restaurants dishing out polished traditional dishes in a sleek, candlelit atmosphere. Large mirrors and ample shrines lining the walls mean that Shiva the Destroyer will be watching your every bite. Delicious vegetarian options like spicy mashed eggplant *baigan bhurta (1445Ft)* will even tempt carnivores. Go for the cheap lunch buffet and dine with area bankers or join the local crowd for a semi-fancy dinner.

🚇 *M1: Oktogon. Head south on Teréz krt for 3 blocks and turn right on Dob utca.* ℹ *Reservations recommended.* $ *Lunch 1100-1350Ft. Vegetarian options 1050-1750Ft. Vindaloo 2140-2550Ft. Entrees 2140-4100Ft.* ⏰ *Open daily noon-4pm and 6pm-midnight.*

**400 LOKAL** 💳♿🍸☁ CAFE, BAR [1]

Kazinczy utca 52/b ☎776 07 65

What starts as a low key cafe with small bites by day turns to a chill evening where the cheap drinks keep comin' and the moody music flows until the wee morning hours. With a striking red floor adorned with imposing windows and a homey wooden bar, Lokal begs you to stay for awhile.

🚇 *M1, M2, OR M3: Deák tér. Head north on Király and turn right on Kazinczy.* $ *Salads from 680Ft.* ⏰ *Open M 11am-3am, Tu-Th 11am-4pm, F-Sa noon-5am, Su noon-3am.*

**PORTH ART KOCSMA ÉS ÉTTEREM** 💳🚭🍸 RESTOBAR [3]

Dohány utca 7. ☎351 84 06 💻www.porth.hu

A retro restaurant and bar. Great place to go for dinner if you are looking to combine your meal with the start of a night out. Three different spaces create three separate atmospheres: from the green cellar, great for sipping wine, to the white baby-doll room, where you can eat pastries and sip tea with your pinky up, to the swanky red flat, where ball lamps and glove chairs make you feel as if you've stumbled upon a revamped Hungarian '50s diner. While not for the ravenous due to smaller portions, it's more than acceptable for a joie-de-vivre-type evening.

🚇 *M2: Astoria. Head east on Rákóczi út, left on Sip utca and a quick left on Dohány.* ℹ *Salads from 1100Ft. Meat dishes 1250Ft. Beer from 680Ft.* ⏰ *Open M-W 4pm-2am, Th 4pm-3am, F-Sa 4pm-4am.*

## TERÉZVÁROS

**MENZA** 🚭♿📶☁ HUNGARIAN [3]

Liszt Ferenc tér 2 ☎413 14 82 💻www.menza.co.hu

Makes you feel like you're one of the locals eating the cuisine of champions. Don't be deterred by the large crowds— this *menza* (canteen) is packed for a reason. Large portions of real Hungarian lunch food in an atmosphere that can't be any more mundane (in the best sense). Go for the daily menu *(890Ft)* and you'll get a real bang for your buck, with meals like fried turkey breast and a rice-and-peas side.

🚇 *M2: Oktogon. From the Metro, take Andrássy út west and then turn left onto Liszt Ferenc tér; the restaurant is at the corner with Paulay Ede utca.* $ *Salads 1390-1690Ft. Pasta 1290-1990Ft. Entrees 1890-3990Ft.* ⏰ *Open daily 10am-1am.*

**FŐZELÉK FALO** 🚭♿📶☁ HUNGARIAN [1]

Nagymező utca 18

You can't go to Hungary and not try *főzelék*—a truly Hungarian everyman dish composed of vegetables and spices cooked into a thick soup. This tiny place boasts every kind of *főzelék* and makes you feel like you've dropped in at grandma's. Be sure to try the squash *(380Ft);* those looking to bypass the nostalgia for something a little more hearty should try the *weiner schnitzel (350Ft).*

🍴 *M1: Oktogon. Head south from the Metro on Andrássy and right on Nagymező.* Ⓢ *Főzelék 380Ft. Entrees 390-690Ft.* 🕐 *M-F 10am-9:30pm. Sa noon-8pm.*

## KAJA.HU
🍴♿⊛✿ HUNGARIAN ❷

Nagymező utca 41 ☎374 04 68 🖥www.kaja.hu

One of the cheapest deals in the city. A simple canteen-style eatery serving traditional and delicious Hungarian fast food in huge portions to a local student and working crowd. Order the fried camembert with blueberry sauce *(950ft)* and you'll fit right in. A great place for lunch, but also for a quick starter drink and meal before a night out.

🍴 *M1: Oktogon. Head south from the Metro on Andrássy and right on Nagymező.* 𝒾 *Delivery available.* Ⓢ *Menus 640Ft. Salads 890Ft. Entrees from 990Ft.* 🕐 *Open daily 10am-midnight.*

## ZSÁKBAMACSKA
🍴♿✿ HUNGARIAN ❸

Lovag utca 3 ☎354 18 10 🖥www.zsakbamacska.hu

Finally some decent Hungarian sit-down food without the inauthentic gypsy music drilling in the background. A simple cellar setting invites guests almost as warmly as the staff does. Hit some Hungarian fish soup *(1250Ft)* for a spicy time and couple it with crispy duck topped with sour cherry sauce *(2750Ft).* The prices are just as spicy as the food, but you can save by getting a hearty soup or a small meat dish with a salad.

🍴 *M3: Arany János utca. From the Metro, take Bajcsy-Zsilinszky út north, then make a sharp right onto Nagymező utca, and then turn left onto Lovag utca.* Ⓢ *Appetizers 1350-2350Ft. Soups 750-1150Ft. Salads 550-950Ft. Entrees 1950-4550Ft. Vegetarian entrees 1550-2150Ft.* 🕐 *Open M-F 5pm-midnight, Sa-Su noon-midnight.*

## CSIRKE CSIBÉSZ
🍴♿✿ FAST FOOD ❶

Nagymező utca 35 ☎269-39 62

The haunt for locals after a night of drinking. Open until the wee hours, this place serves up sizzling whole chickens for you to devour (with your hands, if you wish). Stand at the counters or sit in a high stool and be amazed at how great the fare tastes—even during the day in a sober state of being.

🍴 *M1: Oktogon. Head south from the Metro on Andrássy and right on Nagymező.* Ⓢ *Sandwiches and entrees from 290Ft.* 🕐 *M-F 7am-6pm and W-Sa 7:30pm-5am.*

## CACTUS JUICE
🍴⊗✿❄ HUNGARIAN, AMERICAN ❸

Jókai Tér 5 ☎302 21 16 🖥www.cactusjuice.hu

As you pull up to this little joint you might be thinking, why in the great heavens did you send me to some Western pub in the middle of Budapest!? Don't you worry! Just head on downstairs and join the hoards of chilled-out local 20-to-30-somethings enjoying cheap beer and feasting on a Hungarian-American fare that's truly unlike any other restaurant in the city. If you're scrimping, go for the goulash *(860ft).* If you're in the mood to dole out a little more loot, take a stab at the tenderloin steak and *lecsó,* Hungarian tomato and pepper sauté *(2990Ft).*

🍴 *M1: Oktogon. Head south on Andrássy and turn right on Jókai.* 𝒾 *Often hosts DJs. Check online for listings.* Ⓢ *Salads from 1490Ft. Entrees from 1590Ft.* 🕐 *Open M-Th noon-2am, F-Sa Noon-4am, Su 4pm-2am.*

## CAFÉ ALOÉ
🍴⊗✿❄ CAFE ❶

Zichy Jenő utca 37 ☎269 45 36

Some of the cheapest booze around in a cozy ruin-pub-style cellar that also serves light meals during the day and most nights. Bookshelves stocked with classic novels (some in English left by travelers) line the walls; read on one of the stylishly ratty couches or just admire them from afar as you down basically free Jager, the house specialty *(360Ft).* Fill your gullet with similarly giveaway-

budapest

priced pizza *(780Ft).*

*🚇 M1: Oktogon. Head south from the Metro on Andrássy and right on Nagymező, then right again on Zichy. $ Beer from 280Ft. Wine from 250Ft. 🕐 Open Daily 2pm-2am*

**ARRIBA TAQUERIA** 💳♿📶☀ MEXICAN ❸

Teréz körút 25 ☎374 00 57 💻www.arriba.hu

Mexican cuisine quite reminiscent of something you'd find in the States. Friendly servers stand behind a counter and pile up heavy doses of traditional ingredients per your request. The colorful walls and furniture construct a funky, hippie kind of vibe reflecting much of the clientele. Chill out with your computer (free Wi-Fi) to catch up on some chat dates or try to recover with the mellow soundtrack after that gigantic burrito.

*🚇 M1: Oktogon. From the Metro, take Teréz körút west; the restaurant will be on your right. $ Tacos 400-550Ft. Quesadillas 1050-1350Ft. Burritos 1120-1490Ft. Mexican beer 950Ft. 🕐 Open daily 11am-midnight.*

**KIADÓ KOCSMA** 💳☀🍸🚭 CAFE, BAR ❷

Jókai tér 3 ☎331 19 55

Delicious light meals served in a seriously cool venue where Tibetan prayer flags hang with an unpretentious earthy style. Head downstairs for a more dining-oriented experience or ascend to the lounge where you will be served cheap drinks and can give your gut and mind a rest. Equipped with worn, wooden tables and chairs, this place is bound to make you feel down-to-earth—just look at the paper menu that offers "bio menus" like Hungarian cauliflower casserole *(550ft)* for a barely-there price.

*🚇 M1: Oktogon. From the Metro, take Andrássy toward downtown and then turn right onto Jókai tér; the cafe will be on your left. $ Pasta 1350-1500Ft. Entrees 1650-2600Ft. Beer from 280Ft. Tea and coffee from 250Ft. Mixed drinks 900-1800Ft. Shots 360-630Ft. 🕐 Open M-F 10am-1am, Sa-Su noon-1am.*

**MARQUIS DE SALADE** 💳🚭🍸☀ AZERBAIJANI ❸

Hajós utca 43 ☎302 40 86 💻www.marquisdesalade.hu

This Azerbaijani restaurant has the occasional Russian dish (or pun) thrown in for good measure. Relax on soft benches surrounded by pillows, bottles, and draperies as you browse an impressive salad selection. The meat of choice here is lamb—try the grape leaves stuffed with minced lamb *(2800Ft)* and grilled lamb liver and heart *(3400Ft)*. For the less adventurous, the original Marquis de Salade *(chicken breast with grapefruit, shrimp, and fresh vegetables in a grapefruit dressing; 2600Ft)* will satisfy your soul.

*🚇 M3: Arany János út. From the Metro, take Bajcsy-Zsilinszky út north and then make a sharp right onto Hajós. $ Salads 1300-2500Ft. Vegetarian options 2600-2800Ft. Entrees 2500-3900Ft. 🕐 Open daily noon-1am.*

**PARÁZS PRESSZÓ** 💳📶🍸☀ HUNGARIAN-THAI FUSION ❷

Szobi St 4 ☎950 37 70 💻www.parazspresszo.com

A titillatingly shocking Hungarian-Thai fusion prepared by a husband and wife team. Roomy floor cushions, couches, and chairs ensure that everyone's seating preferences are accommodated. Especially popular with students and backpackers from nearby hostels. The fried camembert with blueberry jam and jasmine rice *(1580Ft)* is a specialty.

*🚇 M1, M2, or M3 Nyugati. Head east on Teréz and turn left on Szobi. $ Appetizers 680-1350Ft. Soups 750-1100Ft. Entrees 1580-2350Ft. Vegetarian options 750-1750Ft. 🕐 Open daily noon-midnight.*

**BALETTCIPŐ ESZPRESSZÓ** 💳♿🍸☀ INTERNATIONAL ❷

Hajós utca 14 ☎269 31 14

This friendly little restaurant in the heart of District VI serves up an international cuisine for every taste bud. From the Philly cheese steak *(1850Ft)* to a hummus and pita plate *(690Ft)* to a chicken baguette sandwich with curry mayonaise *(1580Ft)*, it will be hard not to find something to satify your appetite. Expansive windows let in the light and energy of the main Hajós street and make you happy you've chosen such a great deal for lunch.

*M1: Oktogon. From the Metro, take Andrássy toward downtown and then turn right onto Nagymező, left onto Ó utca and left on Hajós utca. $ Salads from 990Ft. Coffee from 330Ft. ⏰ Open M-F 10am-midnight. Sa 11am-11pm, Su noon-11pm.*

**FRICI PAPA KIFŐZDÉJE** — FAST FOOD [1]

Király utca 55 — ☎0620 955 59 08

A tiny Hungarian-type fast food place serving delicious meals in the fashion of Hungarian mothers when they're in a bind. A bit more dolled up than most canteens in terms of decor, the place manages to maintain an authenticity and unassuming aura. Don't forget to try the *diós tészta*, pasta in a sweet walnut paste, *(459Ft)* and pretend to be nostalgic—this dish is a favorite of schoolchildren.

*M1: Oktogon. East on Teréz, right on Király. $ Entrees from 399Ft. ⏰ Open M-F 11am-9pm.*

**ARTESANO** — TAPAS BAR [1]

Ó utca 24-26 — ☎688 16 96 www.artesano.hu

Tucked away on unassuming Ó street, this stylish tapas bar is a favorite of classy locals and discerning expats. Spend the evening sampling a variety of creative original and Spanish-inspired dishes, such as king prawn wrapped in ham *(1690Ft)* or Spanish pancakes *(480Ft)*.

*M1: Opera. From the Metro, Take Hajós utca past the opera house and then turn left onto Ó utca; the restaurant is on the right. $ Tapas 400-1690Ft. Paella 1800Ft. Seafood 2100Ft. ⏰ Open M-Sa noon-midnight.*

## JÓZSEFVÁROS

**SIRIUS KLUB** — TEA HOUSE [1]

Bródy Sándor utca 13. — ☎266 17 08

A giant selection of teas served through a small window connected to the main seating area, Tibetan prayer flags, and floor cushions invite you to kick off your walking shoes and mellow out. If you're starved you might head to a restaurant, but for a quick nosh try their chocolate cookies.

*M3: Kálin tér. From the station, head north on Múzeum krt and turn right on Bródy Sándor. $ Tea from 540Ft. Cookies 250Ft. ⏰ Open daily noon-10pm.*

**DARSHAN UDVAR** — INTERNATIONAL [2]

Krúdy Gyula utca 7. — ☎266-5541 www.darshan.hu

Housed in a mosaic-tiled building with a magnificent inner courtyard, this restaurant boasts a menu as eclectic as its decor. From Buddha statues to Hungarian-style tablecloths, this place combines world cuisine with Hungarian spice. Relax in the courtyard over a meal, or stay for a beer and live music in the later hours.

*M3: Ferenc körút. From the station, head north on József krt and turn left on Krúdy Gyula. $ Soups from 690Ft. Entrees 990-2350Ft. Dessert 590-720Ft. ⏰ Open daily 11am-midnight.*

**BÉCSISZELET** — HUNGARIAN [2]

Üllöi út 16/a. — ☎267 49 37

Be prepared to be amazed at the gigantic portions paired with miniscule prices and maximum flavor. The turkey stuffed with chicken liver *(1190Ft)* is a speciality, and the enormous *wiener schnitzel (2290Ft)* will keep you satisfied for a week.

🚇 *M3: Kálvin tér. From the station, head east.* $ *Soup 290-490Ft. Entrees 850-1350Ft. Specialties 1090-3000Ft.* ⏰ *Open M-Sa 11am-11pm, Su 11am-10pm.*

**VENDÉGLÖ HÁRY** HUNGARIAN [3]

Bródy Sándor utca 30/a. ☎338 48 78 💻www.haryvendeglo.hu

One of the few places in the area where you can get a filling, hot breakfast. Traditional Hungarian cuisine is served in a cool basement by personable waiters. Don't miss the breaded vegetables *(900-1100Ft)* or the spicy goulash *(990Ft)*. Live dulcimer musicians add a charming noise to the otherwise mellow tone.

🚇 *M3: Kálvin tér. From the station, head north on Múzeum krt and turn right on Bródy Sándor.* **i** *Changing menü provides a good deal. Takeout meals 50-100Ft. Check website for events and concerts.* $ *Appetizers 950-2350Ft. Entrees 1550-3250Ft.* ⏰ *Open daily 10am-10pm.*

## FERENCVÁROS

**PINK CADILLAC PIZZERIA** ITALIAN [2]

Ráday utca 22 ☎216 14 12 💻www.pinkcadillac.hu

Pink Cadillac is a stylish pizza joint that offers some of the best pies in the city. Its specialties include the *Pirata*, *Dolce Vita*, and the massive signature Pink Caddy *(mushroom, ham, salami, olives; 2860Ft)* after which you may need a forklift to exit the building. The decor includes some vintage advertisements as well as the front of the eponymous pink Cadillac, sticking out of the wall with headlights on.

🚇 *M3: Kálvin tér. From the station, take Kálvin tér toward the river and turn left on Ráday.* $ *Pizza 750-2860Ft. Pasta 1140-1900Ft.* ⏰ *Open daily 11am-1am.*

**PASTA NEGRA** TAPAS [3]

Kálvin tér 8 ☎215 56 16 💻www.patanegra.hu

This wonderful tapas joint in the middle of Kálvin tér will make you happy you chose Budapest over Madrid for a summer vacation. Tapas range from the banal Catalan bread *(350Ft)* to the exotic crispy fried baby squid *(950Ft)*. Don't let the big scary bull standing outside frighten you—the patio is where it's at if you want a true fusion of Spanish slow-cooking in the bustle and noise of Hungary's capital.

🚇 *M3: Kálvin tér. From the station, walk across the street.* $ *White wine from 690Ft. Red wine from 750Ft. Entrees 840-1300Ft. Tapas 350-1950Ft.* ⏰ *Open M-W 11am-midnight, Th-F 11am-1am, Sa noon-1am, Su noon-midnight.*

**BERLINER SÖRÖZŐ** HUNGARIAN [3]

Ráday utca 5 ☎217 67 57 💻www.berliner.hu

A refreshingly low-key Hungarian-type pub in the middle of an all-too-often snobby Ráday utca. Come here for a relaxing lunch, a sip in the evening hours, or enjoy a dinner under the stars in a prime people-watching location. Traditional Hungarian fare will be found, including breaded turkey breast, mixed with such accoutrements as almond and peaches *(1680Ft)*, and the tasty but questionably named crunchy roast pig *(1980Ft)* will satisfy the gluttonous.

🚇 *M3: Kálvin tér. From the station, take Kálvin tér toward the river and turn left on Ráday.* $ *Traditional Belgian drafts from 400Ft. Appetizers 1120-2150Ft. Salads 360-400Ft. Entrees 1680-3250Ft.* ⏰ *Open M-Sa noon-1am.*

**ZOË CAFÉ** CAFE [3]

Ráday utca 20

A younger, sexier crowd sporting stunnah shades lounge at this stylish two-level red and black cafe. Those who like to pretend they're clubbing at all hours of the day will also appreciate the continuously playing R and B beats. The gnocchi with veal *(1990Ft)* gives people with more reasonable sensibilities a reason to stop by as well.

🚇 *M: Kálvin tér. From the station, take Kálvin tér toward the river and turn left on Ráday.* $ *Soups 780-980Ft. Salads 1180-1380Ft. Pasta 1620-1890Ft. Appetizers 890-2180Ft. Entrees 1980-3580Ft.* ⏰ *Open daily noon-1am.*

**JAFFA CAFÉ** CAFE ❷

Ráday utca 39 ☎219 52 85 💻www.jaffakavehaz.hu

The flourescent orange walls almost buzz with electricity, or perhaps that's just the excitement of the mixed clientele who flock to this friendly and fun cafe-turned-nightlife-spot after hours. Plush red velvet booths make you feel like you've stumbled into a funky version of the Moulin Rouge, but the alternative-type live music will bring you back down to the moment.

🚇 *M3: Kálvin tér. From the Metro, take Kálvin tér toward the river and turn left on Ráday.* ℹ *Free Wi-Fi.* $ *Coffee 290Ft. Tea 400Ft. Salads 990-1790Ft. Entrees 1790-2190Ft. Vegetarian options 1590-1690Ft.* ⏰ *Open M-Th 10am-1am, F 10am-2am, Sa noon-2am, Su 2pm-midnight.*

**SHIRÁZ PERZA ÉTTEREM** PERSIAN ❸

Mátyás utca 22 ☎ 218 08 81 💻www.shirazetterem.hu

A fabulous alternative to the somewhat ritzy rip-offs offered along Ráday. A Persian restaurant with choice of floor seating on plush authentic throws and pillows as you eat with your hands and enjoy a fruity waterpipe. If you're not alone, go for a mixed plate of kebab meats *(9500Ft)* and some Persian rice *(380Ft)*. It's a great option for vegetarians, too—try the Alibaba *(eggplant rice plate, 1950Ft)*.

🚇 *M3: Ferenc körút. From the station, head towards the river on Üllői út, then left on Köztelek which runs right into Ráday. The restaurant is on the corner of Ráday and Mátyás.* $ *Khoresh 1750Ft. Kebab plates 2400Ft.* ⏰ *Open daily noon-midnight.*

**MARIE KRISTENSEN SZENDVICSBÁR** SANDWICHES ❷

Ráday utca 7 ☎218 16 73

Some of the best hot sandwiches in the city and wholeheartedly recommended by local students and adults alike. Choose the size of sandwich you want and customize it to your liking. Also a good place to go if you want a hot breakfast for a wildly delicious low price--a rare phenomenon in Budapest. Its laid-back atmosphere is refreshing amongst the throngs of Ráday tourists and trend-seekers.

🚇 *M3: Kálvin tér. From the Metro, head east to Ráday.* $ *Sandwiches from 600Ft.* ⏰ *Open daily 9am-6pm.*

**VÖRÖS POSTAKOCSI ÉTTEREM** HUNGARIAN ❸

Ráday utca 15 ☎217 67 56 💻www.vorospk.com

Interesting decor choices make you feel like you're back at your crazy aunt's house. Hungarian cuisine sizzling in all its paprika glory comes fresh from the oven and close quarters make you friendly with your neighbors as you clap for occasional musicians or bounce along with folk dancers. A must-try is the classically delicious Hungarian dish most under the tourist radar, ox-tail soup *(890ft)*.

🚇 *M3: Kálvin tér. From the Metro, head east to Ráday.* $ *Fish 1700Ft. House specials 2290Ft. Vegetarian 1700Ft.* ⏰ *Open daily 11:30am-midnight.*

## THE VÁROSLIGET *City Park*

**ROBINSON RESTAURANT** HUNGARIAN ❸

Városligeti tó ☎663 68 71

Certainly commands one of the more interesting locations in Budapest atop an artificial pond in the middle of City Park. Serves a mix of Hungarian and international dishes. Grilled goose liver *(2790Ft)* is the house specialty.

🚇 *M1: Hősök tere. From the station, walk through Heroes' Sq. and then turn left; the restaurant is in the park across from the zoo.* $ *Soups 1200-1400Ft. Entrees 1900-5890Ft.* ⏰ *Open daily noon-4pm, 6pm-midnight.*

**GUNDEL ÉTTEREM** 💳♿🍸⛅❄ CLASSY ❹

Állatkerti út 2 ☎603 24 80 🖥www.gundel.hu

If you dare to enter, remember your best posh accent and pretentious gaze—this is the only area restaurant classy enough for both the Queen of England and Pope John Paul II to have graced it with their presence. Most of the menu is well outside a backpacker's budget, and the style probably diverges as well. The best deal is the three course lunch menu *(3800Ft)*, which comes with a glass of house wine.

*🚇 M1: Hősök tere. From the station, walk through Heroes' Square and then turn left; the restaurant is right next to the zoo.* ***i*** *Men must be in blazers or sport jackets. Reservations not required, but recommended.* $ *Sandwiches 1990-2190Ft. Salads 3190-3790Ft. Entrees 3980-6200Ft.* ⏰ *Open daily noon-4pm and 6:30-midnight.*

**BARAKA** 💳♿❄🍸 INTERNATIONAL ❸

Andrássy út 111 ☎483 13 55

Located on the ground floor of a former historic hotel, Baraka is one of Budapest's most celebrated restaurants. The exterior overlooks the beautiful boulevard and Heroes' Square, while the interior has the feel of a sleek New York lounge. Start off with the Thai-marinated salmon *tataki* in coconut crust *(1800Ft)*. The five-spice duck breast *(4900Ft)* is one of the chef's specialties.

*🚇 M1: Bajza utca. Walk toward Heroes' Sq.; the restaurant is on the right.* ***i*** *Reservations recommended.* $ *Appetizers 1500-1900Ft. Entrees 2400-6200Ft.* ⏰ *Open M-Sa noon-3pm and 6-11pm, Su noon-3pm.*

**BAGOLYVÁR ÉTTEREM** 💳♿🍸❄ HUNGARIAN ❸

Állatkerti út 2 ☎468 3110 🖥www.bagolyvar.com

Vine-covered exterior prepares you for the elegance inside. High-end Hungarian cuisine proudly prepared by generations of Hungarian mothers and grandmothers. The small menu changes daily, though specialties like the rump steak *(2350Ft)* and the goose liver *(4390Ft)* are mainstays. Strictly for those who can afford a splurge.

*🚇 M1: Hősök tere. From the station, walk through Heroes' Sq. and then turn left; the restaurant is right next to the zoo.* ***i*** *Reservations required.* $ *Appetizers 660-930Ft. Entrees 1880-4390Ft.* ⏰ *Open daily noon-11pm.*

**KERTEM** 🚫💳♿🍸⛅ CAFE ❷

Olof Palme sétány 3 ☎3630 225 13 99 🖥www.kertemfesztival.hu

Prepare to be greeted by bicycles hooked onto the fence when you enter this triple threat that functions as a cafe by day and a pub and music venue by night. Don't go here if you're starved, but do if you're ready to escape the snobby City Park restaurants.

*🚇 M1: Hősök tere. Behind the Palace of Art* ***i*** *Check online for concert and program listings.* $ *Coffee from 280Ft. Sandwiches from 660Ft. Crepes from 290Ft.* ⏰ *Open daily 11am-4am. Kitchen open 4pm-4am.*

**CAFE KARA** 🚫💳♿🍸 CAFE ❷

Andrássy út 130 ☎269 4135 🖥www.cafekara.hu

A favorite of young Hungarians and backpackers, this Turkish cafe serves some of the tastiest and most reasonably priced food in the area. The toasted turkey and cheese sandwiches *(950Ft)* are perfect after a day of walking around the park. When you've finished with your coffee and hummus, you can wind down with a waterpipe and a variety of fruity tobacco flavors *(pipe and tobacco; 1300Ft)* as well as a few more unconventional varieties like Cola and Red Bull.

*🚇 M1: Hősök tere. At the corner of Andrássy and Heroes' Square.* $ *Turkish coffee 360Ft. Salads 900-1500Ft. Sandwiches 950-1500Ft.* ⏰ *Open daily 10am-10pm. Bellydancing F-Sa 8pm.*

## ◙ DAUBNER CUKRÁSZDA                     ⊛♿☕ CAFE ❷

Szépvölgyi út 50                     ☎335 22 53 🖳www.daubnercukraszda.hu

While locals rave about the cakes and ice cream, the place is all too easy for tourists to miss due to its off-the-beaten-path location. A sweet place to get something to go and eat in the privacy of your hostel bed; or stay a while and couple a chocolate cake *(380Ft)* with some nutty coffee *(300Ft)*. While the glass cases are stocked with more things than you could ever work off at the gym, don't stand and slobber too long—the line of people out the door will slip into a premature sugar coma.

⚑ *Tram 17: Kolosy tér. From the tram stop, walk a few blocks up Szépvölgyi út; the cafe will be on your left.* ⑤ *Sweets from 300Ft. Coffee from 300Ft.* ☒ *Open daily 9am-7pm.*

## ARANYSZARVAS BISZTRÓ                     ⊛♿🍷❄☕ HUNGARIAN ❹

Szarvas tér 1                     ☎375 64 51 🖳www.aranyszarvas.hu

An enormous gilt deer head greets guests at this fancy coffeehouse where many of the 18th century's most renowned literary luminaries gathered to reinvigorate the Hungarian language and invent modern Serbian. For decades, this revered Buda landmark was the only restaurant in Budapest that served game. Nearly 40 years later, venison, boar, and pheasant are still the only game in town. Don't be petrified after a cursory glance at the menu—it is possible to keep the price down if you go for a fairly filling starter like smoked pork joint salad with horseradish *(1450Ft)* or a schmancy after-dinner dessert like baked yogurt with raspberry ice cream *(990Ft)*.

⚑ *Trams 18 or 19: Döbrentei tér. From the tram stop, take Döbrentei tér away from the river, turn right onto Attila út, and then veer left; the restaurant is on the corner.* ⓘ *Reservations recommended.* ⑤ *Appetizers 1200-1800Ft. Entrees 1600-2900Ft. Desserts 990-1400Ft.* ☒ *Open daily noon-11pm.*

## NAGYI PALACSINTÁZÓJA                     ⊛♿☕ FRENCH ❷

Hattyú utca 16                     ☎212 48 66

Literally "your grandmama's creperie," this tiny joint fries up thin pancakes Hungarian-style, stuffing them with delicious fatteners like sweet cocoa powder, rice pudding, and sour-cherry sauce. It's a perfect early-morning place to soak up all that booze from a raunchy night and watch the sun rise over Parliament.

⚑ *M2: Moszkva tér. From the station, walk toward the river; at the big intersection, veer right on Hattyú utca.* ⓘ *Another location is at Batthyány tér 5.* ⑤ *Sweet crepes 130-640Ft. Savory crepes 240-620Ft.* ☒ *Open 24hr.*

## TABÁNI TERASZ                     ⊛♿☕🍷 HUNGARIAN ❸

Apród utca 10                     ☎201 10 86 🖳www.tabaniterasz.hu

A century-old Hungarian restaurant housed in a 250-year-old inn. Long tables run vertically along the walls of the cellar to create an intimate space accented by traditional red seat covers. The outdoor wooden deck opens during the warm months, welcoming guests to enjoy a lush garden-green oasis. The goulash soup *(980Ft)* is particularly tasty, and the "homestyle" smoked silver carp filet *(1950Ft)* will leave you properly bloated for relatively cheap.

⚑ *Tram 18 or 19: Döbrentei tér. From the tram stop, take Döbrentei tér away from the river, turn right onto Attila út, and then veer right onto Apród utca.* ⑤ *Appetizers 1100-2980Ft. Soups 860-980Ft. Pasta 2100-2900Ft. Entrees 2500-4600Ft.* ☒ *Open daily noon-midnight.*

## SEOUL HOUSE                     ⊛⊗ KOREAN ❷

Fő utca 8                     ☎201 74 52

Bam! A Korean restaurant smack-dab in the quasi-center of Budapest. Now we've seen everything. Sizzling barbecue is served in a bamboo setting a panda bear would envy. Specialties include sliced and broiled ox tongue *(3000Ft)* and barbecue spare ribs *(3100Ft).*

🚊 *Tram 19: Lánchíd. From the tram stop, cross the street, take Jégverem utca to the corner, and turn left on Fő utca.* Ⓢ *Soup 500-1400Ft. Entrees 2300-3900Ft.* 🕗 *Open M-Sa noon-11pm.*

## BISTRO MANAMANA
●((ŋ))♈⚐ CAFE ❷

Zivatar utca 11 ☎3630 680 87 41

An inviting little place nestled into the hills of Buda, Bistro Manamana is an unaffected, inexpensive option for the Buda traveler looking for a quick sandwich or a lazy coffee. Don't be deterred by the hike up the hill, which will reward you with a view of the city found nowhere else among the throngs of fanny-pack-toters.

🚊 *Tram 4 or 6: Margit híd. From the tram stop, walk straight up the hill until Margit utca cros Zivatar; the bistro is on the left on the corner of Rómer Flóris.* i *TV showing sporting events. Poker and games available.* Ⓢ *Salads from 990Ft. Coffee 400Ft. Afternoon menus from 500Ft.* 🕗 *Open M-F 8am-8pm, Sa 9am-3pm.*

## NÁNCSI NÉNI VENDÉGLŐJE
●🕹♈⚐ HUNGARIAN ❸

Ördögárok utca 80 ☎398 71 27 💻www.nancsineni.hu

Quite a trek uphill, but if you're devoted enough to work for a treat like "my mother's green pea soup" *(980Ft),* you won't be sorry. Light floods the cozy family run little restaurant through pink curtains and the tables are adorned with traditional red-and-white checkered cloths. Gorge on delectable Hungarian cuisine suitable for carnivores and vegetarians alike: omnivores, try the vegetable ragout of lamb *(2650Ft).*

🚊 *M3: Arany János utca. From the station, take bus #157: Nagyrét utca. The restaurant is across the street on Ördögárok utca.* Ⓢ *Soups from 850ft. Entrees 1750-2850ft.* 🕗 *Open daily noon-11pm.*

## PLATÁN
●⊗((ŋ))⚐ CAFE ❷

Döbrentei tér 2 ☎3620 361 22 87

Platán provides a pleasant view of **Elizabeth Bridge** and the **Liberty Monument,** which makes up for the sparsity of available foodstuffs. While the baguettes are on par, don't expect a sizzling home-cooked meal. Come for the coffee and stay for the company—many moody locals frequent the establishment to write.

🚊 *Tram 18 or 19: Döbrentei tér. From the tram stop, head south toward the square.* Ⓢ *Espresso 310Ft. Tea 350Ft. Beer from 320Ft.* 🕗 *Open daily 10am-midnight.*

## TRANZIT ART CAFÉ
●((ŋ))♈⚐ CAFE ❶

Bukarest utca 5 ☎209 30 70 💻tranzitcafe.com

The funky glass building that houses this cafe—which is more like a cultural center –is hard to miss amid the towering communist-era apartment buildings. Swing back and relax in the hammocks that hang outside or take part in childen's fingerpainting classes. Oh yeah, and eat something too—the changing daily menu offers a deliciously cheap deal like a whopping bowl of soup with a Hungarian canteen-style entree *(1200Ft).*

🚊 *Tram 49: Kosztolányi Dezső tér. From the stop head south on Bartók Béla út and turn left on Ulászló utca; the cafe will be in the 1st inlet on your right.* i *Check online for special event listings and occasional art classes.* Ⓢ *Menus 900-1200Ft. Coffee 310Ft.* 🕗 *Open daily 9am-9pm.*

## MARXISM
●♈⊗ PUB ❷

Kis Rókus utca 23 ☎316 02 31

A pizza place that will make you see stars—big, red, scary ones. We guess it's not too soon to draw phallic Stalin cartoons and muscular working-types in Hungary. Don't worry, the pizza is just as good as the humor. Take a bite out of a saucy Stalin bloodbath and wash it down with a tangy Molotov cocktail.

🚊 *M2: Moszkva tér. From the station, head toward Millenáris Park on Lövőház utca, turn right on Fény utca just before the park, and veer left on Kis Rókus utca; the pizzeria is on the right.* 🕗 *Open M-Th noon-1am, F-Sa noon-2am, Su 6pm-1am.*

food · várhegy, central buda, and the vizivaros

## ÓBUDA

### 👍 EMIL CUKRÁSZDA

⊘♿⛅ CAFE ❶

Bécsi út 314 ☎240 75 35 💻www.emilcukraszda.hu

While it may seem like a random shop thrown in between some other odd shops on a main road leading out of the city, beware this type of dismissive thinking! Don't miss out on one of the best confectionaries in the land, stocked with finger- (and if it drops on the ground, ground-) licking good treats. Limited seating area (i.e., a bench next to the entrance) means it's an in-and-out sort of ordeal, but the courageous traveler will not be disappointed once he's taken his first bite of triple chocolate cake with raspberry filling and buttercream accents.

*➡ Bus #260: ATI. Keep walking a bit in the direction of the bus and cross the road. $ Sweets from 250Ft. Coffee from 210Ft. ⏰ Open daily 10am-6pm.*

### CSÜLÖK CSÁRDA

⊘♿🍸⛅ HUNGARIAN ❸

Szentendrei út 89 - 95 ☎240 02 54 💻www.emilcukraszda.hu

Csülök Csárda is for the real meat lover. A sea of wooden tables greets ravenous guests ready to mangle their prey, and traditional Hungarian cuisine served in an interesting decor makes you wonder where these Hungarians get their decorators. The food is delicious, despite its surroundings' lack of aesthetic beauty, and the giant portions come at an unbeatable price.

*➡ HÉV: Köles Street. From the stop, backtrack on Szentendrei út 1 block. $ Soups 500-620Ft. Entrees 1100-2500Ft. ⏰ Open M-F 10am-10pm, Sa-Su 11am-11pm.*

## MARGIT-SZIGET

### 👍 HOLDUDVAR

💳♿🍸⛅ HUNGARIAN, MEDITERRANEAN ❷

Margit Sziget ☎236 0155 💻www.holdudvar.net

Orange lanterns and hipster-type furniture welcome the hungry traveler. If it's not enough that this place turns into one of the coolest open-air venues come nightfall with film screenings, live music, and dancing 'til dawn, it also serves up some of the most delicious fare in the middle of the river. The food is Hungarian with a Mediterranean tinge. Try the Mediterranean tomato soup with mozzarella *(850Ft)* and you'll leave happy and satisfied. Turns into a fun bar come nightfall.

*➡ From the Margit Bridge entrance, take the main road; the garden will be on your right, across from the Hajós Alfréd Swimming Pool. ℹ Film screenings in the open-air cinema Su 9pm. $ Appetizers 1700-2500Ft. Pasta 1700-2900Ft. Entrees 1500-4500Ft. ⏰ Open daily in summer 11am-5am.*



### CHAMPS SPORTS PUB

💳♿🍸⛅ PUB ❷

Margit Sziget ☎413-1655 💻www.champs.hu

An expansive wooden deck invites guests to sip beer or relax and chat with friends on beanbags. More than 30 plasma TVs broadcast the latest game and the kitchen serves up wholesome portions of pizza, Mexican food, and other delicious odds and ends.

*➡ Tram 1: Jászai Mari tér, walk across the bridge to the island. The pub is across the way from Holdudvar. $ Pizza 900-1500Ft. Quesadillas 1000Ft. ⏰ Open in summer daily 11am-2am.*

# nightlife

## THE BELVÁROS

### 👍 KATAPULT

💳⊗🍸 PUB

V, Dohány u. 1 ☎01 266 7226

Local 20-somethings squeeze into this tiny but lively pub that functions as a cafe by day. Red walls and trippy lamps bring a range of evenings, from political debates to head-banging and grinding; the space leaves it up to the clientele to decide its vibe for the night. Try to eat beforehand as the kitchen closes in the afternoon.

*M2: Astoria. Walk west up Károly krt from the Metro and backtrack to the right onto Dohány. $ Beer from 500Ft. Open daily 9am-2am.*

### scrub pub

Ruin pubs—the number one trend in nightlife in Budapest these days—are installed in the courtyards and gardens of empty, crumbling old communist-era residential buildings. You won't see anything from the outside (except people drifting in and out with their plastic beer glasses, or perhaps a beefy guard controlling the noise levels of these residential party pads), but the inner courtyard is decorated with a hodgepodge of hipster-eque furniture: bathtubs for sofas, a table with eight different chairs, etc. Concerts, DJs, films, and alternative exhibits provide the entertainment at these hot hangouts.

**GÖDÖR KLUB** CLUB

V, Erzsébet Tér ☎01 201 3868 www.godorklub.hu

The conspicuously bare concrete walls of the club, situated in the former foundation of what was supposed to be the new National Concert Hall, might seem unfinished, but on weekends you can hardly move in the crowded concert arena where rock, jazz, world, techno, and folk deafen patrons. If you arrive early enough you might snag a table on the long staircase or a seat on one of the benches along the retaining walls. For a more relaxing time head there during the week for Pilates.

*M1-3: Deák Tér. $ Beer from 350Ft. Shots 200-1000Ft. Open M-Th 10am-2am, F-Sa 10am-4am, Su 10am-2am*

**CAPELLA CAFE** GAY CLUB

V, Belgrád rakpart 23 ☎70 328 6775 www.capellacafe.hu

Budapest's first gay discotheque draws a crowd of all orientations to its three levels even during the week. Themed dance rooms, a variety of music and occasional drag nights promise an evening unlike any other in the city. Upstairs you'll find a laid-back bar with a balcony surrounding the dance floors for those wallflower types.

*Trams 2 and 2a: Március 15 tér. Follow the river towards the castle. [i] Cover W Sa usually 1000ft. $ Beer and wine 600Ft. Shots from 800Ft. Open daily M-Sa 10am-5am.*

**CSENDES** BAR

V, Ferenczy István utca 5 www.kiscsendes.hu

Across the street from the university, this local artist haunt is more like a deranged child's bedroom. The walls are festooned with picture frames, mannequins, and a bicycle. Six chandeliers float above, and mismatched chairs and tables bring you down to earth. Check the website for weekly specials like film screenings and live concerts.

*M2: Astoria. From the Metro take Múzeum krt toward the National Museum and turn right on Ferenczy István utca; the bar is on your left. $ Beer from 250Ft. Shots 290-850Ft. Open Tu-Sa 3pm-2am.*

## LIPÓTVÁROS

### BECKETT'S IRISH PUB

PUB

V, Bajcsy-Zsilinszky út 72 ☎01 311 1035 www.becketts.hu

The only Irish pub in Budapest that is owned and operated by an actual Irishman, it's mostly expats with hearty laughs and iron livers here. Get a kick out of Irish culture juxtaposed with Hungarian locals debating politics or soccer. Fall and winter months bring live concerts in the form of Oasis cover bands.

*M3: Nyugati. From the Metro walk south. The pub is on the right. $ Sandwiches 950-1950Ft. Beer from 600Ft. Shots from 445Ft. 10% discount with student ID. Open M-Th noon-midnight, F-Sa noon-2am, Su noon-midnight. Kitchen open until midnight.*

### LE CAFE M

GAY BAR

V, Nagysándor József utca 3 ☎01 312 1436 www.lecafem.com

Stylish, small gay bar in the heart of district V. Caters to a low-key crowd and draws a mix of locals and tourists with subdued conversation and tasteful drinking. Brick walls, leather booths, and atmospheric lighting set a similar mood. While anyone can have a good time here, the bar is frequented mostly by gay men.

*M3: Arany János utca. From the Metro take Bajcsy-Zsilinszky north and turn left on Nagysándor. $ Beer from 450Ft. Shots from 300Ft. Mixed drinks from 990Ft. Open M-F 4pm-4am, Sa-Su 6pm-4am.*

### CAFE NEGRO

BAR

V, Szent István Tér 11 ☎01 302 0136

The sleek black interior and reflective silver wallcovering behind the bar emit a pricey air. Bring your sunglasses to look cool and join the other foreigners for a finger-snapping evening.

*M1: Bajcsy-Zsilinszky út. From the Metro take József Attila west, right on Sas and right into courtyard. $ Mixed drinks 1450-2200Ft. Open daily 11am-4am.*

## ERZSÉBETVÁROS

### SZIMPLA KERT

RUIN PUB

Kazinczy utca ☎352 41 98 www.szimpla.hu

Graffiti designs adorn the crumbling walls, a hodgepodge of furniture ranging from your grandmother's Victorian love-seat to the old beach lounger you threw in the garage, colorful lighting, a movie screen, and concert stage make for a chilled out night in hipster glory at Budapest's original ruin pub. Smoke in the courtyard, eat crepes by the bar, or make out upstairs in the bathtub. Mind-blowing films screened almost every night nicely compliment the dream-like atmosphere.

*M2: Astoria. Head east on Rákóczi út and turn left on Kazinczy. i Check the website for event listings. $ Beer from 350Ft. Shots from 600Ft. Mixed drinks 1400-2500Ft. Open daily noon-3am.*

### MUMUS

RUIN PUB

Dob utca 18.

If you can figure out how to keep mellow at this laid-back bar where the booze runs cheaper than penny candy, shoot us an email. Local students and artists along with the occasional with-it backpacker haunt the place with an off-the-grid atmosphere: non-sloppy, all-night boozing. A classy ruin pub with a simple decor that invites an intelligent clientele to sip, chat, and listen to floaty music.

*M2: Astoria. Head north on Károly krt and turn right on Dob utca. $ Beer from 240Ft. Shots 250-500Ft. Wine from 200Ft. Open M-Sa 3pm-3am, Su 4pm-midnight.*

### GARZON

PUB

Wesselényi utca 24. ☎0630 438 77 88 www.garzoncafe.com

A brand-new, up-and-coming cafe and pub with a funky interior design and a local student vibe. Sit in a worn leather chair at an oddly-shaped table, or relax in the tiled booth that looks like one of Home Depot's bathroom show rooms.

*M2: Blaha Lujza. Head north on Erzsébet krt and turn left on Wesselényi. i Check online for event listings. $ Beer 300Ft. Wine from 200Ft. Coffee 250Ft. ⏰ Open M-W 10am-1am, Th 10am-2am, F 10am-3:30am, Sa 4pm-3:30am, Su 4pm-midnight.*

**SZÓDA** BAR

Wesselényi utca 18. ☎3670 389 64 63 🖥www.szoda.hu

Still a fun and lively place to go, despite its change in atmosphere from bumping party spot to lounge-like booze-sipping locale. Bathed in red light, with ceiling covered in life-sized manga comics, the place is moody and opinionated. The downstairs area sees DJs on a weekly basis and draws local crowds from the city's universities.

*M2: Astoria. Head east on Rákóczi and turn left on Kazinczy; the bar is near the corner of Kazinczy and Wesselényi. i Check online for event listings. $ Beer from 300Ft. Shots 350-650Ft. ⏰ Open M-F 9am-5am, Sa-Su 2pm-5am.*

**KLUB VITTULA** BAR

Kertész utca 4. ☎20 527 7069 🖥www.vittula.hu

Tiny place in a brick cellar whose walls are splattered with a mix of graffiti and Asian murals. DJs amp up the crowd, who would otherwise be chillin' over a glass of wine, with energy. Great in summer if you're looking for a cool underground retreat.

*M2: Blaha Lujza tér. Head north on Erzsébet krt, turn left after 1 block and make a swift right onto Kertész. i Check website for music listings. $ Beer from 340Ft. Shots from 450Ft. ⏰ Open M-Sa 6pm-4am.*

**ELLÁTÓ** CLUB

Klauzál tér 1-2

Another happening club in line with the new trend of mellow hipster-type places. Smoke over a political debate or be the guy with sunken cheeks and tired eyes drowning in vino next to the conversation. Not bad for lunch or dinner; the kitchen serves up cheap and easy Hungarian home-cooking.

*M2: Blaha Lujza tér. Head west on Rákóczi and turn right on Nagy Diófa which takes you right to the square; the bar is on the right. $ Salads 400-900Ft. Entrees 1100-1500Ft. Beer from 220Ft. Shots 300Ft. ⏰ Open M-Sa 2pm-2am, Su 4pm-midnight.*

## TERÉZVÁROS

**MOST** RUIN PUB

Zichy Jenő utca 17

A new take on the ruin pub, Most offers a diverse array of styles; classic grunge furniture to sleeker decor on the terrace means a good night for everyone. Three venues, each with its own personality, guarantee to serve a clientele base just as unique. Head upstairs to the balcony for a romantic drink, chill indoors on the first floor amidst the books and odds-and-ends to get your hipster on, or never leave the unassuming garden where you entered—a plot of land transformed into a quiet oasis of happy conversation and cheap drinking.

*M1: Opera. East on Andrássy, left on Nagymező and left on Zichy Jenő. $ Beer 550Ft. Wine 450Ft. ⏰ Open daily 11am-3am.*

**SZILVUPLÉ** RUIN PUB

Ó utca 37 ☎3620 992 51 15 🖥szilvuple.hu

A more refined remake on the ruin-pub decor with (gasp!) matching tables and chairs. A frightening female doll sitting at the entrance will freak you out, while quirky murals hiding the crumbling walls will convince you that the building won't collapse in a matter of minutes. This will especially feel true after you've downed the area's cheapest booze. Go upstairs to witness salsa dancing performances or just to get a little higher.

*M1: Oktogon. South on Andrássy, right on Nagymező and right on Ó utca.* *i* *Check online for event listings.* $ *Beer from 290Ft. Wine from 230Ft.* ⏰ *Th-Sa 6pm-4am, Su 6pm-2am.*

**PÓTKULCS** RUIN PUB

Csengery utca 65/b ☎269 10 50 💻www.potkulcs.hu

One of Budapest's most difficult-to-find ruin pubs, but well worth the effort. The terrace is full of greenery and surrounded by the old brick from a former apartment building. Live music and DJs inspire spontaneous dancing in the main room. Don't be surprised if you have to move because people have started to use your table as a dance floor. The expansive, inexpensive drink list (which includes honey *pálinka*) gives you ample reason to stick around.

*M1: Vörösmarty utca. From the Metro, take Vörösmarty toward the train station and turn left at Szondi; the bar is on the corner of Csengery and Szondi.* $ *Beer from 450Ft. Wine from 190Ft. Shots from 500Ft.* ⏰ *Open daily 5pm-3am.*

**TŰZRAKTÉR** CULTURAL CENTER, PUB

Hegedű utca 3 💻www.tuzrakter.hu

A 3-story high mural of a girl riding a bicycle greets you at the entrance to this cultural center situated in an old high school; Tűzraktér also happens to be one of the best pubs around. If you get there during business hours, take a look around the galleries, where artists freely exhibit their work. At night, occasional house and techno DJs bid the lounging clientele to dance with varying degrees of success.

*M1: Oktogon. From the Metro, take Teréz körút south 2 blocks, turn left on Király, and then right on Hegedű.* $ *Beer from 230Ft. Shots 280-800Ft.* ⏰ *Bar open daily 3pm-2am.*

**PIAF** LOUNGE

Nagymező utca 25 ☎312 38 23

Head to the address, find the black door, knock on the window, marvel at the little old lady who demands the cover charge and then relax on the red velvet couches that make you feel like you've stumbled upon a sexless brothel. Yeah, we're serious. This joint gets poppin' after 3am, and even that's a little early to show up. Haunted by young and old, Budapest's oldest nightclub will guarantee you an experience unlike any other and help you recover after a night of ruin pub rendezvous with a refreshingly old style. Bounce around downstairs to an eclectic mix of dance music, or lounge up the stairs until you hear the city's sorry saps start heading to work in the morning.

*M1: Oktogon. Head south on Andrássy út and right on Nagymező.* $ *Beer from 650Ft. Wine from 450Ft.* ⏰ *Open Tu-Th 3am-6am, F-Sa 3am-7am.*

**INSTANT** RUIN PUB

Nagymező utca 38 💻www.instant.co.hu

A ruin pub with an inner courtyard covered in vines and a basement filled with secret alcoves for more intimate meetings. Definitely one of the more laid-back bars in the area, constantly pumping out concerts, live music and DJs to keep the clientele on their feet. Feels like you've come to a stylish friend's house party where people mingle and double-fist cheap booze.

*M1: Opera. From the Metro, take Andrássy toward Oktogon and turn left on Nagymező.* $ *Beer from 270Ft.* ⏰ *Open daily 6pm-2am.*

## JÓZSEFVÁROS

**CORVINTETŐ** CLUB

Blaha Lujza tér 1-2 ☎772 29 84 💻www.corvinteto.hu

As you're walking up in anticipation of what's to come, don't be fooled by the graffiti-stained stairs and concrete monstrosity in front of you: this dance-and-drink party place on top of a former state-owned department store is a stylish club offering one of the most breathtaking views in Budapest. Regular DJs and live acts are a popular draw in the red-lit lounge area, but head outside in the summer to the three bars and non-stop grooving.

*M2: Blaha Lujza tér. From the station, walk towards the Corvin building, the entrance is along Somogy Béla út, up the stairs. $ Beer from 320Ft. Shots 600-950Ft. ⏰ Open daily 6pm-5am.*

**KAMRA** — RESTAURANT, BAR

Lőrinc pap tér 4. ☎3620 565 61 21

The ancient French horns hanging from the ceiling seem to lure in a music-obsessed clientele. Local bands and solo artists show their goods in this laid-back venue that serves Hungarian cuisine by day and transforms into a happening party joint by night.

*M3: Ferenc krt. From the station, head north on József krt and left on Krúdy Gyula utca. The pub will be on the left across from the Catholic church. i $ Beer from 200Ft. Wine from 250Ft. ⏰ Open M-Th noon-midnight, F-Sa noon-4am.*

**KÖNYVTÁR (THE LIBRARY)** — BAR

Múzeum krt 4. ☎509 01 89 www.knoyvtarklub.hu

A giant student population from the neighboring university flocks this "library" for some hardcore "studying" at the bar. The underground club hosts live acts every single night throughout the year and the summer months draw kids to the breezy outdoor terrace adorned with glowing lanterns and accented by the occasional older type.

*M2: Astoria. From the station, walk toward the university; the club is through the gate and down the stairs to the left. $ Beer from 300Ft. Shots from 500Ft. ⏰ Open M-F 7pm-3:30am, Sa 6pm-3:30am.*

## FERENCVÁROS

**RUMBA CAFÉ** — BAR

Lónyay utca 27 ☎3670 503 69 69 www.rumbacafe.hu

A super-relaxed bar that makes you feel like you're in your best friend's den. Worn sofas, an eclectic mix of posters, '70s-esque armchairs, and wooden tables offer a nice flashback as you sip island drinks—the house specialty is Sex on the Rumba *(rum, pineapple juice and apricot brandy; 950Ft).*

*M3: Ferenc körút. From the station, head west on Üllői and left on Kinizsi and right on Lonyay utca. $ Shots from 660Ft. ⏰ Open Tu-Sa 6pm-midnight.*

**KÖZGÁZ KLUB** — CLUB

Fővám tér 8 ☎0630 992 96 44 www.schoolclub.hu

One of the coolest student nightclubs in the city, literally run out of a cellar in an economics department building. Expect lots of bodies grooving to hip American—and occasionally Hungarian—music, and cheap drinks in a well-hidden venue. Special events and local bands play constantly, but their viral information is hard to come by, so check out the place during the day for listings.

*South of the green Liberty Bridge. i 1000ft cover for men. $ Beer from 300Ft. Wine 250Ft. ⏰ Only open during term time, Sept 1-June 1. Open M-Sa 10am-2am.*

## VÁRHEGY, CENTRAL BUDA, AND THE VIZIVAROS

**ZÖLD PARDON** — ENTERTAINMENT COMPLEX

Goldmann György tér ☎279 1880 www.zp.hu

"Green" Pardon has gained a bit of a bad name over the past few years for catering primarily to 16-year-olds yearning to escape their parents and have a night of unrestricted smoking and paying their elders to buy them drinks. Contrary to stereotype, however, the rising number of savvy Budapestians who know what's up would wholeheartedly recommend this expansive open-air venue to anyone young, old, short, or tall looking for a good time. The summer months bring countless DJs, rappers, hip-hop stars, and dancers, while the constantly changing drink specials at the multiple bars will have you seeing green elephants well into the morning hours.

✸ *Trams 4 or 6: Petőfi híd, budai hídfő.* ⓘ *Check website and Facebook for event listings.* ⓢ *Cover 300Ft. Beer from 350Ft. Mixed drinks from 1000Ft.* ⓣ *Open Apr-Oct daily 11am-5am.*

## A38
⬥●⊗�♿ CLUB

Near Petöfi Bridge, Buda side ☎464 3940 🖳www.a38.hu

A radically *sui generis* venue, this club-on-a-boat offers magical views of the Chain Bridge and Parliament in all their brilliant midnight glory. This trendy place pumps "house" or electronica-type tunes for its well-dressed clientele who drink fruity cocktails and smoke light slims. The giant dance floor in the center is the perfect place for those who enjoy claustrophobia and the best place to meet new people by bumping elbows and pouring drinks on their freshly starched shirts.

✸*Tram 4 or 6: Petőfi híd. Walk past Zöld Pardon and cross the street.* ⓢ *Beer from 450Ft. Mixed drinks 1100-1850Ft. Cover around 500Ft.* ⓣ *Open M-Sa 11am-11pm.*

## RUDAS ROMKERT
●♿�♿ RUIN PUB

9 Döbrentei square ☎3630 351 5217 🖳www.rudasromkert.hu

A relatively new open-air ruin pub housed in actual Roman ruins at the foot of Gellért Hill. Caters to a bit more of an upscale clientele than would most ruin pubs and feels more like a club than a chill hangout. Colorful paper lanterns strung from one end to the other bring down the pretentiousness a notch, but the posse of bouncers at the door checking IDs and instituting face control might make Birkenstock-wearing backpackers think twice about entering.

✸ *Bus 7: Rudas gyógyfürdő.* ⓢ *Beer from 450Ft. Mixed drinks from 900Ft.* ⓣ *Open daily 5pm-late.*

# MARGIT-SZIGET

## ▨ HOLDUDVAR
⬥●♿�♿ OUTDOOR BAR

Margit Sziget ☎236 01 55 🖳www.holdudvar.net

Built on 13th century ruins, this giant garden venue doles out the best tunes, tastiest fare, and wildest nights on the island. Hit up the place during the day and gorge on such tasty things as "paprika chicken breast with curded ewe cheese dumplings" *(1900Ft)* and come back by the midnight hours to watch a film outdoors, dance like there's no tomorrow, and, most importantly, drink the cheapest beverages on the island until you forget what tomorrow means.

✸ *From the Margit Bridge entrance, take the main road; the garden will be on your right, across from the Hajós Alfréd Swimming Pool.* ⓘ *Film screenings on the open-air cinema Su 9pm.* ⓢ *Beer from 300Ft. Shots 790-1400Ft. Appetizers 1700-2500Ft. Pasta 1700-2900Ft. Entrees 1500-4500Ft.* ⓣ *Open in summer daily 11am-5am.*

## CHA CHA CHA TERASZ
●♿�♿ OUTDOOR BAR

Margit Sziget ☎329 27 88 🖳www.chachacha.hu

Yes, that "music" you've been hearing for the past three hours has indeed been the exact same beat. Not to worry though, because this friendly dance club has plenty of tables to take a break from all that grinding and enjoy a cheap draft or chat with newly acquired friends under the stars.

✸ *From the Margit Bridge entrance, take the main road and turn left at the entrance to the athletic complex; the garden is on your left.* ⓢ *Beer from 350Ft. Shots 350-700Ft. Some high-end drinks go for 3500Ft.* ⓣ *Open in summer daily 11am-late.*

### SZIGET KLUB TERASZ
&#9992;&&#9866;&#9986; OUTDOOR BAR

Margit Sziget &#9743;3620 203 74 88 &#9632;www.szigetklubterasz.hu

Deserving more credit than it typically gets, this open-air bar is the unsung hero of the island. The smallest of its counterparts, this mellow hangout on the Buda-side shore of the island is delicately hidden in an outward nook, allowing the club to expand its quarters onto a deck that almost reaches the water. While the atmosphere is less assuming and the populace may seem small, it's simply a reflection of weeding out the worst.

&#9223; *From the Margit Bridge entrance, take the main road; the garden will be on your left just past the bus stop.* &#9412; *Beer from 350Ft. Shots 700-900Ft. Mixed drinks 650-900Ft. Appetizers and salads 850-1500Ft. Entrees 1150-1500Ft.* &#9419; *Open in summer daily 11am-late.*

# arts and culture

## MUSIC AND OPERA

### ▣ ACADEMY OF MUSIC
&#9992;& TERÉZVÁROS

Liszt Ferenc tér 8 &#9743; 342 0179 &#9632;www.zeneakademia.hu

Find the nation's young musical prodigies all in one room at the prestigious Academy of Music. Pray to the music gods to make you lucky enough to catch a concert in the majestic Art Nouveau building that houses the school in Franz Liszt's honor.

&#9223; *M1: Oktogon. From the station, head east on Teréz krt and turn right on Király utca; the academy will be on your right one block down.* &#9432; *Check the website or call for concert listings. Schedules vary and there are rarely concerts in summer.* &#9412; *Prices vary.* &#9419; *Box office open daily 2-8pm.*

### MAGYAR ÁLLAMI OPERAHÁZ (STATE OPERA HOUSE)
&#9992;& TERÉZVÁROS

Andrássy út 22 &#9743;353 0170 &#9632;www.opera.hu

Housed in a magnificent Neo-Rennaissance building that took nine years to construct, the Hungarian State Opera hosts some of the continent's finest op-eras, ballets, and classical performances. While some tickets sell out a year in advance, rush tickets are sometimes available at a fraction of the normal price one hour before the performance.

&#9223; *M1: Opera.* &#9432; *Call for show schedules, or check the poster at the gate.* &#9412; *Tickets 1000-9000Ft.* &#9419; *Box office open M-Sa 11am-7pm, Su 4-7pm. Closes at 5pm on non-performance days.*

## THEATER

### ▣ MADÁCH SZÍNHÁZ
&#9992;&&#9866; ERZSÉBETVÁROS

Erzsébet körút 29 &#9743;478 2041 &#9632;www.madachszinhaz.hu

A local favorite, Madách Színház is one of the few theaters in the city that suits all tastes. From *Cats* to *Monty Python* to *Anna Karenina*, you can get your fill of culture in all its many shades.

&#9223; *Tram 4 or 6: Wesselényi utca. From the station, walk across the street.* &#9432; *Check online for listings and prices.* &#9412; *Prices vary; approximately 800-5200Ft.* &#9419; *Box office open daily 1pm-6:30pm.*

### MAGYAR SZÍNHÁZ
&#9992;&&#9866; ERZSÉBETVÁROS

Hevesi Sándor tér 4 &#9743;341 3849 &#9632;www.magyarszinhaz.hu

A small but legendary theater house, this funky building is host to a wide variety of performances from opera to "prosaic," from classical Hungarian to Russian drama. Opened in the late 19th century, this venue paved the way for Hungarian theater culture across the nation.

&#9223; *M1: Vörösmarty utca. From the station, walk east on Izabella utca; the theatre is where Izabella forks with Szövetség utca. [S] Prices vary according to season and shows. ⏰ Box office open daily 1-7pm, and 10am-7pm in the event of a matinee showing.*

## DANCE

**NEMZETÍ TÁNCSZÍNHÁZ (NATIONAL DANCE THEATRE)** 💳♿ BELVÁROS

Színház utca 1-3 ☎201 4407 💻www.dancetheatre.hu

The only 18th century theater building in Hungary that's still a theater has been home to many key events in Hungarian cultural history. The first Hungarian-language play was performed here in 1790, and many of classical music's luminaries, including Beethoven, played here. Today the theater is home to Budapest's dance performances, which encompasses ballet, modern dance, and folk.

*‡ Castle Hill, just north of the royal palace. Facing the castle, the theater is to the right, up the stairs. [S] Tickets 2500Ft. ⏰ Box office open M-Th 10am-6pm, F 10am-5pm.*

# shopping

## MUSIC

**FERENC LISZT MUSIC SHOP** ⊘♿ TERÉZVÁROS

Andrássy út 45 ☎322 4091

Named after Hungary's most famous composer, the store mostly carries classical music as well as musical necessities like sheet music and instructional how-to tapes.

*‡ M1: Oktogon. From the station, walk south towards the Opera. ⏰ Open M-F 10am-6pm, Sa 10am-1pm.*

**WAVE MUSIC** 💳♿ TERÉZVÁROS

Révay köz 1 ☎269 0754 💻www.wave.hu

A carefully selected collection of CDs, LPs, and DVDs to satisfy tastes that range from alternative punk to jazz.

*‡ M1: Bajcsy-Zsilinszky út. From the station, head north on Bajcsy-Zsilinszky and turn right on Révay köz. ℹ Check out the online library coming soon. ⏰ Open M-Sa 10am-8pm.*

**CONCERTO** 💳♿ ERZSÉBETVÁROS

Dob utca 33 ☎268 9631

Some new, some old, but always unique and thoughtfully organized in a multitude of categories satifying even the snootiest classicist.

*‡ M2: Astoria. Walk north on Károly körút from the Metro and turn right on Dob utca. ⏰ Open M-F noon-7pm, Su noon-4pm.*

**INDIEGO** ⊘♿ JÓZSEFVÁROS

Krúdy Gyula utca 7 ☎266 5541

An alternative music store hidden in a small side street. Expect to find colorful hair and lots of tattoos accompanying the variety of tunes.

*‡ Tram 4 or 6: Krúdy Gyula utca. ⏰ Open M-Th 11am-1am, F 11am-2pm, Sa 6pm-2am, Su 6pm-midnight.*

**RÓZSAVÖLGYI** ⊘♿ BELVÁROS

Szervita tér 5 ☎318 3500

One of the coolest places to buy Hungarian folk music and other locally made jams.

*‡ M1, M2, or M3: Deák Ferenc. From the station, head south on Bárczy István utca until you hit the square. ⏰ Open M-F 9:30am-7pm, Sa 10am-5pm.*

# BOOKS

### PENDRAGON
●‑& TERÉZVÁROS
Pozsonyi út 21-23
☎340 4426
A diverse selection of English novels and travel guides, neatly stacked by a helpful and friendly staff.
✂ *Tram 4 or 6: Jászai Mari tér. From the station, walk up Pozsonyi út.* ✆ *Open M-F 10am-6pm, Sa 10am-2pm.*

### KÓDEX
●‑& BELVÁROS
Honvéd utca 5
☎331 6350
A pleasant selection of English books and travel guides, including the very best travel guide out there (wink, wink).
✂ *M2: Kossuth Lajos tér. From the station, head east on Báthory utca, then left on Honvéd.* ✆ *Open M-W 9am-5pm, Th 9am-6pm, F 9am-4pm.*

### OXFORD UNIVERSITY PRESS BOOKSHOP
●‑& BELVÁROS
Gerlóczy utca 7
☎318 8633 ▣www.oupbooks.hu
You don't have to make good marks and pass your A-levels to enter! Just another ol' bookshop for those English-speaking types.
✂ *M2: Astoria. From the station, head north on Károly körút and turn left on Gerlóczy utca.* ✆ *Open M-F 10am-6pm.*

### ATLANTISZ BOOK ISLAND
●‑& BELVÁROS
Gerlóczy utca 4
☎266 3870
Part of a movement to heighten intellectual curiosity and exposure to foreign cultures with the written word, this book store aims to offer students knowledge in the social sciences at affordable prices.
✂ *M2: Astoria. From the station, head north on Károly körút and turn left on Gerlóczy utca.* ✆ *Open M-F 10am-6pm, Sa 10am-2pm.*

### WRITERS' BOOKSHOP
●‑& TERÉZVÁROS
Andrássy út 45
☎322 1645
Once a popular cafe for literary types, Writers' Bookshop now aims to spread Hungarian literature by selling English translations of famous Hungarian works.
✂ *M1: Oktogon. From the station, head south on Andrássy út.* ℹ *Often hosts lectures and book readings; check with the store for details.* ✆ *Open M-F 10am-6pm, Sa 10am-1pm.*

# CLOTHES

### JAJCICA
●‑& ERZSÉBETVÁROS
Dohány utca 94
☎321 2081 ▣www.jajcica.hu
Hip, alternative clothing and an awesome selection of retro shoes and leather boots.
✂ *M2: Blaha Lujza tér. From the Metro walk north on Erzsébet körút, turn right on Dohány utca, the store will be on your left.* ✆ *Open M-F 10am-7pm, Sa 10am-2pm.*

### G-STAR RAW
●‑& BELVÁROS
Andrássy út 2
☎484 6484 ▣www.g-star.com
Stylish denim that's quite pricey, but the store itself is worth a gander. Gives new meaning to the word Metro-polis.
✂ *M1: Bajcsy-Zsilinszky. From the station, walk across the street.* ✆ *Open daily 10am-6pm.*

### TISZA MÁRKABOLT
●‑& BELVÁROS
Károly körút 1
☎266 3055
Old communist-era clothing and shoes that were once considered repressive and stifling are now fashionable. Get yours today for probably 20 times the price they once were.
✂ *M2: Astoria. From the station, walk across the street.* ✆ *Open M-F 10am-7pm, Sa 9am-1pm.*

shopping • clothes

## ÁRKÁD PLÁZA
♦♿♥♨☼<sup>(p)</sup> DISTRICT X

Örs Vezér tér 25 ☎433 1414 ▣www.arkadbudapest.hu

According to locals, the best mall in town. Can fulfill all of your desires, and then some.

✈ *M2: Örs vezér tere M + H. Across the street from the Metro.* 🕐 *Open M-Sa 6:30am-10pm, Su 7:30am-9pm.*

## H AND M
♦♿ JÓZSEFVÁROS

Váci utca 12 ☎235 4040

A trusty old friend. Great for those who wish to feel as though they never left the comfort of cheap colors and dainty Rheinstone jewels. Basically the only affordable store in Váci utca.

✈ *M1: Vörösmarty tér. From the station, walk up Váci utca.* 🕐 *Open M-F 10am-8pm, Sa 10am-7pm, Su 11am-5pm.*

## RETROCK
♦♿ BELVÁROS

Henszlmann Imre utca 1 ☎0630 556 2814 ▣www.retrock.com

Local designers and one-of-a-kind clothing stock this boutique decorated with "tasty kitsch."

✈ *M3: Ferenciek tere. Head south from the Metro on Ferenciek tere until it crosses Henszlmann Imre.* 🕐 *Open M-F 10:30am-7:30pm Sat 10:30am-3:30pm.*

## ECSERI PIAC
♦♿♨ DISTRICT XIX

Nagykőrösi út 156 ☎282 9563

A heavy trek from the city center, but also a guaranteed adventure. A giant flea market where you'll find all your basic necessities: Soviet army watches, porcelain vases that probably belonged to St. Stephen, and a portable well.

✈ *Bus #54 or #55: Alvinc utca.* ⓘ *At least a half hour from the city center.* 🕐 *Open Tu-Sa 6am-1pm.*

## MAMMUT I AND II
♦♿♥♨☼<sup>(p)</sup> DISTRICT II

Lövőház utca 2 ☎345 8024 ▣www.mammut.hu

This Buda shopping mall is the biggest in the city. Upon entering, one feels as if he or she has entered a new world, fully equipped with foodstuffs and survival tools—why ever leave?

✈ *Tram 4 or 6: Széna tér. From the station, walk up the hill.* 🕐 *Open daily 10am-11pm.*

## HASZNÁLT RUHA ÁRUHÁZ
♿ JÓZSEFVÁROS

Üllői út 6

Can't miss this place if you're walking around the city. Characteristic blue sign with UK flag and giant writing. Though it's a chain, these places have tons of one man's trash just waiting to be your treasure.

✈ *M3: Kálvin tér. From the station, walk across the street.* ⓘ *Thrift store runs for the entire block.* 🕐 *Open M-F 10am-8pm, Sa 10am-7pm, Su 11am-5pm.*

# FOOD

## 🍴 LEHEL PIAC
♦♿♨ TERÉZVÁROS

Lehel tér

The best open-air market to buy fruit and veggies for pennies or less. All local growers and the lack of a middle man makes it an authentic price.

🕐 *Open M-F 6am-6pm, Sa 6am-2pm, Su 6am-1pm.*

# SPECIALTY

## 🍴 LEKVÁRIUM
♦♿ ERZSÉBETVÁROS

Dohány utca 39 ☎321 6543

This place sells homemade jam almost as good as your grandmother makes. Try the strawberry jam—the older, the tastier.

✈ *M2: Blaha Lujza tér.* 🕐 *Open M-F 10am-6pm.*

## FÜGGŐÁGYBOLT

⊛& DISTRICT XI

Fehérvári út 29 ☎3630 992 8600

An earthy store that sells every color and patterned hammock you could imagine. Get your swing on.

🚊 *Tram 4: Fehérvári út. The shop is down the street from the stop.* 🕗 *Open M-F 10:30am-6:30pm, Sa 10:30am-2pm.*

## RODODENDRON

⊛& BELVÁROS

Madách Imre út 3 ☎3670 419 5329 📧www.rododendron.hu

A random gem you'd be hard-pressed to match, Rododendron is a small store that sells illustrations of famous Hungarian artist Irisz Agócs in game, Christmas card, and book form, at an affordable price.

🚇 *M1, M2, or M3: Deák Ferenc tér. From the station, head north on Király utca, right on Rumbac Sebestyén and right again on Madách Imre.* 🕗 *Open M-F 11am-7pm, Sa-Su 11am-3pm.*

## LE PARFUM

⊛& BELVÁROS

Cukor utca 1 ☎3630 470 0248

The owner of this tiny perfume shop can judge how you should smell after a 15-minute conversation. Stop by for a "consultation" and pick up your one-of-a-kind perfume a few days later.

🚇 *M3: Ferenciek tere. From the station, head south on Ferenciek tere and turn right at the second street to reach Cukor utca.* 🕗 *Open M-F 10am-7pm, Sa-Su 10am-5pm.*

## LOKOMOS CSEMEGE

🌐&♈ BELVÁROS

Váci utca 48 ☎267 8544

Come here for all your fancy Hungarian booze needs. Stock up on fruit *pálinkas* and globes and globes of Unicum.

🚇 *M3: Ferenciek tere. From the station, follow the throngs of tourists to Váci utca.* 🕗 *Open M-F 7am-8:30pm, Sa-Su 7am-7pm.*

# essentials

🔁

essentials · practicalities

## i am number one

The phone code for Budapest is ☎1.

## PRACTICALITIES

- **TOURIST OFFICES: TourInform** arranges tours and accommodations. *(V, Sütő u. 2.* ☎429 97 51. 📧*incoming@vista.hu)* Ⓢ **Budapest Card** (Budapest Kártya) provides discounts, unlimited public transportation, and admission to most museums *(2-day card 6300Ft, 3-day 7500Ft.* 🕗 *Open M-F 9am-6:30pm, Sa 9am-2:30pm.)*

- **DOMESTIC OPERATOR:** *(☎190)*

- **INFORMATION:** *(☎199)*

- **GLBT RESOURCES: GayGuide.net Budapest** posts an online guide and runs a hotline with info and a reservation service for GLBT-friendly lodgings. *(☎06 30 932 33 34.* 📧*www.budapest.gayguide.net.* 🕗 *Hotline open daily 4-8pm.)* **Na Végre!** publishes an up-to-date guide to gay nightlife, available at any gay bar. *(📧www. navegre.hu.)*

- **POST OFFICE:** *(V, Városház utca 18 ☎318 4811. i Poste Restante, Postán Mar, is in office around the right side of the building. Ⓐ Open M-F 8am-8pm, Sa 8am-2-pm.)* Alternative branches at Nyugati station, VI, Teréz körút; 105/107 Keleti Station, VIII, Baross tér 11/c; and elsewhere. Open M-F 7am-8pm, Sa 8am-2pm.

- **POSTAL CODE:** *(Depends on the district—postal codes are 1XX2, where XX is the district number.)*

## EMERGENCY!

- **TOURIST POLICE:** *(V, Sütő utca 2, inside the Tourinform office. ☎438 80 80. ✈ M1, M2, or M3: Deák tér. i Beware of imposters demanding to see your passport. Ⓐ Open 24hr.)*

- **PHARMACIES:** *(II, Frankel Leó út 22 ☎314 36 95. i Generally, look for green signs labeled Apotheke, Gyógyszertár, or Pharmacie. Ⓐ Open M-F 7:30am-9pm, Sa 7:30am-2pm. Minimal after-hours service fees apply.)*

- **MEDICAL SERVICES: Falck (SOS) KFT** *(II, Kapy út 49/b. ☎224 90 90. i The US embassy maintains a list of English-speaking doctors.)*

## GETTING THERE

### By Plane
**Ferihegy Airport** *(BUD; ☎235 38 88).* From the airport to the center, take bus #93 *(Ⓢ 270Ft. Ⓐ 20min., every 15min. 4:55am-11:20pm)*, then #3 to Kőbánya-Kispest (15min. to Deák tér, in downtown Budapest). **Airport Minibus** *(☎296 85 55)* goes to hostels *(Ⓢ 2990Ft).*

### By Train
The major stations, **Keleti Pályaudvar, Nyugati Pályaudvar,** and **Déli Pályaudvar,** are also Metro stops *(☎3640 49 49 49).* Most international trains arrive at **Keleti Station,** but some from Prague go to **Nyugati Station.** For schedules, check ◆www.mav.hu, part of which is in English. Prices change often and sometimes depend on time of day and time of year. To: **Berlin** *(Ⓢ 15,800Ft. Ⓐ 12-13hr., 4 per day);* **Bucharest, ROM** *(Ⓢ 23,600Ft. Ⓐ 14hr., 5 per day);* **Prague** *(Ⓢ 16,300Ft. Ⓐ 7-8hr., 5 per day);* **Vienna, AUT** *(Ⓢ 3600Ft. Ⓐ 3hr., 17 per day);* **Warsaw, POL** *(Ⓢ18,500Ft. Ⓐ 11hr., 2 per day).* The daily **Orient Express** stops on its way from Paris, FRA to Istanbul, TUR. Trains run to most major destinations in Hungary. Purchase tickets at an **International Ticket Office** *(Ⓐ Keleti Station open daily 8am-7pm; Nyugati Station open M-Sa 5am-9pm; info desk 24hr.).* Or try **MÁV Hungarian Railways,** VI, Andrássy út 35. *(☎461 55 00. Branches at all stations. Open Apr-Sept M-F 9am-6pm, Oct-Mar M-F 9am-5pm.)* The **HÉV Commuter Railway Station** is at Batthyány tér, opposite Parliament. Trains head to Szentendre *(Ⓢ 460Ft. Ⓐ 45min., every 15min. 5am-9pm).* Purchase tickets at the station for transport beyond the city limits.

### By Bus
Buses to international and some domestic destinations leave from the **Népliget Station,** X, Üllői út 131. *(✈ M3: Népliget. ☎329 14 50. Ⓐ Cashier open 6am-8pm.)* Check ◆www.volanbusz.hu for schedules.

## GETTING AROUND ▣

### By Train
The **HÉV Commuter Rail Station** is across the river from Parliament, one Metro stop past the Danube in Buda at Batthyány tér. On the list of stops, those within the city limits are displayed in a different color. For these stops, a regular Metro ticket will suffice. Purchase tickets at the counter to travel beyond the city limits. Békásmegye is the final stop within the city limits.

budapest

## hot ticket

Student discounts are NOT available for trains; you will get fined if you purchase a student ticket with your ISIC card, so beware of scams. There is typically a discount for travelers under 26 on afternoon and weekend trains. Ask at the register.

### By Budapest Public Transit

The **subways** and **trams** run every few minutes. **Buses** are generally on time and some run 24hr.; schedules are posted at stops. **Budapest Public Transport** *(BKV;* ☎*3680 40 66 86* ▪*www.bkv.hu)* has information in Hungarian and an English website. Single-fare tickets for public transport *(one-way on 1 line* Ⓢ *320Ft)* are sold in Metro stations, Trafik shops, and by sidewalk vendors at tram stops. Punch them in the orange boxes at the gate of the Metro or on buses and trams; punch a new ticket when you change lines, or face a fine of 6000Ft from the undercover ticket inspectors. *(*Ⓢ *Day pass 1550Ft, 3-day 3850Ft, 1-week 4600Ft, 2-week 6200Ft, 1 month 9400Ft.)*

The Metro has three lines: **M1 (yellow), M2 (red),** and **M3 (blue).** M1 runs west to east from downtown Pest past City Park along Andrássy út. M2 runs west to east and connects **Deli Train Station** in Buda with **Keleti Train Station** in Pest along Rákóczi út. M3 runs north to south through Pest and provides a transfer bus to the airport from the southern terminus (Kőbánya-Kispest). A fourth Metro line is currently under construction that will connect southern Buda to northeastern Pest, though it is not expected to open until 2012. The Metro runs 4:30am-11:30pm.

Most buses and trams stop running at 11pm. After you've missed the last tram, transportation is available in the form of **night (É) buses** which run midnight-5am along major routes: #7É and 78É follow the 2 route; #6É follows the 4/6 tram line; #14É and 50É follow the 3 route.

# budapest 101

## HISTORY

### Make Way for Magyars

Modern-day Budapest was founded as Aquincum, a Roman engineering marvel, which used the Danube to power waterworks for amphitheaters, steam baths, and a sewer system. Aquincum was also known as the "people's highway" for its advantageous position on Baltic and Black Sea trade routes. This title likely inspired pride until the Huns decided to make a permanent pit stop in the fifth century; Attila and friends evicted the Romans, but were soon ousted themselves by a parade of central Asian nomadic powers including the Ostrogoths, the Lombards, the Gepids and the Avars. This last group managed to control the region for 250 years, from about 560 to 700CE, until the Slavs rolled in and dominated through the sixth and seventh centuries.

The nomadic **Magyar** tribe conquered Hungary in 896, under a warlord named Arpad. A decentralized clan system prevailed until the end of the 10th century, when Arpad's less exotically named descendent, **Stephen,** decided to go Western. Stephen subjugated the tribal aristocracy and instituted Christianity, proclaiming himself the first King of Hungary. For more than 200 years his descendants ruled over a relatively prosperous Hungary, and slowly developed Buda and Pest. In 1541 the city met its new family when the Ottomans moved in, leading to the construction of some fine Turkish baths and the enmity of the **Habsburg** empire, which had conquered Western

*budapest 101 . history*

## C. 1100
King Coloman declares that witches don't exist, but fails to convince the rest of Europe.

## 1200S
The royal seat moves from Székesfehérvár to Buda, presumably due to lack of international ability to pronounce Székesfehérvár.

## 1241-42
The Mongolian Invasion. Like the British Invasion but with less teenage fans.

## 1472
András Hess sets up one of Europe's first printing presses in Buda.

## 1500S
Paprika, Hungarians' soul spice, first introduced

**budapest**

# facts and figures

- **POPULATION:** 1,696,000 (city); 2,475,740 (metropolitan area).
- **NUMBER OF DISTRICTS:** 23.
- **TIME ZONE:** UTC/GMT +1.
- **COUNTRY DIALING CODE:** +36.
- **ELEVATION:** 185m/607ft.
- **NUMBER OF CITIES:** 2. Separated by the Danube, Buda and Pest still have autonomy though their compound name came into use more than a century ago. Just like Minneapolisstpaul.
- **NUMBER OF THEATRES:** 86.
- **NUMBER OF GEOTHERMAL HOT SPRINGS:** 80.
- **NUMBER OF BRIDGES ACROSS THE DANUBE:** 9.
- **SEATS IN THE DOHÁNY STREET SYNAGOGUE:** 3000.
- **AGE OF THE MILLENNIUM UNDERGROUND:** 114 years old in 2010.
- **"TIME WHEEL" TURNOVER TIME:** Exactly one year. The sand in this 8m-tall hourglass takes a full year to sift down. How they flip it over is another story.

Hungary but had failed repeatedly in their efforts to claim the capital. In 1686 the Hapsburgs finally got their way, destroying most of Buda in the process and, after some tricky treaties, kicking the Ottomans out of Hungary entirely in 1718. Not everyone was a happy Hapsburg, though, and repeated uprisings of the native Magyars and disgruntled bourgeoisie occurred over the next 150 years, culminating in the 1848 revolution. Put down within a year, it was a little anti-climactic.

### Austria-Hungary: A Monarchy Makeover
In 1867, the **"Year of Reconciliation,"** Austria and Hungary teamed up and Buda/Pest was chosen as the capital of this dual monarchy. In 1873 Buda combined with Pest and Óbuda (old Buda) to officially rebrand as Budapest. Until 1914 Budapest expanded like a loaf of **kálacs** (Let's Go recommends this delish Hungarian sweet bread, by the way), becoming the political and cultural heart of central Europe. The good times stopped rolling with WWI, when Austria-Hungary collapsed; by 1918, Hungary was flying solo as an independent republic. Things only got worse during WWII—38,000 civilians were killed during the 1944-45 **Battle of Budapest**, and 20-40% of the Budapest area's 250,000 Jews were murdered.

## Back in the USSR

In 1949 Budapest became a communist **"People's Republic,"** with "people" meaning Stalin. Monuments of the former regime (such as the old Buda castle) were destroyed and Hungarian-national identity was down-played. In 1956, peaceful protests in Budapest heated up into the **Hungarian Revolution,** which was thoroughly crushed, leaving 3000 dead. Soviet tanks invaded the capital, enduring as emblems of Soviet repression and resentment. From the '60s to the '80s much of Budapest's war-damaged infrastructure was repaired, and the city was dubbed the "happiest barrack" of the Eastern bloc countries. Few denied that its citizens looked even happier when the **Iron Curtain** fell in 1989-90. Since 1990, Budapest has served as the capital of the Hungarian Republic. Although the country joined the European Union in 2004, the capital hails Hungary's unique cultural heritage with monuments, festivals, museums and, of course, that delightfully indecipherable language.

## The City Today

Hungary's capital is undoubtedly the heart of this newly enfranchised republic (so long, Soviets!) and the nexus of national pride. The lauded **Blue Danube** makes a glamorous centerpiece to this 525 sq. km, two-part Metropolis, with Pest's more modern buildings stretching along the river's flat Eastern bank, and the Buda's old-world charm crowning the Western bank's hills. Various bridges connect the two cities, while three islands, **Óbuda, Margaret** and **Csepel,** sit in the river. Years of Soviet industrialization have blackened the façades of many of Budapest's older buildings, but a massive cleaning effort is underway to restore them.

Hungary's massive parliament building is in unmissable, though some believe the bloated edifice symbolizes inefficient and overblown bureaucracy. The local government is two-tiered, with a central city council as well as leaders for each of the city's districts, a system which some say makes for chaos and interior squabbling. Whatever the criticisms, the city was ranked 'most liveable' of Central and Eastern European cities on the EU's quality of life index in both 2009 and 2010. Although the spas and comfort food may have had more to do with that rating than the government...

# FOOD AND DRINK

## Food

Hungarians don't take food lightly. Accordingly, traditional Hungarian fare is as heavy as it comes, usually starring meat, potatoes and **paprika** (the Hungarian kind, which is HOT). No city does savory stews and meaty pancakes better than Budapest, but for those adverse to eating things that once had hooves, there are definitely options. Fortunate constants among most Budapest eateries are generous portions and reasonable prices, no matter what the cuisine. Some local specialties:

- **FŐZELÉK.** A hearty vegetable stew. Vegetarians, rejoice! It

**1800S**
Mass production of sweet paprika begins.

**1866**
Strauss composes the Blue Danube Waltz, the soundtrack to all boat tours ever after.

**1873** Budapest is born.

**1874**
Hungarian-American magician Harry Houdini is born in Budapest.

**1937** Hungarian scientist Albert Szent-Győrpi receives the Nobel Prize for discovering vitamin C in researching (guess what) paprika.

**JULY-DEC. 1944**
Raoul Wallenberg saves thousands of Hungarian Jews by issuing fake Swedish passports and creating safehouses throughout.

can be flavored with bacon or sausage, though; so ask first, then rejoice.

- **HORTOBÁGY PANCAKES.** (*Hortobágyi Palacsinta*) An ooey-gooey amalgam of fried pancakes, veal chunks, sour cream and paprika.
- **GOULASH.** The ubiquitous meat, potatoes and paprika stew. Hard to mess up, but beware if you're sensitive to heat.
- **KOLBÁSZ.** Hungarian sausage.
- **FATÁNYÉROS.** A barbeque dish of mixed meat, including mutton, beef, veal, and/ or pork.
- **HALÁSZLÉ.** This "fisherman's soup" is a spicy showcase of river fish, heated up with (yep) a good dose of paprika.

## Drinks

Hungary has become an active **wine** producer in recent years (especially since the fall of the Soviet Union), a point of pride among modern Budapestians—so much so that a national wine festival is celebrated in the city each September. To impress the locals or expand your palate, try ordering a *Budai Zöld, Furmint, Juhfark, Hárslevelu, Kadarka, Kéknyelu,* or *Királyleányka* (and if you successfully get one, make sure to toast your pronunciation skills). Budapest also boasts numerous *czardas* (old-fashioned taverns), *pinces* (beer/wine cellars) and *sorozos* (pubs) that serve as good a selection of local and international beers as anywhere on the continent. Just be careful to order what you want by name—order just *sor* (beer), and restaurants will often automatically bring you their expensive imported beer, instead of a cheaper Hungarian brand.

# SPORTS AND RECREATION

## Football

Soccer is Hungary's most popular spectator sport, despite an international team that has failed to dominate the European circuit since the 1950s. But Budapestians are no fair-weather fans: thousands flock to the 68,000-seat **Puskás Ferenc Stadion** to watch MTK Hungária, Budapest Honvéd or Újpest.

## Margaret Island

The entirety of this sprawling island is a public recreation institution in itself. Aside from the public pools and park, the island has miles of jogging trails along the river, public tennis courts, playgrounds, a football field, and even a track and field complex.

## Water Sports/The Baths

With the Danube running through its heart and natural hot springs fueling a lucrative spa business, it's only natural that water sports have made a big splash (sorry, sorry) in Budapest. Swimming, water polo, and canoeing are perennially popular. Public swimming and bathing venues are particularly tourist-friendly, with their dual roles as fitness centers and hangout spots. Popular watering holes include the **Alfréd Hajós Swimming Complex** (Nemzeti Sportuszoda), on Margaret Island, and the **Palatinus Strand**, a huge complex also on Margaret Island (both open May 1-Sept 15 daily 8am-7pm; 1800Ft. for the day, 1600Ft. for students). Prominent bathhouses include the **Széchenyi Baths** and the Gellért Baths, open year-round.

# MEDIA

Hungarian media has a life all its own, but for a foreigner not versed in the same language system that brought us cult classics like **Finnish** and **Basque**, it can look and sound like a jumble of k's and z's. Luckily, there are plenty of media options for the English-speaking traveler to stay in touch.

## Internet

If your laptop is like your child but your hotel doesn't provide Wi-Fi, there are a number of efficient Internet cafes catering to you. **Café Szóda**, VII. Wesselényi u. 18, will let you browse for as long as you want for just a cup of coffee, and has plenty of outlets. **Farger**, V. Zoltán u. 18, is another popular place. For the artsy and eco-friendly, try **Treehugger Dan's Bookstore Café**, VI. Csengery u. 48 for fair trade coffee, or **Kávészünet**, V. Tátra u. 12/b, which hosts local artist shows. If your laptop didn't fit in your backpack, try **Ami Internet Coffee**, V. Váci u. 40, or **Yellow Zebra Bikes**, Sütő u. 2. V. District, both of which have a number of terminals.

## Publications

*The International Herald Tribune, USA Today, Guardian, The Economist, Financial Times, Times of London, European, Newsweek, The Wall Street Journal Europe*, and *Time* are all often available in high-end hotels, newsstands and bookstores in central Pest. Less common are *People, Vogue, Harper's*, and a rare but possible find is *The New York Times*. **Sajtó Térkép** has a particularly good English periodicals selection, with locations at V. Kálvin tér 3 and V. Városház u. 3-5. For a Hungarian take that's still comprehensible, check out the weekly *Budapest Sun* or the *Budapest Times*, both available in English.

# ART AND ARCHITECTURE

Budapest's architecture is nothing if not varied, showcasing the city's many-layered past. The Buda **Castle District** is a medieval town, with winding cobblestone streets and tipsy two-storied shops. Don't miss the Royal Palace, which crowns the hill (Let's Go recommends the funicular ride to get up there—it's got fun in the name, for goodness' sake), **Matthias Church's** immense gothic spire and patterned roof, and **Fisherman's Bastion**, a lookout platform with spectacular views of the Danube, and a turret for each of the seven Hungarian tribes. The much flatter and more modern Pest side is characterized by its uniform, Eastern-bloc urban planning (thanks, Soviets), but has its highlights as well. The boulevard **Andrássy út** runs through the city's heart, showcasing Budapest's best architecture while connecting it with the city park (Városliget) via **Hero's Square**—a rearing testament to Budapesters' fierce national pride. Also notable are Budapest's most sizeable structures. These include the world's third largest Neo-Gothic Parliament building (best seen from the Danube or Buda); the **Dohány Street Synagogue**, the world's second largest synagogue; the Esztergom Basilica, Europe's third largest church, and the Széchenyi Medicinal Bath, Europe's largest such spa. The entire country is slightly smaller than Indiana. Compensating for anything, Hungary?

Budapest takes an active interest in fostering the arts, from the city's Cultural Way (Budapest's rebuttal to New York City's Museum Mile, mostly along Andrássy út) to its numerous music and dance festivals. The Museum of Fine Arts and the Palace of Art, both located in Hero's Square, are definitely worth a look, as is the National Gallery in the Buda Palace. Another highlight is the **Budapest Opera**, which has played host to the likes of Gustav Mahler and stages over 50 performances a year.

# HOLIDAYS AND FESTIVALS

There's nothing Budapestians take more seriously than celebrating, especially when their city is the star of the party. Consequently, Budapest's calendar is filled with festivals featuring everything from wine tasting to gladiator fights.

- **INTERNATIONAL BOOK FESTIVAL (APRIL 23-26).** The name says it all.

- **FLORALIA FESTIVAL (MAY 22-23).** Party like it's 50CE! Held at the Aquincum **Museum in Óbuda** (Old Buda, district 3), this event revives an ancient Roman tradition, including theatre, flower exhibitions and even gladiator fights (the family-friendly kind).

- **NATIONAL GALLOP (JUNE 5-6).** Heroes' Square, Andrássy Ut. If you don't mind being inundated with Hungarian national pride, this exhibition of traditional equestrian skills is worth the trek.

- **SUMMER ON THE CHAIN BRIDGE (JUNE 27-JULY 19).** This Budapest institution takes over the famous Chain Bridge with various performances and programs against the cerulean backdrop of the Danube.

- **SZIGET ROCK MUSIC FESTIVAL (AUGUST 11-16).** College students and motorcycle dudes descend on the city for this four-day rock-out, which has attracted crowds of over 300,000.

- **FESTIVAL OF FOLK ARTS (AUGUST 20-22).** Explore Buda's castle district to hear traditional Hungarian folklore and see handicraft demonstrations. The festival kicks off with celebrations for St. Stephen's Day on August 20 that include an artisans' parade and the "blessing of the bread" in front of St. Matthias' church.

- **JEWISH SUMMER FESTIVAL (AUGUST 30-SEPTEMBER 6).** Part celebration and part education, this festival is a full introduction to Hungarian Jewish culture, centered around (where else?) the Dohány Street Synagogue.

- **WINE FESTIVAL (FIRST WEEK IN SEPTEMBER).** Beginning with the harvest parade, this week-long toast to Hungarian vinters includes traditional costumes, dance, handicrafts, and of course lots of refreshments. Every year's a good year.

**budapest**

# EXCURSIONS

If you've been huffing and puffing your way through Berlin, Prague, or Budapest, been almost hit by a speeding Mercedes multiple times, and gotten lost in seemingly endless museum hallways, while muttering Lenny Kravitz's "Fly Away," it's time to escape. Kick back in royal paradises. Canoe and hike through forests that will have you tra-la-la-ing to *Sleeping Beauty* tunes. Experience more of the history of World War II. Travel through a picturesque town so small that there is absolutely no way to get lost. It's time to relax! Hop on that train or bus and travel back to a slower time.

## greatest hits

- **HIGH ON A MOUNTAIN TOP.** Hike up to the Karlštejn Castle (p. 222), the fortress built by Charles IV in 1348 to guard the crown jewels.

- **CHILLED TO THE BONE.** Check out the Bone Church Ossuary (p. 226) on your daytrip to Kunta Hora.

- **BREATHE EASY.** Trek across the 3km preservation of traditional country towns at the Hungarian Open Air Museum (p. 228).

- **WALKING ON BROKEN GLASS.** Peer through the (unbroken!) glass floor at the Basilica excavation (p. 230) to see the ruins of the castle where St. Stephen was born.

- **BUILD CASTLES IN THE SKY.** Dreams really do come true in Potsdam (p. 218), where Friedrich II's schloßes, gardens, and tea houses will provide the perfect backdrop for your fairy tale romance.

Is your head throbbing from from a techno overdose? Can't bear to eat any more street food? Escape the city hustle on a daytrip to the 'burbs of these major metropolises. Beriln, Prague, and Budapest are the hubs of history-rich country that's only a short bus ride away. Take advantage of the student discount at Kutná Hora's Czech Museum of Silver and climb 35m into the earth. Not trying to shell out any money? Put your wallet away and climb to the top of Church Hill in Szentendre to capture striking panoramas of the Danube below. Spreewald—a forest just outside of Berlin—also offers some amazing trails if you still haven't worn out your walking boots.

# germany

## SPREEWALD AND LÜBBENAU ☎03542

About 100km southeast of Berlin, the Spree River splits into an intricate maze of small streams and canals, weaving between meadows, forests, and farmland that were once home to the **Sorbs,** Germany's native Slavic minority. In broad terms, the 1000 sq. km of this area is termed the **Spreewald** (*Spree Forest*), and, of the many small villages scattered around the area, the most famous is **Lübbenau.**

Spreewald is a popular daytrip destination for Berliners seeking their pastoral-idyllic fix in its hiking trails, gondola rides, and kayaks. Tourists drift down scenic canals lined with thatched roofs and birch trees, catching glimpses of the wildlife. For quaint German towns, Lübbenau simply can't be beat. Even as it's increasingly corrupted by the knick-knack shops that sell decorated eggs and jars of pickles, there is still something refreshingly authentic about the ambience. Many of the buildings from the original Sorb settlement have either been preserved or recreated, and the virtue of simplicity and wholesome living are echoed in the rough-hewn wood siding and bare floors of the homes. And however tourist-oriented the city centers may be, there's no denying the incredible beauty of the Spreewald landscape. Vast meadows of tall grasses and pockets of densely packed birches make for an endlessly refreshing view as you tramp across hiking trails or paddle through streams in your canoe.

A small second town, officially considered part of Lübbenau, is 3km away from city center. **Lehde** is truthfully less of a town, and more of a sight; it's here that you'll find a higher concentration of preserved homes clustered together in a densely forested area.

### Accommodations 🛏

The only things outnumbering gondolas in Lübbenau are the **hotel pensions** literally shoulder-to-shoulder along cobblestone streets, and sometimes on top of each other. Just five minutes of walking through the streets of Lübbenau will bring you in contact with seven or so pensions, each almost identical in price, appearance, and location. Expect to pay €45-55 for a double room, or, at the slightly lower end of the spectrum, about €20 per person. Your best bet is to check out the comprehensive catalog of pension listings available in the tourist office; in the busy summer months, it's likely that your decision will be determined by availability. Though there's little diversity in accommodation options, we've listed the least expensive hostels in Lübbenau, as places you might want to contact first when inquiring about a room. Or go **camping;** there may be no better place than Spreewald to dust off your tents and break out the mosquito repellent.

### CAMPINGPLATZ AM SCHLOSSPARK

CAMPGROUND ❶

Schlßbezirk 20 ☎03542 35 33 🖳www.spreewaldcamping.de

125 tent plots with cooking and bathing facilities on site, as well as a convenience store, make this beautiful campground a little more comfortable to boot.

*From the tourist information office, follow Ehm-Welk-Str. to the left, as it turns into Schloßbezirk. $ €6 per person; 2- to 4-person bungalows €20-50. ⏰ Reception 7:30am-12:30pm and 2-10pm.*

### PENSION SCHERZ

PENSION ❷

Bergstr. 9A ☎03542 465 78 🖳www.pensionscherz.de

Coral walls and mismatched lawn furniture give this pension the feel of a laid-back family lake house. This pension might be worth checking first because of its low prices and wonderfully kind staff.

*From the tourist information office, walk down Ehm-Welk-Str. until it turns into Karl-Marx-Str. Turn right onto Bergerstr. The pension is at the end of the street. ℹ Breakfast included. $ Singles €38; doubles €45. Per-person rates €19-24 per night.*

### PENSION AM ALTEN BAUERNHAFEN

PENSION ❸

Stottof 5 ☎03542 29 30 🖳www.am-alten-bauernhafcn.de

Pine paneled walls and red-checked curtains make this pension an unusually well-decorated riverside retreat. The outdoor patio backs right up to a canal, and guests lounge in the shade. Prices vary, so check ahead.

*From the tourist information office, follow Ehm-Welk-Str. as it turns into Karl-Marx-Str., and then turn left onto Stottof. The pension will be on your left. $ Doubles from €44; triples from €55; 4-person rooms €50-80.*

## Sights

Luckily for travelers, Lübbenau's biggest sight is always free and open. **Spreewald Forest's** winding paths and quaint canals are yours for the taking, so explore the woods at will. If you're looking to relax and enjoy a view of Spreewald in true Sorb fashion, and don't mind the company of many a senior citizen, gondola rides are the way to go. Tours of the forest (in German) depart from the **Großer Hafen** (larger port) and the **Kleiner Hafen** (smaller port). The Großer Hafen, along Dammstr. behind the church, offers a wider variety of tours, including 2-3hr. trips to Lehde. The boats take on customers starting 9-10am and depart when full (about 20 passengers) throughout the day. **Genossenschaft der Kahnfährleute** *(Dammstr. 77a. ☎03542 22 254 🖳www.grosser-hafen.de $ €8.50, children €4.25; 3hr. €10/5; 5hr. tour of the forest €13/6.50. ⏰ Open Mar-Oct daily 9:30am-6pm)* is the largest gondola company in Lübbenau. They offer 2hr. round trips to Lehde. From the Kleiner Hafen, less-touristed but nearly identical wilderness trips are run by the **Kahnfährmannsverein der Spreewaldfreunde** *(Spreestr. 10a. ☎03542 40 37 10 $ €8-20, children €4-10. ⏰ Open Apr-Oct daily 9am-6pm.)*

There's no better view of Lübbenau than from the river, and perhaps no better way than on a kayak or canoe. Where gondola rides are restrictive for those looking to explore on their own, paddling your own boat lets you wander through streams and canals as you please. Kayaks, canoes, and paddleboats can be rented from the **Campingplatz Am Schloßpark** (above) for €5 per hr. *(single person)*, or €15 per day. **Kajak-Sports.** *(Dammstr. 76a. ☎03542 37 64 🖳www.bootsverleih-richter.de $ Single paddleboats for €5 per hr., €14 per day. Doubles for €6 per hr., €15 per day. Kayaks for €9 per hr., €12 for 2 hr., €18 per day. ⏰ Open daily from 9am.)*

### FREILANDMUSEUM LEHDE (OPEN-AIR MUSEUM LEHDE)

MUSEUM

Located in Lehde, behind the aquarium. ☎03542 24 72 🖳www.freiland-museum-lehde

**Lehde** itself is a sight to see. Just 3km away from Lübbenau along a tree-shaded path, this UNESCO-protected landmark is accessible by foot, boat, or bike. The Freilandmuseum is a small community of recreated houses and workshops with exhibits that illustrate the 19th century lifestyle of the Sorbs, when whole families slept in one room, and newlyweds would go out back for a literal "romp in the hay." Though the unfortunately creepy mannequins performing typical Sorbian tasks are more off-putting than enlightening, the overall effect of this small cluster of buildings is pleasant; the buildings are authentically constructed, and the handicraft is observable in the rough timbers lining the walls and the uneven clay-brick floors. Artisans have set up workshops in some the buildings, making pots and decorative eggs in the Sorbian tradition.

*Follow the signs from Altstadt or Groß Harbor to Lehde.* [$] *€5, students €4, children under 16 €1.* [⏰] *Open daily Apr-Sept 10am-6pm, last entry 5:30pm; Oct 10am-5pm.*

**SPREEWALDMUSEUM** MUSEUM

Topfmarkt 12 ☎03542 24 72 www.spreewald-web.de

While community history museums often fall flat, Spreewaldmuseum rotates fascinating exhibits on clothing, yarn-spinning, art, and toys from the beautiful Spreewald region. The thatched roofs of Lehde are captured in oil on hanging canvases, and intricately woven dresses, antique looms, and, of course, original steins with Sorbian history are on display on the upper levels. Aside from the requisite uninteresting pottery shards, this museum does an excellent job of capturing the history of a fascinating culture whose influence still permeates Lübbenau. Visit here before the Freilandmuseum, to gain a little more knowledge and perspective on the Sorbs as you walk through the reconstructed houses in Lehde.

*From the tourist information office, follow Ehm-Welk-Str. to just before it turns into Karl-Marx-Str.* [$] *€4, students €3, children under 16 €1.* [⏰] *Open Apr-mid-Oct Tu-Su 10am-6pm.*

## Food

Although virtually every restaurant in Lübbenau caters to tourists, with moderately overpriced menus and hordes of 60-year-olds crowding outdoor patios, there's still pleanty of cheap food available. Check out the *Imbiße* (snack bars) and stands that line the **Großer Hafen,** and other main town squares. The local specialties are pickles and fresh fish, so if you're itching to eat like the Sorbs, go for one of those. The irrepressible bratwurst is a good fallback for a filling meal, and the sausage-and-beer combo feels fitting in this quintessentially German town.

## Essentials

### Practicalities

- **TOURIST OFFICE:** *(Ehm-Welk-Str. 32. ☎03542 4 66 47* [⏰] *Open M-F 10am-5pm.)*

### Getting There

Lübbenau is a 2hr. bus and train ride away from Berlin, through beautiful farmland and pine forests. Don't let the distance scare you; the trip is pleasant. Take the **Regional Express, line 2** toward **Königs Wusterhausen.** Trains run every 2hr. from Zoologischer Garten, Berlin Hauptbahnhof, and Berlin Ostbahnhof *(tickets €13).* At Königs Wusterhausen you'll need to transfer to a bus; exit the train station, turn right, and then take the first right about 30m from the train station, and walk under the bridge. **Bus B,** the second leg of the the trip, departs from there (dir. Lübbenau). Lübbenau is about 1hr. from the station, the last stop on the bus line.

### Getting Around

There's not much to be said for internal transportation in little Lübbenau. Buses run M-F early morning-3pm *(single ride €1.30),* but luckily, you won't need them. The whole area is easily covered on foot, or, if you prefer, on bike. Bike rentals are all over the city; expect to pay €8-10 for a day rental. For rentals, try **Kowalsky's,** near the train station *(Poststr. 6. ☎03542 28 35* [$] *€8 per day.* [⏰] *Open M-F 9am-12:30pm and 2-6pm, Sa 9am-noon, Su call in advance),* or **Michael Metzdorf,** across from the tourist office.

# POTSDAM ☎0331

Imagine Disneyland. Now swap out the the rollercoaster rides for exquisite old palaces, the long lines for winding gravel pathways, and the acres of concrete parking lots for fields of tall grass, towering trees, and serene lakes. That's Potsdam. Just an S-Bahn ride away from a decidedly un-royal Berlin, Potsdam is the glittering city of

Friedrich II, and one of our candidates for the most beautiful towns on earth. If you have the time, low cost and accessibility make Potsdam an absolute must-see for anyone visiting Berlin. The extraordinary sights are concentrated in the Park Sanssouci, which overflows with yellow ochre palaces and perfectly manicured gardens. You can barely walk 10m without hitting your head on a hanging crystal chandelier. The smaller Neuer Park to the north is also home to beautiful palaces and monuments, and has the added advantage of a lakeside setting.

## Accommodations

Budget options are extremely limited in Potsdam. Luckily, it's easy to commute from your hostel in Berlin, meaning you most likely won't need to find accommodations.

### JUGENDHERBERGE POTSDAM (HI) — HOSTEL ❶

Schulstr. 9 ☎0331 581 31 00 🖥www.jh-potsdam.de

The closest hostel is one S-Bahn stop before Potsdam. Far less sterile than many HI hostels, Jugendherberge is warmed up with pine bunks and light yellow walls, even if it still mostly lacks decoration and character. Rooms are a little crowded, but clean and neat, with personal lockers and ensuite baths.

*🚆 S7: Babelsberg. ℹ Breakfast and linens included. Wi-Fi €2 per hr. $ Dorms from €15, over 27 €18; singles €31.50/34; doubles €26.5/29.50. ⏰ Reception 24hr.*

### CAMPINGPLATZ SANSSOUCI-GAISBERG — CAMPGROUND ❶

An der Pirschhiede 41 ☎0331 951 09 88 🖥www.campingpark-sanssouci-potsdam.de

Located on the banks of the beautiful Templiner See, this campsite is far removed from the sights in Potsdam. The *campingplatz* isn't a convenient place from which to explore Potsdam or Berlin, but its relaxed, lake-side living style might make it a destination itself.

*🚆 S7: Potsdam Hauptbahnhof, then tram #91:Bahnhof Pirschheide. Call 8:45am-10:45am, or 5:30-9pm for free shuttle to the campsite from "Pirschheide." ℹ Internet €2 per day. $ €12.30 per person. ⏰ Phone reception 8am-1pm and 3-8pm.*

## Sights

The **Premium Day Ticket** will get you into all the sights in the Parks *(€19, students €14)*, and the **Day pass** will get you in everywhere except the Schloβ *(€14/10)*. The **Premium Family Ticket** is good for two adults and up to three children *(€49)*, as is the **Family ticket without Schloß** *(€24)*.

### Park Sanssouci Sights

If you only go one place in Potsdam, make it **Park Sanssouci.** The park's full of winding paths and yellow palaces that will keep you wandering in awe for days, and more small palaces, monuments, and little teahouses than you could imagine. Next to the Schloß Sanssouci, the collection of Caravaggio, van Dycke, and Reubens crowd the wall of an exquisitely guilded **Buildergalerie.** *(☎0331 969 4181 $ €3, students €2.50. Audio guide €1. ⏰ Open Apr-Oct Tu-Su 10am-5:30pm.)* The stunning **Sizllianer Garten** (Sicilian Garden) is next door. Overlooking the park from the north, the pseudo-Italian **Orangerie** is famous for its 67 dubious Raphael imitations that replace originals swiped by Napoleon. Climb to the top of the tower for a view of the whole park *($ Tours €3, students €2.50. Tower only €2. ⏰ Open mid-May to mid-Oct Tu-Su 10am-12:30pm and 1-5pm.)*. Romantic **Schloß Charlottenhof,** whose park surroundings were a Christmans gift from Friedrich Wilhelm III to his son Friedrich Wilhem IV, flows from landscaped gardens to grape arbors *($ €4, students €3. ⏰ Open May-Oct Tu-Su 10am-6pm.)*. Nearby is the **Römische Bader** (Roman bath), which sits beside a reedy pond with small bridges. The park's single and mystifyingly Asian-inspired building, the **Chinesisches Teehaus,** is complete with a parasol-laden Buddha on the rooftop and 18th-century Chinese pottery inside *($ €3, students €2.50. ⏰ Open May-Oct. Tu-Su 10am-6pm.)*.

**PARK SANSSOUCI** PARK

Access the park from Hegelallee, Weinbergstr., or Gregor-Mendal-Str. ☎0331 969 4200

Schloß Sanssouci's 600-acre "backyard" puts Versailles to shame. The park is done in two distinct styles; half is Baroque, with geometric paths intersecting at topiaries and statues of nude nymphs. The other half is a rolling, almost-but-not-quite-natural landscape of wheat fields, rose trellises, and lush, immaculate gardens. There may be no more magically beautiful garden than this one; be warned that once you start walking, you may never want to leave. For information on the park's many attractions, from Rococo sculptures to beautiful fountains, head to the visitors center next to the windmill, behind the Schloß.

*🚌Buses #606, #612, #614 or #692: Luisenpl. Nord/Park Sanssouci. $ Free. ⏰ Open daily Mar-Oct 8am-10pm; Nov-Feb 9am-8pm.*

**SCHLOß SANSSOUCI** PALACE

Off Zur Historischen Mühle ☎0331 696 42 00

The park's main attraction, the turquoise-domed *schloß Sanssouci* sits atop a terraced hill, looking out over fountains and manicured gardens. Designed in 1747, the palace is small and airy, with ethereal paintings and carvings of the Greek gods in pinks and light greens. Frescoes of Dionysus are right at home in a breezy palace, whose name is French for "without worry." The brainchild of Friedrich, the Francophile, Sanssouci also has the small, exotically decorated **Voltairezimmer** (Voltaire Room), outfitted with carved reliefs of parrots and tropical fruit that climb around walls and down the chandelier. The library reveals another of Friedrich's eccentricities: whenever he wanted to read a book, he had a copy printed for each of his palaces–*en français*, of course. Also on display is Andy Warhol's magnificently magenta-and-lime modern interpretation of the king's portrait.

*🚌 Bus #695 of X15: Schloß Sanssouci. $ Admission €12, students €8. Audio guide (available in English) and ticket to the Buldergalerie included. ⏰ Open Tu-Su Apr-Oct 10am-6pm, last entry 5:30pm; Nov-Mar 10am-5pm, last entry 4:30.*

**NEUES PALACE** PALACE

Located on Lindenavenue ☎0331 96 94 361

Because sometimes one beautiful royal palace just isn't enough. Friedrich the Great built Sanssouci's fourth and largest palace in celebration of the Prussian victory in the Seven Years' War. And because nothing says masculine-military-power like pale magenta, Neues Palace is an expansive, 200-room, proudly pink *schloß*, featuring royal apartments, festival halls, and the impressive Grottensaal, whose shimmering walls are covered with seashells.

*🚌 X5: Neues Palace. $ €5, students €4. Audio guide €1. ⏰ Open Apr-Oct M and W-Su 10am-6pm, last entry 5:30pm; Nov-Mar 10am-5pm, last entry 4:30pm.*

excursions

## Other Sights

**NEUER GARTEN** GARDEN

Schloß Cecilienhof ☎0331 969 42 44

Borded by Holy Lake on the east, and Am Neuen Garten on the west

Neuer Garten, the smaller, less-attraction-packed counterpart to Park Sanssouci that lies to the east, is all free-flowing meadows and beautiful lake beaches. Scattered through the park are several royal residences, including the **Schloß Cecilienhof.** Built in the style of an English Tudor manor, this *schloß* houses exhibits on the Potsdam Treaty, signed at the palace in 1945. Visitors can see the table where the Big Three bargained over Europe's fate, and stand in the room Stalin used as his study. The garden also contains the centerpiece of the park, the **Marmorpalais** (Marble Palace). Classically designed from rust-colored marble, the palace also has a concert hall. Also in the Neuer Garten is the inexplicable **Egyptian pyramid** once used for food storage. At the far north end of the lake, beachgoers bare all, and relieve themselves of the summer humidity in the cool water.

*🚉 Bus #692: Schloß Cecilianhof. $ Garden free. Schloß Cecilienhof €5, students €4. Marmorpalais €4/3. ⏰ Schloß Cecilienhof open Apr-Oct Tu-Su 10am-6pm; Nov-Mar 10am-5pm. Marmorpalais open Apr-Oct Tu-Su 10am-5pm; Nov-Mar Sa-Su 10am-4pm.*

## Food

Altstadt is overflowing with lovely cafes and restaurants, but unfortunately, high prices come with the territory. For fresh produce, try the **flea market** in Bassinpl. *(open M-F 9am-6pm)*, or stock up at the massive **Kaufland** grocery store in the Hauptbahnhof *(open daily 6am-8pm)*. For budget options, your best bet is to try ethnic eateries.

### SIAM
THAI ❶

Friedrich-Ebert-Str. 13 ☎0311 200 9292

For large portions and low prices, Siam is the place to go. Admittedly, it's more than a little strange to watch Thai specialties being cooked up in a bamboo-covered kitchen, with a view of such a quintessentially old European street. But if you embrace the irony, you'll leave Potsdam with a full stomach and wallet.

*🚉 Trams 92 or 96: Brandenbergerstr. $ Entrees €4.70-8. ⏰ Open daily 11:30am-11pm.*

### KASHMIR HAUS
INDIAN ❷

Jägerstr. 1 ☎0331 870 9580

This understated Indian restaurant is removed from the touristy bustle. The weekday lunch special is a fantastic deal, and includes vegetarian options. On a hot day, cool down with mango or lychee smoothies *(€2.50)*.

*🚉 Trams 92 or 96: Nauener Tor. ℹ Lunch special served 11am-4pm. $ Lunch special €4.50-6.50. ⏰ Open M-F 11am-11pm, Sa-Su 11am-midnight.*

### CAFE HEIDER
GERMAN ❸

Friedrich-Ebert-Str. 29 ☎0331 270

If you're looking to spend a little extra for a German meal in this most European of cities, one of your cheapest options is Cafe Heider. Breakfasts run from €4-7.80, and entrees from €8-15. Eat on the expansive patio overlooking Nauen Gate.

*🚉 Trams #92 or 96: Nauener Tor. $ Homemade ice cream €1.30 per scoop. ⏰ Open M-F 8am-midnight, Sa 9am-midnight, Su 10am-midnight.*

## Essentials

### Practicalities

- **TOURIST OFFICES:** *(in the S-Bahn station. ⏰ Open M-Sa 9:30am-8pm, Su 10am-4pm.)* **Second location.** *(Brandenbergerstr. 3 in the city center. ⏰ Open Apr-Oct M-F 9:30am-6pm, Sa-Su 9:30am-4pm; Nov-Mar M-F 9:30am-6pm, Sa-Su 9:30am-2pm.)* Both offices sell **city maps** for €1 (if you don't already have a good map of the parks, you'll definitely want to pick this up), and book rooms for free with cooperating hotels. The tourist offices run 2hr. tours of the Old Town in English and German; inquire at the office *($ €8 ⏰ departs May-Sept daily 3pm)*. They also lead 3½hr. tours of Sanssouci Park *(1½hr. without Sanssouci Palace)* daily at 11am, departing from Potsdam Hauptbahnhof. Reservations required *($ €27, without Sanssouci Palace €16)*.
- **POST OFFICE:** *(Pl. der Einheit. ⏰ Open M-F 9am-6:30pm, Sa 9am-1pm.)* **Postal Code:** 14476.

### Getting There

Getting to Potsdam is wonderfully simple. Take the **S7** toward Potsdam *(40min.)*, or the **RE1** from most major stations, including Berlin Ostbahnhof, Friedrichstr., Alexanderpl., Hauptbahnhof, or Zoologischer Garten *(25min.)*. You'll need to buy a ticket for Zones A, B, and C *(€2.40 single ticket)*, or if you already have a day or week-long pass for Zones A and B, supplement it with an extra ticket to Zone C *(€1.40)*.

### Getting Around

**Public Transportation:** Potsdam is in **Zone C** of Belrin's BVG transit network, so all main-city prices are the same. Special Potsdam-only passes can be purchased on any bus or tram *(€1.40 valid 1hr., €4 all-day)*. The **Berlin Welcome Card** is also valid in Potsdam.

**Bike Rental and Tours:** Potsdam is best experienced by bike. If you choose to rent for the day, be sure to request a map, outlining the best route to see all the sights on wheels. From the Griebnitzsee station, pay to take your bike on the S-Bahn *(special bike pass €1.20 at any BGV ticket office).* **Potsdam Per Pedales.** *(Main location at Rudolf-Breitscheid-Str. 201, in the"Griebnitzsee" S-Bahn station or on the S-Bahn platform at Potsdam Hauptbahnhof. ☎0331 784 0057 💻www.pedales.de i Bike tours in English (reserve ahead) and German. $ Rentals €10, €8.50 for students. Bike tours €10.50, €8.50 students. Audio guide €6. ⏰ Open 9:30am-7pm.)* **Cityrad.** *(Right across from the Babelsbergerstr. exit of the Hauptbahnhof. ☎0177 825 47 46 💻www.cityrad-rebhan.de $ €11 per day. ⏰ Open Apr-Oct M-F 9am-7pm, Sa 9am-8pm.)*

# czech republic

## KARLŠTEJN

Karlštejn Castle was built by Charles IV in 1348 to guard the crown jewels, and unlike its counterpart in Prague, this sucker's actually a full-on castle. We're talking a big-ass wall perched on a mountain top and pawning the cutest little support town you've ever seen, now mostly desperate souvenir shops. The schlep there and back can be done in half a day, and the images of the Czech countryside, run-ins with priceless locals, and the self esteem boost you'll get from imagining you own it all will be some of the most memorable parts of your trip. If you're even thinking of going, make a reservation **now** for the second, extended tour *(available May-Oct)*, which takes guests into the heart of the castle including the **Chapel of the Sacred Heart** and some incredible medieval ruins. Those lucky enough to get a reservation can sleep easy knowing they've seen one of the top three sights in the entire Czech Republic. Travelers in less of a hurry can stay over for lunch or take a hike through the woods, which are jurassically overgrown and green in the summer.

### Sights

#### Karlštejn Castle

**CASTLE TOUR I**

Státní hrad Karlštejn ☎274008154 💻www.hradkarlstejn.cz

The hour-long tour of Karlštejn Castle takes you through Charles's bedroom and throne chambers as well as the nuns' quarters and the lower rooms of the medium-sized Marian tower. While none of the sights are stunning, it's pretty cool to check out Charles's collection of holy relics, the best of which is the head of a dragon St. George killed. Turns out it's a crocodile—imagine that. While the real crown jewels no longer hang in Karlštejn, guests can take a look at some impressive copies. At the height of its power, Karlštejn would hold hundreds of knights at a time, and a few of their original "armor closets" are still on display. Unfortunately, this tour doesn't let visitors into the enormous large tower.

*➔ From Karlštejn, walk up the path to the castle. $ 250Kč, students 150Kč. ⏰ Nov-Mar Tu-Su 9am-3pm; Apr, Oct 9am-4pm; May-June, Sept 9am-5pm; Jul-Aug 9am-6pm. Schedule subject to change; check website to confirm times.*

**CASTLE TOUR II**

Státní hrad Karlštejn ☎274008154 💻www.hradkarlstejn.cz

This tour takes you into the best parts of Karlštejn castle, including the Great Tower, which was never conquered even when the Hussites took the fortification and, as well as the Chapel of the Holy Cross, which was used to store the crown jewels. Best of all, the tour is limited to 15 guests, so you can tap the knowledegable tour guides. Ask questions. They have stories they won't tell you unprompted. For instance, while most castles used wells for water (in case of a siege), Karlštejn couldn't tap its well and had to dig a secret water main from the nearby brook. If anyone found that out, they could poison the brook and take the castle. So, problem solver that he was, Charles IV killed all the workers who built the duct so they wouldn't tell anyone. What makes the tour is the Church of Our Lady, which has an original medieval apocalypse scene violently splayed on its walls. Though some has been destroyed in various sieges, there are still enough nine-headed **dragons,** ghouls made of fire, and skeletons on horses to let you glimpse the horror of the medieval imagination and to haunt your dreams for years to come. The Chapel of the Holy Cross, the final stop on the trek, contains 129 portraits of Bohemian Kings and saints and is covered with the country's largest collection of semi-precious stones. The ceiling, though, is what rocks. It's covered in thousands of glass plates that try (and mostly succeed) to look like a starry sky.

*From Karlštejn, walk up the path to the castle. i All reservations must be made in advance. Reservations for Jul and Aug should be made up to 6 months in advance. $ 300Kč, students 200Kč. Open Tu-Su Jun 1-Oct 31.*

## Food

A dozen or so food shops fill this little village, and all of them are more or less fine. But the only one that offers a different, better experience is listed below.

### RESTAURACE POD DRACI SKÁLOU — CZECH

267 18 Karlštejn 130 ☎311 681 177 www.poddraciskalou.eu

A 5min. walk through the forest from the door to the castle, or a 15min. walk from town, this little forest cafe serves up great authentic food in the middle of what feels like a medieval clearing. None of the items are in English, but a small little picture at the bottom of each section lets you know which animal you're about to eat. If you can find someone to translate, try one of the wild treats like shark steak *(111Kč)* or wild boar *(237Kč).*

*From the castle, turn right immediately after you leave the gate (there'll be a sign directing off into the woods). Follow the path through the woods down the hill. From the town/train station, proceed towards the castle and take the only left that diverts from the main path through the town about 10min. before the castle entrance. Take the road about 10min. through the woods. The restaurant will be on your right. Look for the statue of a* ***dragon.*** *$ Entrees 75-200Kč. Beer 15-35Kč. Open M-Sa 11am-11pm. Su 11am-8pm.*

## Essentials

### Getting There

To get to Karlštejn, take the **Boroun train** *(92Kč)* from Prague's Hlavní Nádraží which leaves every hour *(last train leaves at 7pm).* The train station can be extremely difficult to navigate and the signs poorly marked, so a traveler's best bet is to find any of the information windows and explain your dilemma. The ride takes about 40min. and spends a long time along a river and snaking through the mountains—it's gorgeous. Once you arrive, the castle is a wee bit of a walk *(2km),* but again, except to the very lazy, this walk will be enjoyable. Just head to your right down the road and across the bridge, then up the hill following the signs that read "hrad." If you're thinking of staying until the evening, make sure to check at the train station when the last train for Prague leaves.

# TEREZÍN

Although Terezín's most infamous era was WWII when it served as a prison camp for enemies of the Reich (mainly Jews), it was originally built at the end of the 18th century as a strategic stronghold against invaders from the east. It quickly became apparent however, that Terezín was ineffective as a defensive structure, and it was adapted to serve mainly as a prison. The assassins of Archduke Ferdinand—the man whose death started WWI—were jailed and eventually died in Terezín. During WWII, the camp was first used as a prison for political prisoners of the SS, but was slowly converted into a concentration and transit camp for Jews, Romas, Communists, and homosexuals. Terezín was unique, however, in its designation as a prison for high profile prisoners. The abundance of artists, writers, and intellectuals kept in Terezín would produce some of the war's most striking and stark images of life in a Nazi concentration camp. All in all, 200,000 men, women, and children would pass through Terezín's transit centers; 40,000 died at the camp, while 120,000 moved on to death camps in the east. Only 8,000 of the prisoners to pass through Terezín would survive the war.

## Sights 👁

The essential sights of Terezín are all administered by a centralized organization, **Terezín Memorial.** A universal ticket can be purchased at any of the sites *(200Kč, students 150Kč)*, or tickets can be purchased separately for each *(160Kč, students 130Kč)*. If you have time, start with the **Ghetto Museum.** For travelers short on time, just see the **Small Fortress.** That being said, Terezín is best experienced as an entire morning and afternoon trip, and given the hour-long bus ride a visit to Terezín requires, it makes sense to spend some time there.

### SMALL FORTRESS ♿⊛ MEMORIAL

Principova alej 304 ☎416 782 225 💻www.pamatnik-terezin.cz

Although the information center provides explanatory maps of the small fortress grounds, definitely try to get a guided tour, which groups of 10 or more can call ahead and book for free (and upon which keen Let's Go travelers can usually piggyback). The Nazis built Terezín as a show prison to demonstrate their humane treatment of prisoners to Red Crosss workers. Only a guide can explain, for instance, that the sinks in the main cell block didn't actually work, or that the swallows building mud nests on the light fixtures had built the same nests during the war; they were a symbol of hope for the winter-frozen prisoners. During the 90min. tour, a knowledgeable and able historian shows you the large holding cells, the solitary confinement cells, the showers and delousing stations, and the various execution grounds. After the tour, travelers can visit exhibits on the WWI and WWII history of the fortress or view documentaries and propaganda films that are shown in an extant Nazi cinema. A relaxed tour of the small fortress can easily take 2hr.

*➜ From the bus stop, head east out of the town, over the bridge the bus passed coming in. At the cemetery memorial, take the left fork. $ Combined 200Kč, single 160Kč. Students 150Kč/130. 🕐 Open Nov-Mar daily 8am-4:30pm, Apr-Oct daily 8am-6pm.*

### GHETTO MUSEUM ♿⊛🍸 MUSEUM

Komenského ulice ☎416 782 225 💻www.pamatnik-terezin.cz

The Ghetto Museum contains a permanent exhibit on the Jewish "Final Solution," specifically with regard to its implementation in Czechoslovakia. Not only does the museum put this tragedy in context, but it contains the most moving exhibit of the entire monument: hundreds of drawings by children who were briefly allowed to attend school during the occupation of the ghetto. The museum also screens a documentary about the memorial and the various events and souls that contributed to the tragedy.

*➜ From the bus stop, walk east around the corner from the information center. ℹ A well-stocked cafe in the basement sells lunch and snack fare. Open daily 11am-4pm. $ Combined 200Kč, single 160Kč. Students 150Kč/130. 🕐 Open daily Nov-Mar 9am-5:30pm, Apr-Oct 9am-6pm.*

### CREMATORIUM ⊛♿ CEMETERY

Principova alej 304 ☎416 782 225 💻www.pamatnik-terezin.cz

The crematorium, where the remains of prisoners were burned, suffered heavy damage in the flooding of 2004. While the facilities have been restored, they have been uncomfortably "over-restored" so that the crematorium now appears to be almost functional. But that's just the inside. From the oustide, the unassuming crematorium could be a small synagogue in the middle of a Jewish graveyard, where a giant stone menorah and various other urns and monuments commemorate the murdered Jews of the Final Solution.

*➜ From the bus stop, head across the square to the southwest corner of the Terezín. Continue walking 3-5min. out of town, following the signs that say "Krematorium." ℹ Men should cover their heads before they enter the grounds. Yarmulkes can be purchased inside the crematorium for 20Kč. $ Combined 200Kč, single 160Kč. Students 150Kč/130. ⏰ Open Nov-Mar daily 10am-4pm, Apr-Oct daily 10am-5pm.*

### MADGEBURG BARRACKS — MUSEUM

Komenského ulice — ☎416 782 225 💻www.pamatnik-terezin.cz

The Madgeburg Barracks house a collection of paintings, drawings, manuscripts, and artisan works produced by Terezín's unusually high proportion of artists, performers, and writers who made these works in the Ghetto—the camps and the Nazi administration buildings where artists were employed to illustrate various announcements. While these secretly produced images were intended to alert the outside world of the atrocities being commited at Terezín, attempts to transmit the pictures were discovered and brutally punished, and most of these images were not uncovered until after the war. The barracks additionally hold the various manuscripts, set pieces, and costumes from the show performances that the Jews were forced to put on for the Red Cross workers.

*➜ From the bus station head across the square along Komenského. The barracks is to the left at the end of the street. $ Combined 200Kč, single160Kč. Student 150Kč/130. ⏰ Open daily 9am-5pm.*

## Food

### RESTAURACE NA HRADBÁCH — CZECH ❶

Bohušovická brána 335 — ☎0723 287 738

A little tiny place where the owners are more than likely to sit down and have a beer with you, Na Hradbách should give you a delicious taste of what it's like to be from the Czech countryside—and it will hardly cost you a dime. Although everything on the menu is great (and virtually free), one surprisingly delicious dish is the fried bread and mustard *(10Kč)*, which could be a meal in itself.

*➜ Head to the southwest corner of the garrison. The restaurant is just after you leave the town proper on your way to the Crematorium. $ Entrees 50-95Kč. ⏰ Open M-F noon-10pm Sa-Su noon-8pm.*

## Essentials

### Getting There

Buses leave regularly from **Nádraží Holešovice** off the metro's C line. The bus station can be difficult to navigate for first-timers. Your best best is to find an information booth, tell them you're trying to get to Terezín, then let them point you in the direction of the proper platform. Tickets are purchased on the bus and cost 80Kč one way. The bus ride takes about 1hr. and drops you directly in front of the Terezín tourist office, 25m from the entrance to the Ghetto Museum. Check the tourist office for the time of return buses. Be warned: the last bus leaves Terezín for Prague around 6pm on most days.

# KUTNÀ HORA

Kutnà Hora might be the perfect day trip, with cheap grub, untamed countryside, and a set of sights that range from the bone art of 40,000 dead humans to a jaunt 100ft. below the surface of the earth make afternoons here unforgettable. Plus there's one of the most beautiful Gothic cathedrals in central Europe. Even though Kutnà Hora was once a popping city wealthy from its silver mines, the community is now small, quiet, and peaceful, unlike anything you can find in Prague.

## Orientation

If you took the bus here, and you should have, the city center (*Palackého náměstí*) sits to the southwest, just up the hill. From there, the tourist center can point you to the nearby Silver Mine Museum and Santa Barbara Cathedral farther up the hill. On your way you can check out St. James Cathedral and the Jesuit College, which are both worth walking by. Visiting the **Cathedral of Our Lady of Assumption** and the **Bone Church** requires a 15min. local bus ride from the bus station.

## Sights

### ST. BARBARA'S CATHEDRAL ◉♿ CHURCH

Barborská ☎327 512 115 🖥www.chramsvatebarbory.cz

From the outside, St. Barbara's looks like an ecclesiastical horn toad with spikes and spires jutting willy-nilly. Examined closely, these horns become gargoyles shaped like men or ghouls or rabbits. Inside the church has its own non-traditional charms, like the crests of moneyed families conspicuously floating on the ceiling or the comic book Bible scenes hodgepodged in the gaps between the arches. Then there's the golden organ with its angel band stroking harps and blasting bugles. The Church of St. Barbara (the patron saint of mining) was founded in 1388, and is still worth it today.

*➜ From Palackého náměstí, head west on Husova, then take a left on Mincířská another quick right onto Komenského náměstí and another quick left onto Barborská. Follow it as it snakes up the hill and ends at the Cathedral. [S] 50Kč, students 30Kč. ⏰ Open daily Nov-Mar 10am-4pm; Apr-Oct 9am-6pm.*

### THE BONE CHURCH/OSSUARY/ALL SAINTS CHURCH ◉♿ CHURCH

Zámecká 127 ☎327 561 143 🖥www.kostnice.cz

In the 15th century the Black Death caused the death of a significant portion of the European population. Rumor spread that some traveling monk brought soil to All Saints church from the Holy Land and suddenly, All Saints was *the* place to die and be dead. There were so many people wanting to rest in peace at the church that they decided to expand it. This meant digging up nearly 40,000 bodies. And as everyone knows, when you've got 40,000 exhumed bodies, the only thing to do is give them to a half-blind monk so he can arrange them into crazy designs. The ossuary has skull chandeliers, femur mobiles, streamers of human heads. Try to remember as you're enjoying these decorations that each once had a mother who loved it. Ask to see the hand-pumped organ on the top floor of the church—it's mildly entertaining.

*➜ From the bus station, take local bus #1 Bus M-F, #7 Bus Sa-Su to Sedlec. [S] 40Kč, students 30Kč. ⏰ Open daily Nov-Feb 9am-4pm; Mar 9am-5pm; Apr-Sept 8am-6pm; Oct 9am-5pm.*



### CZECH MUSEUM OF SILVER - HRÁDEK ◉⊗ MINE

Barborská 28 ☎327 512 159 🖥www.cms-kh.cz

Rivaling the Bone Church in coolness, this tour of an abandoned silver mine shaft wraps you in miner gear and sends you 35m below the surface of the Earth. The experience is gritty and dirty: ground water streams freely from the rocks around you and in some parts of the tour, vistors must duck and squeeze through the rock. The 1½hr. tour also covers the history of mining in the city and a lot of other stuff that seems weak-sauce compared to the tour of the mine.

*➜ From Palackého náměstí, head west on Husova, then take a left on Mincířská another quick right onto Komenského náměstí and another quick left onto Barborská. **i** Not reccomended for people with even mild claustrophobia or people who have trouble with stairs. [S] 120Kč, students 80Kč. ⏰ Open daily Tu-Su Apr, Oct 9am-5pm; May-Jun, Sept 9am-6pm; July-August 10am-6pm. Nov Sa-Su 10am-4pm, M-F through prior booking.*

### CATHEDRAL OF THE ASSUMPTION OF OUR LADY ◉⊗ CHURCH

Zámecká, 284 03 ☎327 561 143 🖥www.sedlec.info

A relatively large and empty church, the Cathedral of the Assumption of our

Lady definitely won't be the thing you remember from Kutnà Hora, but it's worth a stop in, especially with the combined ticket described below. A group of happy Hussites burned the cathedral down during the war, but it was rebuilt in the Baroque style in the 18th century.

*From the bus station, take local bus #1 M-F, #7 Sa-Su to Selecs. $ 30Kč, students 20Kč. Joint ticket to the ossuary and the cathedral 70/40Kč. ⏰ Open Apr-Oct M-Sa 9am-5pm, Su 12pm-5am; Nov-Mar by appointment only.*

## Food

Authentic. Almost free. Delicious.

### MCK FAST FOOD

CAFE

Kollárova 590, 284 01

☎327 512 127

Despite the idiotic name, McK will be an amazing gastronomical experience for you, if only because the food is basically free. Baguettes of good sizes *(20-30Kč)* and toast *(12-16Kč)* go for a pittance. Entire hamburger meals with fries and a drink are what they could have cost at McDonalds in 1994, and if you just want the hamburger, expect to pay as much as you would for bubble gum *(55Kč)*. Also, the food is good. Vegetarians can dig the big salads *(40Kč)*.

*From Palackého náměstí, head down Kollárova. $ Meals 20-50Kč. ⏰ Open M-F 7:30am-5:30pm, Sa 9am-2pm.*

## Essentials

### Practicalities

- **TOURIST OFFICES:** *(Palackého náměstí 377/5 🖥http://kutnahora.cz i Contains maps and information, and has an incredibly eager staff. ⏰ Open Mar-Sept M-Su 9am-6pm, Oct-Feb M-F 9am-5pm, Sa-Su 10am-4pm.)*

### Getting There

It seems weird, but Kutnà Hora is best reached by bus and best left by train. Buses leave less-than-frequently from Prague's **Florenc** bus station (Metro: B, C) and cost 83Kč each way. For a full day in Kutnà Hora, it's best to be to the train station by 10am. It's 90min. to the Kutnà Hora bus station, and from there it's just a short walk up the hill to the information center and most of Kutnà Hora's sites. Reaching the Ossuary (All Saints Church) from the center of town requires a 20min. bus ride to **Selecs** *(weekdays: # 1, weekends: # 7 $ 10Kč)*. From there, it's a 10min. walk to the train station, where trains leave to Prague *(each way 127Kč)*. The train ride takes about 1hr. The last train leaves at 9pm. A trip to Kutnà Hora can be properly done in 5hr., not including travel, but most of the city shuts down at 5pm, so a trip to Kutnà Hora should begin with an early morning.

Kutnà Hora, with a decidedly smaller English-speaking population, can be a bit more difficult to navigate than Prague. The best advice is to look for signs, and remember that everything important is in the same basic area.

# hungary

## SZENTENDRE

☎06 26

This tiny town of 20,000 is home to many Budapest businessmen and their families seeking refuge from the commotion of the big city. Its cobblestone streets and tiny little nooks under lush greenery give it something of a romantic character. A small trek up to the top of Church Hill will give you the perfect pictures to send home, and the tiny art galleries and museums are perfect for any troubled genius.

## Orientation

Boats (☎484 40 00) leave from the pier below **Vigadó tér** (Ⓢ 2000Ft. ☒ 1½hr., 2 per day.). The train and bus stations are 10min. from Fő tér; descend the stairs past the HÉV tracks and through the underpass up Kossuth utca. At the fork, bear right on Dumtsa Jenő utca. From the ferry station, turn left on Czóbel sétány and left on Dunakorzó utca.

## Sights

### ⬛ CHURCH HILL (TEMPLOMDOMB) ⊗ VIEW

The best place to capture panorama photos of old houses, tons of church spires and a majestic Danube below.

☞ Walk up the hill from the Town Hall.

### ⬛ HUNGARIAN OPEN AIR MUSEUM ⬤&⌂ MUSEUM
Sztaravodai út ☎502 500

This museum is a 3km preservation of traditional Hungarian country towns and villages from the end of the 18th century to the beginning of the 20th. Traditional feasts, everyday tasks, and craft-making are also represented to teach foreigners about Hungarian pastoral life.

Ⓢ 600Ft, students 400Ft, family 1600Ft. ☒ Open daily 9am-4pm.

### SZAMOS MARZIPAN MUSEUM AND CONFECTIONERY ⬤& MUSEUM
Dumtsa Jenő utca 12 ☎412 626 ▣www.szamosmarzipan.hu

Have you ever seen a life-sized replica of the Hungarian crown jewels, scenes from the *Wizard of Oz*, and a 160cm long replica of the Hungarian parliament— all made from marzipan? If that won't get you to make the trip, maybe the 80kg white-chocolate statue of Michael Jackson will be a draw—a thriller even. On your way out, it's hard to resist getting at least a little something from the confectionery or the adjoining cafe.

☞ 2 blocks down the street from Tour Inform. Ⓢ 400Ft. ☒ Open daily May-Oct 10am-7pm, Nov-Apr 10am-6pm.

### CZÓBEL MUSEUM ⬤& MUSEUM
Templom tér 1 ☎26 310 244

The Czóbel Museum exhibits work by noted artist Béla Czóbel, including his bikini-clad "Venus of Szentendre." Admission includes access to the adjoining exhibit of works by the Szentendre Artists' Colony, which are either hit-or-miss.

☞ Head west from Fő tér. ⓲ English captions. Ⓢ 500Ft, students 300Ft. ☒ Open W-Su 10am-6pm.

### PARISH CHURCH OF SAINT JOHN & CHURCH
Church Hill

One of the few surviving medieval churches in Hungary that was rebuilt after Ottoman occupation in the 18th century. The holy ghosts have put a curse on all those hoping to snap a photo from inside the church, which costs 100Ft to evade.

☞ On Church Hill. Ⓢ Free. 100Ft to take pictures. ☒ Open Tu-Su 10am-4pm. Services Su 7am.

### NEMZETI BORMÚZEUM (NATIONAL WINE MUSEUM) ⬤&⌣ MUSEUM
Bogdányi utca 10 ▣www.bor-kor.hu

The grandiose National Wine Museum consists of little more than a cellar with some displays set up to elaborate on Hungary's various wine regions. The museum tour is available with a wine-tasting course, which features eight Hungarian wines as well as Hungarian appetizers. During the hot, sticky summer, the mercifully cool wine cellar is worth the trip alone, even if you wine connoisseurs might be less than impressed.

Ⓢ Exhibit 200Ft. Tasting and English-language tour 2200Ft. ☒ Open daily 10am-10pm.

excursions

## Food

### CAFE CHRISTINE
HUNGARIAN [3]

Görög utca 6 ☎369 7008 www.cafechristine.hu

Enjoy reasonably priced tourist food right by the Danube. In the summer, the small cafe opens up onto the sidewalk with plenty of seating and shade with a mix of umbrellas and trees. Those with little regard for their arteries will spring for the traditional Hungarian beef stew with ewe cheese gnocchi *(2100Ft)*.

*From Fő tér walk towards the river; the restaurant is on your right. $ Entrees 900-4100Ft. 🕐 Open daily 8am-11:30pm.*

### LÁNGOS
FRIED DOUGH [1]

Dumsta Jenő utca

For some delicious fried dough, stop at this little lunch counter on your way to the tourist office.

*Next to Tourinform. $ Lángos 165-250Ft. 🕐 Open daily 10am-8pm.*

### ART CAFÉ
CAFE [2]

Fő tér 11 ☎311 285

The best pastries in town, as well as gigantic, out-of-this-world ice cream sundaes. Much less assuming than the other places in the main square.

*On the right as your heading to the main square. $ Sundaes from 800Ft. Sandwiches from 650Ft. 🕐 Open daily 10am-10pm.*

## Essentials

### Practicalities

- **POST OFFICE** on Fő tér *(☎06 26 310 011 🕐 Open M-F 8am-5pm, Sa 8am-noon).*
- **POLICE** *(2000 Szentendre Dunakorzó ☎06 26 310 233).* In the neighboring city of **Dunakeszi** *(Tábor utca 2 ☎06 27 341 055).*
- **HOSPITAL** *(Kanonok utca 1 ☎06 26 501 440).*
- **TOURINFORM** *(Dumtsa Jenő út. 22, ☎02 631 79 65)* is between the center and the stations. Open from mid-Mar to Oct daily 9:30am-1pm and 1:30-4:30pm; from Nov to mid-Mar M-F 9:30am-1pm and 1:30-4:30pm.

### Getting There

HÉV **trains** go to **Szentendre** *($ 480Ft. 🕐 45min. 3 per hr.)* depart from Budapest's Batthyány tér station. **Buses** run from Szentendre to Budapest's **Árpád híd** metro station *($ 280Ft. 🕐 30min., 1-3 per hr.)*, **Esztergom** *($ 660Ft. 🕐 1hr., 1 per hr.)*, and **Visegrád** *($ 375Ft. 🕐 45min., 1 per hr.)*. **Boats** *(☎484 4000)*leave from the pier below Vigadó tér *($ 2000Ft. 🕐 1½hr., 2 per day.)*.

# ERSZTERGOM ☎033

Atop the **Esztergom Basilica,** as the breeze of a thousand years cools your face, looking out at the hills in the distance and the domed bridge that whisks travelers effortlessly across the border into Slovakia, you might feel a bit light-headed. The city of Esztergom produces a kind of ethereal haze, giving it a glow that extends far beyond its historical significance as the birthplace of King St. Stephen. It's the perfect "city upon a hill," nestled in the Danube Bend, where the awe-struck traveler will be surprised when he or she runs into locals who live day-to-day in the magical land; many will scramble to share their town and the stories of their great past.

## Orientation

Just down the street from the train station is St. Anne Church (Szent Anna Templom), a domed yellow church with a lovely green-lined walkway. On the way from the station to the Basilica you can take a detour to the left at **Árok utca** and check out the **Prímás island** for a view of the river. Just a little ways down from Árok you'll find **Lőrinc utca,** which will take you to **Párkányi híd,** the bridge that crosses the border to **Slovakia.** If you continue down **Kiss János altábornagy út** from the station, past **Hősök Tere,** you should keep left towards **Bajcsy-Zsilinszky Endre utca** to hike up to the fortress and Basilica.

## Sights 👁

### BASILICA OF ESZTERGOM

🚫⊗ BASILICA

☎033 40 23 54 💻www.bazilika-esztergom.hu

The nave lacks much of the ornamentation of other cathedrals, which gives it a sense of quiet stoicism. The organ, adorned with angelic statues, is one of the largest in Hungary. To one side you can find the millennia-old skull of Saint Stephen, founder of the Kingdom of Hungary. The beautiful Bakócz Chapel, to the left of the nave, is the only surviving chapel from the Middle Ages. The builders disassembled the chapel into 1,600 pieces and reincorporated it into the new church while preserving its original form. The church crypt, also a worthy sight, contains the remains of Hungary's archbishops. Perhaps the greatest attraction is the hike up to the cupola. Four hundred stairs whisk travelers up a tightly wound spiral staircase (not for the agoraphobic) to a magnificent view of the city and neighboring area. On clear days you can see the beautiful pine-covered peaks of the Slovak Low Tatras.

$ *Chapel free. Cupola 400ft. Crypt 200ft.* ⏰ *Open Mar-Oct Tu-Su 9am-4:30pm; Nov-Dec Tu-F 9am-4:30pm, Sa-Su 10am-3:30pm.*

### CASTLE RUINS

RUINS, MUSEUM

☎033 41 59 86

Around the Basilica you can see the ruins of the castle where St. Stephen was born, which once dominated the same hilltop. A museum now occupies the former ruins and showcases many artifacts from the medieval and Renaissance periods. Some areas allow you to look through the 👍**glass floor** into the excavation site below.

$ *800Ft.* ⏰ *Open Tu-Su 10am-4:45pm.*

## Food 🍎

### CSÜLÖK CSÁRDA

🚫⛅🍸❄ HUNGARIAN ❷

Batthyány Lajos utca 9 ☎33 41 24 20 💻www.csulokcsarda.hu

Traditional, but somewhat over-played, here you'll find Hungarian cuisine in a picnic-esque atmoshphere. Dishes range from the ancient recipe of smoky ox tongue *(1390Ft)* to aquatic treasures like the Hungarian classic, mixed fish soup *(1890Ft).* Don't be turned off by the restaurant's logo—the ghost from *Ghostbusters*—the restaurant is usually packed with hungry tourists and locals alike, especially during the summer.

$ *Appetizers 790-1395Ft. Entrees 1690-3990Ft.* ⏰ *Open July-Aug M-F 8am-5pm, Sa 9am-noon; Sept-June M-F 8am-4pm.*

## Essentials ℹ

### Getting There ↗

Trains run from Budapest's **Nyugati station** *($ 750Ft. ⏰ 1½hr, 22 per day).* The train station is about a 15min. walk from town. Facing away from the station, go left on the main street. Follow the street around the bend to the left and turn right at **Kiss János Vezérezredes út.** Buses run from **Szentendre** *($ 500Ft. ⏰ 1½hr, 1 per hr.)* and **Visegrád** *($350Ft. ⏰ 45min., 1 per hr.).* From the bus station, walk by **Simor János út** toward the market. The most spectacular way to get there is by 👍**MAHART ferry** *(☎484 40 13 💻www.mahartpassnave.hu),* which leaves the pier at Gőzhajó utca on **Prímás Sziget** for Budapest *($ 2985Ft. ⏰ 5hr., 6 per day).*

excursions

# ESSENTIALS

You don't have to be a rocket scientist to plan a good trip. (It might help, but it's not required.) You do, however, need to be well prepared, and that's what we can do for you. Essentials is the chapter that gives you all the nitty-gritty you need to know for your trip: the hard information gleaned from 50 years of collective wisdom (and those phone calls to Germany, the Czech Republic, and Hungary the other day that put us on hold for an hour). Planning your trip? Check. Staying safe and healthy? Check. The dirt on transportation? Check. We've also thrown in communications info, meteorological charts, and a ▣phrasebook, just for good measure. Plus, for overall trip-planning advice from what to pack (money and as little underwear as possible) to how to take a good passport photo (it's physically impossible; consider airbrushing), you can also check out the Essentials section of ▣www.letsgo.com.

We're not going to lie—this chapter is tough for us to write, and you might not find it as fun of a read as 101 or Discover. But please, for the love of all that is good, read it! It's super helpful, and, most importantly, it means we didn't compile all this technical info and put it in one place for you (yes YOU) for nothing.

## greatest hits

- **WORK IT.** You need a visa and a work permit to secure employment as a foreigner in Berlin, Prague, or Budapest (p. 232).

- **PUFF PUFF PASS.** The possession of small quantities of marijuana is decriminalized in Germany and the Czech Republic (p. 239).

- **PHONE HOME.** Skype is a most popular way of staying in touch while abroad (p. 244).

- **SPEAK EASY.** Not fluent in German, Czech, or Hungarian? Not a problem. Check out the phrasebook. (p. 247).

# planning your trip

- **PASSPORT:** Required for citizens of Australia, Canada, Ireland, New Zealand, the UK, and the US.
- **VISA:** Required for visitors who plan to stay in the Schengen area for more than 90 days.
- **WORK PERMIT:** Required for all foreigners planning to work in Berlin, Prague, or Budapest.

## DOCUMENTS AND FORMALITIES

You've got your visa, your invitation, and your work permit, just like Let's Go told you to, and then you realize you've forgotten the most important thing: your passport. Well, we're not going to let that happen. **Don't forget your passport!**

### Visas

Citizens of Australia, Canada, Ireland, New Zealand, the UK, and the US need a valid passport for entrance into the Schengen areas. EU citizens do not need a visa to globetrot through Berlin, Prague, or Budapest. Citizens of Australia, Canada, New Zealand, and the US do not need a visa for stays of up to 90 days, but this three-month period begins upon entry into any of the countries that belong to the EU's **freedom of movement** zone. For more information, see **One Europe** (below). Those staying longer than 90 days may purchase a visa at your local embassy or consulate. The cost of a visa and length of stay that it permits varies.

## one europe

The EU's policy of freedom of movement means that most border controls have been abolished and visa policies harmonized. Under this treaty, formally known as the Schengen Agreement, you're still required to carry a passport (or government-issued ID card for EU citizens) when crossing an internal border, but, once you've been admitted into one country, you're free to travel to other participating states. Most EU states are already members of Schengen (excluding Cyprus), as are Iceland and Norway. For more consequences of the EU for travelers, see **The Euro** feature later in this chapter.

Double-check entrance requirements at the nearest embassy or consulate of Germany, the Czech Republic, or Hungary (listed below) for up-to-date information before departure. US citizens can also consult ▇http://travel.state.gov.

Entering the Schengen area to study requires a special visa. For more information, see the **Beyond Tourism** chapter.

### Work Permits

Admittance to a country as a traveler does not include the right to work, which is authorized only by a work permit. For more information, see the **Beyond Tourism** chapter.

essentials

- **GERMAN EMBASSY IN CANBERRA:** *(119 Empire Circuit, Yarralumla ACT 2600, Canberra, Australia* ☎*61 262 70 19 11* ▪*www.canberra.diplo.de* ☺ *Open M-F 9am-noon.)*

- **GERMAN EMBASSY IN OTTAWA:** *(1 Waverley Street, Ottawa, ON, K2P 0T8* ☎*001 61 32 32 11 01* ▪*www.ottawa.diplo.de* ☺ *Open M-F 9am-noon.)*

- **GERMAN EMBASSY IN DUBLIN:** *(31 Trimleston Avenue, Booterstown, Blackrock, Co. Dublin* ☎*353 12 69 30 11* ▪*www.dublin.diplo.de* ☺ *Open M, Tu, and F 8:30-11:30am, Th 8:30-11:30am and 1:30-3:30pm.)*

- **GERMAN EMBASSY IN WELLINGTON:** *(90-92 Hobson St., Thorndon, 6011 Wellington, New Zealand* ☎*64 44 73 60 63* ▪*www.wellington.diplo.de* ☺ *Open M-Th 7:30am-4:30pm, F 7:30am-3pm.)*

- **GERMAN EMBASSY IN LONDON:** *(23 Belgrave Square, SW1X 8PZ, London, United Kingdom* ☎ *020 78 24 13 00* ▪*www.london.diplo.de* ☺ *See website for a detailed service schedule.)*

- **GERMAN EMBASSY IN WASHINGTON:** *(4645 Reservoir Road, NW, Washington DC, District of Columbia, USA 20007-1998* ☎*1 20 22 98 81 40* ▪*www.germany.info* ☺ *Open M-Th 8:30am-5pm, F 8:30am-3:30pm.)*

- **AUSTRALIA:** *(Wallstraβe 76-79, 10179 Berlin, Germany* ☎*49 308 80 08 80* ▪*www.germany.embassy.gov.au/beln/home.html* ☺ *Open M-Th 8:30am-5pm, F 8:30am-4:15pm.)*

- **CANADA:** *(Leipziger Pl. 17, 10117 Berlin, Germany* ☎*49 30 20 31 20* ▪*www.canadainternational.gc.ca/germany-allemagne* ☺ *Open M-F 8:30am-5pm.)*

- **IRELAND:** *(Jägerstraße 51, 10117 Berlin, Germany* ☎*49 30 22 07 20* ▪*www.embassyofireland.dehome.html* ☺ *Open M-F 9:30am-12:30pm and 2:30-4:45pm.)*

- **NEW ZEALAND:** *(Friedrichstr. 60, 10117 Berlin, Germany* ☎*49 30 20 62 10* ▪*www.nzembassy.com/germany* ☺ *Open M-Th 9am-1pm and 2-5:30pm, F 9am-1pm and 2-4:30pm.)*

- **UNITED KINGDOM:** *(Wilhelmstr. 70, 10117 Berlin, Germany* ☎*49 30 20 45 70* ▪*http://ukingermany.fco.gov.uk/en/.html* ☺ *Open M-Th 9am-1pm and 2-5:30pm.)*

- **UNITED STATES:** *(Pariser Pl. 2, 14191 Berlin, Germany* ☎*49 30 08 30 50* ▪*http://germany.usembassy.gov* ☺ *Open M-F 8:30am-noon.)*

**planning your trip · documents and formalities**

- **CZECH EMBASSY IN CANBERRA:** *(8 Culgoa Circuit, O'Malley, Canberra, ACT 2606, Australia ☎61 262 90 13 86 🖳www.mzv.cz/canberra ⏰ Open M-F 9am-noon and 1:30-3pm.)*
- **CZECH EMBASSY IN OTTAWA:** *(251 Cooper Street, Ottawa, Ontario, Canada K2P 0G2 ☎613 562 38 75 🖳www.mzv.cz/ottawa ⏰ Open M-F 9am-noon.)*
- **CZECH EMBASSY IN DUBLIN:** *(57 Northumberland Road, Ballsbridge, Dublin 4 ☎003 531 668 11 35 🖳www.mzv.cz/dublin ⏰ Open Tu and Th 9am-noon and 1:30-4pm.)*
- **CZECH CONSULATE IN AUCKLAND:** *(Level 3, BMW Mini Centre,11-15 Great South Road and cnr Margot Street, Newmarket, Auckland, New Zealand ☎0064 95 22 87 36 ⏰ Open M-F 9am-5pm.)*
- **CZECH EMBASSY IN LONDON:** *(26-30 Kensington Palace Gardens, London W8 4QY ☎44 20 72 43 11 15 🖳www.mzv.cz/london ⏰ See website for a detailed service schedule.)*
- **CZECH EMBASSY IN WASHINGTON:** *(3900 Spring of Freedom St. NW, Washington, DC 20008 ☎202 274 91 00 🖳www.mzv.cz/washington ⏰ Open M-F 8:30-11:30am.)*

- **AUSTRALIA:** *(6th Floor, Solitaire Bldg, Klimentska ul. 10, Prague 1, Czech Republic ☎ 420 296 57 83 50 🖳www.dfat.gov.au ⏰ Open M-F 9am-1pm and 2-5pm.)*
- **CANADA:** *(Muchova 6, 160 00 Prague 6 ☎420 272 10 18 00 🖳www.canadainternational.gc.ca/czech-tcheque ⏰ Open M-F 8:30am-12:30pm and 1:30-4:30pm.)*
- **IRELAND:** *(Embassy of Ireland, Tržiště 13, 118 00 Prague 1 ☎420 257 53 00 61 🖳www.dfa.ie ⏰ Open M-F 9:30am-12:30pm and 2:30-4:30pm.)*
- **NEW ZEALAND:** *(Dykova 19, Prague 10, 101 00 ☎222 51 46 72 ⏰ Office hours by appointment only.)*
- **UNITED KINGDOM:** *(Thunovska 14 ,118 00 Prague 1 ☎420 257 40 21 11 🖳http://ukinczechrepublic.fco.gov.uk/en/ ⏰ Open M-F 8:30am-5pm.)*
- **UNITED STATES:** *(Tržiště 15, 118 01 Prague 1 - Malá Strana ☎420 257 02 20 00 🖳http://prague.usembassy.gov ⏰ Office hours by appointment only.)*

essentials

## hungarian embassies and consulates abroad

- **HUNGARIAN EMBASSY IN CANBERRA:** *(17 Beale Crescent, Deakin, ACT 2600* ☎*61 262 82 32 26* ▤*http://www.mfa.gov.hu/emb/canberra* ☿ *Open M-F 9am-1pm.)*
- **HUNGARIAN EMBASSY IN OTTAWA:** *(299 Waverley Street, Ontario, K2P 0V9* ☎*613 230 27 17* ▤*www.mfa.gov.hu/kulkepviselet/CA/en* ☿ *Open M, W, and F 9am-noon.)*
- **HUNGARIAN EMBASSY IN DUBLIN:** *(2 Fitzwilliam Place, Dublin 2* ☎*01 661 29 02* ▤*www.mfa.gov.hu/kulkepviselet/IE/en* ☿ *Open M, W, and F 9am-noon.)*
- **HUNGARIAN CONSULATE IN WELLINGTON:** *(P. O. Box 29-039, Wellington 6443* ☎*64 49 73 75 07* ☿ *Office hours by appointment only.)*
- **HUNGARIAN EMBASSY IN LONDON:** *(35 Eaton Place, SW1X 8BY, London* ☎*44 20 72 01 34 40* ▤*www.mfa.gov.hu/kulkepviselet/UK/en* ☿ *Open M-F 9:30am-noon.)*
- **HUNGARIAN EMBASSY IN WASHINGTON:** *(3910 Shoemaker Street, N.W., Washington, D.C. 20008* ☎*(202) 362-6730* ▤*www.huembwas.org* ☿ *Open M, W, and F 10am-1pm.)*

## embassies and consulates in budapest

- **AUSTRALIA:** *(Kiralyhago ter 8-9, Budapest 1126* ☎*36 14 57 97 77* ▤*www.hungary.embassy.gov.au* ☿ *Open M-F 8:30am-4:30pm.)*
- **CANADA:** *(1027 Budapest, Ganz u. 12-14* ☎*36 13 92 33 60* ▤*www. hungary.gc.ca* ☿ *Open M-Th 8am 4:30pm and F 8am-1:30pm.)*
- **IRELAND:** *(Budapest 1054, Szabadsag ter 7, Bank Center, Granit lower, V. Floor* ☎*36 13 01 49 60* ▤*www.dfa.ie* ☿ *Open M-F 9:30am-12:30pm and 2:30-4pm.)*
- **NEW ZEALAND:** *(1065 Budapest VI, Nagymező utca 47.* ☎ *36 13 02 24 84* ▤*sardi@t-online.hu* ☿ *Office hours by appointment only.)*
- **UNITED KINGDOM:** *(Harmincad Utca 6, Budapest 1051* ☎*36 12 66 28 88* ▤*http://ukinhungary.fco.gov.uk/en/* ☿ *Open M-F 9:30am-12:30pm.)*
- **UNITED STATES:** *Szabadság tér 12, H-1054 Budapest* ☎*36 14 75 44 00* ▤*http://hungary.usembassy.gov/* ☿ *Open M-F 8am-5pm.)*

planning your trip

## TIME DIFFERENCES

Germany, the Czech Republic, and Hungary are one hour ahead of Greenwich Mean Time (GMT) and observe Daylight Saving Time. This means that they are six hours ahead of New York City, 9 hours ahead of Los Angeles, one hour ahead of the British Isles, 9 hours behind Sydney, and 10 hours behind New Zealand.

# money

## GETTING MONEY FROM HOME

Stuff happens. When stuff happens, you might need some money. When you need some money, the easiest and cheapest solution is to have someone back home make a deposit to your bank account. Otherwise, consider one of the following options.

### pins and atms

To use a debit or credit card to withdraw money from a cash machine (ATM) in Europe, you must have a four-digit Personal Identification Number (PIN). If your PIN is longer than four digits, ask your bank whether you can just use the first four or whether you'll need a new one. Credit cards don't usually come with PINs, so if you intend to hit up ATMs in Europe with a credit card to get cash advances, call your credit card company before leaving to request one.

Travelers with alphabetic rather than numeric PINs may also be thrown off by the absence of letters on European cash machines. Here are the corresponding numbers to use: 1 = QZ; 2 = ABC; 3 = DEF; 4 = GHI; 5 = JKL; 6 = MNO; 7 = PRS; 8 = TUV; 9 = WXY. Note that if you mistakenly punch the wrong code into the machine multiple (often three) times, it can swallow (gulp!) your card for good.

### Wiring Money

Arranging a **bank money transfer** means asking a bank back home to wire money to a bank in Berlin, Prague, or Budapest. This is the cheapest way to transfer cash, but it's also the slowest and most agonizing, usually taking several days or more. Note that some banks may only release your funds in local currency, potentially sticking you with a poor exchange rate; inquire about this in advance. Money transfer services like **Western Union** are faster and more convenient than bank transfers—but also much pricier. Western Union has many locations worldwide. To find one, visit ▪www.westernunion.com or call the appropriate number: in Australia ☎1800 173 833, in Canada and the US ☎800-325-6000, in the UK ☎0800 735 1815, in Germany ☎0800 180 7732, in the Czech Republic ☎221 105371, or in Hungary ☎01 456 6030. To wire money using a credit card in Canada and the US, call ☎800-CALL-CASH; in the UK, ☎0800 833 833. Money transfer services are also available to **American Express** cardholders and at selected **Thomas Cook** offices.

### US State Department (US Citizens only)

In serious emergencies only, the US State Department will forward money within hours to the nearest consular office, which will then disburse it according to instructions for a US$30 fee. If you wish to use this service, you must contact the Overseas Citizens Services division of the US State Department. (☎+1-202-501-4444, from US 888-407-4747)

essentials

## the euro

Despite what many dollar-possessing Americans might want to hear, the official currency of 16 members of the European Union—Austria, Belgium, Cyprus, Finland, France, Germany, Greece, Ireland, Italy, Luxembourg, Malta, the Netherlands, Portugal, Slovakia, Slovenia, and Spain—is the euro.

Still, the currency has some important—and positive—consequences for travelers hitting more than one eurozone country. For one thing, money-changers across the eurozone are obliged to exchange money at the official, fixed rate (below) and at no commission (though they may still charge a small service fee). Second, euro-denominated traveler's checks allow you to pay for goods and services across the eurozone, again at the official rate and commission-free. For more info, check a currency converter (such as ◼www.xe.com) or ◼www.europa.eu.int.

## TIPPING AND BARGAINING

### Berlin

Service staff is paid by the hour, and a service charge is included in an item's unit price. Cheap customers typically just round up to the nearest whole Euro, but it's customary to tip 5-10% if you are satisfied with the service. If the service was poor, you don't have to tip at all. To tip, mention the total to your waiter while paying. If he states that the bill is €20, respond "€22," and he will include the tip. Do not leave the tip on the table; hand it directly to the server. It is standard to tip a taxi driver at least €1, housekeepers €1-2 a day, bellhops €1 per piece of luggage, and public toilet attendants around €.50. Germans rarely barter, except at flea markets.

### Prague

Tipping in Prague is not mandatory, and service staff will not chase after tips. However, it is polite to tip around 5-10% if you're satisfied with your sevice. Touristy restaurants in the center of town will expect a 15-20% tip, but you have Let's Go to help you avoid those places.

### Budapest

Tipping is customary in all situations where the customers and service workers—waiters, taxi drivers, and hotel porters—come face to face. Depending upon how satisfied you are with the service, plan to tip 10-15%.

## TAXES

Most goods in the Schengen area are subject to a Value-Added Tax of 19% (a reduced tax of 7% is applied to books and magazines, foods, and agricultural products). Ask for a VAT return form at points of purchase to enjoy tax-free shopping. Present it at customs upon leaving the country, along with your receipts and the unused goods. Refunds can be claimed at Tax Free Shopping Offices, found at most airports, road borders, and ferry stations, or by mail (Tax-Free Shopping Processing Center, Trubelgasse 19, 1030 Vienna Austria).

money · taxes

# BACKPACKING
## by the numbers:

**117** photos snapped

**41** gelato flavors (3 lbs gained)

**23** miles walked (in the *right* direction)

**6** buses missed

**4** benches napped on

**2½** hostel romances

**1** Let's Go Travel Guide

**0** REGRETS.

# LET'S GO

# safety and health

## GENERAL ADVICE

In any type of crisis, the most important thing to do is **stay calm.** Your country's embassy abroad is usually your best resource in an emergency; registering with that embassy upon arrival in the country is a good idea. The government offices listed in the **Travel Advisories** feature at the end of this section can provide information on the services they offer their citizens in case of emergencies abroad.

### Local Laws And Police

You should not hestitate to contact the police in Berlin (☎110), Prague (☎158), or Budapest (☎107) if you are the victim of a crime. Be sure to carry a valid passport, as police have the right to ask for identification. Travelers to Berlin may find that the police are keen to ticketing jaywalkers. Police in Prague and Budapest can sometimes be unhelpful if you are the victim of a currency exchange scam; in that case, you might be better off seeking advice from your embassy or consulate.

### Drugs And Alcohol

If you carry insulin, syringes, or any prescription drugs in these cities, you must carry a copy of the prescriptions and a doctor's note. Avoid public drunkenness as it will jeopardize your safety. The drinking age in Germany is 16 for beer and wine and 18 for spirits. In Hungary and the Czech Repubic, drinking is permitted at age 18. Marijuana is entirely illegal in Budapest, but the possession of small quantities is decriminalized in Berlin and Prague. Carrying drugs across an international border—considered to be drug trafficking—is a serious offense that could land you in prison.

Smoking is incredibly popular in Berin, Prague, and Budapest. If you are sensitive to cigarette smoke, ask for a non-smoking room in a hotel or hostel, or to be seated in the non-smoking area of a restaurant.

## SPECIFIC CONCERNS

### Natural Disasters

Relatively weak earthquakes occur regularly in Germany, primarily in the seismically active Rhein Rift Valley or in coal mining areas where blasting can set them off. In the event of an earthquake, drop and take cover if indoors. If outside, move away from buildings and utility wires. Flooding occurs fairly frequently in Prague and Budapest, but city officials are quick to warn residents, and relief efforts are swift and effective.

## PRE-DEPARTURE HEALTH

Matching a prescription to a foreign equivalent is not always easy, safe, or possible, so if you take **prescription drugs,** carry up-to-date prescriptions or a statement from your doctor stating the medications' trade names, manufacturers, chemical names, and dosages. Be sure to keep all medication with you in your carry-on luggage. Some drugs—like pseudoephedrine (Sudafed) and diphenhydramine (Benadryl)—are not available in Germany, the Czech Republic, or Hungary, or are only available with a perscription, so plan accordingly.

### Berlin

Drugs such as aspirin (*Kopfschmerztablette* or *Aspirin*), acetaminophen or Tylenol (*Paracetamol*), ibuprofen or Advil, antihistamines (*Antihistaminika*), and penicillin (*Penizillin*) can be found at any local German pharmacy (*apotheke*).

## Prague

Drugs such as aspirin, acetaminophen or Tylenol, ibuprofen or Advil, antihistamines (*antihistaminika*), and penicillin can be found at any local Czech pharmacy (*lékárna*).

## Budapest

Drugs such as aspirin (*aszpirin*), acetaminophen or Tylenol (*paracetamol*), ibuprofen or Advil, antihistamines (*antihisztaminok*), and penicillin can be found at any local Hungarian pharmacy (*gyógyszertár*).

## Immunizations And Precautions

Travelers over two years old should make sure that the following vaccines are up to date: MMR (for measles, mumps, and rubella); DTaP or Td (for diphtheria, tetanus, and pertussis); IPV (for polio); Hib (for *Haemophilus influenzae* B); and HepB (for Hepatitis B). For recommendations on immunizations and prophylaxis, check with a doctor and consult the **Centers for Disease Control and Prevention (CDC)** in the US or the equivalent in your home country. (*☎+1-800-CDC-INFO/232-4636 ▣www.cdc.gov/travel*)

## budget airlines

The recent emergence of no-frills airlines has made hopscotching around Europe by air increasingly affordable. Though these flights often feature inconvenient hours or serve less popular regional airports, with ticket prices often dipping into single digits, it's never been faster or easier to jet across the continent. The following resources will be useful not only for crisscrossing the Schengen area but also for those ever-popular weekend trips to nearby international destinations.

- **BMIBABY:** Departures from multiple cities in the UK to Paris, Nice, and other cities in France. (☎0871 224 0224 for the UK, +44 870 126 6726 elsewhere ▣wwww.bmibaby.com)

- **EASYJET:** London to Bordeaux and other cities in France. (☎+44 871 244 2366, 10p per min. ▣wwww.easyjet.com Ⓢ UK£50-150.)

- **RYANAIR:** From Dublin, Glasgow, Liverpool, London, and Shannon to destinations in France. (☎0818 30 30 30 for Ireland, ☎0871 246 0000 for the UK ▣wwww.ryanair.com)

- **SKYEUROPE:** Forty destinations in 19 countries around Europe. (☎0905 722 2747 for the UK, ☎+421 2 3301 7301 elsewhere ▣www.skyeurope.com)

- **STERLING:** The first Scandinavian-based budget airline connects Denmark, Norway, and Sweden to 47 European destinations, including Montpellier, Nice, and Paris. (☎70 10 84 84 for Denmark, 0870 787 8038 for the UK ▣www.sterling.dk)

- **TRANSAVIA:** Short hops from Krakow to Paris. (☎020 7365 4997 for the UK ▣www.transavia.com Ⓢ From €49 one-way.)

- **WIZZ AIR:** Paris from Budapest, Krakow, and Warsaw. (☎0904 475 9500 for the UK, 65p per min. ▣www.wizzair.com)

essentials

# getting around

For information on how to get to Berlin, Prague, or Budapest and save a bundle while doing so, check out the Essentials section of **www.letsgo.com.** (In case you can't tell, we think our website's the bomb.)

## BY PLANE

### Commercial Airlines

For small-scale travel on the continent, *Let's Go* suggests **budget airlines** (below) for budget travelers, but more traditional carriers have made efforts to keep up with the revolution. The **Star Alliance Europe Airpass** offers low economy-class fares for travel within Europe to 220 destinations in 45 countries. The pass is available to non-European passengers on Star Alliance carriers, including bmi, Brussels Airlines, and Lufthansa. *(www.staralliance.com)* **EuropebyAir's** snazzy FlightPass also allows you to hop between hundreds of cities in Europe and North Africa. *(☎+1-888-321-4737 www.europebyair.com $ Most flights US$99.)*

In addition, a number of European airlines offer discount coupon packets. Most are only available as tack-ons for transatlantic passengers, but some are standalone offers. Most must be purchased before departure, so research in advance. For example, **oneworld,** a coalition of 10 major international airlines, offers deals and cheap connections all over the world, including within Europe. *(www.oneworld.com)*

### rail resources

- **WWW.RAILEUROPE.COM:** Info on rail travel and railpasses.
- **POINT-TO-POINT FARES AND SCHEDULES:** www.raileurope.com/us/rail/fares_schedules/index.htm allows you to calculate whether buying a railpass would save you money.
- **WWW.RAILSAVER.COM:** Uses your itinerary to calculate the best railpass for your trip.
- **WWW.RAILFANEUROPE.NET:** Links to rail servers throughout Europe.
- **WWW.LETSGO.COM:** Check out the Essentials section for more details.

## BY TRAIN

Trains in the Schengen area are generally comfortable, convenient, and reasonably swift. Second-class compartments, which seat from two to six, are great places to meet fellow travelers. Make sure you are on the correct car, as trains sometimes split at crossroads. Towns listed in parentheses on European train schedules require a train switch at the town listed immediately before the parentheses.

You can either buy a **railpass,** which allows you unlimited travel within a particular region for a given period of time, or rely on buying individual **point-to-point** tickets as you go. Almost all countries give students or youths (under 26, usually) direct discounts on regular domestic rail tickets, and many also sell a student or youth card that provides 20-50% off all fares for up to a year.

## BY BUS

Though European trains and railpasses are extremely popular, in some cases buses prove a better option. Often cheaper than railpasses, **international bus passes** allow unlimited travel on a hop-on, hop-off basis between major European cities. **Busabout,** for instance, offers three interconnecting bus circuits covering 29 of Europe's best bus hubs. *(☎+44 8450 267 514 💻www.busabout.com $ 1 circuit in high season starts at US$579, students US$549.)* **Eurolines,** meanwhile, is the largest operator of Europe-wide coach services. We get misty-eyed just thinking about their unlimited 15- and 30-day passes to 41 major European cities. *(Berlin ☎+49(0)69 7903-501. Prague ☎+420 245 005 245. Budapest ☎+36/1 382 0888. 💻www.eurolines.com $ High season 15-day pass €345, 30-day pass €455; under 26 €290/375. Mid-season €240/330; under 26 €205/270. Low season €205/310; under 26 €175/240.)*

## travel advisories

The following government offices provide travel information and advisories by telephone, by fax, or via the web:

- **AUSTRALIA: Department of Foreign Affairs and Trade.** *(☎+61 2 6261 1111 💻www.dfat.gov.au)*
- **CANADA: Department of Foreign Affairs and International Trade (DFAIT).** Call or visit the website for the free booklet *Bon Voyage...But. (☎+1-800-267-8376 💻www.dfait-maeci.gc.ca)*
- **NEW ZEALAND: Ministry of Foreign Affairs.** *(☎+64 4 439 8000 💻www.mfat.govt.nz)*
- **UK: Foreign and Commonwealth Office.** *(☎+44 20 7008 1500 💻www.fco.gov.uk)*
- **US: Department of State.** *(☎888-407-4747 from the US, +1-202-501-4444 elsewhere. 💻http://travel.state.gov)*

### BY BICYCLE

Some youth hostels rent bicycles for low prices, and in Berlin, Prague, and Budapest, train stations often rent bikes and often allow you to drop them off elsewhere. In addition to **panniers** (US$40-150) to hold your luggage, you'll need a good **helmet** (US$10-40) and a sturdy **lock** (from US$30). For more country-specific books on biking through the Schengen area, try **Mountaineers Books.** *(1001 SW Klickitat Way, Ste. 201, Seattle, WA 98134, USA ☎+1-206-223-6303 💻www.mountaineersbooks.org)*

# keeping in touch

### BY EMAIL AND INTERNET

Hello and welcome to the 21st century, where you can check your email in most major European cities, though sometimes you'll have to pay a few bucks or buy a drink for Internet access. Although in some places it's possible to forge a remote link with your home server, in most cases this is a much slower (and thus more expensive) option than taking advantage of free **web-based email accounts** (e.g., 💻**www.gmail.com**). **Internet cafes** and the occasional free Internet terminal at a public library or university are listed in the **Practicalities** sections of cities that we cover.

**Wireless hot spots** make Internet access possible in public and remote places. Unfortunately, they also pose security risks. Hot spots are public, open networks that use unencrypted, unsecured connections. They are susceptible to hacks and "packet sniffing"—the theft of passwords and other private information. To prevent

problems, disable "ad hoc" mode, turn off file sharing and network discovery, encrypt your email, turn on your firewall, beware of phony networks, and watch for over-the-shoulder creeps.

## international calls

To call the Schengen area from home or to call home from the Schengen area, dial:

- **1. THE INTERNATIONAL DIALING PREFIX.** To call from **Australia,** dial ☎0011; **Canada** or the **US,** ☎011; **Ireland, New Zealand,** or the **UK,** ☎00; **Germany, Czech Republic,** and **Hungary** ☎00.

- **2. THE COUNTRY CODE OF THE COUNTRY YOU WANT TO CALL.** To call **Australia,** dial ☎61; **Canada** or the **US,** ☎1; **Ireland,** ☎353; **New Zealand,** ☎64; the **UK,** ☎44; **Germany,** ☎49, **Czech Republic** ☎420, or **Hungary** ☎36.

- **3. THE CITY/AREA CODE.** Let's Go lists the city/area codes for Berlin, Prague, and Budapest opposite the city or town name, next to a ☎, as well as in every phone number. If the first digit is a zero, omit the zero when calling from abroad to the Schengen area.

- **4. THE LOCAL NUMBER.**

## BY TELEPHONE

### Calling Home From Berlin, Prague, and Budapest

**Prepaid phone cards** are a common and relatively inexpensive means of calling abroad. Each one comes with a Personal Identification Number (PIN) and a toll-free access number. You call the access number and then follow the directions for dialing your PIN. To purchase prepaid phone cards, check online for the best rates; ▇www.callingcards.com is a good place to start. Online providers generally send your access number and PIN via email, with no actual "card" involved. You can also call home with prepaid phone cards purchased in Berlin, Prague, or Budapest.

If you have Internet access, your best—i.e., cheapest, most convenient, and most tech-savvy—bet is probably our good friend **Skype.** (▇www.skype.com) You can even videochat if you have one of those new-fangled webcams. Calls to other Skype users are free; calls to landlines and mobiles worldwide start at US$0.021 per minute, depending on where you're calling.

Another option is a **calling card,** linked to a major national telecommunications service in your home country. Calls are billed collect or to your account. Cards generally come with instructions for dialing both domestically and internationally.

Placing a collect call through an international operator can be expensive but may be necessary in case of an emergency. You can frequently call collect without even possessing a company's calling card just by calling its access number and following the instructions.

### Cellular Phones

The international standard for cell phones is **Global System for Mobile Communication (GSM).** To make and receive calls in Germany, the Czech Republic, and Hungary, you will need a GSM-compatible phone and a **SIM (Subscriber Identity Module) card,** a country-specific, thumbnail-size chip that gives you a local phone number and plugs you into the local network. Many SIM cards are prepaid, and incoming calls

**essentials**

are frequently free. You can buy additional cards or vouchers (usually available at convenience stores) to "top up" your phone. For more information on GSM phones, check out ◙www.telestial.com. Companies like **Cellular Abroad** *(◙www.cellularabroad. com)* and **OneSimCard** *(◙www.onesimcard.com)* rent cell phones and SIM cards that work in a variety of destinations around the world.

## BY SNAIL MAIL

### Sending Mail Home From Berlin, Prague, or Budapest

**Airmail** is the best way to send mail home from Germany, the Czech Republic, or Hungary. **Aerogrammes,** printed sheets that fold into envelopes and travel via airmail, are available at post offices. Write "airmail," *"par avion,""Luftpost"* (German), *"letecky"* (Czech), or *"légiposta"* (Hungarian) on the front. Most post offices will charge exorbitant fees or simply refuse to send aerogrammes with enclosures. Surface mail is by far the cheapest and slowest way to send mail. It takes one to two months to cross the Atlantic and one to three to cross the Pacific—good for heavy items you won't need for a while, like souvenirs that you've acquired along the way.

### Sending Mail To Berlin, Prague, or Budapest

In addition to the standard postage system whose rates are listed below, **Federal Express** handles express mail services from most countries to Germany, the Czech Republic, and Hungary. *(☎+1-800-463-3339 ◙www.fedex.com).*

There are several ways to arrange pickup of letters sent to you while you are abroad. Mail can be sent via **Poste Restante** (General Delivery; *"Postlagernd"* in German or *"Postán maradó"* in Hungarian) to almost any city or town in the Schengen area with a post office, and it is pretty reliable. Address Poste Restanteletters like so:

Václav HAVEL
Poste Restante
Prague 110 00
Czech Republic

The mail will go to a special desk in the central post office, unless you specify a post office by street address or postal code. It's best to use the largest post office, since mail may be sent there regardless. It is usually safer and quicker, though more expensive, to send mail express or registered. Bring your passport (or other photo ID) for pickup; there may be a small fee. If the clerks insist that there is nothing for you, ask them to check under your first name as well. Let's Go lists post offices in the **Practicalities** section for each city.

**American Express** has travel offices throughout the world that offer a free **Client Letter Service** (mail held up to 30 days and forwarded upon request) for cardholders who contact them in advance. Some offices provide these services to non-cardholders (especially AmEx Travelers Cheque holders), but call ahead to make sure. For a complete list of AmEx locations, call ☎+1-800-528-4800 or visit ◙www.americanexpress. com/travel.

# climate

Germany has a temperate seasonal climate dictated by the North Atlantic Drift. The climate in Berlin is oceanic with maximum rainfall during the summer. The Czech Republic is characterized by hot summers and cold, snowy winters. Its landlocked geographical location accounts for a drastic temperature difference between summer and winter. Hungary's continental climate yields frequent rainshowers, but low overall humidity.

| AVG. TEMP. (LOW/ HIGH), PRECIP. | JANUARY | | | APRIL | | | JULY | | | OCTOBER | | |
|---|---|---|---|---|---|---|---|---|---|---|---|---|
| | °C | °F | mm | °C | °F | mm | °C | °F | mm | °C | °F | mm |
| Berlin | -3/2 | 26/35 | 43 | 4/13 | 39/55 | 43 | 13/23 | 55/73 | 53 | 6/13 | 42/55 | 36 |
| Prague | -4/2 | 26/35 | 24 | 4/13 | 38/56 | 38 | 13/24 | 62/82 | 66 | 5/13 | 41/55 | 31 |
| Budapest | -3/2 | 27/36 | 39 | 7/17 | 44/62 | 47 | 16/28 | 56/75 | 50 | 8/16 | 46/61 | 47 |

To convert from degrees Fahrenheit to degrees Celsius, subtract 32 and multiply by 5/9. To convert from Celsius to Fahrenheit, multiply by 9/5 and add 32.

| °CELSIUS | -5 | 0 | 5 | 10 | 15 | 20 | 25 | 30 | 35 | 40 |
|---|---|---|---|---|---|---|---|---|---|---|
| °FAHRENHEIT | 23 | 32 | 41 | 50 | 59 | 68 | 77 | 86 | 95 | 104 |

# measurements

Like the rest of the rational world, Germany, the Czech Republic, and Hungary use the metric system. The basic unit of length is the meter (m), which is divided into 100 centimeters (cm) or 1000 millimeters (mm). One thousand meters make up one kilometer (km). Fluids are measured in liters (L), each divided into 1000 milliliters (mL). A liter of pure water weighs one kilogram (kg), the unit of mass that is divided into 1000 grams (g). One metric ton is 1000kg.

| MEASUREMENT CONVERSIONS | |
|---|---|
| 1 inch (in.) = 25.4mm | 1 millimeter (mm) = 0.039 in. |
| 1 foot (ft.) = 0.305m | 1 meter (m) = 3.28 ft. |
| 1 yard (yd.) = 0.914m | 1 meter (m) = 1.094 yd. |
| 1 mile (mi.) = 1.609km | 1 kilometer (km) = 0.621 mi. |
| 1 ounce (oz.) = 28.35g | 1 gram (g) = 0.035 oz. |
| 1 pound (lb.) = 0.454kg | 1 kilogram (kg) = 2.205 lb. |
| 1 fluid ounce (fl. oz.) = 29.57mL | 1 milliliter (mL) = 0.034 fl. oz. |
| 1 gallon (gal.) = 3.785L | 1 liter (L) = 0.264 gal. |

# language

## GERMAN (DEUTSCH)

Most Germans speak some basic English, but you will encounter many who don't. Preface any questions with a polite *Sprechen Sie Englisch?* (Do you speak English?) When out at restaurants, bars, and attractions, a simple *Bitte* (please) and *Danke* (thank you) are obviously important magic words. Even if your handle on German is a little loose, most locals will appreciate your effort.

### Pronunciation

German pronunciation, for the most part, is consistent with spelling. There are no silent letters, and all nouns are capitalized.

An umlaut over a letter (e.g., ü) makes the pronunciation longer and more rounded. An umlaut is sometimes replaced by an "e" following the vowel, so that "schön" becomes "schoen." Germans are generally very forgiving toward foreigners who butcher their mother tongue, but if you learn nothing else in German, learn to pronounce the names of cities properly. Berlin is "bare-LEEN," Hamburg is "HAHM-boorg," Munich is "MEUWN-shen," and Bayreuth is "BUY-royt."

Different pronunciations for certain letters and diphthongs are listed below. The German "ß," is referred to as the *scharfes S* (sharp S) or the *Ess-tset*. It is shorthand for a double-s, and is pronounced just like an "ss" in English. The letter appears only in lower case and shows up in two of the most important German words for travelers: Straße, "street," which is pronounced "SHTRAH-sseh" and abbreviated "Str."; and Schloß, "castle," pronounced "SHLOSS."

| PHONETIC UNIT | PRONUNCIATION | PHONETIC UNIT | PRONUNCIATION |
|---|---|---|---|
| a | AH, as in "father" | j | Y, as in "young" |
| e | EH, as in "bet" | k | always K, as in "kelp" |
| i | IH, as in "wind" | r | gutteral RH, like French |
| o | OH, as in "oh" | s | Z, as in "zone" |
| u | OO, as in "fondue" | v | F, as in "fantasy" |
| au | OW, as in "cow" | w | V, as in "vacuum" |
| ie | EE, as in "thief" | z | TS, as in "cats" |
| ei | EY, as in "wine" | ch | CHH, as in "loch" |
| eu | OI, as in "boil" | qu | KV, as in "kvetch" |
| ä | similar to the E in "bet" | sch | SH, as in "shot" |
| ö | similar to the E in "perm" | st/sp | SHT/SHP, as in "spiel" |
| ü | close to the EU in "blue" | th | T, as in "time" |

## Phrasebook

Nothing can replace a full-fledged phrasebook or pocket-sized English-German dictionary, but this phrasebook will provide you with a few of the essentials. German features both an informal and formal form of address; in the tables below, the polite form follows the familiar form in parentheses. In German, all nouns can take any one of three genders: masculine (taking the article **der;** pronounced DARE), feminine (**die;** pronounced DEE), and neuter (**das;** pronounced DAHSS). All plural nouns also take the *die* article, regardless of their gender in the singular.

| ENGLISH | GERMAN | PRONUNCIATION |
|---|---|---|
| Hello!/Hi! | Hallo!/Tag! | Hahllo!/Tahk! |
| Goodbye!/Bye! | Auf Wiedersehen!/Tschüss! | Owf VEE-der-zain!/Chuess! |
| Yes. | Ja. | Yah. |
| No. | Nein. | Nine. |
| Sorry! | Es tut mir leid! | ESS toot meer lite! |
| **EMERGENCY** | | |
| Go away! | Geh weg! | Gay veck! |
| Help! | Hilfe! | HILL-fuh! |
| Call the police! | Ruf die Polizei! | Roof dee Pol-ee-TSFI! |
| Get a doctor! | Hol einen Arzt! | Hole EIN-en Ahrtst! |

## Greetings

| ENGLISH | GERMAN | ENGLISH | GERMAN |
|---|---|---|---|
| Good morning. | Guten Morgen. | My name is... | Ich heiße... |
| Good afternoon. | Guten Tag. | What is your name? | Wie heißt du (heißen Sie)? |
| Good evening. | Guten Abend. | Where are you from? | Woher kommst du (kommen Sie)? |
| Good night. | Guten Nacht. | How are you? | Wie geht's (geht es Ihnen)? |
| Excuse me/Sorry. | Enthschuldigung/Sorry. | I'm well. | Es geht mir good. |
| Could you please help me? | Kannst du (Können Sie) mir helfen, bitte? | Do you speak English? | Sprichst du (Sprechen Sie) Englisch? |
| How old are you? | Wie alt bist du (sind Sie)? | I don't speak German. | Ich spreche kein Deutsch. |

## Useful Phrases

| CARDINAL NUMBERS | | | | | | | | | | |
|---|---|---|---|---|---|---|---|---|---|---|
| 0 | 1 | 2 | 3 | 4 | 5 | 6 | 7 | 8 | 9 | 10 |
| null | eins | zwei | drei | vier | fünf | sechs | sieben | acht | neun | zehn |

| CARDINAL NUMBERS | | | | | | | | | | |
|---|---|---|---|---|---|---|---|---|---|---|
| 11 | 12 | 20 | 30 | 40 | 50 | 60 | 70 | 80 | 90 | 100 |
| elf | zwölf | zwanzig | dreißig | vierzig | fünfzig | sechzig | siebzig | achtzig | neunzig | hundert |

| ORDINAL NUMBERS | | | | | | |
|---|---|---|---|---|---|---|
| 1st | erste | 5th | fünfte | 9th | neunte |
| 2nd | zweite | 6th | sechste | 10th | zehnte |
| 3rd | dritte | 7th | siebte | 20th | zwanzigste |
| 4th | vierte | 8th | achte | 100th | hunderte |

| DIRECTIONS AND TRANSPORTATION | | | |
|---|---|---|---|
| (to the) right | rechts | (to the) left | links |
| straight ahead | geradeaus | Where is...? | Wo ist...? |
| next to | neben | opposite | gegenüber |
| How do I find...? | Wie finde ich...? | It's nearby. | Es ist in der Nähe. |
| How do I get to...? | Wie komme ich nach...? | Is that far from here? | Ist es weit weg? |
| one-way trip | einfache Fahrt | round-trip | hin und zurück |
| Where is this train going? | Wohin fährt das Zug? | When does the train leave? | Wann fährt der Zug ab? |

| ACCOMMODATIONS | | | |
|---|---|---|---|
| Rooms available | Zimmer frei | I would like a room... | Ich möchte ein Zimmer... |
| No vacancies | besetzt | ...with sink. | ...mit Waschbecken. |
| Are there any vacancies? | Gibt es ein Zimmer frei? | ...with shower. | ...mit Dusche. |
| Single room | Einzelzimmer | ...with a toilet. | ...mit WC. |
| Double room | Doppelzimmer | ...with a bathtub. | ...mit Badewanne. |
| Dormitory-style room | Mehrbettzimmer/ Schlafsaal | nonsmoker | Nichtraucher |

| TIME AND HOURS | | | |
|---|---|---|---|
| open | geöffnet | closed | geshloßen |
| morning | Morgen | opening hours | Öffnungszeiten |
| afternoon | Nachmittag | today | heute |
| night | Nacht | yesterday | gestern |
| evening | Abend | tomorrow | morgen |
| What time is it? | Wie spät ist es? | break time, rest day | Ruhepause, Ruhetag |
| It's (seven) o'clock. | Es ist (sieben) Uhr. | At what time? | Um wieviel Uhr? |

| FOOD AND RESTAURANT TERMS | | | |
|---|---|---|---|
| bread | Brot | water | Wasser |
| roll | Brötchen | tap water | Leitungswasser |
| jelly | Marmelade | juice | Saft |
| meat | Fleisch | beer | Bier |
| beef | Rindfleisch | wine | Wein |
| pork | Schweinfleisch | coffee | Kaffee |
| chicken | Huhn | tea | Tee |
| sausage | Wurst | soup | Suppe |
| cheese | Käse | potatoes | Kartoffeln |
| fruit | Obst | milk | Milch |
| vegetables | Gemüse | sauce | Soße |

essentials

| cabbage | Kohl | french fries | Pommes frites |
|---|---|---|---|
| **I would like to order...** | Ich hätte gern... | **Another beer, please.** | Noch ein Bier, bitte. |
| **It tastes good.** | Es schmeckt gut. | **It tastes awful.** | Es schmeckt widerlich. |
| **I'm a vegetarian.** | Ich bin Vegetarier (m)/ Vegetarierin (f) | **I'm a vegan.** | Ich bin Veganer (m)/ Veganerin (f). |
| **Service included.** | Bedienung inklusiv. | **Daily special** | Tageskarte |
| **Check, please.** | Rechnung, bitte. | **Give me a Nutella sandwich.** | Geben Sie mir ein Nutellabrötchen. |

# CZECH (ČESKY)

Cut from the same cloth as many Slavic languages (though cleverly severing the ties of using the Cyrillic alphabet), Czech is the official language of the Czech Republic.

## Pronunciation

Czech pronunciation is tough for the average English speaker. If a word appears vowel-less, try not to panic. In Czech, the stress falls on the first syllable, and an accent (á, é, í, ó, or ú) lengthens a vowel. The table below covers the basics of Czech pronunciation.

| PHONETIC UNIT | PRONUNCIATION | PHONETIC UNIT | PRONUNCIATION |
|---|---|---|---|
| c | TS, as in "gets" | ř | ZH, close to the -ge sound in "luggage" |
| ě | YE, close to "yet" | w | V, as in "very" or "Vaclav" |
| j | Y, as in "young" | Milan Kundera; Václav Havel | MEE-lahn KOON-dehr ah; VAHTS-lahv HAH-vel |

## Phrasebook

| ENGLISH | CZECH | PRONUNCIATION |
|---|---|---|
| Hello | Dobrý den *(formal)* | DOH-bree dehn |
| Yes/No | Ano/ne | AH-noh/neh |
| Please/you're welcome | Prosím | PROH-seem |
| Thank You | Děkuji | DYEH-koo-yee |
| Goodbye | Nashledanou | NAS-kleh-dah-noh |
| Good morning | Dobré ráno | DOH-breh RAH-noh |
| Good evening | Dobrý večer | DOH-breh VEH |
| Good night | Dobrou noc | DOH-broh NOHTS |
| Sorry/excuse me | Promiňte | PROH-meen-teh |
| Do you speak English? | Mluví anglicky? | MLOO-veet-eh ahng-GLEET-skee |
| I don't speak Czech. | Nemluvím Česky. | NEH-mloo-veem CHESS-kee |
| I don't understand. | Nerozumím. | NEH-rohz-oo-meem |
| Please write it down. | Mohl byste to napsat? | MO-huhl BI-ste to NAP-sat |
| When? | Kdy? | gdee |
| **TRAVELING** | | |
| Where is...? | Kde je...? | gdeh yeh |
| ...the bathroom? | ...koupelna? | KOH-pehl-nah |
| ...the nearest telephone booth? | ...nejbližší telefonní budka? | NEY-bleezh-shnee TEH-leh-foh-nee BOOT-kah |
| ...the center of town? | ...centrum města? | TSEN-troom MYEHST-steh |
| toilet | W.C. | VEE-TSEE |
| left | vlevo | VLEH-voh |
| right | vpravo | VPRAH-voh |
| straight ahead | přímo | PRZHEE-moh |
| Do you have a vacancy? | Máte volný pokoj? | MAH-teh VOL-nee POH-koy |
| I'd like a room. | Prosím pokoj. | proh-SEEM PO-koy |
| single room | jednolůžkový pokoj | YEHD-noh-loozh-koh-vee POH-koy |

| double room | dvoulůžkový pokoj | DVOH-loozh-ko-vee POH-koy |
|---|---|---|
| reservation | rezervace | REH-zer-vah-tseh |
| luggage | zavadla | ZAH-vahd-lah |
| station | nádraží | NAH-drah-zhee |
| train | vlak | vlahk |
| bus | autobus | OW-toh-boos |
| bus station | autobusové nádraže | PW-toh-boo-sohv-eh NAH-drazh-eh |
| airport | letiště | LEH-teesh-tyeh |
| I want a ticket to... | Chtěl bych jízdenku do... | khytel bikh YEEZ-den-koo DOH |
| ticket | lístek | LEES-tek |
| round-trip | zpáteční | SPAH-tehch-nyee |
| one-way | jedním směrem | YED-neem SMNYE-rem |
| How much does this cost? | Kolik to stojí? | KOH-leek STOH-yee |
| How long does the trip take? | Jak dlouho ta cesta trva? | yahk DLOH-ho tah TSE-stah TER-vah |
| departure | odjezd | OHD-yehzd |
| arrival | příjezd | PREE-yehzd |
| square | náměstí | NAH-myeh-stee |
| passport | cestovní pas | TSEH-stohv-nee pahs |
| bank | banka | BAHN-kah |
| exchange | směnárna | smyeh-NAHR-nah |
| post office | pošta | POSH-tah |
| stamp | známka | ZNAHM-kah |
| airmail | letecky | LEH-tehts-kee |

| NOM NOM NOM | | |
|---|---|---|
| breakfast | snídaně | SNEE-dahn-yeh |
| lunch | oběd | OHB-yed |
| dinner | večeře | VEH-cher-zheh |
| market | trh | terh |
| grocery | potraviny | POH-trah-vee-nee |
| menu | listek/menu | LEES-tehk/meh-noo |
| I'd like to order... | Prosím... | proh-SEEM |
| bread | chléb | khlep |
| vegetables | zelenina | ZEH-leh-nee-nah |
| meat | maso | MAH-soh |
| coffee | káva | KAH-vah |
| milk | mléko | MLEH-koh |
| hot | teplý | TEHP-leeh |
| cold | studený | STOO-deh-nee |
| beer | pivo | PEE-voh |
| Cheers! | Na zdraví! | nah-ZDRAH-vee |
| I don't eat... | Nejím maso... | NEH-yeem MAH-soh |
| I'm allergic. | Jsem alergický. | ysehm AH-lehr-gits-kee |
| Check, please. | Paragon, prosím. | PAH-rah-gohn proh-SEEM |

| EMERGENCY | | |
|---|---|---|
| Help! | Pomoc! | POH-mots |
| Go away. | Prosím odejděte. | pro-SEEM ODEH-dyeh-teh |
| police | policie | POH-leets-ee-yeh |
| doctor | doktor | DOHK-tohr |
| hospital | nemocnice | NEH-mo-tsnyi-tseh |

essentials

# HUNGARIAN (MAGYAR)

Hungarian is a Uralic language, which means it's basically unrelated to most others in Europe. We've tried to keep it simple in the tables that follow. Just remember that as with Czech, stress falls on the first syllable of each word. After consonants, especially g, l, or n, the y is not pronounced but serves to soften the letter it follows.

## Phrasebook

| ENGLISH | HUNGARIAN | PRONUNCIATION |
|---|---|---|
| Hello | Szervusz (polite)/Szia (informal)/ Hello | SAYHR-voose/see-ya/Hello |
| Yes/No | Igen/nem | EE-gehn/nehm |
| Please/you're welcome | Kérem | KAY-rehm |
| Thank You | Köszönöm | KUH-suh-nuhm |
| Goodbye | Viszontlátásra | VEE-sohnt-laht-ah-shrah |
| Good morning | Jó reggelt | YAW RAHg-gailt |
| Good evening | Jó estét | YAW EHSH-teht |
| Good night | Jó éjszakát | YAW AY-sah-kaht |
| Sorry/excuse me | Elnézést | EHL-nay-zaysht |
| Do you speak English? | Beszél angolul? | BESS-ayl AHN-gawl-ool |
| I don't speak Hungarian. | Nem tudok (jól) magyarul. | nehm TOO-dawk (yawl) MAW-jyah-rool |
| I don't understand. | Nem értem. | ncm AYR tom |
| Please write it down. | Kérem, írja fel. | KAY-rem, EER-yuh fel |
| When? | Mikor | MEE-kohr |

| TRAVELING | | |
|---|---|---|
| Where is...? | Hol van...? | haul vahn |
| ...the bathroom? | ...a W. C.? | ah VAY-tsay |
| ...the nearest telephone booth? | ...a legközelebbi telefonfülke? | ah LEHG-kawz-ehl-ehb-ee teh-leh-FAWN-FOOHL-keh |
| ...the center of town? | ...a városközpont? | ah VAH-rosh-kohz-pohnt |
| toilet | W.C. | VAH-tsay |
| left | bal | bohl |
| right | jobb | yawb |
| straight ahead | egyenesen | EHDJ-ehn-ehshen |
| Do you have a vacancy? | Van üres szoba? | vahn oo-REHSH SAH-bah |
| I'd like a room. | Szeretnék egy szobát | seh-reht-naik ehj SAW-baht |
| single room | egyágyas | EHD-ahd-awsh |
| double room | kétágyas szoba | keht-AHGAHS soh-bah |
| reservation | helyfoglalás | HEY-fohg-lah-DASH |
| luggage | csomag | CHOH-mahg |
| airport | repülőtér | rep-oo-loo-TAYR |
| train | vonat | VAW-noht |
| bus | autóbusz | AU-OO-toh-boos |
| bus station | buszmegálló | boos-mehg-AH-loh |
| I want a ticket. | Szeretnékegy jegyet. | sehr-eht-nayk-ehj yehj-at |
| ticket | jegyet | YEHD-eht |
| round-trip | oda-vissza | AW-doh-VEES-soh |
| one-way | csak oda | chohk AW-doh |
| How much does this cost? | Mennyibe kerül? | MEHN-yee-beh KEH-rool |
| departure | indulás | IN-dool-ahsh |
| arrival | érkezés | ayr-keh-zaysh |
| square | tér | tehr |
| passport | az útlevelemet | ahz oot-leh-veh-leh-meht |

| bank | bank | bohnk |
|---|---|---|
| exchange | pénzaváltó | pehn-zah-VAHL-toh |
| post office | posta | PAWSH-tah |
| stamp | bélyeg | BAY-yeg |
| airmail | légiposta | LAY-ghee-PAWSH-tah |

| IRON CHEF | | |
|---|---|---|
| breakfast | reggeli | REHG-gehl-ee |
| lunch | ebéd | EHB-ayd |
| dinner | vacsora | VAWCH-oh-rah |
| market | piac | PEE-ohts |
| grocery | élelmiszerbolt | AY-lehl-meh-sehr-bawlt |
| I'd like to order... | kérek | KAY-rehk |
| vegetables | zöldségek | ZUHLD-seh-gehk |
| meat | húst | hoosht |
| coffee | kávé | KAA-vay |
| milk | tej | tay |
| hot | meleg | MEE-lehg |
| cold | hideg | HEE-dehg |
| beer | sör | shurr |
| Cheers! | Egészségedre! | ehg-eh-SHEHG-eh-dreh |
| I don't eat... | Nem eszem... | nem eh-sem |
| I'm allergic. | Allergia's vagyok. | ah-lehr-ghee-ahsh vah-jawk |
| Check, please. | A számlát, kérem. | uh SAHM-lot KAY-rehm |

| EMERGENCY | | |
|---|---|---|
| Go away. | Távozzék. | TAH-vawz-zayk |
| police | rendőrség | REHN-doer-shayg |
| doctor | kórház | KAWR-haaz |
| hospital | orvos | AWR-vahsh |

| CARDINAL NUMBERS | | |
|---|---|---|
| one | egy | ehj |
| two | kettő | KEHT-tuh |
| three | három | HAH-rohm |
| four | négy | naydj |
| five | öt | uht |
| six | hat | hawt |
| seven | hét | hayt |
| eight | nyolc | nyawltz |
| nine | kilenc | KEE-lehntz |
| ten | tíz | teehz |

## let's go online

Plan your next trip on our spiffy website, ▪www.letsgo.com. It features full book content, the latest travel info on your favorite destinations, and tons of interactive features: make your own itinerary, read blogs from our trusty Researcher-Writers, browse our photo library, watch exclusive videos, check out our newsletter, find travel deals, follow us on Facebook, and buy new guides. Plus, if this Essentials wasn't enough for you, we've got even more online. We're always updating and adding new features, so check back often!

essentials

# BEYOND TOURISM

If you are reading this, then you are a member of an elite group—and we don't mean "the literate." You're a student preparing for a semester abroad. You're taking a gap year to save the trees, the whales, or the dates. You're an 80-year-old woman who has devoted her life to egg-laying platypuses and figuring out what the hell is up with that. In short, you're a traveler, not a tourist; like any good spy, you don't observe your surroundings—you become an active part of them.

Your mission, should you choose to accept it, is to study, volunteer, or work in Berlin, Prague, and Budapest as laid out in the dossier—er, chapter—below. More general wisdom, including international organizations with a presence in many destinations and tips on how to pick the right program, is also accessible by logging onto the Beyond Tourism section of ▣www.letsgo.com. We leave the rest (when to go, whom to bring, and how many changes of underwear to pack) in your hands. This message will ▣**self-destruct** in five seconds. Good luck.

## greatest hits

- **BE THE NEXT KAFKA:** A three-month literature program in Prague could make you the next "it" author (p. 255).

- **OVERACHIEVE:** Study and intern in Hungary's capital (p. 255).

- **PAPRIKA IT UP!** Learn to spice up your cuisine in Budapest (p. 257).

- **TEACH FOR GERMANY.** Teach English and maybe even pick up some German along the way that involves more than "Bier bitte" (p. 259).

- **ACHIEVE WORLD PEACE.** Or just in Prague, but at least you're one step closer to winning the Miss Universe pageant (p. 258).

# studying

Going overseas to Berlin, Budapest, or Prague as a foreign exchange student might prove anything but. With many programs only offering English-language courses, the immersion factor, especially in Hungary and the Czech Republic, might be a little lacking. But take advantage of these comprehensive programs, with notable educational names like CIEE and AIFS, and enjoy the fact that they practically baby their enrolled students by taking care of all aspects of the semester abroad. Hey, everyone's getting your euro's worth.

## visa information

No visa is needed to enter Germany for European Union nationals or US citizens for up to 90 days. To work in Germany, non-EU citizens usually need a residence permit and a work permit. Work permits are difficult to acquire without a job offer. Employees of European Economic Area (EEA) companies who have "Van der Elst" visas are exempt from work permits. Students have three options for student visas: a language course visa that is void when the course is completed, a student visa that must be converted to a residence visa upon university admission, or a 1yr. student visa along with proof of study.

All visa applications cost €60 and require valid passports for identification. Remember that short-term visas can take 2-10 days to process, while long-term visas can take up to three months. Visa applications should be sent to the German embassy. For additional visa information, refer to Documents and Formalities.

## UNIVERSITIES

### Berlin

While studying abroad is not a foreign concept to Germans who often go abroad themselves, they may scoff at your instinctual and awful attempts to make certain words too guttural. Luckily, most study abroad in Berlin programs offered by U.S. companies require some kind of German language knowledge beforehand, and most immerse students in German-spoken and written classes right away.

**THE EXPERIMENT IN INTERNATIONAL LIVING**

P.O. Box 676, 1 Kipling Rd., Brattleboro, VT 05302 ☎+1 800 345 2929 🖥www.experimentalinternational.org

Offers summer programs in Germany involving language-skill improvement and cultural education.

[$] *$6,500 with international airfare included.*

**ARCADIA UNIVERSITY**

450 S. Easton Rd., Glenside, PA 19038 ☎+1 866 927 2234 🖥 www.arcadia.edu/abroad

Offers summer abroad program in Germany to learn about culture and renewable energy policies and technology.

[$] *$7,600 with airfare included.*

**INTERNATIONAL PARTNERS FOR STUDY ABROAD**

🖥 www.studyabroadinternational.com

Offers summer and semester programs at language schools in major German cities. Programs vary in difficulty and intensity.

[$] *Prices vary widely, starting at around €70 per week for group intensive lesions. Application fee €100.*

## LEXIA

6 The Courtyard, Hanover, NH 03755 ☎+1-800-775-3942 ◼www.lexiaintl.org

Summer or semester programs in Berlin to study architecture, visual culture, and cultural studies.

*i Applicants must have completed at least 1 year of undergraduate studies and have a minimum cumulative grade point average of B- in their field of study.*

## CCIS STUDY ABROAD

2000 P St., NW, Suite 503 Washington, DC 20036 ☎+1-800-453-6956 ◼www.ccisstudyabroad.org

Learn German in summer or semester long programs in Berlin or Heidelberg.

Ⓢ *Semester $5,633-11,453. 8-week summer programs $5,500-6,900.* ♔ *Semester programs offer studies in business administration, foreign language, politics, and history. Range from 8-16 weeks.*

# Prague

Most foreign exchange programs in Prague are conducted in English, but the immersion factor still exists in these cultural programs. Most are designed for students to live in homestays, but dormitory life is available for those envisioning late nights in Czech bars that end with stumbling home into bed.

## AMERICAN INSTITUTE FOR FOREIGN STUDY

College Division, River Plaza, 9 West Broad St., Stamford, CT 06902 ☎+1 800 727 2437 ◼www.aifsabroad.com

The Study Abroad in Prague program introduces students to Czech culture with English classes. Housing in dorms and apartments available.

*i Also offers volunteering opportunities to complement schoolwork.* Ⓢ *All-inclusive program US$13,495. Fulfills maximum of 18 semester credits. Includes traveling around European cities.*

## CULTURAL EXPERIENCES ABROAD (CEA) GLOBAL EDUCATION

2005 W. 14th St., Suite 113, Tempe, AZ 85281 ☎+1 480 557 7900 ◼www.gowithcea.com

Exchange students study at the Anglo-American University, the oldest private higher education institution in the country. All courses offered in English.

*i Apartments are standard, but students can arrange alternate living situations, including homestays.* Ⓢ *Semester curriculum US$10,995.*

## CIEE STUDY ABROAD

300 Fore St., Portland, ME 04101 ☎+1 800 40 STUDY ◼www.ciee.org

A largely liberal arts program, the 12-week Prague syllabus involves a lot of heavy philosophy and literature, so it's best for humanities majors.

*i Requirements include a 3.0 GPA when applying as well as one semester of European studies, including language, culture, and politics.* Ⓢ *Academic year tuition US$25,700, fall and spring semester US$13,500.*

# Budapest

Most programs in collaboration with institutions in the city are conducted in English, which doesn't do much for your Hungarian language prowess. Most companies and universities that liaise with these Hungarian universities take care of all necessities, including accommodations, course schedules, and the like. But given these programs are held in one of the most historically fascinating cities in the world, don't expect to do much studying, if at all.

## BARD COLLEGE

Institute for International Liberal Education, 30 Campus Rd., P.O. Box 5000, Annandale-on-Hudson, New York 12504-5000 ☎+1 718 213 8297 ◼www.bard.edu

Study in Budapest at the Central European University. Subjects range from environmental policy to journalism. An accompanying internship program is also available for those interested in getting work experience during their semester

*studying · universities*

abroad. Summer school and internship programs also available.

*i Maximum 16 credits per semester.*

### WHITTEMORE SCHOOL OF BUSINESS AND ECONOMICS, UNIVERSITY OF NEW HAMPSHIRE

15 Academic Way, McMconnell Hall, Durham, NH 03824 ☎+1 862 3885 💻www.wsbe.unh.edu

In collaboration with Corvinus University of Budapest, UH sends most students over in the fall. Syllabus includes a trip to nearby towns surrounding the greater urban area.

*i Various field trips planned.*

## LANGUAGE SCHOOLS

Despite government policies that encourage English education at a younger age, Eastern Europe still has a lot of distance to catch up to their western counterparts. Currently, Hungarian public schools continue to seek native English-speaking expats to teach at primary schools. Although Berlin's population is fairly bilingual, Budapest and Prague may make ordering a "Big Mac" somewhat difficult. Most language schools in Hungary and the Czech Republic offer homestays to fully immerse enrollees in the culture.

### EUROCENTRES

Seestr., 247, CH-8038 Zürich ☎+41 (0)44 485 50 40 💻www.eurocentres.com

Language programs for beginning to advanced students with homestays in Berlin.

*i Must be 16+. $ Prices begin at roughly US$550-690 for 2 weeks, depending on the intensity of the courses. ⏰ Programs 2-12 weeks.*

### GERMAN LANGUAGE SCHOOL

Kastanienallee 82, 10435 Berlin ☎+030 780089 11 💻www.gls-berlin.de

Berlin-based language school offers variety of language courses with on-site accommodation or homestays, internships, highs school exchanges, and summer camps in Berlin and Munich.

*i Must be 18+. $ Standard 5-week course roughly US$810. 5-week accommodation US$2,160.*

### BWS GERMANLINGUA

Bayerstr. 13, 80335 Munich ☎+089 599 892 00 💻www.germanlingua.com

Berlin-based language school offers variety of language courses with on-site accommodation or homestays, internships, highs school exchanges, and summer camps in Berlin and Munich.

*i Must be 18+. $ German courses €1030. Various accommodation options available, adding an additional charge of €40-550. ⏰ Full- and part-time language classes in Munich and Berlin for up to 1 year. Standard 6 weeks.*



## COOKING SCHOOLS

Not exactly known for its delicious and exciting fare, Berlin won't give adventurous eaters much reason to be excited about gastronomic explorations. But once you head east, get ready to confront carbs like you've never faced before. In Budapest, where meals revolve around sausages, bread, and more sausages, visitors may want to take some gourmet culinary courses to take a break from all the local meat and potatoes. But in a country where spices serve as a foundation of their food pyramid, cooking classes will definitely take advantage of Hungarian cuisine's tanginess. Once in Prague, head over to a baking school to learn what *kolache* and fruit dumplings are all about.

### Berlin

#### KOCHLUST BUCHHANDLUNG BRIT LIPPOLD

Alte Schonhauser Str. 36/37, 10119 Berlin-Mitte ☎+49 (0)30 24 63 88 83 💻www.kochlust-berlin.de

This legit culinary school and catering company also publishes a cookbook regularly.

*i* *Minimum of eight to conduct a class. Tickets can be refunded 10 days in advance.* $ *Reserve and pay for classes two weeks in advance to receive tickets.* ⏰ *Full- and part-time language classes in Munich and Berlin for up to 1 year. Standard 6 weeks.*

### Prague

#### ATELIER MAFAL

Velflikova 12, Prague 6 ☎420 773 22 44 11

If you hate the taste of fast food but can't stand waiting around the oven waiting for it to ding, drop by this school to learn the art of casual cooking. Marketed as a social experience, the school encourages students to bring friends along.

*i* *Lessons offered in both Czech and English.* ⏰ *Call to make reservations ahead of time.*

#### OLA KALA

Korunni 115, Prague 3 ☎420 777 270 199 💻www.olakala.cz

Learn the art of the traditional Czech pastry and its mild soups at this professional culinary institution. Continental cooking lessons also offered. Cook your way into someone's heart, as this place encourages dates and couple lessons. Great Czechoslovakian chefs teach here and rotate on a regular basis.

*i* *Bring up to 12 friends, just try to refrain from having a food fight.* ⏰ *Call ahead of time.*

### Budapest

#### CHEFPARADE COOKING SCHOOL

1094 Budapest, Páva Utca 13 ☎+06 1 210-6042 💻www.chefparade.hu

A top-level culinary school, it also offers classes to the general public. Learn how to make the best soup dishes from guys in tall hats.

*i* *Expect crowds on the weekends.*

# volunteering

Americans may get a lot of flack from other countries for their overeager Samaritan attitude when it comes to saving the world, but that's no reason to stop being your self-righteous, do-gooder self, especially if it benefits the less fortunate. Most opportunities in Eastern Europe involve teaching English as a second language to youngsters, as many have not caught up to their Western European counterparts. Don't be taken aback that some organizations ask you to pay upfront for offering services; fees go toward keeping these opportunities viable.

## BERLIN

- **BUND JUGEND:** This eco-friendly group provides information and organizes events for youth in Germany, incoluding volunteer and internship opportunities. Website in German. *(☎+030 275 86 50 💻www.bundjugend.de)*
- **GEOVISIONS:** Live with a German family while teaching them English for 15 hours per week. *(63 Whitfield St., Guilford, CT 06437 ☎+1-203-453-5838 💻www.geovisions.org/pages/723_conversation_corps_munich.cfm)*

## BUDAPEST

- **ASSOCIATION FOR WOMEN'S CAREER DEVELOPMENT IN HUNGARY:** Promotes women's equality in the work force. Works alongside the United Nations and European Union to further women's employment rights in Hungary. *(H-1118 Budapest, Ugron Gabor u. 28 ☎1 319 5245 💻www.womenscareer.hu)*
- **VOLUNTEER CENTRE FOUNDATION:** Serves as a resource center that spreads volunteerism throughout the country. Connects with multiple NGOs within Hungary.

English-speakers welcome. *(1053 Budapest, Muzeum krt. 23-25, IV/17* ☎*225 0710* ▢*www.okentes.hu)*

- **NIOK FOUNDATION:** An aggregated website that collects information on volunteering in Budapest and Hungary. *(1024 Budapest, Margit krt. 43-45, IV/3* ☎*315 3151* ▢*www.niok.hu)*

- **GLOBAL VOLUNTEERS:** This American organization connects volunteers to multiple organizations in Eastern Europe, including those located near urban Budapest. Most programs involve teaching English to elementary and middle school students. Expect to work with the local bureaucracy and the public school administrations rather than independent language schools. An initial fee must be paid which covers various costs including food, housing, orientation, and medical insurance. *(375 E. Little Canada Rd., St. Paul, MN 55117* ☎*+1 800 487 1074* ▢*www.goabroad.com)*

## PRAGUE

- **INEX CZECH REPUBLIC NATIONAL CENTRE:** This jack-of-all-trades organization offers volunteering jobs in social enterprise, cultural development, and environmental policy. Multiple projects happen simultaneously at any given time of the year, and most last about 14-20 days. With additional branches in Eastern Europe, this organization usually accepts most applicants. *(Senovázné Námesti 24, 116 47 Prague 1* ☎*420 234 621527* ▢*www.inexsda.cz)*

- **KMC:** This non-profit organizes volunteer experiences involving gardening, renovation, and ecological development. Good for those fond of nature and being outdoors. Past experience with manual labor is helpful. *(Karoliny Svetle 30, 110 00 Prague 1* ☎*420-2222-20347* ▢*www.kmc.cz).*

- **MAKE A CONNECTION:** Advocates for democratic values and human rights in Hungary. Focuses on civil society issues. Programs target children and young people. Also supports civic organizations and churches in their charity projects. *(Jelenei 196/15, Prague 1* ☎*420 2 2051 4032* ▢*www.nros.cz)*

- **HESTIA:** A member of VolunteerNet, a network of volunteering organizations in Central-Eastern Europe and the Baltics, Hestia is also affiliated with the Big Brothers Big Sisters, as well as other European non-profits, such as IAVE and Volonteurope. Advocates volunteers and their services around Prague and other major cities in Eastern Europe. Volunteers can visit their website for more application information. *(Na Porici 12, Prague 1* ▢*www.hestia.ecn.cz).*

- **NROS:** This non-profit coordinates research, training, and educational programs to help other non-profits become established enterprises in the Czech Republic. 50 members work here at a time, mostly volunteers. Past projects include the reorganization of the Czech Republic's Big Brothers Big Sisters program, as well as support for the unemployed. NROS also publishes newsletters and helps volunteers get connected to other organizations in search of workers. *(Jeleni 196/15, 118 00 Prague 1* ▢*www.nros.cz)*

- **VIA FOUNDATION:** Helps develop rural Czechoslovakian towns. Invests in non-profits and helps start-ups with business consulting. Also active in philanthropic projects around the country. Applicants should visit the website for more information on submitting materials. *(Jeleni 195/9, Prague 1* ☎*233 113 370* ▢*www.nadacevia.cz)*

- **MUTICULTURAL CENTER PRAGUE:** This cultural organization is always looking for new volunteers to join their ranks and help host cultural and educational events. Volunteers should expect to help out with administrative work. *(Vodičkova 36 Palác Lucerna, 116 02 Prague 1* ☎*420 296 325 345* ▢*www.mkc.cz)*

# working

The usual cop-out of teaching English works in all three cities since native speakers will always be in demand for their language skills. Check online to find some unexpected internships, especially in the agricultural field, as milking cows and other *Heidi*-esque jobs become trendier among college students.

## LONG-TERM WORK

### Teaching English

- **INTERNATIONAL SCHOOLS SERVICES:** A non-profit corporation that builds and manages international schools where they offer teaching and administrative positions. *(15 Roszel Road, P.O. Box 5910, Princeton, NJ 08543 ☎+1 609 452 0990 ▧www.iss.edu)*

- **TEACH INTERNATIONAL:** Offers TESOL (Teaching English to Speakers of Other Languages) programs in New Zealand, Australia, and Canada to be certified to teach English abroad. *(Level 2/370 George St., Brisbane, 4000, Australia ☎+617 3211 4633 ▧www.teachinternational.com)*

- **INSTITUTION OF INTERNATIONAL EDUCATION:** This highly competitive program sends college graduates to teach in western and eastern Europe. *(809 United Nations Plaza, New York, NY 11017 ☎+1 212 883 8200 ▧www.iie.org)*

- **TEACHING ENGLISH AS A FOREIGN LANGUAGE:** Lists various job opportunities to teach English abroad. *(▧www.tefl.com)*

- **OXFORD SEMINARS:** Offers TEFL programs and job placements in Europe. *(244 5th Avenue, Suite J262, New York, NY ☎+1 212 213 8978 ▧www.oxfordseminars.com)*

## more visa information

In the Czech Republic, European Union, Canadian, and United States citizens are not required to have visas for touring or short business trips of up to 90 days in length. However, trips of over 30 days must be registered within 30 days upon arrival with the Alien and Border Police. Visas for over 90 days in the country are available. All applications must be made in person. Traveling to the Czech Republic and applying for visas both require a passport that will be valid for at least 90 days after your arrival in the country. Contact your nearest Czech embassy to acquire more information on all documents required and prices of visa applications required to enter the country.

In Hungary, European Union, Canadian, and United States are not required to have visas for stays of up to 90 days as long as the purpose of the trip does not involve employment, immigration, or studies. Work, student, or self-employment visas are available for those who plan to stay in Hungary for over 90 days or have a separate purpose besides tourism for visiting the country. Single- to multiple-entry visas are also available, and vary in price. A valid passport is required for both tourism travel and visa applications. Contact your nearest Hungarian embassy to inquire into proper documents for travel.

working · long-term work

### Au Pair Work

- **AUPAIRCONNECT:** Database of families looking for au pairs as well as available au pairs. *(▧www.aupairconnect.com)*

- **AU PAIR CARE CULTURAL EXCHANGE:** Provides au pair opportunities in Germany. *(AYUSA International e.V., Giesebrechtstr. 10, 10629 Berlin ☎308 439 39 20 ✉www.aupaircare.de/inbound)*

- **INTEREXCHANGE:** Provides listing of teaching and au pair jobs in Germany. *(161 6th Ave., New York City, NY 10013 ☎+1-212-924-0446 ✉www.interexchange.org)*

- **CHILDCARE INTERNATIONAL:** Lists au pair opportunities available across the globe. *(✉www.childint.co.uk)*

## INTERNSHIPS

- **CA EDUCATION PROGRAMS (CAEP):** Coordinates paid internships and other educational experiences with agricultural organizations. Jobs range from farming to wine-making. College credit also available. *(112 E. Lincoln Ave., Fergus Falls, MN 56538 ☎+1 218 739 3241).*

- **INTERNATIONAL WEITERBILDUNG UNT ENTWICKLUNG GGMBH:** Professional training for students and young people from Germany and abroad. *(Inwent – Capacity Building International, Germany, Friedrich-Ebert-Allee 40, 53113 Bonn ☎+49 228 4460-0 ✉www.inwent.org).*

- **CDS INTERNATIONAL:** Offers professional development programs and long-term paid internships in several countries, for students and recent graduates of accredited U.S. colleges and universities. *(440 Park Avenue South, New York, NY 10016, USA ☎+1 212 497 3500 ✉www.cdsintl.org)*

- **INTERN ABROAD:** Search engine for internships abroad. *(✉www.internabroad.com)*

### Other Long-Term Work

- **INTERNATIONAL COOPERATIVE EDUCATION:** Finds summer jobs for students ages 18-30 in Germany. Semester- and year-long commitments also available. Costs include a $250 application fee and $900 placement fee. *(15 Spiros Way, Menlo Park, CA 94025 ☎+1 650-323-4944 ✉www.icemenlo.com)*

## SHORT-TERM WORK

- **BUNDESAGENTUR FÜR ARBEITG:** The federal employment bureau, which handles student applications from abroad, offers various job opportunities. German fluency required. *(✉www.arbeitsagentur.de)*

- **TRANSITIONSABROAD.COM:** Lists various short-term work opportunities, including au pair jobs, farmwork, and other summer jobs.*(✉www.transitionsabroad.com)*

beyond tourism

## tell the world

If your friends are tired of hearing about that time you saved a baby orangutan in Indonesia, there's clearly only one thing to do: get new friends. Find them at our website, ✉www.letsgo.com, where you can post your study-, volunteer-, or work-abroad stories for other, more appreciative community members to read. There's also a Beyond Tourism section that elaborates on non-destination-specific volunteering, studying, and working opportunities. If you liked this chapter, you'll love it; if you didn't like this chapter, maybe you'll find the website's more general Beyond Tourism tips more likeable, you non-likey person.

# INDEX

## a

Andrássy Út 174
Aquincum Ruins 180
Au Pair Work 259

## b

baths 175
  Hotel Gellért And Gellért Baths 178
  Király Baths (Király Fürdő) 177
  Széchenyi-Gyógyfürdő (Széchenyi Baths) 175
beer gardens 85
  Cassiopia 71
  Heinz Minki 73
  Jägerklause 71
  Levetské sady 117
  Prague Exhibition Ground 117
  Prater Garten 69
  Tempelhofer Park 51
Belváros, District V 160
Berlin 15
  accommodations 24
  arts and Culture 74
  essentials 80
  food 53
  nightlife 63
  orientation 16
  shopping 76
  sights 35
Berliner Weiße 85
Berlin Wall 84
breweries
  Klášterní Pivovar a Restaurace 3v. Norbert 132
  Staropramen 118
  U Fleků 106
bridges
  Charles Bridge 107
  Oberbaumbrücke 51
  Széchenyi Chain (Széchenyi Lánchíd) 177
Budapest 159
  accommodations 165
  arts and Culture 203
  essentials 207
  food 182
  nightlife 196
  orientation 160
  shopping 204
  sights 172
budget airlines 240

## c

Castle Labyrinths (Budavári Labirintus) 178
castles
  Karlštejn Castle 222
  Pražský Hrad (Prague Castle) 114
  Royal Palace 176
  Schloß Charlottenburg 35
  Schloß Bellevue 43
Charlottenburg 16
Checkpoint Charlie 85
cheeses 120
churches
  Church of Our Lady before Týn 107
  Church of Saint Nicholas 111
  Katedrála sv. Víta (Saint Vitus's Cathedral) 114
  Matthias Church (Mátyás Templom) 176
Citadella 179
climate 245
cooking schools 256
Currywurst 85

## d

Defenestration 155
Dejvice 94

## e

embassies
  abroad
    Czech 234
    German 233
    Hungarian 235
  in Berlin 233
  in Budapest 235
  in Prague 234
Ersztergom 229
Erzsébetváros, District VII 160

euro 237
excursions 215
  Czech Republic 222
  Germany 216
  Hungary 227

## f

Ferencváros, District IX 163
festivals
  in Budapest 158, 214
  in Prague 158
film
  in Berlin 75
Franciscan Gardens 106
Friedrichshain 21

## g

Gellért Hegy (Gellért Hill) 165
getting around 241
  by bicycle 242
  by bus 241
  by plane 241
  by train 241
Goulash 212
Grand Market Hall (Nagycsarnok) 172

## h

history
  of Berlin 83
  of Budapest 209
  of Prague 154
Holešovice 94
Hradčany 94

## i

international calls 244
internships 260

## j

Josefov 92
Józsefváros, District VIII 163

index

# k

KaDeWe 76
Kafka, Franz 8, 108, 111, 113, 115
Karlštejn 222
knedlik 156
Kreuzberg 21
Křižík's Fountain 117
Kutnà Hora 225

# l

language 246
  Czech 249
  German 246
  Hungarian 251
Lipótváros, District V and XIII 160

# m

Magyar Állami Operaház 174
Malá Strana 94
Margit-Sziget (Margaret Island) 165
memorials
  Homosexual Memorial 40
  Memorial to the Murdered Jews of Europe 40
  Small Fortress 224
microbreweries 60, 119
Mitte 87
money 236
  Pins and ATMs 236
  Taxes 237
  Tipping and Bargaining 237
  Wiring 236
monuments
  Berliner Mauer Dokumentationzen- trum 48
  Dancing House 106
  East Side Gallery 50
  Fisherman's Bastion (Halászbástya) 176
  Hősök tere (Heroes' Square) 175
  Liberty Monument (Szabadság Szobor) 178
  Memento Park (Szoborpark) 180
  Széchenyi-Gyógyfürdő (Széchenyi Baths) 175
  Vyšehrad National Cultural 117
museums
  Alfons Mucha Museum 105

Deutsches Technikmuseum Berlin 51
Franz Kafka Museum 113
Ghetto Museums 224
Hungarian Open Air Museum 228
Käthe-Kollwitz-Museum 35
Neue National Gallerie 45
Pergamon Museum 39
Royal Palace 176
Topography of Terror 39
music and opera
  in Berlin 74
  in Budapest 203

# n

New Town Hall 105
Nové Město (New Town) 90

# o

Óbuda 165
Országhaz (Parliament) 172

# p

Pál-Völgyi And Mátyás Caves 179
parks
  Erzsébet Tér 172
  Grunewald and the Jagdschloß 38
  Levetské sady 117
  Nyugati Pályaudvar 174
  Tiergarten 44
  Volkspark 50
planning your trip 232
  Documents and Formalities 232
    Visas 232
    Work permits 232
  Entrance requirements 232
Potsdam 218
Potsdamer Platz 45
Prague 89
  accommodations 96
  arts and Culture 149
  essentials 153
  food 119
  nightlife 141
  orientation 90
  shopping 150
  Sights 104
Prenzlauer Berg 17

# r

rail resources 241
Reichstag 43

ruin pubs 197

# s

safety and health 239
  Drugs and Alcohol 239
  Immunizations and Precautions 240
  Local Laws and Police 239
Saint Henry Tower 104
Sandwich of Death 179
Schloßplatz 42
Schöneberg and Wilmersdorf 17
Smichov 96
Spreewald and Lübbenau 216
Stare Město 92
studying abroad 254
suggested itineraries 6
synagogues
  Spanish Synagogue (Španělská Synagoga) 110
  Synagogue and Jewish Museum 173
Szentendre 227

# t

Terezin 223
Terézváros, District VI 163
theater 76
  in Berlin 76
  in Budapest 203
  in Prague 149
time differences 236
travel advisories 242

# v

Várhegy, Central Buda, and the Vizivaros 163
Városliget (City Park) 163
Vinohrady 94
Volunteering abroad 257

# w

walking tour 46
working abroad 259

# z

Žižkov 94

# MAP INDEX

## BERLIN
Charlottenburg  16
Friedrichshain  22
Kreuzberg  23
Mitte  19
Overview  IV-V
Prenzlauer Berg  20
Schöneberg and Wilmersdorf  18

## PRAGUE
Hradčany  95
Josefov  92
Malá Strana  93
Nové Město  90
Overview  VI-VII
Stare Město  91

## BUDAPEST
The Belváros  161
Overview  VIII-IX
Terézváros  162
Várhegy, Central Buda, and the Vizivaros  164

map index

---

## MAP LEGEND

| | | | |
|---|---|---|---|
| ▪ Sight/Service | ♖ Castle | 🖥 Internet Cafe | ▧ Police |
| ✈ Airport | ⛪ Church | 📚 Library | ✉ Post Office |
| ⊓ Arch/Gate | ⚑ Consulate/Embassy | Ⓢ Ⓤ Metro Station | ⚐ Skiing |
| $ Bank | ⛪ Convent/Monastery | ⛰ Mountain | ✡ Synagogue |
| ⚱ Baths | ⚓ Ferry Landing | ☪ Mosque | ☎ Telephone Office |
| 🚌 Bus Station | (347) Highway Sign | 🏛 Museum | ♉ Theater |
| ✪ Capital City | ⊞ Hospital | ℞ Pharmacy | ⓘ Tourist Office |
| | | | 🚆 Train Station |

The Let's Go compass always points NORTH.

⋯⋯ Pedestrian Zone
▨▨▨ Stairs

■ Park   ■ Water   ⬚ Beach

# THE STUDENT TRAVEL GUIDE

## These Let's Go guidebooks are available at bookstores and through online retailers:

### EUROPE
Let's Go Amsterdam & Brussels, 1st ed.
Let's Go Berlin, Prague & Budapest, 2nd ed.
Let's Go France, 32nd ed.
Let's Go Europe 2011, 51st ed.
Let's Go European Riviera, 1st ed.
Let's Go Germany, 16th ed.
Let's Go Great Britain with Belfast and Dublin, 33rd ed.
Let's Go Greece, 10th ed.
Let's Go Istanbul, Athens & the Greek Islands, 1st ed.
Let's Go Italy, 31st ed.
Let's Go London, Oxford, Cambridge & Edinburgh, 2nd ed.
Let's Go Madrid & Barcelona, 1st ed.
Let's Go Paris, 17th ed.
Let's Go Rome, Venice & Florence, 1st ed.
Let's Go Spain, Portugal & Morocco, 26th ed.
Let's Go Western Europe, 10th ed.

### UNITED STATES
Let's Go Boston, 6th ed.
Let's Go New York City, 19th ed.
Let's Go Roadtripping USA, 4th ed.

### MEXICO, CENTRAL & SOUTH AMERICA
Let's Go Buenos Aires, 2nd ed.
Let's Go Central America, 10th ed.
Let's Go Costa Rica, 5th ed.
Let's Go Costa Rica, Nicaragua & Panama, 1st ed.
Let's Go Guatemala & Belize, 1st ed.
Let's Go Yucatán Peninsula, 1st ed.

### ASIA & THE MIDDLE EAST
Let's Go Israel, 5th ed.
Let's Go Thailand, 5th ed.

# ACKNOWLEDGMENTS

**SARAH THANKS:** Germany/BPB runs on Fun Pod. Bro-tastic Colleen(ie bear) for always being patient with her freshman Ed. Meagan for musicals "busting out all over" on the daily. Matt for his melodic Jamaican Patois. Daniel for the jajajas. Marykate for fielding questions despite disagreements on cuisine. Joey G for the bear hugs. Prod for solving multiple computer issues while jamming on the ukulele and sharing stories. Ashley, Nathaniel, and Joe for the inspiration and comedy, the best combination an employee could ask for. Everybody else at Let's Go; you're all incredible. My researchers for putting their best foot forward for this book. My friends who dealt with the antics and rain checks. Big sis' Becca, who's a trooper and a role model, and little sis' Nina, the light of my life. My parents for going the extra mile for me. And for feeding me, which is a full-time job.

**COLLEEN THANKS:** My RWs for killer copy and staying in touch. Sarah for supering (and being super). FUN POD. Daniel for pep talks. Matt for letting me be Ari. Meg for Massachusetts and summer theater. Marykate for laying the smackdown at Crema. Nathaniel for hiring me. Joe for family dinners. Joe for marketing moves. Sara and Dan for fixing my lazy RIVER. Edward-Michael for treats on crebit. Trace for loving life and being a bestie. Iris for labbits. Aaron for tweeting at me and reminding me that my boyfriend is gay. Court and Cathy for being all-star Gato Girlz. Travis for that free drink (call me!). Unos for snack hours and karaoke. Winnie and Logan for SF. Katie for NYC. Mr. Cronin for my first Red Sox game. My proctees for being good. Brendy for buying great birthday presents. Mom for everything.

**DIRECTOR OF PUBLISHING**   Ashley R. Laporte

**EXECUTIVE EDITOR**   Nathaniel Rakich

**PRODUCTION AND DESIGN DIRECTOR**   Sara Plana

**PUBLICITY AND MARKETING DIRECTOR**   Joseph Molimock

**MANAGING EDITORS**   Charlotte Alter, Daniel C. Barbero, Marykate Jasper,  Iya Megre

**TECHNOLOGY PROJECT MANAGERS**   Daniel J. Choi, C. Alexander Tremblay

**PRODUCTION ASSOCIATES**   Rebecca Cooper, Melissa Niu

**FINANCIAL ASSOCIATE**   Louis Caputo

**DIRECTOR OF IT**   Yasha Iravantchi

**PRESIDENT**   Meagan Hill

**GENERAL MANAGER**   Jim McKellar

LET'S GO
masthead

# ABOUT LET'S GO

## THE STUDENT TRAVEL GUIDE

Let's Go publishes the world's favorite student travel guides, written entirely by Harvard students. Armed with pens, notebooks, and a few changes of clothes stuffed into their backpacks, our student researchers go across continents, through time zones, and above expectations to seek out invaluable travel experiences for our readers. Because we are a completely student-run company, we have a unique perspective on how students travel, where they want to go, and what they're looking to do when they get there. If your dream is to grab a machete and forge through the jungles of Costa Rica, we can take you there. If you'd rather bask in the Riviera sun at a beachside cafe, we'll set you a table. In short, we write for readers who know that there's more to travel than tour buses. To keep up, visit our website, www.letsgo. com, where you can sign up to blog, post photos from your trips, and connect with the Let's Go community.

## TRAVELING BEYOND TOURISM

We're on a mission to provide our readers with sharp, fresh coverage packed with socially responsible opportunities to go beyond tourism. Each guide's Beyond Tourism chapter shares ideas about responsible travel, study abroad, and how to give back to the places you visit while on the road. To help you gain a deeper connection with the places you travel, our fearless researchers scour the globe to give you the heads-up on both world-renowned and off-the-beaten-track opportunities. We've also opened our pages to respected writers and scholars to hear their takes on the countries and regions we cover, and asked travelers who have worked, studied, or volunteered abroad to contribute first-person accounts of their experiences.

## FIFTY-ONE YEARS OF WISDOM

Let's Go has been on the road for 51 years and counting. We've grown a lot since publishing our first 20-page pamphlet to Europe in 1960, but five decades and 60 titles later, our witty, candid guides are still researched and written entirely by students on shoestring budgets who know that train strikes, stolen luggage, food poisoning, and marriage proposals are all part of a day's work. Meanwhile, we're still bringing readers fresh new features, such as a student-life section with advice on how and where to meet students from around the world; a revamped, user-friendly layout for our listings; and greater emphasis on the experiences that make travel abroad a rite of passage for readers of all ages. And, of course, this year's 16 titles—including five brand-new guides—are still brimming with editorial honesty, a commitment to students, and our irreverent style.

## THE LET'S GO COMMUNITY

More than just a travel guide company, Let's Go is a community that reaches from our headquarters in Cambridge, MA, all across the globe. Our small staff of dedicated student editors, writers, and tech nerds comes together because of our shared passion for travel and our desire to help other travelers get the most out of their experience. We love it when our readers become part of the Let's Go community as well—when you travel, drop us a postcard (67 Mt. Auburn St., Cambridge, MA 02138, USA), send us an email (feedback@letsgo.com), or sign up on our website (www.letsgo.com) to tell us about your adventures and discoveries.

For more information, updated travel coverage, and news from our researcher team, visit us online at www.letsgo.com.

# THANKS TO OUR SPONSORS

- **MOSAIC HOUSE.** ▣www.mosaichouse.com.
- **MISS SOPHIE'S.** ▣miss-sophies.com.
- **CZECH INN.** ▣czech-inn.com.
- **SIR TOBY'S.** ▣sirtobys.com.
- **CITYSTAY HOSTEL.** Rosenstrasse 16, 10178 Berlin-Mitte. ☎49 30 23 62 40 31. ▣www.citystay.de.
- **HELTER SKELTER HOSTEL.** Kalkscheunenstr. 4-5, 10117 Berlin. ☎0049 0 30 280 44 99 7. ▣www.helterskelterhostel.com.
- **SUNFLOWER HOSTEL.** Helsingforser Str. 17, 10243 Berlin. ☎0049 0 30 440 44 250. ▣www.sunflower-hostel.de.
- **HEART OF GOLD HOSTEL.** Johannisstr. 11, 10117 Berlin. ☎0049 0 30 29 00 33 00. ▣www.heartofgold-hostel.de.
- **ODYSSEE GLOBETROTTER HOSTEL.** Grünberger Str. 23, 10243 Berlin. ☎0049 0 30 29 0000 81. ▣www.globetrotterhostel.de.
- **FIVE ELEMENTS HOSTEL.** Moselstr. 40, 60329 Frankfurt. ☎0049 0 69 24 00 58 85. ▣www.5elementshostel.de.
- **EASY PALACE CITY HOSTEL.** Mozartstr. 4, 80336 Munich. ☎0049 0 89 55 87 97 0. ▣www.easypalace.de.
- **PRAGUE CENTRAL HOSTELS.** ▣www.praguecentralhostels.com; ▣www.praguesquarehostel.com; ▣www.oldpraguehostel.com.
- **HOTEL HANSABLICK.** Flotowstr.6, 10555 Berlin, Germany. ☎49 030 390 48 00. ▣www.hansablick.de.
- **ALETTO KREUZBERG.** Tempelhofer Ufer 8/9, 10963 Berlin, Germany. ☎49 030 25 96 04 80. ▣www.aletto.de.
- **ALETTO SCHÖNEBERG.** Grunewaldstraße 33, 10823 Berlin, Germany. ☎49 030 25 96 04 80. ▣www.aletto.de.

notes

**HELPING LET'S GO.** If you want to share your discoveries, suggestions, or corrections, please drop us a line. We appreciate every piece of correspondence, whether a postcard, a 10-page email, or a coconut. Visit Let's Go at **www.letsgo.com** or send an email to:

**feedback@letsgo.com, subject: "Let's Go Berlin, Prague & Budapest"**

Address mail to:

**Let's Go Berlin, Prague & Budapest, 67 Mount Auburn St., Cambridge, MA 02138, USA**

In addition to the invaluable travel advice our readers share with us, many are kind enough to offer their services as researchers or editors. Unfortunately, our charter enables us to employ only currently enrolled Harvard students.

Distributed by Publishers Group West.
Printed in Canada by Friesens Corp.
Maps © Let's Go and Avalon Travel
Design Support by Jane Musser, Sarah Juckniess, Tim McGrath

ISBN-13: 978-1-59880-712-7

Second edition
10 9 8 7 6 5 4 3 2 1

**Let's Go Berlin, Prague & Budapest** is written by Let's Go Publications, 67 Mt. Auburn St., Cambridge, MA 02138, USA.

# quick reference

## YOUR GUIDE TO LET'S GO ICONS

| | | | | | |
|---|---|---|---|---|---|
| ☎ | Phone numbers | ⊗ | Not wheelchair-accessible | ❄ | Has A/C |
| 🖳 | Websites | ((ŋ)) | Has Internet access | ⇄ | Directions |
| 💳 | Takes credit cards | ☂ | Has outdoor seating | *i* | Other hard info |
| ® | Cash only | ▼ | Is GLBT or GLBT-friendly | Ⓢ | Prices |
| ♿ | Wheelchair-accessible | ⚲ | Serves alcohol | 🕐 | Hours |

## PRICE RANGES

*Let's Go* includes price ranges, marked by icons ❶ through ❺, in accommodations and food listings. For an expanded explanation, see the chart in How To Use This Book.

| BERLIN | ❶ | ❷ | ❸ | ❹ | ❺ |
|---|---|---|---|---|---|
| ACCOMMODATIONS | under €15 | €15-24 | €24-30 | €30-35 | over €35 |
| FOOD | under €4 | €4-9 | €9-13 | €13-20 | over €20 |

| PRAGUE | ❶ | ❷ | ❸ | ❹ | ❺ |
|---|---|---|---|---|---|
| ACCOMMODATIONS | under 440Kč | 440-650Kč | 650-800Kč | 800-1100Kč | over 1100Kč |
| FOOD | under 110Kč | 110-220Kč | 220-340Kč | 340-450Kč | over 450Kč |

| BUDAPEST | ❶ | ❷ | ❸ | ❹ | ❺ |
|---|---|---|---|---|---|
| ACCOMMODATIONS | under 3000Ft | 3000-4000Ft | 4000-5700Ft | 5700-9000Ft | over 9000Ft |
| FOOD | under 1200Ft | 1200-1800Ft | 1800-2400Ft | 2400-3500Ft | over 3500Ft |

## IMPORTANT PHONE NUMBERS

### BERLIN EMERGENCY: POLICE ☎110, FIRE ☎112

| Poison Control | ☎030 192 40 | Drug Crisis | ☎030 192 37 |
|---|---|---|---|

### PRAGUE EMERGENCY: POLICE ☎158, FIRE ☎150

| Prague Ambulance Service | ☎155 | Toxicology Information Center | ☎224 915 402 |
|---|---|---|---|

### BUDAPEST EMERGENCY: POLICE ☎107, FIRE ☎105, AMBULANCE ☎104

| General Emergency | ☎112 | Pharmacy | ☎314 36 95 |
|---|---|---|---|

## USEFUL PHRASES

| ENGLISH | GERMAN | CZECH | HUNGARIAN |
|---|---|---|---|
| Hello!/Hi! | Hallo!/Tag! | Dobrý den *(formal)*. | Szervusz/Szia |
| Goodbye! | Auf Wiedersehn!/Tschüss! | Nashledanou | Viszontlátásra. |
| Yes. | Ja. | Ano. | Igen. |
| No. | Nein. | Ne. | Nem. |
| Sorry! | Es tut mir leid! | Promiňte. | Elnézést. |
| Help! | Hilfe! | Pomoc! | Segítsen! |
| police | Polizei | policie | rendőrség |
| doctor | Arzt | doktor | kórház |

## MEASUREMENT CONVERSIONS

| | |
|---|---|
| 1 foot (ft.) = 0.305m | 1 meter (m) = 3.28 ft. |
| 1 mile (mi.) = 1.609km | 1 kilometer (km) = 0.621 mi. |
| 1 pound (lb.) = 0.454kg | 1 kilogram (kg) = 2.205 lb. |
| 1 gallon (gal.) = 3.785L | 1 liter (L) = 0.264 gal. |